Modeling and Simulating Software Architectures

Modeling and Simulating Software Architectures

The Palladio Approach

Ralf H. Reussner, Steffen Becker, Jens Happe, Robert Heinrich, Anne Koziolek, Heiko Koziolek, Max Kramer, and Klaus Krogmann

The MIT Press
Cambridge, Massachusetts
London, England

This book was set in Stone Sans and Stone Serif by Toppan Best-set Premedia Limited. Printed and bound in the United States of America.

Library of Congress Cataloging-in-Publication Data

Names: Reussner, Ralf, editor.
Title: Modeling and simulating software architectures : the Palladio approach / edited by
    Ralf H. Reussner, Steffen Becker, Jens Happe, Robert Heinrich, Anne Koziolek, Heiko Koziolek,
    Max Kramer, and Klaus Krogmann.
Description: Cambridge, MA : MIT Press, [2016] | Includes bibliographical references and index.
Identifiers: LCCN 2016004419 | ISBN 9780262034760 (hardcover : alk. paper)
Subjects: LCSH: Software architecture. | Computer software—Computer simulation. | Palladio
    (Computer program)
Classification: LCC QA76.758 .M585 2016 | DDC 005.1/2—dc23 LC record available at
    https://lccn.loc.gov/2016004419

10 9 8 7 6 5 4 3 2 1

Contents

Foreword

Composing software systems out of smaller parts is a daunting task. At the foundations of this process is common programming—the composition of programs from primitives provided by runtime environments and made available in programming languages. The high degrees of freedom at the level of general programming enable all that is in the world of software today. Division of labor is facilitated by means of libraries, frameworks, and packages of pre-built software. As powerful as the approach is, general programming makes it very difficult to predict the functional correctness, the meeting of qualitative requirements such as security properties, and the meeting of quantitative requirements such as performance properties.

Composing software out of larger-grained and well-specified units that bring along stronger functional and other properties has thus long been seen as a major step forward in more efficient software construction that yields more predictable outcomes. There are different kinds of such larger-grained units, including those that are sufficiently independent and thus retain their inherent structure in a composed system. These latter units are referred to as software components.

Planning to compose software from given as well as purpose-built components raises the desire to understand the functional and other properties of the system to be built, before actually building it. However, predicting properties of systems built from such components is not automatic. Both the architecture of a system to be composed as well as the individual properties of the components used or built need to be captured and methods and tools are needed to leverage such captured specifications.

This brings us to the topic area of the book at hand. Palladio is a system simulator that operates over a given software architecture and allows for the dependable prediction of properties such as performance and reliability characteristics, but also maintainability and cost. Furthermore, the Palladio simulator is itself built in a compositional fashion, making it extensible and configurable.

The Palladio project has been a pillar in this area of science and engineering for well over a decade and this book gathers the profound lessons learned. The authors present a comprehensive view of what Palladio is—a tool, a method, and a practice. The approach presented allows practitioners to move from the building of numerous prototypes that are subjected to measurements in possibly questionable environments to a clean engineering method that allows for the model-driven analysis of to-be-built systems. Problems, such as performance bottlenecks or untenable cost, can be spotted early and corrected by adjusting the architecture, selecting different components, or developing specific components where the need is now understood.

Clemens Szyperski
Redmond, Washington
February 2016

Preface

Another Book on Software Architecture?

There are many good books available about software architecture. This is no surprise, as software architecture became an established field in research and practice nearly two decades ago.

So, why another book about software architecture? Well, because all the other books are about "documenting software architectures," whereas this one is about "simulating software architectures." There is nothing wrong with documenting software architectures. Several software engineering activities can benefit considerably from documented software architectures, such as cost planning, component definition, work plan derivation, or planning of reuse and planning for reuse. One of the more recent uses of documented software architectures, however, is their simulation. This use of software architectures is very important for software engineers because the ability to predict the properties of an artifact on the basis of its design without actually having to realize it is one of the central characteristics of an engineering discipline. From this perspective, "software engineering" is barely an engineering discipline. Too often, we lack an understanding of the impact of design decisions on quality attributes, such as performance or reliability. As a result, we try to test quality in costly and risky trial-and-error cycles. The problem with this is testing of software means that we have already put effort into its implementation, and late architectural performance improvements lead to additional costs. This book explains how software architectures can be modeled and simulated to automatically obtain quantitative quality predictions for a software system before it is actually implemented and documented.

Who This Book Is For

This book on quality modeling and simulation of software architectures is intended for graduate students, their instructors, and practitioners with an academic background in software engineering. At universities, instructors and students may use it as a primary textbook in graduate courses on quality engineering, performance engineering, or as supporting material for specialized sections of more general courses on software architecture.

This book qualifies computer science students and practitioners to become quantitative software engineers that master the performance and reliability of software architectures:

• Understand how to build quantitatively better software architectures.
• Simulate and predict the impact of software architectures.
• Avoid and fix performance and reliability problems.
• Understand the quality implications of changes in software architectures.
• Circumvent typical pitfalls in the creation process and design of software.

What This Book Is About

This book is about simulating software architectures to understand their impact on software quality. It explains in detail how quality attributes of software systems, such as performance or reliability, can be modeled, analyzed, and improved before the eventual rollout. This book shows how software architects can profit from architectural simulation and provides dependable and well-validated modeling and prediction techniques. It does not formulate software architecture documentation as a means to its own end but describes the world's first simulator for software architectures: Palladio. With the presented engineering approach to software design, you get to know how to overcome costly testing cycles that are bound to trial and error. Step by step, you learn and experience how to model reusable, parameterized components and configured, deployed systems in order to analyze quality of service in early design stages.

The text details the key concepts of a domains-specific modeling language for software architecture and presents the corresponding development and analysis process. It describes how quality information can be used to calibrate architectural models from which detailed simulation models are automatically derived for quality predictions. The use and benefit of the prediction results obtained is explained in general terms along established and innovative processes, such as round-trip engineering or design space exploration, and is illustrated using three industrial case studies.

What do you get from reading this book? Simply speaking, you learn how to systematically answer questions such as the following:

• Does my system scale?
• What hardware resources are required to achieve performance goals?
• How do I design my software for high efficiency or reliability?
• What kind of service-level agreements do I need to settle with my service provider?

With this book, you can answer these questions by modeling and analyzing the quality of service of reusable, parameterized components and configured, deployed systems in early design stages.

How This Book Is Organized

Running Example
The book features a running example (chapter 2) that models and analyzes the Media Store system, in which media files can be uploaded and downloaded. Parts of this running example appears in several chapters to illustrate specific tasks and methods. In addition, three industrial case studies are comprehensively presented and discussed in part V.

Questions, Exercises, Further Reading, and Takeaways
At the end of each chapter of parts II, III, and IV, there are three special sections that allow you to assess your understanding, to obtain additional information from external sources, and to check whether you retained all key points. First, a set of questions is provided in order to give you the ability to check directly after each chapter whether you understood the presented material correctly. Then, you can gain further practical insights to the presented topic using exercises. Both questions and exercises are classified according to the required cognitive effort: reproduction (*), reorganization (**), transfer (***), or creation (****) of knowledge. The answers to these questions and solutions to these exercises are available on the book's companion website (discussed later), which also features tutorials and screencasts. Next, sources of additional information are provided in a "Further Reading" section. It briefly lists recommended literature that either covers fundamental concepts in more detail or completes the presented material in advanced topics. Finally, each of the chapters of parts II, III, and IV is concluded by a section on "Takeaways," which briefly summarizes the key points that can be learned from the chapter.

Definitions, Digressions, and Index
Where disputed terminology makes it necessary, brief definitions are used to clarify important terms. Additional information that completes the presented material but that is not necessary for further comprehension is provided in separate "Digression" boxes. To allow you to navigate quickly to a certain keyword, the most important terms are indexed and listed at the end of the book.

Companion Website
Because many of the topics presented in this book are already taught in university courses and in the seminars of several industrial partners, we are able to provide extensive online material in the form of tutorials, recorded screencasts, and lecture material at our MIT Press companion website:

https://mitpress.mit.edu/books/modeling-and-simulating-software-architectures

Palladio Website

The main source of information about Palladio as an approach, tool, and architectural language is:

www.palladio-simulator.com

Here you can download the tool "PCM Workbench" and also tutorials, screencasts, and various publications and case study documentations.

Acknowledgments

The authors would like to express their gratitude to many people helping to write this book. First of all, Marie, Kathleen, Katherine and the whole team at MIT Press guided us safely through the writing and editing process. Our families, partners, and children deserve thanks, as so often in the past three years they saw us writing "the book" instead of being with them.

In a broader context, we also have to thank all those who enabled the creation of Palladio. Among the funding agencies that supported our work, we want to emphasize the German Research Foundation (DFG), which invested in the initial Palladio project in the form of a young investigator Emmy Noether grant when the success of the whole story was not so clear. All those who wrote this book contributed in various forms to the Palladio project; however, there are many contributors even beyond the authors of this book. Many former employees, as well as students who worked as research assistants or wrote their master's or bachelor's theses, helped to make Palladio what it is: the world's first working software architecture simulator and—hopefully—a step toward making software design an engineering discipline. Many thanks to all of you!

About the Editors

The editors of this book are a group of scientists and engineers in academia and industry that developed, extended and successfully applied architectural quality simulations and predictions.

• *Prof. Dr. Ralf H. Reussner* — Full Professor of software engineering, Chair of Software Design and Quality at the Karlsruhe Institute of Technology (KIT), Executive Director of the Research Center for Information Technologies (FZI)

• *Prof. Dr.-Ing. Steffen Becker* — Full Professor of software engineering, Chemnitz University of Technology (TU)

• *Dr.-Ing. Jens Happe* — Senior Researcher at SAP Research and co-founder of the software start-up avenyou

• *Dr. rer. nat. Robert Heinrich* — Head of Quality-driven System Evolution Research Group at the Chair of Software Design and Quality, Karlsruhe Institute of Technology (KIT)

• *Jun.-Prof. Dr.-Ing. Anne Koziolek* — Junior Professor of software engineering and head of the Architecture Driven Requirements Engineering Group at the Karlsruhe Institute of Technology (KIT)

• *Dr.-Ing. Heiko Koziolek* — Principal Scientist and Global Research Area Coordinator at ABB Corporate Research

• *Max E. Kramer* — Scientist at the Chair of Software Design and Quality, Karlsruhe Institute of Technology (KIT)

• *Dr.-Ing. Klaus Krogmann* — Manager quality engineering platform with Citrix, GetGo

Part I   An Engineering Approach to Software Architecture

Part I describes the simulation of software architectures through application scenarios and explains the role of software architecture–based quality prediction in an engineering approach to software design. The Palladio approach is introduced, and the basic elements and concepts of the software architecture modeling language of Palladio are briefly summarized in relation to an example software system. An overview of the structure of this book is presented, and possible reading paths for different readers are discussed.

1 Introduction

Ralf H. Reussner, Jörg Henss and Max Kramer

This chapter discusses the need for simulating software architectures through application scenarios and explains the role of software architecture–based quality prediction in an engineering approach to software design. It introduces the Palladio approach, its main metrics, its modeling language, the underlying process, and the corresponding roles and responsibilities. The chapter concludes with an overview of the structure of the book and a discussion of possible reading paths for different readers.

Many good books about software architecture are available. This is no surprise, as software architecture became an established field in research and practice nearly two decades ago.

As noted in the preface, the specific property of this book is its concern with documenting *and simulating* architectures.

Why should we simulate a software architecture? For engineers, it is common practice to simulate a model of an artifact before physically realizing it. Design models of cars, electronic circuits, bridges, and so forth, are simulated to understand the impact of design decisions on various quality attributes of interest, such as safety, energy consumption, or stability. The ability to predict the properties of an artifact on the basis of its design, without actually having to realize it, is one of the central characteristics of an engineering discipline. From this view of the established engineering disciplines, "software engineering" is barely an engineering discipline. Too often, software engineers lack an understanding of the impact of design decisions on quality attributes, such as performance or reliability. As a result, they try to "test in" quality in costly trial-and-error cycles.

What happens if we do not simulate? Not understanding the impact of design decisions can be costly and risky: testing of software means that we have already put effort into its implementation. For example, if testing reveals performance problems, it is likely that the architecture needs to be changed, which leads to additional costs. These costs arise because in enterprise software systems, low performance is mainly the effect of inappropriate architectures rather than the effect of weak code.

The list of failed or challenged software projects is long (Glass 1998). A number of recent projects were significantly delayed or significantly over budget. Such adverse results can partly be traced back to problems with software architecture and quality attributes, such as performance or reliability. Thus, the problems originate in the high-level organization of systems. Prominent examples concerning performance are provided by Schmietendorf and Scholz (2001) and Koziolek (2008): the automated baggage-handling systems at Denver International Airport and Heathrow Airport and SAP's Business by Design project.

Baggage-handling systems: Problems with its baggage-handling system caused Denver International Airport to open 16 months later than scheduled, almost $2 billion over budget, and without an automated baggage system. Here, the system was planned to serve one terminal of the airport at the outset and ultimately to serve all terminals (Montealegre and Keil 2000). The system was not able to cope with this increased demand, which means that it was not sufficiently scalable. Similar problems on a smaller scale occurred at Heathrow's newly built Terminal 5 in 2008: the number of messages generated by the baggage system was too high for the system [24], so that during the initial weeks of operation, 23,000 bags were lost, and more than 500 flights were canceled, causing losses of £16 million (Thomson 2008). The number of passengers of the carrier British Airways dropped by 220,000 in the month afterward, which is mostly attributed to the baggage-handling problems (Robertson 2008).

SAP's Business by Design: This project is an Enterprise Resource Planning (ERP) solution targeting medium-size enterprises. In contrast to previous solutions, Business by Design is a software-as-a-service solution: the application is hosted by SAP (or a specialized provider), and enterprises rent it, paying per use or per user. The project was announced in 2007 [23], planned to be launched at the beginning of 2008 [22], and planned to win 10,000 customers by 2010 leading to $1 billion in sales [38]. Performance problems, however, delayed the start of the project. An early implementation was significantly slower than SAP's standard solution and was only able to handle 10 concurrent users instead of the desired 1,000 users [22]. As a result, the project start was delayed until mid-2010 [27]. At the beginning of 2011, Business by Design had 400 customers [25]. The costs of this delay are not known but are probably high due to the project's large planned volume.

In all cases, the lack of predicted quality properties (here, performance) led to high losses both financially and in reputation and demonstrates the need to adopt engineering principles in software engineering. It also shows that quality properties need to be considered early in the life cycle of a software project.

What is meant by "simulating" software architectures? As a software architecture does not contain the exact execution semantics of the software, simulating the architecture cannot mean the execution of the computer program written according to the architecture. Rather, the simulated architecture reveals the quality attributes of the software developed according to the software architecture. This means the simulation is "quality equivalent" to the code written according to the architecture. In the case of performance simulation of a software architecture, this means the simulation reveals information on throughput, response times of methods, and utilization of resources such as the code would exhibit once it were written, deployed, and executed as specified in the architecture.

How can that be? A software system's quality attributes, such as performance (e.g., response time, throughput, and utilization) or reliability (e.g., mean time to failure, probability of failure on demand), are influenced by its architecture. For some domains, such as enterprise information systems, this influence is so strong that knowledge of the architecture is sufficient to make a good prediction of performance or reliability of the executing software, even if only the architecture is used for prediction. Note that this does not generally need to be the case: for some domains, such as those worked with in high-performance computing, the main influence factor on performance is the execution platform and the algorithm, while the architecture of such applications remains simple and without a strong impact on performance.

For what can we use the simulation of architectures? There are several activities that benefit from simulation results. When making design decisions, such as pattern selection, system structuring, or definition of component boundaries, prediction enables one to foresee the implications of such design decisions on the quality of the later executing software. Such decisions are made not only in forward engineering but also during refactoring and software evolution. The benefit of simulation is that exploring the impact of design decisions is easier by changing the architecture and simulating it than by changing the code and reinstalling the system.

In capacity planning, predictions help to estimate the right amount of resources needed to fulfill given quality requirements. Before ordering and installing the hardware, we can simulate the influence of network bandwidth, processor capacities, replication, and so forth. The simulation can also explore the influence of software resources, such as virtual machines, server replication, and so forth, before actually changing the real configuration. Moreover, we can systematically optimize different deployment options (i.e., how software components are mapped to virtual and physical resources) without costly trial-and-error evaluations in the real world. Here again, the benefits are the reduced costs compared to those of installing and benchmarking the system to understand its performance. In addition, we can make purchase decisions with much higher confidence that the ordered configuration will indeed fulfill the given performance or reliability requirements.

Scalability analyses are also of practical interest. Here, we investigate the impact of varying workload. For enterprise information systems, this mainly means an increase of the number of concurrently served users. The main question is to what extent the workload can be increased while not violating any given performance requirement. Questions like this emerge in various contexts, ranging from capacity planning to service-level management in cloud-computing environments.

1.1   An Engineering Approach to Software Design

The creation of artifacts can be seen as one of the specific abilities of mankind. Not all artifacts, however, are created with an engineering approach. Shaw and Garlan introduce a model of different approaches to creation of artifacts (Shaw and Garlan 1996). Craftsmanship is the oldest approach where the quality of the artifact (and its process of creation) solely depends on the experience of the craftsman. Examples are basically any artifacts created before the Iron Age. Later in history, the creation and use of artifacts further differentiated, and more elaborate production processes came into focus. At those times, complex artifacts were created in manufacturing facilities. Here, the process of creation was split into several steps to be performed manually by specialists. These specialists were basically skilled craftsman dedicated to specific steps of the production process. A prominent example of this preindustrial production approach is how textile fabrics were created in manufacturing facilities during the baroque period in France. But this is still different from an engineering approach. For many artifacts, it is desirable to have predictability: a predictable process in creation and predictable properties of the artifact. Predictability means the ability to foresee relevant quality properties (e.g., costs, time, and resources for the process or specific quality attributes for the product). This ability is the prerequisite for goal-driven designs of products and processes and ultimately their optimization. Without predictability, engineers will stick with trial-and-error approaches to improve processes and products. As said, this is not only costly but also increases the risk of not getting a satisfying product at the late phases of development. This predictability requires scientific theories: theories that enable a forecast, a kind of what-if analysis, on a model level before things are actually realized.

What does this have to do with software engineering, or more specifically with software design? Nowadays, software is developed in a kind of manufacturing style (Shaw and Garlan 1996). Skilled craftsmen develop software according to their specific roles. Still, and even in agile processes, personal experience, talent, and dedication play a major role for the success of the development of software. There is nothing wrong with benefiting from experience and talent. But lacking a theory of the software, engineers cannot perform resource dimensioning without having bought and set up the hardware of the execution environment, cannot make statements on the scalability of the software, and have difficulty systematically designing the software according to quality requirements.

In contrast, this book aims to lay the foundation of an engineering approach to software design. It presents a language to describe software architectures and a simulator to make predictions of the influence of the architecture on performance and reliability. The language offers the "vocabulary" to express software architectures with details required for simulation but allows modeling of software architectures according to general best practices. The simulation and additional analytical tools are seamlessly integrated into the modeling environment. This integration allows engineers to design the architectures and immediately start an analysis to understand the effects of design decisions. There are several "knobs" to be "turned":

• The architecture itself
• The execution environment
• The usage profile

While turning these "knobs," we can perform what-if analyses as mentioned in the application scenarios above. That means by changing the architecture, we evaluate different design alternatives (e.g., which variant of a pattern; effects of the separation or merging of components or of different interface designs). When changing the execution environment, we can evaluate the effects of differently sized hardware, such as server or network capacities or different deployment options (i.e., different mappings of components to physical or virtual resources). By changing the usage profile, we can evaluate the scalability (i.e., the change of performance if the data volume or the number of concurrent users is increased).

1.2   The Role of Software Architecture

Given these scenarios of an engineering approach to software engineering, the architecture of the software plays an important role for two reasons: First, all of the above scenarios finally affect the design of the software. Second, the architecture itself is the input for the simulator. But how does this relate to the general role of software architecture?

According to the ISO/IEC/IEEE 42010 standard, a *software architecture* comprises the "fundamental concepts or properties of a system in its environment embodied in its elements, relationships, and in the principles of its design and evolution." While the first part of this definition is according to the general understanding of architecture as the structural plan of a system, the latter part, "principles of its design," may subsume another understanding of software architecture; namely, the architecture as a set of documented design decisions. This understanding is beneficial, for example, when communicating software architectures (as a set of design decisions) or when evolving software. For example, when requirements change, one could reflect whether parts of the architecture are still appropriate by checking whether the rationale of former design decisions is still fitting to the changed requirements. Positively or negatively, the IEEE definition does not prescribe a fixed level of abstraction of how to model software architecture. In general, there is no one single correct level of abstraction for a software architecture. Much more, the abstraction of how software architectures are specified depends on several factors, such as the domain, company culture, software development processes, needs of later life-cycle phases, the execution, platform, or even a part of the software, as some parts need more specific details in the architecture than others. When simulating the software architecture, however, some information is required. Still, the level of abstraction, including how coarse grained a component is, is variable. But, essentially, we need information about three properties of a system: first, the structure of the system, including components, interfaces, and their dependencies; second, the deployment describing the mapping of components and connectors to virtual or physical resources, including a description of these resources; third, the control and data flows through the system.

While the first of these three *view types* is common for what we intuitively assume as architecture, the latter two may need some comments. The second view type may depend on the local installation of software and therefore might be beyond the control of the software architect. We see it as part of the architecture, first because the architect implicitly defines potential deployment options through the structure of the system, and second because the deployment strongly influences the performance simulation and hence the design decisions relating to the structure of the system. The last view type on the control and data flows includes parallelism, synchronization, and dependencies on the data flow and is documented as control flow within components as well as control flow between components.

The usage profile, as a kind of fourth view type, is not part of the architecture of the system, but much more the interaction with the system.

1.3   The Role of Software Components

Software components (McIlroy 1969) are building blocks for software. Hence, besides modules and classes, they are a means to structure software. While modules (Parnas 1972a) are thought to encapsulate design decisions and classes are thought to model data and behavior of domain entities in software (Meyer 1992), software components are thought to be a technical means to separate two development processes: the process of component development and the process of system development using components. Therefore, components are software building blocks that can be used without understanding their internals (i.e., the black-box principle).

Many interesting challenges arise from the distinction of developing and using components; namely, how to intersect the two development processes. For example, should components be there before the system is designed? Can components be created by the system designer by composing other components? In the context of this book, two different properties of components are of interest: first, the ability to reuse results of component quality predictions, and second, the ability to reuse component quality descriptions. The first ability is also called *compositional reasoning*. This means that one can reuse the quality prediction results of a component "in combination" with the quality prediction results of other components (without having to recompute them) in order to infer the quality of the component composition (i.e., a composed component). The "combination" of quality prediction results is possible when information about the way components are composed is sufficient to combine the component quality prediction results to predict properties of the composed component. The concept of compositionality means that the quality of a composition can be computed by composing the quality properties of single components.

The second property is concerned with the specification of component quality by defining the input for the prediction. This reusability of quality specifications requires that all external factors influencing the quality of a component occur in the specification as parameters and are not hardwired.

While compositional reasoning (property 1) is important for scalability (i.e., analyzing large systems), the reuse of quality specifications is the prerequisite for practical feasibility of quality predictions. Without reusable, component-specific quality specifications, one always has to create quality models by hand as input for predictions, and these models are not related to the system's structural architecture (componentization). As soon as the system evolves, the whole specification has to be re-created.

1.4   The Palladio Approach

In this book, the Palladio approach to modeling and analysis of software architecture is presented. It is named after the Italian Renaissance architect Andrea Palladio (see figure 1.1). Palladio is a software component modeling approach that focuses on the prediction of quality attributes of a software architecture. The idea is to avoid costly changes to a software architecture by performing quality analysis during the early design stages of the software. Commonly in software design, decisions are made on the basis of experiences or, when lacking those, by making an educated guess. But, through the information gained via the Palladio approach, the best-suited design alternatives can be chosen.

This is well aligned with classical engineering where first a blueprint is constructed and then a structural analysis is performed for the given design.

While the approach initially targeted the modeling of business information systems, it is not limited to this domain and has been successfully applied to several other domains.

1.4.1   What Quality Attributes and Metrics Can the Palladio Approach Predict?

From a set of software quality attributes, the Palladio approach supports the prediction of performance and reliability of a modeled system. Both performance and reliability are inherently important, as they are commonly understood as part of the externally visible quality of a system. These external attributes can only be predicted with respect to how the system relates to its environment (i.e., its deployment and usage).

During analysis, several metrics are captured to reflect the performance of the system:

Response time: The response time of a system is the time it takes between sending a request to the system and getting the corresponding response. Fast response times are often mission critical and the key to success, especially for web-based information systems.

Throughput: Throughput is a metric that denotes the number of requests the system can process per unit of time. It is especially important when checking whether a system scales to a distinct number of parallel users. Although in some cases low response times can lead to high throughput, response time and throughput are in general not correlated.

Digression 1.1

Andrea Palladio

Our approach is named after the Italian Renaissance architect Andrea Palladio (1508–1580; figure 1.1), who, in a certain way, tried to predict the aesthetic impact of his buildings in advance. He is nowadays recognized for having a strong influence on Western architecture. The Palladian architectural style was adapted by many other architects and is still noticeable in modern architecture.

Figure 1.1

Resource utilization: Resource utilization denotes the fraction of time a hardware resource is kept busy processing requests on the system. Shared resources can be a bottleneck for a system. In many settings, it is desirable to keep the utilization of a resource below a certain threshold (e.g., 80%). An overall utilization that is too high can lead to undesired peaks in the response time as a result of congestion effects.

While performance is the key quality attribute, it is also possible to predict the reliability of a software architecture using Palladio. Reliability is about faults and failure occurring in the software and hardware. It is usually specified as mean time to failure and mean time to repair of certain parts of a system. Furthermore, for software components, the probability of failures is used. The Palladio approach can predict the reliability of a system using the following metrics:

Probability of failure on demand: The probability of failure on demand specifies the likelihood that a request to the system will result in a failure of the system.
Failure rate: The failure rate denotes the overall occurrence rate of failures. It is dependent on the usage rate of the system.

Many performance-prediction approaches have strong limitations on the statistics they provide (e.g., only mean values are provided). A key feature of analysis in the Palladio approach is that quality metrics are evaluated using probability distributions. This means a certain probability is shown for each interval of values. These probability densities can be visualized as a chart, for example, and thus be used for detailed quality assessment.

1.4.2   What Parts Constitute the Palladio Approach?
The Palladio approach is composed of three essential parts that are designed to work hand in hand. First, the Palladio Component Model (PCM), a domain-specific language (DSL), is targeted at specifying and documenting software architectural knowledge. Second, on the basis of this DSL, multiple analytical techniques ranging from queuing network analysis to discrete event simulation can be used to predict the quality of the modeled system. Finally, the Palladio approach is aligned with a development process model specifically tailored for component-based software systems.

The Palladio DSL   So what exactly is a domain-specific language? The definition given by Fowler states that DSLs are languages of limited expressiveness that are focused on "one particular aspect of a system" (Fowler and Parsons 2010). According to Fowler, DSLs are especially useful when having a "clear focus on a small domain." The PCM DSL fulfills both criteria as it is limited to the domain of software architecture and focuses on the quality prediction thereof.

Why can't we use an existing general-purpose modeling language, such as the Unified Modeling Language (UML)? While using the UML in software development is common, the use of a DSL for describing software architectures has the distinct advantage of omitting unnecessary information. This makes understanding and correctly applying the Palladio approach much easier than using the UML for this purpose. Furthermore, general-purpose modeling languages, such as UML, often have to cope with ambiguities in their use.

The Palladio Component Model is backed by a meta-model that covers structural views, component behavior specifications, resource environment, component allocation, and the modeling of system use. Furthermore, a graphical syntax can be used to define all aspects of the software architecture.

Model-Driven Analyses   *How are analyses performed in the Palladio approach?* Besides using a dedicated DSL for software architecture and its quality, the Palladio approach differentiates between the design model and the analytical model. In consequence, the model resulting from designing the system is not directly used for analysis, but another model is derived therefrom that is used for analysis.

How is the generation performed? In the Palladio approach, model-driven technologies are used for generating the analytical model. This means the modeled system is transformed by applying a chain of model transformations to it. The result of a model transformation can be, for example, another model or a code when using a model-to-code transformation.

What kinds of analyses are supported? To simulate a system's performance, usually executable simulation code will be generated by the transformation. This kind of code generation can also be used to create performance prototypes of the system. Furthermore, analytical models representing formalisms such as queuing Petri nets (QPNs) and layered queuing networks (LQNs) can be generated as well.

What are the advantages of generating the specific analytical model? In general, this helps engineers to keep the design model simpler and free of details specific to one of the analytical methods. In addition, the process of designing the system stays simple, as no expert knowledge of analysis is required. Moreover, analysis can be performed without manual steps, and existing analytical tools can be put to use. Furthermore, the derived analytical model can include additional information required for performing an analysis. This additional information can then be woven in by a model transformation.

The Palladio Development Process   The Palladio development process explicitly distinguishes between component development and design of the software architecture. While the *component developer* is responsible for specifying and implementing the components, the *software architect* designs architectures that are reusable by assembling components.

To evaluate quality attributes at an early development stage, we need additional information about the usage and the deployment environment of the system. Therefore, further developer roles are defined in the Palladio development process: The *system deployer* is responsible for specifying the concrete execution environment of the system. The environment describes the available processing resources and the connections between servers. The *domain expert* is mainly responsible for identifying and modeling important use cases, each representing the behavior of a typical user class.

1.4.3 Relation to Legacy Systems

Reengineering is a special development scenario for which Palladio is applicable. Reengineering means that existing software is taken as input for the development of an improved version. This is usually necessary when no extensive documentation of the corresponding software architecture has been created. Reengineering tries to identify the component structures in the existing software by analyzing the code. After a software architecture has been extracted this way, the Palladio approach can be applied to find design flaws and test for potential optimizations of the architecture. This is similar to the creation of a floor plan for an existing building.

1.5 Structure of the Book and Reading Paths

This book is structured into five individual parts that provide insights into the Palladio approach for modeling and analysis of software architecture from different perspectives. Part I describes the central motivation and rationale for this book and the Palladio approach. Part II explains the architectural modeling capabilities of Palladio in a general way that largely applies to other component-based approaches. Part III describes how such architectural models can be analyzed in order to predict qualities such as performance or reliability. Part IV explains how these modeling and analytical activities can be prepared and how to embed them into the overall software engineering process. Part V presents three industrial case studies that exemplify how the Palladio approach and its tools can be applied in practice.

In part II, chapter 3 describes how software architectures can be modeled from different perspectives to represent the structure, behavior, deployment, and the corresponding design decisions. Chapter 4 discusses how artifacts and decisions can be reused for several architectures; for example, using styles, patterns, reference architectures, and product lines.

In part III, chapter 5 demonstrates how individual quality attributes can be modeled in a goal-driven way. Chapter 6 discusses how we obtain the necessary data using code analysis, instrumentation, and tests. Chapter 7 explains the use of the data and analysis in order to analyze, compare, and choose design alternatives. Chapter 8 concludes this part by providing a glimpse on the simulations and transformations that are performed under the hood in order to predict quality attributes.

In part IV, chapter 9 describes how architectural quality predictions with Palladio can be integrated into different engineering processes and how they influence them. Chapter 10 discusses the relation of software architecture and requirements. Chapter 11 shows how Palladio can be used in evolution scenarios; for example, with forward and reverse engineering techniques.

In part V, chapter 12 demonstrates how Palladio was used to analyze a large and distributed system of the web-hosting company 1&1 Internet using only monitoring data. Chapter 13 presents an application of Palladio in business information systems to analyze storage virtualization at International Business Machines Corporation (IBM). Chapter 14 shows how a cost-efficient architecture was determined using Palladio for a distributed software system of the automation corporation ABB.

Readers may choose different ways to read this book and its five parts depending on their backgrounds and interests. Experienced software architects, for example, will probably skip part II and directly jump into part III on architectural analysis and quality prediction. Software engineers who are not yet completely familiar with software architectures could

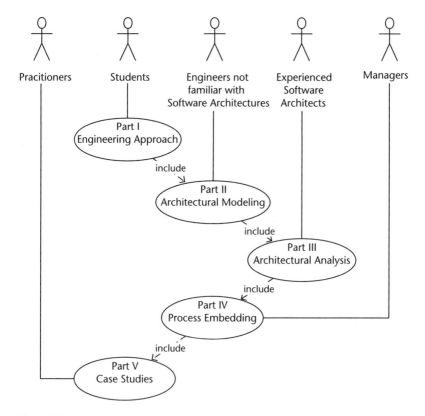

Figure 1.2
Illustration of some reading paths different readers may take.

start with part II and decide afterward where to continue reading. Managers might start with part IV, which explains the impact of the Palladio approach on other steps in the software engineering process. Practitioners with a very precise application scenario in mind could start with the case studies in part V to see whether Palladio was already applied in a similar setting. Students, however, should read everything or at least everything their professor told them to read. A visual guide to these individual reading paths through the book is shown in figure 1.2.

2 Palladio in a Nutshell

Ralf H. Reussner, Kiana Rostami, Misha Strittmatter, Robert Heinrich, and Philipp Merkle

In this chapter, we present the application of the Palladio approach "in a nutshell." On the basis of a running example called Media Store, we illustrate how Palladio helps in understanding the consequences of architectural design decisions on resource consumption and scalability. Starting with an initial architecture, potential design alternatives are discussed. Using Palladio, a software architect can analyze these design alternatives in order to select the appropriate one. Furthermore, we explain the role of architectural models using Media Store in prediction of quality of service properties.

2.1 Media Store

Media Store resembles a file-hosting system for audio files. It serves as a running example throughout this book because first, one can roughly understand its purpose without reading reams of documentation; second, it is small enough to be fully grasped within teaching courses; and third, it still has many properties of real-world information systems and hence plays an exemplary role.

On the basis of this running example, one will see the role of Palladio for getting immediate feedback on the fulfillment of performance requirements while designing software systems. At design time, a software architect faces major challenges in designing a software system. Such challenges include meeting the functional and quality requirements as well as satisfying development efficiency considerations such as reuse of existing components. In our scenario, typical to many real-world projects, components can either be implemented or already exist in a repository. This repository contains components that were developed from a third-party vendor or were implemented in-house. To understand how Palladio is used to analyze the performance of a system at design time, one will see a small example based on a set of initial requirements with some design decisions discussed. On the basis of simulation results, a system architect can decide which design decision is appropriate. In the subsequent parts of the book, we will explain architectural modeling and quality modeling with Palladio as well as use of Palladio in the development process in greater detail.

2.1.1 Media Store's Requirements

The primary use case of Media Store is that users can download audio files. In addition, users can also share their own audio files with others. Thus, Media Store allows users to upload audio files as a second use case. On the basis of these two main use cases, the Media Store requirements analysts have collected functional requirements. The functional requirements that are relevant for the architectural analysis in this chapter are the following:

- Users can download audio files from Media Store after selecting them.
- Users can select the preferred bit rate while downloading the audio files.
- If a user selects more than one audio file to download, the files shall be compressed to one archive file before download.
- Users can also upload audio files to share them with other users.
- Users can specify the meta-data of an audio file when uploading it.
- Users can browse in the store and get a list of all available audio files.

Furthermore, the requirements analysts have collected a set of quality requirements and constraints in order to achieve a good user experience, low development costs, and low maintenance costs, as well as to comply with legal regulations:

Performance: The response time shall be as low as possible, but less than 60 seconds for 95% of all requests for the expected workload, as introduced later. In the following, the response time is defined as the time span between arrival of a request in a component and the response of the component to that request.

Maintainability: The components of Media Store shall be loosely coupled to facilitate evolution. They should communicate with each other only using interfaces. This shall avoid a change to a software component propagating through the system.

Reusability: Components that are developed from scratch for Media Store shall be reusable in future projects, if appropriate.

Reuse: Media Store shall be, if possible, implemented using reused components from third parties to save development costs and future maintenance effort. Thus, when designing the interfaces between components, existing components shall be taken into account.

Security: Only authenticated users should access the system and thus the audio files. Furthermore, passwords should be encrypted before being stored in the database.

Compliance: Copyright is an important concern, and Media Store shall comply with respective laws and regulations. Therefore, any copyright violation shall be detected. For example, an unauthorized download of copyrighted audio files should be avoided.

We focus on the performance of the system as the main aspect with respect to the expected user workload. Potential implementations of requirements influence the performance of our Media Store. The domain expert expects the following usage profile, which describes client behavior, and the workload can be approximated as an open workload with the properties that follow:

• The domain expert assumes that the workload is memoryless. This means the previous states of the workload are irrelevant to the current state. Therefore, he or she models the distribution of interarrival times of the requests using exponential distribution with a rate parameter $\lambda = 0.03$.

• The domain expert expects that the file size of audio files ranges between 5 and 11 megabytes (MB).

• The domain expert analyzes the characteristics of audio collection, such as the number of downloaded requests, and considers them in the model.

2.1.2   User Interaction with Media Store

The usage model includes the following types of user interaction with the system:

SaveNewUsers: After users have submitted the registration form, the UserManagement component hashes and salts passwords and forwards their credentials to the UserDBAdapter component. The UserDBAdapter component then sends the corresponding queries to the Database component to store the users' information.

LogIn: The registered users can log into the system per the WebGUI component. The users' log-in information is forwarded to the Database component via the UserManagement and the UserDBAdapter components.

Upload: If a user uploads an audio file, the corresponding meta-data is saved in the DataStorage component without any changes.

Download: When users select an audio file with a certain bit rate to download, the WebGUI component sends the corresponding request to the MediaManagement component, which forwards the request to the MediaAccess component. The MediaAccess component creates an associated query for the corresponding meta-data. On the basis of the answer of the Database component, the MediaAccess component fetches the associated file from the DataStorage. After the ReEncoder component encodes the audio file at the selected bit rate, the TagWatermarking component writes the log-in identifier of the user into the comment of the audio file, which is sent back to the user. If more than one audio file will be downloaded at once, the MediaManagement component forwards the watermarked audio files to the Packaging component, which combines the audio files into a single compressed file.

GettingFileList: After the user has logged into Media Store, a request is sent to the MediaManagement component to get a list of all audio files. Then, the MediaManagement component forwards the request to the MediaAccess component, which creates the corresponding query und fetches the list from the Database component.

2.1.3   Initial Design

Performance is, across most application domains, among the most important quality aspects in the software life cycle, as it directly affects the usability of the software. During design time, an early detection of potential system bottlenecks reduces the costs of fixing

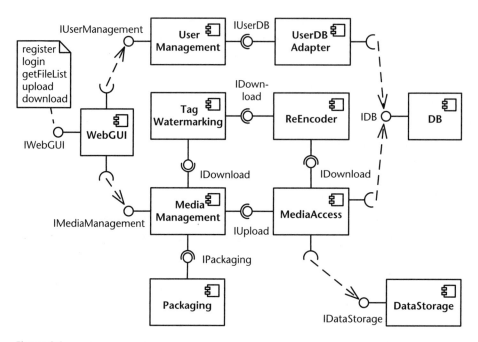

Figure 2.1
The initial architecture of Media Store.

performance issues compared to such costs in later development phases. Therefore, using Palladio, a software architect can model the software architecture in order to predict the performance at design time and identify performance issues in early development phases (Smith et al. 2001; Happe et al. 2011). Thus, before implementing Media Store, the performance of the architecture can be examined on the basis of the expected workload.

An overview of Media Store's architecture is illustrated in figure 2.1. Each component addresses a group of related concerns. While designing the system and components, the software architect divides the components into three groups. He or she then chooses a three-layer software architecture because of the type of components and for flexible deployment of the application on multiple physical tiers (Fowler et al. 2002):

Presentation layer: One of the main components of Media Store is a server-side web front end, namely the WebGUI component, which delivers websites to the users and provides session management. To meet the user authentication requirement, registration and log-in have to be offered. To this end, the WebGUI component delivers the corresponding registration and log-in pages to users. After the user has logged into the system, he or she will be forwarded to a site to list the audio files. The main functionality, however, is provided by other components. In addition, users can browse, download, and upload audio files using the WebGUI component.

Domain layer: Application business logic is provided by a central business logic component, called the MediaManagement component. The MediaManagement component coordinates the communication of other components. Furthermore, it fetches audio files from a specific location (e.g., a dedicated file server or a local disk) when processing download requests. As described above, to communicate with the system, users' registration and authentication are needed. The UserManagement component answers the requests for registration and authentication. The UserDBAdapter component queries the database. When a user logs into the system, Media Store does not store the password in plain text, but rather the UserManagement component implements further functions to hash and salt the passwords. To reduce the risk of copyright infringements, all downloaded files are watermarked. To this end, the requested files are first re-encoded. The re-encoded files are then digitally and individually watermarked by the TagWatermarking component. Afterward, the MediaManagement component forwards these audio files from the TagWatermarking component to the user. Hence, each downloaded audio file is uniquely connected to a user ID and can be associated with the user if the audio file should ever appear on the public Internet. To allow users to download several files at a time, we provide the Packaging component, which archives multiple audio files into a single compressed file. The ReEncoder component converts the bit rates of audio files. This can result in reduction of file sizes.

Data source layer: The persistence tier contains components that are concerned with the storage of audio files and their meta-data. The Database component represents an actual database (e.g., MySQL). It stores user information and meta-data of audio files such as the name and the genre. After the user calls the page to list all available audio files, AudioAccess creates a query that is sent to the Database component. When a user uploads an audio file, the MediaAccess component stores it at the predefined location. The MediaAccess component encapsulates database accesses for meta-data of audio files. Furthermore, it fetches a list of all available audio files. By contrast, the UserDBAdapter component provides all functions required in order to encapsulate database accesses for the user data. The UserDBAdapter component creates a query based on the user's request. The Database component then executes the actual query for files. All salted hashes of passwords are also stored in the Database component. By contrast, all audio files are stored in a specific location (e.g., a dedicated file server or a local disk) to decouple the DataStorage from the database. When a user requests files to download, the MediaAccess component fetches the associated meta-data from the Database. Afterward, based on the user request and the corresponding meta-data, the file will be retrieved from the DataStorage. When a user uploads a file, it will be stored in the DataStorage without any change; however, a download can cause re-encoding of the audio file.

2.1.4 Initial Design Decisions
Roughly, any functional requirement can be fulfilled by any architecture; however, the architecture strongly affects the possibility to fulfill quality requirements. Hence, while designing

the initial architecture of Media Store, the software architect has to be concerned with performance and other quality requirements. More concretely in Media Store, the quality-concerned architect wonders whether, for instance, the disk or the CPU could become a bottleneck to resources. In the case of the disk, an I/O-intensive component such as the database may be the root cause for a bottleneck, as it reads and writes data most frequently. In the case of the CPU, a CPU-intensive component such as the TagWatermarking or the ReEncoder component may result in a CPU bottleneck, as the watermarking and re-encoding of the audio files cause CPU load. The main questions for the architect are: If the workload increases, which resource would become the bottleneck, and when could the system no longer meet the quality requirements?

Additional design decisions arise. Although we can generally assume that adding a Cache component (e.g., logically or physically) would improve the performance of a system by decreasing the load on the disk. A logical Cache component may result in increasing the load on the server, and it may build a bottleneck. In addition, in case of many cache misses, the Cache component even may result in a performance overhead. Also, cache misses and page swapping would impair the quality properties of the system. Furthermore, addition of a new Cache component implemented in-house might also result in a high implementation overhead. The software architect can therefore opt for use of commercial-off-the-shelf (COTS) components to reduce the development overhead and increase the maintainability. The questions of interest are: Could the choice of a Cache component decrease the average response time? Would the new Cache component be a potential bottleneck?

Another influencing parameter is the TagWatermarking component, which adds the user ID to the meta-data of audio files. It is a simple and fast way to implement a Watermarking component. Such a watermark, however, can be easily removed from an audio file. Thus, the software architect might consider replacing the TagWatermarking component with a more secure one that makes it more difficult for a malicious user to remove the watermark and illegally redistribute the audio file. The software architect would replace the TagWatermarking component with an existing Watermarking component, which decodes an audio file, embeds an inaudible watermark into the audio information, and encodes the file again. Therefore, the ReEncoder component would also be replaced. Embedding an inaudible watermark rather than writing the user log-in information in the comment tag of the audio file improves the protection against illegal redistribution, as such watermarks are not removable by editing the comment tag. But, would the choice of a secure Watermarking component result in overloading the CPU of the system or, on the contrary, improve the quality properties of the system?

2.2   The Role of Palladio

There are basically three approaches to meet performance requirements: one is to build the software first and then to measure its performance and, if the performance is not satisfying, to try to optimize the software afterward. Although it is a very commonly used approach (due to lack of knowledge of the following approaches), it is obviously very risky, as performance problems are detected late, and their resolution may create high additional costs in changing the implemented software. The second approach uses performance prototypes (instead of the actual system to be developed) to learn about the performance of the execution environment and to draw conclusions on how to develop the software and how to design it to meet performance goals. This approach is also widely used but requires at least an understanding of the similarities of the test environment and the later execution environment and the creation of a realistic load driver. In practice, this can be very challenging. The third approach uses performance models that are simulated to learn about the performance impact of design decisions. The main drawback of this approach is that traditional performance modeling approaches require the manual creation of performance models. This not only requires specific performance modeling knowledge, but also the high manual modeling effort hinders the exploration of many different architectural alternatives and an agile adaptation of the architecture. Hence, in practice, performance models are often outdated or so abstract that they are only helpful in very specific cases.

This drawback of manual performance modeling is avoided (or at least minimized) in Palladio. Palladio is designed to use models as input for its automated performance simulation that are as close as possible to regular architectural models, which should be used anyhow when designing complex software systems. Palladio is a well-validated (Becker et al. 2009; Brosch et al. 2011; Rathfelder et al. 2013) and widely used approach for the prediction of quality properties of component-based software architectures.

In the following, one will observe which kinds of models these are in the Palladio Component Model (PCM). The PCM is one of the core assets of Palladio. It is designed to enable early performance, reliability, and cost predictions for software architectures and is aligned with a component-based software development process (detailed in section 9.2).

The PCM captures the software architecture with respect to static structure, behavior, deployment/allocation, resource environment/execution environment, and usage profile. The PCM describes software in terms of components, connectors, interfaces, individual service behavior models, servers, middleware, virtual machines, network, the allocation of components to servers, and models of the user interaction with the system. Overall, the PCM captures multiple views of software systems with special focus on elements that affect the systems' quality properties (e.g., performance and reliability). The PCM is partitioned into five submodels, each supporting a specific developer role:

Component Repository Model: The Component Repository Model contains components and interfaces. It can be used by component developers who are responsible for the implementation of individual components and interfaces. The component developer can also specify the Service Effect Specification (SEFF) for a component. The service effect specification is an abstraction of component behavior embedded in the Component Repository Model. A service effect specification abstracts from the control flow through the component and the component's source code by focusing on information relevant for analysis. For performance analysis in the Media Store example, the service effect specification expresses Internal Actions representing the resource consumption of the component's services in dependence on its context as well as external service calls. The component developer specifies the quality properties of the component developed by him or her. As a system or component can also be composed of other components, Palladio supports two types of compositions:

1. **Vertical composition:** Components are vertically composed by encapsulating other components into composite components, subsystems, and systems.

2. **Horizontal composition:** The required and provided interfaces of two components are connected via assembly connectors.

System Model: The System Model characterizes the component assembly. This submodel supports a software architect who is responsible for defining the intercomponent structure by assembling components (i.e., wiring components by connectors). A software architect estimates the performance of Media Store's architecture with respect to different components.

Execution Environment Model: The Execution Environment Model defines hardware nodes and network and is described by the component deployer. In the initial version of Media Store, there is only one server. If we plan to distribute Media Store and add another server to the first server, the network as well as the second server should be considered.

Component Allocation Model: The Component Allocation Model describes how components are deployed on hardware nodes. The component deployer allocates components to the resource environment (i.e., he or she defines which component is executed on which part of the execution environment). As noted, all components of Media Store's initial architecture are deployed to only one physical server; however, multiple server deployments can easily be modeled and analyzed.

Usage Model: The Usage Model defines how users interact with a system. The domain expert knows how users interact with a system and which parameters are used in the control flow. In the context of Media Store, the workload is assumed to be an open workload that is specified by interarrival times of requests. A user can either register or log into the system if he or she is already registered. Therefore, if the probability of the user registration is p_1, the probability of the user log-in is $1 - p_1$. Then, the user gets a list of all available files. The domain expert specifies that the user can only download files and upload a file. The sum of the probability of downloads and the probability of uploads should be one. The average number of files downloaded at once and the distribution of downloaded file size or at least its approximation should also be known.

In the following, we simulate the performance properties of the initial design of Media Store and each alternative using Palladio. The major goal of applying Palladio is to determine the best possible architecture with regard to performance properties of the whole system.

2.3   Simulation Result

The system architect models the underlying system with the expected workload as described earlier. He or she simulates the response time of the system for a specific usage model involving provided services (i.e., download, upload, getFileList, LogIn, and SaveNewUser) using Palladio. The goal is to identify the potential performance problems of the system.

Observation of the response-time simulation results reveals a performance problem. The results show that user registration, log-in, and listing the audio files have very low response times. The 90th percentile of response times of user registration, log-in, and getting the list of all files are all below 10 milliseconds. The 90th percentile of response time values is a response time below which 90% of response time values occur.

Observation from the response time results (i.e., figure 2.2) shows that upload has high average response time. The 90th percentile of upload response times is 0.2 second. Download requests have even higher response times. The 90th percentile of download response times reaches 146 seconds.

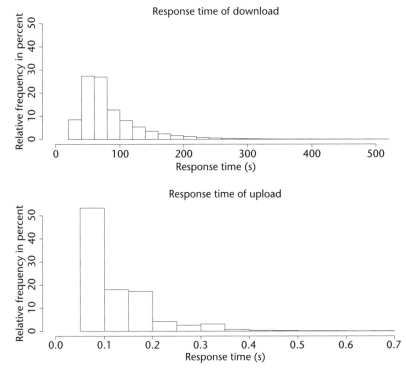

Figure 2.2
Response times of Media Store for download and upload.

This means the response times of upload and download requests are too high and thus do not meet the quality requirement. In the following, we discuss various design decisions and their influences on quality properties. The question of interest is whether the design decisions will improve the response times of download and upload requests.

2.4   Capacity Planning

Our results predict that most services of Media Store have very low mean response time with a 90th percentile below 10 milliseconds, so they fulfill our requirements. The services download and upload, however, have a high average response time. Consequently, we discuss only the simulation results for both services.

The software architect simulates the response time of the initial architecture under various interarrival times to identify when the performance requirements for download and upload requests could no longer be met. A shorter interarrival time leads to more requests that arrive per unit of time. Thus, the arrival ratio of the requests can be increased by reducing the interarrival time. To analyze the impact of interarrival time on response time, we vary the average interarrival time from 25.0 to 71.4 simulation time units. In this case, time units are equal seconds. Figure 2.3 shows that the average simulated response time per request rises sharply when the average interarrival time falls below 45 seconds.

The question of interest is which component causes the bottleneck? Using Palladio, the software architect is able to localize the root cause of such a performance issue. Although a download request is passed through all components similar to an upload request and additionally through the TagWatermarking and ReEncoder components, the SEFFs could be different. Thus, it is not enough to consider only the components when analyzing the cause of the bottleneck. The software architect should simulate the response times of calls to each provided interface of the affected components. In figure 2.4, the response times of calls to the IDownload interface of the TagWatermarking versus the ReEncoder components and of the ReEncoder versus the MediaAccess components are plotted.

Both histograms are right skewed. A pair of side-by-side bars in the histogram at the top indicates a call to the IDownload interface of the TagWatermarking component (i.e., dark gray bars) and a call to the IDownload interface of the ReEncoder component (i.e., light gray bars), respectively. A pair of side-by-side bars in the histogram at the top indicates a call to the IDownload interface of the ReEncoder component (i.e., dark gray bars) and a call to the IDownload interface of the MediaAccess component (i.e., light gray bars), respectively. Comparison of calls to other components is similar to both interlaced histograms at the left-hand side. Therefore, the results from simulation show that an IDownload call to the ReEncoder component causes the high response times of downloads. Therefore, the ReEncoder component is the cause of the bottleneck in the system.

Palladio can also help to find out the source of the bottleneck. As the ReEncoder component is a CPU-intensive task, the software architect assumes that the CPU would build the

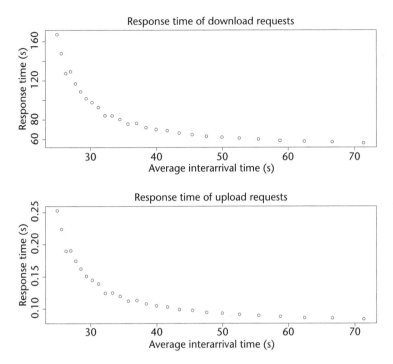

Figure 2.3
Average response times of download and upload requests versus interarrival times of these requests.

bottleneck. To prove this assumption, the software architect simulates the CPU utilization while increasing the workload (figure 2.5). The results indicate that the CPU utilization increases sharply if the interarrival time of requests decreases. Thus, the software architect analyzes design alternatives to improve the response times.

2.5   Media Store: Design Alternatives

In this section, we consider three potential design alternatives, which the software architect analyzes, and discuss the trade-offs between the prespecified quality requirements. Especially, the software architect determines the design questions with respect to the expected impact of each decision on performance. Therefore, he or she simulates the performance of the default and the resulting architectures using Palladio to identify this impact. Note that the following design alternatives do not capture all capabilities of Palladio such as reliability prediction.

In this section, the software architect simulates the aforementioned design alternatives using Palladio to assess the impact of each decision on performance. The main question is:

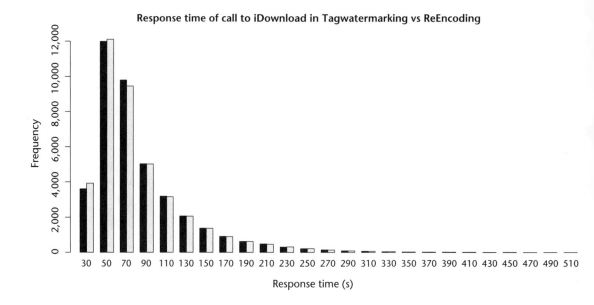

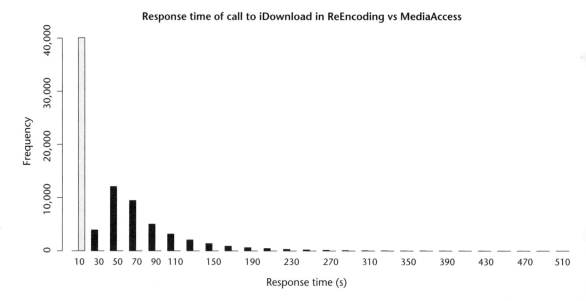

Figure 2.4
Response time of call to IDownload of TagWatermarking versus ReEncoder and ReEncoder versus MediaAccess.

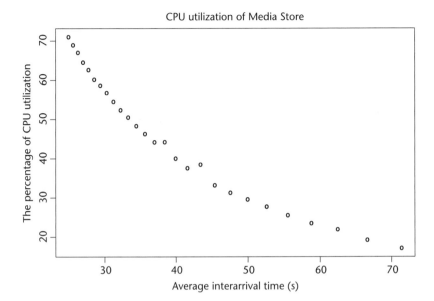

Figure 2.5
The CPU utilization of Media Store while increasing the workload.

Which design decisions will improve the overall performance of Media Store's architecture? Performance can be determined in terms of a range of metrics, such as response time, utilization, and throughput. Specifying response time as a performance metric allows determination of of fulfillment of several requirements, as clients must be able to download and upload files in a short period of time. Depending on design decisions, the software architect selects performance metrics for each scenario.

2.5.1 Reallocating the ReEncoder Component to Another Server
The component deployer is interested in balancing workload across all servers in order to optimize resource usage. Thus, different allocations of components to the underlying hardware lead to different quality properties of the whole system. Appropriate deployment avoids overloading of resources. Below, the software architect determines possible bottlenecks in Media Store due to different allocation of components to physical tiers. As components are interchangeable and could be deployed independently, the component developer expects less development overhead in this design decision. Several bottlenecks can occur in our system depending on the number and the size of files transforming through the network.

As seen in section 2.4, download requests have the highest response times due to high processing time in the ReEncoder component. Furthermore, as the underlying server realizes the whole business logic, too, it might be prone to overload. To reduce the CPU load on the application server, we can redeploy the ReEncoder component to a new server. To this end, we set up a new server with the same hardware and software specification. Before the ReEncoder component is deployed, however, we simulate the performance of both architectures to assess whether the deployment context of the DataStorage may reduce the response times. Figure 2.6 refers to both response-time predictions before and after implementing this design decision at the architectural level. The y axis of both histograms represents the percentage of download requests falling in each group (e.g., bar), whereas the response times of the overall system for download requests is graphed on the x axis. By the initial architecture, the 90th percentile of requests can be processed in less than 146 seconds, whereas this percentile of requests has response times of less than 138 seconds after the ReEncoder component is allocated to the second server. The results indicate that reallocating the ReEncoder component does not improve the download response times. Thus, the software architect allocates all components to only one server.

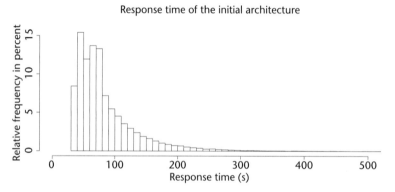
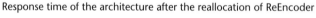
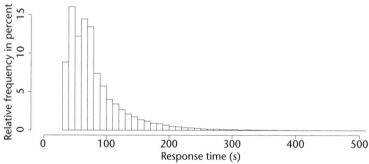

Figure 2.6
Download response times of Media Store for the initial architecture and for the architecture after reallocation.

2.5.2 Adding a Cache Component

To minimize response times, a logical Cache component can be used. The Cache component needs to be able to estimate whether a file might be downloaded in the near future. One method to achieve this is to apply an algorithm, which stores the recently used files temporarily. The hit rate of the Cache component depends on the cache size, the number and size of available audio files, and the distribution of audio files requested. As discussed in section 2.4, the ReEncoder component causes the high response times of download requests. To address this issue, the software architect adds the new Cache component between the TagWatermarking and the ReEncoder components, as seen in figure 2.7.

Thus, the frequently downloaded audio files after re-encoding can then also be cached and individually watermarked for each new user. On that score, it could be advantageous, if only a certain bit rate of an audio file would frequently be downloaded. The software architect is interested in the response-time prediction for both scenarios with and without a Cache component.

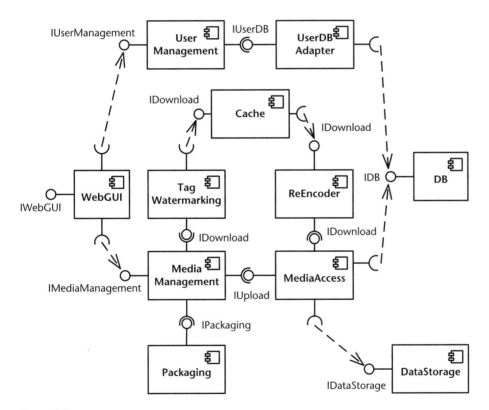

Figure 2.7
The architecture of Media Store after adding a new Cache component.

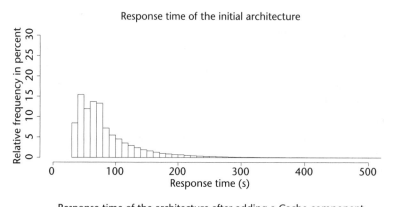

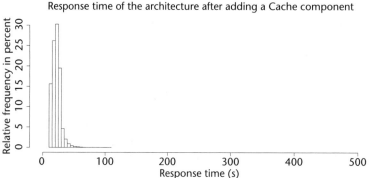

Figure 2.8
Download response times of Media Store for the initial architecture and for the architecture after implementing a new Cache component.

The histogram in figure 2.8 shows the influence of the Cache component on download
response times. In this scenario, the usage model causes a hit rate of approximately 60% and
decreases the average response time of users by 73.06%. Because the new Cache component
keeps recently downloaded media files in a certain bit rate and avoids fetching these files
again, it reduces external calls to the ReEncoder component, which was the root cause of
high response times of download requests. Thus, the software architect opts for a design
alternative with a Cache component.

2.5.3 Replacing the TagWatermarking and the ReEncoder Components
Deployment of various implementations of a component to a certain resource leads to different resource utilization. This results in different I/O and CPU utilization, as a specific implementation of a component could be CPU intensive, whereas another implementation of this
component could be I/O intensive. Component-based implementation allows for a higher

flexibility by component selection. In this case, the ReEncoder and the TagWatermarking components qualify as COTS components, as many encoder and Watermarking components already exist. As seen in section 2.3, the ReEncoder component is a CPU-intensive task and leads to a higher CPU usage of the application server and slows the reaction time for download requests. Using COTS components enables us to select several implementations of the ReEncoder and the TagWatermarking components. As already discussed in section 2.1.4, the software architect opts for replacing the ReEncoder and the TagWatermarking components with a more secure AudioWatermarking component that provides both functionalities, as shown in figure 2.9. The new AudioWatermarking component decodes an MP3 to a WAV audio file, embeds inaudible information about the user log-in in the audio signal, and encodes it back to an MP3 audio file. After deploying the existing component on a representative test server, its resource demand can be measured and estimated. We use these measurements to parameterize the Palladio model.

The choice of components depends on the performance of the system. Thus, the software architect simulates the architecture with these components to ascertain which one would improve the overall performance before he or she selects a certain component. Simulating the response times with the workload discussed in section 2.3 shows that the CPU utilization

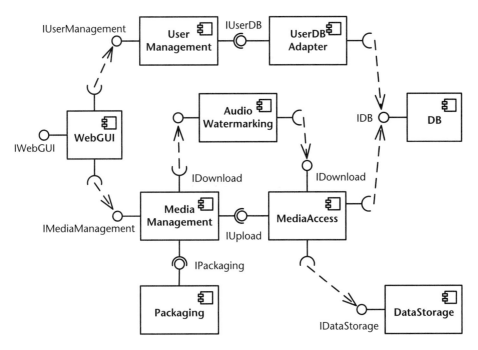

Figure 2.9
The architecture of Media Store after replacing the ReEncoder and the TagWatermarking components.

is more than 95%, and the response times of 10% of the download requests is even higher than 10 minutes due to CPU overload. These results indicate that the new AudioWatermarking component leads to even higher response times.

The results show that the choice of the new AudioWatermarking component would not improve the response times of download requests. Thus, the performance requirement cannot be met. As the software architect is concerned about the performance of the system, he or she would opt for the ReEncoder and TagWatermarking components.

2.6 Conclusion

"Palladio in a nutshell" demonstrates the usefulness of Palladio as a simulation-based approach for the estimation of quality properties of component-based software architectures (e.g., response time or utilization). With regard to Media Store, we summarized the main concepts of Palladio, which will be detailed throughout the remainder of the book. Furthermore, this chapter illustrates the different roles of Palladio in modeling and evaluating the performance of a system in the early design phase using Media Store as an example. To this end, we compare the design alternatives in order to improve the performance of a system. As shown in section 2.5.2, a new Cache component could help to improve the performance of Media Store.

In this chapter, we illustrated various developer roles in the software life cycle. Chapter 3 describes each of these roles along with their tasks, as well as view-based modeling in the context of Palladio. We presented architectural reuse in terms of the COTS concept. Chapter 4 describes further approaches to reuse of various architectural elements. If one is interested in calibrating the Palladio model of Media Store, please read chapter 6, which gives a summary of approaches on getting the data. In addition, we discussed three design decisions and their impact on performance. An explanation of interpreting the simulation result with regard to performance and identifying the potential problems at design time is given in chapter 7. Chapter 9 focuses on the role of the software architect with regard to building a system model using components and illustrates the software development process.

Part II Architectural Modeling

Part II describes the modeling process for software architectures, which is the foundation of all later engineering activities. It introduces the modeling concepts and principles that are needed for software architecture analyses in early design phases in which no implementation exists. It presents and discusses the different viewpoints (static, dynamic, deployment, usage) and the corresponding views of architectural models. Quality descriptions and annotations, which need to be added to models before performing quality analyses and predictions, are not explained in this part but in the subsequent part on architectural analyses.

3 Architectural Viewpoints

Axel Busch, Robert Heinrich, Jörg Henss, Martin Küster, Sebastian Lehrig,
Misha Strittmatter, Max Kramer, Erik Burger, and Ralf H. Reussner

In this chapter, we describe the architectural concepts of the Palladio Component Model (PCM). In section 3.1, we introduce the term *software architecture*, which is fundamental to the whole book. In section 3.2, we give an introduction to the principle of view-based modeling and explain its terminology and its use in Palladio. In the remaining sections, we present the architectural viewpoints in Palladio. Each section contains a description of the view types and model elements that belong to the respective viewpoint.

3.1 Overview

Definition 1 (Software architecture) *A software architecture is the result of a set of design decisions relating to the structure of a system with components and their relationships as well as their mapping to execution environments.*

These *architectural* design decisions play a crucial role in software architecture; for example, during design, development, evolution, reuse, and integration (Jansen and Bosch 2005). Architectural decisions are made primarily in the early phase of the software development process, often overlapping with requirements analysis. But also in later phases, when the influence of the execution environment usually becomes clearer, architectural decisions can be made or changed. Of course, in iterative development processes, the terms "earlier" and "later" roughly mean "requirements oriented" or "code oriented."

It is a specific property of software (different from physical engineering artifacts) that any design decision can be deferred to later phases in the software life cycle; for example, deployment time, configuration time, or run time. But not all decisions can be deferred together, and the decision to defer a decision is itself a design decision. Therefore, even in software systems there always exist early decisions.

Usually, it is the human software developer making these decisions, but this could happen with tool support at design time (e.g., Martens et al. 2010). It is debated whether non-design-time decisions (e.g., run-time reconfigurations) can affect the architecture. On the one hand, component allocations can be changed, which can be seen as an alteration of the architecture. On the other hand, the run-time reconfigurations are always foreseen as an explicitly designed degree of freedom at design time. In our Media Store example, the multiple instantiations of the database on a server farm in case of high load could be an example of such an explicitly designed degree of freedom. Hence, the architecture is actually not changed, as the early design decision to include the degree of freedom is not changed at all.

Software architectures should be documented with dedicated languages in dedicated artifacts. The code can only contain a rather incomplete "image" of the software architecture, as programming languages were never designed to document architectural decisions. But also independent of the capabilities of programming languages, conceptually software systems may have been growing over time in an ad hoc manner without guiding principles or organization. According to the definition here, such systems do not have an architecture. Hence, the architecture is not a somewhat implicit internal structure of the system. Much more, it needs to be explicitly designed.

Palladio is an approach for the definition of software architectures with a special focus on performance properties.

3.2 Models, Viewpoints, View Types, and Views

The Palladio approach is *model centric*: models of the structure, the behavior, and the deployment are first-class entities in Palladio, meaning that they are the primary elements that represent information about a software system.

The Palladio Component Model (PCM) is structured along the modeling process of Palladio (see section 9.2). Several architectural *viewpoints* frame the concerns of the developer

---

Digression 3.1

Software Architecture

In the literature, there exist two general understandings of what a software architecture is. The ISO 42010 standard (*ISO/IEC/IEEE Std 42010:2011 – Systems and software engineering – Architecture description* 2011) defines a software architecture as the "fundamental concepts or properties of a system in its environment embodied in its elements, relationships, and in the principles of its design and evolution." This definition understands the software architecture as a set of artifacts in terms of elements and relationships. Taylor et al. (2009) understand a software architecture as the set of principal design decisions made about the system. Jansen and Bosch (2005) share this understanding. Bass et al. (2003) understand the software architecture as the set of structures needed to reason about the system, which includes software elements, relations among them, and properties of both. The different understandings see a software architecture either as a set of artifacts or as a set of design decisions. The definition of a software architecture in this book brings the different understandings together.

Digression 3.2

Interface Models

Different interface models have been proposed in the literature. The interface model of Beugnard et al. (1999) consists of four levels. The first level defines syntactical properties such as the operations a component can perform, input and output parameters, as well as possible exceptions. The second level defines behavioral properties (i.e., the effect of operations through preconditions and postconditions). The third level targets synchronization aspects and describes dependencies between the provided services of a component such as sequences or parallelism. The first three levels define behavioral properties. The fourth level defines the quality of service properties of the provided services. Beugnard and colleagues consider that the four levels define increasingly negotiable properties.

The interface model of Canal et al. (1999) considers a syntactical level, a protocol level, and a semantic level. The syntactical level defines the provided services in terms of the names and signatures. The protocol level defines the expected call order of provided services and blocking conditions. The semantic level defines the meaning of operations.

---

roles in the process. This section contains definitions for basic terms that are used throughout the book. Section 3.2.1 introduces modeling and meta-modeling terminology. Section 3.2.2 presents the terminology for views, viewpoints, and view types. The use of these principles in Palladio is described in section 3.2.3.

3.2.1 Models and Modeling Languages

Model-driven software engineering (MDSE) is a software development paradigm that raises the level of abstraction in development processes: models describe a software system under development in different stages of the process at different levels of abstraction and maturity. MDSE is not a paradigm with clear boundaries. Many software development processes are model *based* but not model *driven*: models often only play the role of intermediate elements, which are used before or in addition to the implementation of the system in a general-purpose programming language, such as Java. In any case, common model types in software engineering are class diagrams, software architecture models, and models that describe the execution semantics, such as sequence diagrams, state machines, or block diagrams.

The notion of a *model* has very different semantics in the various fields of science (e.g., mathematics, biology, or philosophy). In this book, the term *model* is used according to the definition of the *general model theory* of Stachowiak (1973). This definition matches the understanding of the term *model* in Palladio and also in MDSE in general.

Definition 2 (Model) *A model is a* representation *of a natural or artificial original and has the features* reduction *(omission of information compared to the original) and* pragmatism *(the model serves a specific purpose).*

> **Digression 3.3**
>
> **The General Model Theory**
>
> Herbert Stachowiak noticed that the term *model* was used in many fields of science with very different meanings and complained about its use without a proper definition. The definition of the term in Stachowiak (1973) is supposed to be intuitively understandable; based on it, he develops a systematic theory of models.
>
> In this book, only the basic definition of the term *model* is used, which names three features that any model possesses. In German, these features have been originally named *Abbildungsmerkmal* (representation), *Verkürzungsmerkmal* (reduction), and *Pragmatisches Merkmal* (pragmatism). Note that Stachowiak uses the term *original* rather than *entity of the real world* or similar terms, which are often found in software engineering definitions of the term *model*. Distinguishing between a "model world" and the "real world" is problematic, as models may also represent other models. Thus, the term *original*, which does not make any assumptions on the "reality" of such an entity, is also used in this book.

Following definition 2, even program code can be seen as a very detailed model of the structure and semantics of a software system. Developers usually identify program code as "the system," which implies that it should contain all the information about the system and serves as the "final truth" in development. There are, however, also types of information that are not specified in the code; for example, the allocation or configuration of software. Thus, program code is just one possible reduction of a software system.

Model-driven development combines two main concepts (Schmidt 2006): first, domain-specific languages (DSLs) are used to express domain concepts, with the goal of reducing the complexity in the modeling of systems. A DSL is defined by an abstract syntax and a mapping to at least one concrete syntax. The abstract syntax describes the structure of a language in a way that is independent of its actual depiction or encoding. A concrete syntax defines the textual or graphical depiction or encoding of elements of the abstract syntax. For example, consider the Media Store (see section 2.1.1): a very simple abstract syntax could define that a song has the properties title, artist, and year. There are several concrete syntaxes for this abstract syntax: a list that displays the information in textual form, a graphical representation as dots on a timeline, or the ID3 container format, which is a standard for the description of audio files.

The abstract syntax of DSLs is usually not defined by a grammar but by a *meta-model*.

Definition 3 (Meta-model) *A meta-model is a model that represents models. The models that are represented by a certain meta-model conform to this meta-model. A meta-model serves the purpose of defining the properties that conforming models can possess, and the rules that conforming models have to obey.*

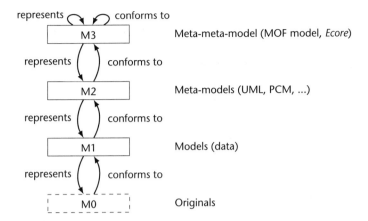

Figure 3.1
The modeling layers in the Meta Object Facility (MOF) standard.

The levels of representation in meta-modeling are theoretically unlimited but are usually set to a fixed number for practical reasons. For example, the Meta Object Facility (MOF) standard [29] defines three stages of representation with four levels M0–M3 (figure 3.1).

• M0 is the most special level and contains the originals. In the music example, the originals are performed songs, or audio files that contain recordings of the songs, or songs in the imaginations of composers.
• M1 contains the models, which represent the originals. In the music example, a Song element with the title "Stairway to Heaven," the artist "Led Zeppelin," and the year "1971" is part of the M1 level.
• M2 contains the meta-models, which represent the models. In the music example, the music meta-model is part of this level. It contains a class called Song with the attributes "title," "artist," which are of the type String, and "year," which is of the type Integer.
• M3 contains a single meta-meta-model. This meta-model defines the concepts "class," "attribute," the data types String, Integer, and so on.

Elements of a certain level conform to levels on the next higher level and represent elements on the next lower level. Because the elements on M0 are originals, they do not represent any other elements. The M0 level is displayed as a dashed element in figure 3.1 because the originals are the elements of consideration and are not created or modified by the modeler. These originals need not be physical entities, but can also be concepts and ideas, such as a piece of music. The elements on M3 are self-describing, so that they represent themselves and conform to themselves. This property is at first very confusing but can be easily explained: as the most general concept for modeling information, MOF defines classes, attributes, relations, and so on. Thus, the MOF meta-meta-model provides these concepts, so that meta-models on M2 can be created, which conform to the MOF meta-meta-model. The MOF meta-meta-model itself, however, is also described and organized with classes, attributes, and relations, as this is already the most abstract concept in MOF.

In the terminology of object-oriented design, the concepts of representation and conformance are called *typing* and *instantiation*. In MOF, these terms are also often used for elements of the levels M1 to M3. In our example, the song "Stairway to Heaven" in M1 can be called an instance of the class "Song" in M2, while this class serves as the type of the song.

According to this terminology, the Palladio Component Model is a meta-model at the M2 level, which defines a domain-specific language for the modeling of software systems. The actual instances of PCM are models at the M1 level.

3.2.2 Views, View Types, and Viewpoints

The ISO 42010 standard contains a definition for the terms *architecture view* and *architecture viewpoint*. The term *architecture view* is defined as a "work product expressing the architecture of a system from the perspective of specific system concerns." This work product can be a formal document, an electronic file in the format of an architecture modeling tool, or a description in natural language. The term *concern* is used for the interests and expectations of certain roles or persons in the development process. The term *architecture viewpoint* is defined as a "work product establishing the conventions for the construction, interpretation and use of architecture views to frame specific system concerns." These conventions may include "languages, notations, model kinds, design rules, and/or modeling methods, analysis techniques and other operations on views."

These definitions are, however, quite broad, as they only establish the relationship of concerns and architectural views and do not differentiate between a type level and an instance level for views. The notion *model kind* is part of the standard and can be understood as the meta-model of an architectural view. To distinguish between modeling levels precisely, the terminology of Goldschmidt et al. (2012) and Burger (2013) is used in this book. It deviates from the ISO standard by introducing the term *view type*.

Definition 4 (View type) *A view type defines the set of meta-classes whose instances a view can display and comprises a definition of a concrete syntax plus a mapping to the abstract meta-model syntax.*

The term *meta-class* denotes a class on the M2 level of the MOF hierarchy. An actual *view* is an instance of a view type showing an actual set of objects and their relations using a certain representation. In the MOF hierarchy, it is at the M1 level. A *viewpoint* defines a concern. This definition is not limited to software architectures but can be used on any kind of meta-model.

The relations of the terms *view*, *view type*, and *viewpoint* are depicted in figure 3.2: a view is a special kind of model that conforms to a special kind of meta-model, which is the view type. The view type meta-model defines the *projectional* properties of the views, while the

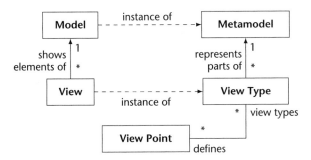

Figure 3.2
Relation of views, view types, and viewpoints. Modified from Burger et al. 2014.

actual view instance defines the *selectional* properties. A view type can serve several viewpoints, and a viewpoint may have several view types.

To illustrate the terms viewpoint, view type, and view, imagine that the meta-model for the Media Store, which was used to illustrate the modeling layers in the previous section, has been extended to not just represent songs but also albums, playlists, users, uploads, downloads, and so on. In this scenario, there are several viewpoints; for example, the user viewpoint, the database administrator viewpoint, the music producer/artist viewpoint, and so on. Each of these viewpoints contains several view types. For example, a registered user may use a "track listing" view type, which has the projectional properties that all the tracks of an album and their playing time are displayed, or a "downloaded items" view type, which defines that the names of single items, their size, and their date of download should be contained. The instances of these view types are views that define a selectional property; for example, an actual music album or the downloaded items of user John Doe. The database administrator viewpoint, in contrast, may use a "user list" view type that defines the projectional properties user names, date of registration, disk quota used, e-mail addresses, and so on. An actual view could select all users that have registered within the past 6 months.

The terminology that this section has just presented is used in Palladio to structure the meta-model. It is important to know that Palladio uses these specific definitions of the terms *view* and *viewpoint*, as they are also used in the literature with different meanings. (Please refer to the further reading section of this chapter for an overview of the different notions.)

3.2.3 Architectural Viewpoints

This subsection gives an overview of the viewpoints in Palladio, which will be explained in detail in sections 3.3 to 3.5. In table 3.1, you can see the Palladio viewpoints arranged in two orthogonal dimensions: the sections that follow are organized by the viewpoints in

Table 3.1

View types in Palladio arranged by viewpoints

	System Specific	System Independent
Structural	Assembly	Repository
	Structural decision	
Behavioral	Sequence diagrams	Service effect specifications (SEFFs)
	Usage model	
	Behavioral decision	
Deployment	Allocation	Resource environment
	Deployment decision	

the first column. The other viewpoint dimension is represented by the first row, and the entries of the table represent the view types in Palladio, which are described in detail in the respective subsections.

The view types are decomposed into the three main viewpoints *structural, behavioral,* and *deployment.* The structural view types contain information about the static properties of a system. They can be differentiated into system-specific and system-independent types. The *repository* view type is the only system-independent view type; it shows all components and interfaces that may be reused within multiple systems. The *assembly* view type shows how components are instantiated in a given system and how these instances are connected. The *behavioral* view types contain information about the functional (*sequence diagrams*) and extra-functional (SEFF) execution semantics of the systems. Furthermore, the behavior of users or other systems that interact with the system is characterized using the *usage model* view type. Finally, the *deployment* viewpoint contains two view types: The *allocation* view type contains information about which component instances of the assembly view type are allocated on which containers of the environment view type. The *resource environment* view type depicts all containers and the links between them. For each of the viewpoints *structural, behavioral,* and *deployment,* there is a respective view type that captures the design decisions.

3.3 Structural Viewpoint

The concern of the structural viewpoint is the dependency structure of systems as well as the specification of their building blocks. It includes two view types: the repository view type (section 3.3.1) and the assembly view type (section 3.3.2). The repository view type contains interfaces (which in turn contain signatures), components, and information about which components provide and require which interfaces. Please note, that interfaces do not pertain to components (Rhinelander 2007) and that we use the term *component* in terms of a PCM element in this section. The assembly view type contains assembly contexts and connectors. The assembly connectors realize linking of call dependencies between assembly contexts.

The role primarily concerned with the structural viewpoint is the system architect and to a lesser extent the component developer. (For a thorough explanation of the Palladio developer roles, please see section 9.2.1.) When designing a system's architecture, the software architect takes existing components from a repository and assembles them into a system. If the software architect needs new functionality, he or she can create new abstract components (see section 3.3.3). Meanwhile, a component developer can take abstract components as a blueprint and specify concrete components. To conform, the interfaces of the concrete component have to adhere to the constraints of the abstract component (section 3.3.3 explains this in detail). The software architect can then replace the preliminary abstract components within the system by conforming concrete components. (For detailed information about the software engineering process with Palladio, please see Chapter 9.)

The remainder of this section presents the repository and assembly view types. The hierarchy of abstract component types, its purpose, and its use are explained. Excerpts of the Media Store running example illustrate the subject matter.

3.3.1 Component Repository

A *repository* is system independent. It contains data types, interfaces, and components. Data types are used as types for parameters within interfaces. The software architect uses the repositories to retrieve components and specify new interfaces and abstract components. Component developers also use it to create and deposit concrete components. Figure 3.3 shows an excerpt of a repository. The following subsections explain the entities of the repository view type and their relations.

Interfaces

Definition 5 (Interface) Interfaces *are abstract descriptions of units of software. They can be used as points of interaction between components.*

Within the Palladio approach, an *interface* has a name and contains a list of signatures. Each signature represents an operation and has a name, a return data type, and a list of parameters that are typed and named. There is a list of predefined data types available, and the developers may specify new ones in the repository. Interfaces are first-class entities, which means that they exist and are specified independently from their potential use by components.

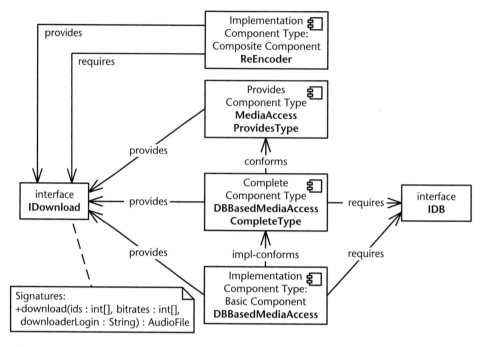

Figure 3.3
Selection of components and interfaces from the Media Store as example content of a repository.

Components

Definition 6 (Software component) *A software* component *is a contractually specified building block for software, which can be composed, deployed, and adapted without understanding its internals.*

Within the PCM, the basic characteristics of a *component* are its name and its relation to interfaces. For each interface a component stands in relation with, the component plays a *provides* or *required* role (i.e., whether the interface is provided or required through the component). A component has to provide at least one interface. One interface can play the required role of one component (A) and the provided role of another component (B). This means that component B provides the functionality required by component A.

An interface can be provided as well as required, even from the *same* component. For example, multiple components providing and requiring the same interface can be linked to a chain (cf. the chain of responsibility pattern by Gamma et al. [1995]). Figure 3.3 illustrates these concepts by an incomplete excerpt from the Media Store example. For instance, the DBBasedMediaAccess requires the IDB interface and provides the IDownload interface.

Figure 3.3 uses the relationship notation, in which relations are shown as arrows. This type of notation illustrates nicely, that interfaces can be used multiple times by several components. There is also an alternative notation (figure 3.4), where the usage of an interface is depicted by lollipops ("provides") and sockets ("requires"). Within this notation, it is not directly apparent if two interfaces are of the same type: it is more suited to display the wiring

---

Digression 3.5

Software Component

"Contractually specified" means that preconditions and postconditions are specified. If the preconditions are fulfilled by the context of the component, it can guarantee the postconditions. The scope of these conditions may be functionality and even quality properties.

In contrast to modules and interfaces, which were used to encapsulate design decisions, the component concept was motivated by reuse. This includes reuse within the same software system, as a component may be used in several places, as well as reuse within completely different software systems. Such third-party reuse means that the internals of the component do not have to be understood (black-box principle). This does not imply, however, that no information about the internals of the component can be provided. For execution, of course component code is required in addition to the interfaces. The information about the functionality and nonfunctional properties should be specified within the interfaces of the component. But the black-box principle does clash with the concept of inheritance in object orientation because inheritance requires insights into the internals of the class from which one wants to inherit. This becomes clear, for example, if a method is overwritten in a subclass: the developer should know where the method is called by other methods in the superclass, as not knowing this could result in unexpected behavioral changes of methods of the superclass.

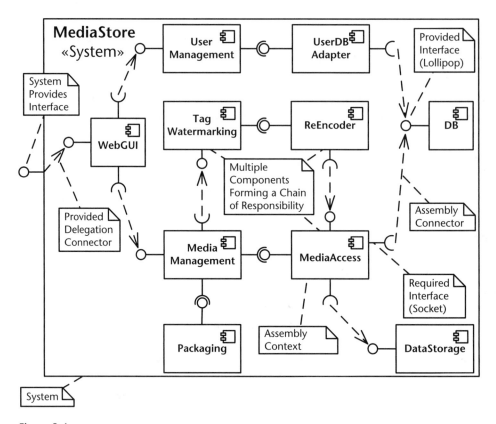

Figure 3.4
The Media Store system as an example of an assembly view.

of components within a system. That is why within the Palladio approach, we use the relationship notation for repositories and the lollipop notation for composite structures.

Components are either abstract or concrete. Abstract components only specify their interfaces, and the software architect uses them as placeholders in the assembly view. We explain their use in section 3.3.3. Concrete components are either basic or composite. A *basic component* specifies a (resource demanding) behavior for each operation of each of its provided interfaces. We explain the modeling of these behaviors in detail in section 3.4. A *composite component* is composed of a collection of connected assembly contexts. The interfaces of a composite component are delegated to interfaces of contained assembly contexts. In general, a component developer creates basic and composite components. Concerning software artifacts, a basic component is implemented through code, hence an actual implemented component. But there may even exist several implementations of a basic component (e.g., different algorithms are used internally). With regard to software artifacts, a composed component is the implementation through composition.

A component can be put into a context within a composite structure, resulting in an assembly context. The aspects of assembly creation and allocation are explained later (section 3.3.2 and section 3.5). When an assembly context of a component is created, the assembly context inherits all the roles of its component. Within graphical notions of composite structures (i.e., systems or composite components), roles will be displayed using the lollipop notation. For reasons of simplicity, however, we refer to roles as interfaces within this book. A component that provides an interface provides an operation for each signature of that interface. To realize these operations, the component may use operations declared within the interfaces it requires. The specification of internal behavior of operations is explained later (section 3.4).

3.3.2 Assembly

The *assembly* view type is used to specify the inner structure of a composite entity (either a system or a composite component). An assembly view contains assemblies and connectors. For example, figure 3.4 shows an assembly view of the system of the Media Store running example. Software architects use the assembly view type to assemble systems, as do component developers, who assemble composite components. In the following, the entities of the assembly view type are explained in detail.

Assembly Contexts   An *assembly context* is an instance of a component within a composite structure. An assembly context has a name and obtains the provided and required interfaces of the components it stands for. In figure 3.4, the system contains multiple assembly contexts. For example, the assembly context of the Packaging component is marked. Its provided and required interfaces are shown in the lollipop notation. Please note that in the notation used, it is not directly apparent that interfaces can be of the same type. It is possible for a composed structure to contain multiple assembly contexts of the same component. In the figure, however, components are assembled only once. This is also the reason why the assembly contexts are named identical to their respective components.

Assembly Connectors   An *assembly connector* links a required interface of an assembly context to a provided interface of another assembly context. Required interfaces can only be linked to a provided interface of the same type or to a provided interface that is a subtype of the required interface. In figure 3.4, for instance, an assembly connector between interfaces of the DB and MediaAccess assembly contexts is highlighted. For illustrative purposes, assembly connectors are not shown if the lollipop and the socket are directly connected. This is the case, for example, between MediaManagement and Watermarking.

The sole functionality of assembly connectors is linking and forwarding requests from the required to the provided interface. This is a major distinction from some other component-based architecture description languages where connectors are first-class entities and may provide additional functionality. Within the PCM, functionality-providing connectors would be a problem, as they should be applicable to arbitrary interfaces, which is not possible in general. So, within the Palladio approach, if there is any other functionality expected within the connection between two assemblies, it should be modeled using additional components. Such components can then be reused within other connections and even other systems, where the same functionality is required. Assemblies of such components may be automatically inserted to minimize the manual modeling effort. Programs that alter models are called model transformations. Transformations that solely add more elements to a model (e.g., more detail) are called completions. An example of model completion is the addition of encryption and decryption components at the ends of a connection.

Delegation Connectors   A *delegation connector* is used to connect an interface of a composite structure to an interface of an assembly context within the composite structure. There are two types of delegation connectors: the *provided delegation connector* links an outer provided interface to an inner provided interface; the *required delegation connector* links an inner required interface to an outer required interface. Similar to assembly connectors, the sole functionality of delegation connectors is linking and request forwarding. In figure 3.4, for example, a provided delegation connector is highlighted. It connects the provided interface of the system with the provided interface of the WebGUI assembly context. The figure does not feature a required delegation connector because the system does not require any functionality; however, required delegation connectors are illustrated analogously.

Systems   Within the PCM, a system entity represents a whole software system that is to be modeled. A system entity is very similar to a composite component, because it features provided and required interfaces and contains assembly contexts. They differ, however, with respect to their allocation (see section 3.5). A composite component can only be deployed on a single resource container. A system, in contrast, can be distributed over several resource containers.

A system has to provide at least one interface. Through the provided interfaces of a system, user interaction with the system can be modeled (see section 3.4). A system may also require interfaces. At these interfaces, quality of service annotations may be specified (e.g., response time), which describe the provided functionality in a high-level, non-parameterized way. For the Media Store running example, the Media Store system is depicted in figure 3.4. It is the outer structure and features one provided interface. The assembly contexts contained in this system are named identical to their components.

3.3.3   Component Type Hierarchy
Software architects have essentially two options when assembling components within system architectures: they can use existing components or let component developers refine and implement new components. While architects can assemble existing components directly, they generally have to wait for component developers to provide new components. Such

waiting is counterproductive in situations where software architects already have a rough idea of new components and would like to draft a system architecture without being deferred by component developers.

For example, a software architect may already know that a database access component for managing database connections needs to be assembled (e.g., DB in figure 3.3). On the basis of this knowledge, the architect could assemble and evaluate a preliminary system with a preliminary database access component (e.g., to provide some early quality estimates). Later on, the software architect could substitute the preliminary database access component with its actual implementation to get more accurate estimates (e.g., with a new component MySQL for accessing a MySQL database).

PCM's component type hierarchy provides dedicated support for such an iterative specification of components and systems. The basic idea is that components can be specified at different levels of abstraction on the basis of the amount of knowledge currently available for these components. Software architects can assemble components at each level of abstraction and substitute more abstract components when more concrete compatible components become available. Therefore, software architects can create an early draft for a system architecture even before component developers provide the final component specification.

Figure 3.5 exemplifies this component type hierarchy of the PCM. If software architects only know the functionality the component should provide, they create and use *provides component types* (highest level of abstraction). For a *provides component type*, architects have to specify all provided interfaces. Architects may also specify required interfaces if they already foresee that certain operations will be required to provide the functionality; this

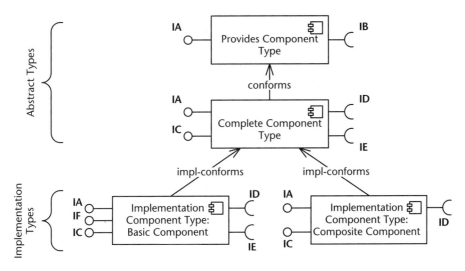

Figure 3.5
Component type hierarchy and *conforms* relation.

allows them to resolve expected assembly context dependencies early. Once specified, software architects can hand *provides component type* specifications over to component developers such that the developers can start refining and implementing more concrete variants of the specified types. Meanwhile, the architects can already assemble systems on the basis of *provides component types*.

As soon as component developers know all required interfaces for certain (in addition to the provided functionality), they should specify a *complete component type*. A *complete component type* features a full specification of provided and required interfaces. This full specification allows software architects to create a complete assembly of their systems and provides for more accurate quality estimates.

But software architects still lack behavior specifications for *complete component types*. Component developers provide such behavior specifications in terms of *implementation component types* (basic and composite components are such implementation components) that refine *complete component types* by adding their behavior. Architects can substitute assembly contexts of *complete component types* by corresponding assembly contexts of matching *implementation component types*. Such a substitution finally allows software architects to conduct fully automated quality analyses with Palladio.

The PCM specifies the *conforms* and *impl-conforms* relations as clear relations between *provides*, *complete*, and *implementation component types*. These relations establish the hierarchy among the component types and, thus, state in which cases software architects can substitute a component with another.

The *conforms* relation indicates that a *provides component type* may be substituted by a *complete component type*. For the relation to be valid, it is required that the *complete component type* provides all the interfaces the *provides component type* provides (e.g., IA). Furthermore, the *complete component type* may provide additional interfaces (e.g., IC) and introduce or alter required interfaces.

An *implementation component type impl-conforms* to a *complete component type* if the two following requirements are fulfilled. First, all interfaces provided by the *complete component type* have to be provided by the *implementation component type* as well (e.g., IA and IC). Second, the *implementation component type* may only require interfaces also required by the *complete component type*. Similar to the *conforms* relation, the *implementation component type* may provide more (e.g., IF) or require fewer interfaces as specified by the *complete component type* (e.g., IE).

In the MediaStore example discussed earlier, DB could also be modeled as *provides component type* that is refined to a hypothetical MySQL component, a *complete component type* additionally requiring a hypothetical IMySQLConnector interface. A component developer may inform a software architect of this additional dependency once it is discovered. Therefore, the software architect may replace the assembly context of DB with a new assembly context for MySQL. Assuming that a component MySQLConnector (implementing

IMySQLConnector) was already available, the software architect could satisfy the additional dependency by assembling MySQLConnector. Once the component developer provides the *implementation component type* MySQL, the software architect can directly substitute the assembly context for DB with a new assembly context for MySQL.

3.4 Behavioral Viewpoint

Behavioral viewpoints usually focus either on intracomponent behavior or intercomponent behavior. The first option describes the internal behavior of each component individually and is also concerned with isolated behavior that is independent of any other components. The second option emphasizes the interactions between components and abstracts from the internal behavior of components. In addition, scenario behaviors describe the usage of a system by users or other systems.

3.4.1 Intracomponent Behavior

Definition 7 (Service effect specification) *A service effect specification (SEFF) describes the intracomponent behavior of a component operation on a highly abstract level by specifying the relationship between provided and required services of a component.*

The main reason for specifying SEFFs is to enable an architecture-level analysis of the software. Therefore, SEFFs include abstract information of intracomponent "wiring." The actual abstraction level of how to describe this wiring depends on the kind of intended analysis. Analogous to different levels of interface abstraction, we can distinguish the following three levels:

• *Signature-list-based interfaces*: for each offered service, the set of potentially called required services forms the SEFF.
• *Protocol-modeling interfaces*: for each offered service, the set of all potential call sequences to required services forms the SEFF. Note that this set is potentially infinite, and also infinite call sequences are possible. Various formalisms can be used to specify this set (exactly or as approximation), such as, for example, state machines, push-down automata, or Büchi automata (Khoussainov and Nerode 2001).
• *Quality-of-service-modeling interfaces*: for each offered service, a "resource demanding" SEFF is specified (see chapter 5).

As this chapter is concerned with architectural modeling, it considers an SEFF as an abstraction of the control flow through the component by reflecting the externally visible behavior of a provided service while hiding its internal computations. For component protocol analysis and adaptation, SEFFs can be translated into finite state machines (FSMs) where transitions denoting external service calls are modeled as state transitions and hence can be expressed as regular expressions in sequences, branches, and loops (Reussner 2003).

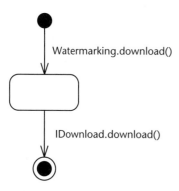

Figure 3.6
Example SEFF as FSM.

Figure 3.6 depicts an SEFF modeled as an FSM for the provided service TagWatermarking. download(). Edges represent calls to required services and are annotated with the name of these services, here IDownload.download(). The states abstractly represent the internal computations of a service after or before executing a required service. Notice that the SEFF only contains the call to the required service, while the component internal activity of adding the watermark is abstracted.

Although SEFFs reveal the inner dependencies between provided and required interfaces of a component, they do not violate the black-box principle. First, architects do not need to understand SEFFs while assembling the static system architecture as SEFFs are only used by tools performing analyses. Second, SEFFs strongly abstract from the component's source code as they do not reveal the intellectual property of component developers encoded in the service's algorithms. Third, SEFFs frequently can be generated out of byte code components, which are generally considered black-box components.

Component developers can specify SEFFs for basic components and then compute the specifications for composite components out of the modeled intracomponent SEFFs (Reussner 2001). For quality modeling and prediction, SEFFs are extended by quality-specific parameters as further described in chapter 5.

3.4.2 Intercomponent Behavior

When having defined the inner behavior of a component, it is desirable to define how components can interact. The intercomponent behavior, sometimes also called intercomponent control flow, describes how components communicate with each other. While the signature-based interfaces of a component define which services a component provides and requires, further information is required to specify the set of valid sequences of service calls. Furthermore, the dependency between calls to provided and required interfaces should not solely be defined as inner behavior of a component but as interplay of components. All services used by the intercomponent behavior can be mapped to corresponding intracomponent specifications. The intercomponent behavior can often be derived from the combined specification of component internal behaviors.

Sequence diagrams can be used to define and visualize intercomponent relationships (figure 3.7). They are commonly used to describe valid sequences of method invocations on an interface. The following elements are used in an intercomponent sequence diagram:

Components are the primary entities in a sequence diagram. Each component is assigned to a lifeline that shows the activity of the component. Bars on the lifeline denote the active phases of a component's service.

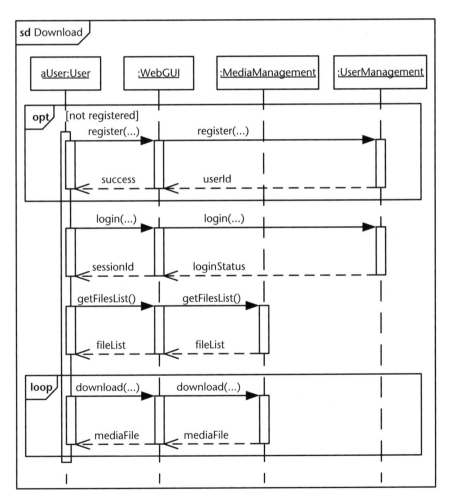

Figure 3.7
Sequence diagram for the Media Store download interaction.

Messages are used to define interactions between components. They are shown as arrows between the components. Usually, the operation name of the called service is assigned to the message. Furthermore, a message can carry the arguments of the service call or a return value. Messages can be sent synchronously or asynchronously.

Combined fragments are used to describe a set of similar sequences in a compact way. They are used to define parts of a sequence that are repeated (*loop*), alternatives (*alt*), optional (*opt*), or parallel (*par*). A combined fragment can have parameters (*guards*); for example, to specify the condition for an optional part. The notation is a box in the diagram containing the respective parts of the sequence.

In figure 3.7, a simplified sequence diagram for the download interaction of the Media Store example is shown. The presented sequence starts with an optional combined fragment executed when a user performs a registration if he or she is not registered yet. Then, the user logs in using his credentials, which are forwarded to the UserManagement component. Afterward, the list of available files is retrieved from the MediaManagement component. The sequence ends with a looping combined fragment that resembles the download of several files from the server. One can learn from the sequence diagram that four components are involved in the interaction. Furthermore, one has learned that the registration is optional, and the log-in services have to be called before doing any downloads.

In general, sequence diagrams should be kept small and focused to foster their understandability. Therefore, different kinds of interactions should be split up into multiple sequence diagrams. For a component-based system, commonly a sequence diagram for each distinct usage scenario is created.

3.4.3   Scenario Behavior

In addition to the intracomponent and intercomponent behaviors, domain experts can specify the behavior for usage scenarios in Palladio. These scenarios describe the interaction between certain user types and the modeled software system. User types can be either human users or other systems. Often, scenarios can be derived from existing requirement documents.

A scenario definition usually is a sequence of actions that occur during typical use of the system. This means methods of the provided interface of the system are invoked. Commonly, usage scenarios are defined using activity diagrams that have call actions referring to the called methods of the system. Each method call can be enriched with information on parameter values and input data. Furthermore, similar to SEFFs, there also can be alternatives, loops, and delays in the sequence of actions. In figure 3.8, a usage scenario resembling the sequence from figure 3.7 is shown. The register method is called with a probability of 30%, and the download method is executed randomly, one to 10 times, in a loop. Moreover, the execution is delayed for 1 second during each repetition.

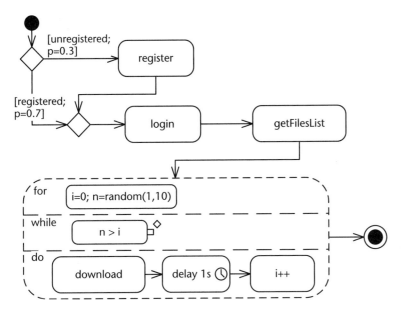

Figure 3.8
Activity diagram for a Media Store usage scenario.

The Usage Model usually contains multiple usage scenarios, reflecting different types of users. In addition, a Workload description supplements each scenario definition. It defines the occurrences of a scenario within a certain time period, that is, the usage intensity of a system.

3.5 Deployment Viewpoint

The *deployment viewpoint* is handled and developed by the system deployer. In Palladio, it covers the specification of the execution environment and the allocation of software components on resources of this execution environment. Such resources can be either physical (e.g., processors, servers, hard disks, communication links) or virtual (e.g., virtual machines, virtual disks, virtual networks). Palladio treats physical and virtual resources equally (specific properties of virtual resources, such as changing performance properties, are currently subject to research).

The execution environment is described by the *resource environment* view type. The *resource environment* defines *resource containers* (i.e., physical or virtual nodes) and their *linking resources* (e.g., network connections using LANs or WANs). A resource container contains several *processing resources*, each having its specific *processing resource types*. Palladio uses the resource type concept to define specific properties of such a class of resources. A resource type repository contains a set of resource types common for component developers and deployers. Finally, a linking resource connects the resource containers with each other.

Figure 3.9 shows a simplified view of a resource environment with two resource containers; namely, an application server and a database server. The stereotypes in angled brackets refer to classes of the PCM. The resource container representing the application server differs from that representing the database server in the *processingRate* of the *processingResourceType*. The application server is equipped with a more powerful processor with a clock speed of 3.5 GHz, as well as a disk with a higher throughput, compared to the database server. Both resource containers are connected by a linking resource.

In addition, figure 3.9 shows the *allocation* of the assembly contexts of the components assembled in the system. These components represent the piece of software to be allocated. For each system assembly context, a corresponding *allocation context* has to exist. The allocation context describes the allocation of the respective assembly context on one of the available resource containers.

Figure 3.9 shows two allocation contexts. The first allocation context contains the MediaAccess component's assembly context that is allocated on the resource container application server. The second allocation context contains the DB component's assembly context that is allocated on the database server.

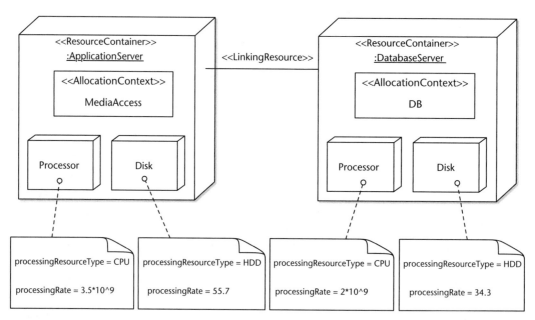

Figure 3.9
Example of a resource environment and component allocation.

Further aspects of execution environments specifically relevant for quality modeling, especially the quality annotations, are described in section 5.5.

3.6 Decision Viewpoint

From the initial design phase of the development of a software system, in which different alternatives are considered, to the evolution phase, in which restructuring of the software may be discussed and planned, architects always make implicit or explicit decisions. Usually, the already implemented features or parts of the system form the basis of such a decision-making process. Further input may come from a new or changed requirement or project constraint; for example, new quality of service requirements that need to be fulfilled or out-dated software that cannot be used in the future. Additional sources are platform changes of the execution environment, which have implications for the architecture of the application software. For example, parts of Media Store that should run in a cloud environment would be such a platform alteration.

The decision viewpoint (figure 3.10) supports software architects in these decisions by connecting all other viewpoints. In general, decisions can be taken on different elements of the architectural model. This makes it hard to integrate the decision viewpoint with the other viewpoints. If architectural decisions are documented only informally, on a very

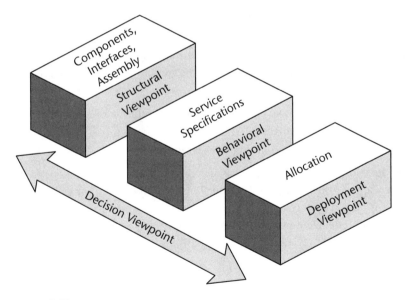

Figure 3.10
Decision view: Architectural decisions are orthogonal to the other viewpoints outlined so far. Decisions can be taken concerning any element of the architectural model.

abstract level, it is impossible to reason about the set of decisions automatically. If the architecture is modified (e.g., by adding a connector), architects cannot be sure if the change violates any of the decisions taken so far. The only way to check for this is to manually reconsider all decisions, which becomes a problem when the number of decisions grows.

In the Palladio Component Model, architects can therefore choose from a set of frequent decision types and apply them to the system's architecture. A decision type defines templates for a model-based documentation of design decisions. Architects can choose from a catalog of frequent decision types or can create decision types of their own. Each decision, which is modeled as an instance of the decision type, links to specific elements of the PCM and is equipped with invariants that have to be fulfilled as long as the decision holds. The benefit of this approach is that automatic reasoning can be done when the architecture is changed. In the above example of adding a connector, the change could invalidate a decision (e.g., layered architectural style). This constraint violation can be detected automatically. The challenge is that the set of possible decision types (together with meaningful invariants) must be specified in advance. The solution is detailed later in section 3.6.2.

3.6.1 Classification of Decision Types

With this classification according to Kruchten et al. (2006), we can distinguish four different categories of decision types that should be recorded.

Existence decisions: If an element is added or introduced to the system's architecture, an *existence decision* states why it has been introduced. This is the easiest kind of decision as the decision's details can be attached directly to the model elements (component, interface, deployment, etc.) and be found easily from these elements.

Example: An architect decides to separate two components and introduce a message-oriented middleware between them to increase scalability and average response times. An existence decision is attached to the newly introduced middleware component.

Ban or nonexistence decisions: When a decision is taken to exclude some element from the system's architecture, a *nonexistence decision* is taken. This kind of decision often leads to project constraints. In a modeled system architecture, nonexistence decisions are harder to express because the affected model element is not present. We can, however, include banned elements in the architectural model as additional information and state the nonexistence decision.

Example: An older version of a component needs to be replaced throughout the system. An architect may state a nonexistence decision saying that the old version of the component is replaced and banned from the architecture.

Property decisions state qualities of a system that are not linked to a particular element of the architecture but are general guidelines, design rules, or constraints. Often, they are the basis for further, more fine-grained decisions. If this kind of decision is neglected, architects have a hard time understanding why other decisions have been taken.

Example: Avoiding license fees by using free third-party software only is an example of a property decision. It can be stated as a constraint as well: the decision is taken to exclude third-party software that is not free.

Executive decisions are decisions that are related to organizational aspects (people, training) or to the business environment. Usually, they are not bound to specific design elements but more to the development process.

Example: Technology decisions such as "use Java EE" or a specific tool are examples of executive decisions. Assignment of people to a project or decisions about the development process (RUP or Scrum) are further examples.

It is important to understand the different categories of decisions. A chain of succeeding decisions is only useful if *all* decisions are recorded. In most cases, the underlying architectural model helps in documenting the architectural decisions correctly, which is explained in the following subsections.

3.6.2 Modeling Decisions
The idea to formalize the structure of documented decisions is fairly old. The first incarnations of such formalizations were decision templates. Text documents that capture the essence of a decision in a structured way were a major step.

More recent ideas included the use of semantic wikis or models, such as the Palladio Component Model, to capture architectural decisions. By using explicit models, architects have the benefit that they can directly link decisions to architectural models. A second benefit is that models can be used for automatic constraint checking. This becomes more important when the number of decisions grows and not all decisions that have been made before can be checked manually.

Purposes of Decision Modeling   Decision models can be used in software development in the early stages of the development process to support architects in decision making and, for the documentation of these decisions, to help developers understand former design decisions when software evolves.

Decision making: To make the right choice between different alternatives in the early stages of development, an abstraction of the various alternatives is needed. Architects can then focus on the important aspects, abstracting from technical considerations, by modeling different architectural designs and comparing them. The model of these designs can be partial in the sense that they focus on a specific aspect of the system's architecture; for example, only depict the deployment of a specific component to different servers of virtual machines (see section 3.5). Discussing the different options with the team or stakeholders is often much easier when using such partial views depicting different alternatives. We can consider architectural decisions as *first-class entities* and lift them to the same level as components and interfaces. Approaches from traceability, such as traceability matrices, are usually much harder to maintain.

Documentation and understanding: When using models for documentation of a system, architects usually work on one model that captures the current version of the implemented or intended architecture. To understand why a system was built the way it was, not only the current design but also earlier versions of the architecture are important. Here, design decisions come into play.

Definition 8 (Architectural knowledge [Kruchten et al. 2006]) *Architectural knowledge = design decisions + design.*

If architectural design decisions are connected to the architectural model, architects get more value by creating architectural knowledge as illustrated by Kruchten and colleagues in the equation of definition 8. It expresses that architectural knowledge is about not only the representation of the result (design) but also the decisions made. It is important to combine the two: by linking the outcome of a decision with the reasons and assumptions, architectural knowledge is created. Using models (and their history) and additional decision information, this knowledge can be used in later phases or by people that were not involved in the initial development process. This is an important aspect of documenting design decisions with architectural models.

We will see in the next subsection that an architectural model can be attached to the decision model. This gives us a link to the actual, formal solution of the decision.

3.6.3 Decision View Types

The preceding subsection contained an outline of how decisions can be represented on a generic level. The approach of recording decisions with this model can be applied on different abstractions of the system, because decisions are not bound to a specific viewpoint. They are independent of a model-based representation of the system (an architectural model, for instance), so the decision model can exist on its own.

In section 3.2.2, a viewpoint has been defined as an entity that is associated with different view types, which themselves are bound to a meta-model (or subset of a meta-model). By introducing or reusing elements of a meta-model, we define a new view type that can be used in different viewpoints. The decision viewpoint is very similar. It combines information from different meta-models (especially the decision meta-model) and from parts of the associated architectural meta-model. The way in which the connection is carried out must, however, be specified in a specific view type.

Example 1

Example Model of a Decision-Making Process

The Media Store system from the example in figure 2.1 is to be deployed on resource containers. The software architect can now decide whether to deploy the components UserManagement and MediaManagement on the same resource container or to deploy them separately on different containers.

A *Decision* element records the discussed alternatives, the pros and cons, and the outcome of the decision in a model (figure 3.11). While the deployment on one machine reduces cost, as less hardware is needed, it has a negative impact on the performance of the system. The various consequences must be discussed and written down in *Alternative* elements so that the decision can be reproduced and traced to the *User* who was responsible for the decision. The model-based approach of recording the decision makes it possible to note relations to other decisions and to the initial issue as well as the current status of the decision.

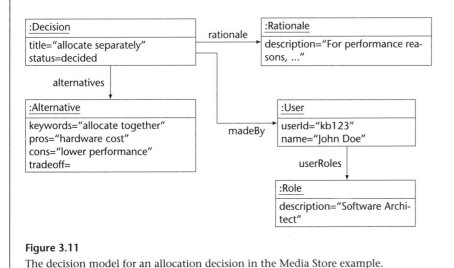

Figure 3.11

The decision model for an allocation decision in the Media Store example.

Figure 3.12 shows the connection between the different architectural viewpoints, the associated decision view types, and the decision viewpoint. It illustrates that specific decision view type elements are connected to specific parts of the PCM. Altogether, they represent the decision viewpoint.

The major benefit of modeling decision types on the meta-level and introducing specific view types is that we can reason about the model and the connected architectural elements. Some decisions recur very often in architectural design. They can be captured as first-class entities in one of the decision view types (i.e. decision meta-models). Invariants that must be

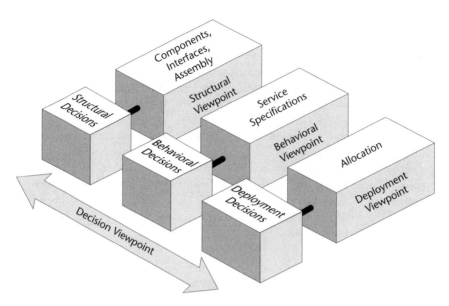

Figure 3.12
Decision view types: By introducing decision view types for all architectural view types (introduced in section 3.2), type safety of the different elements is obtained. This enables automatic checking of the decisions using invariants.

fulfilled by the architecture as long as the decision holds and is valid can be formalized and be stated as part of the decision view type. When the architectural model is altered, these invariants can be checked automatically. The tedious task of checking all decisions manually is replaced by an automatic checking process.

Structural Decision View Types   Structural decisions are concerned with the decomposition of a software system. In a component-and-connector view of an architecture, an architect needs to identify the borders and interactions of components. For that, interfaces need to be specified and connected. Dependencies on libraries or external services must be specified. If similar functionality was already implemented, the decision to reuse and modify or rebuild needs to be taken. With the proposed modeling approach, we record not only the motivation, the trade-offs, and the pros and cons of alternatives, but also the result as a formal artifact (the instance of the decision taken).

Structural decisions are connected to structural elements of the architectural model (i.e., component types, component instances, subsystems, interfaces, assemblies, and connections). Section 3.3 has detailed the structural viewpoint and the associated view types. In this section, we will give typical (=recurring) structural decisions.

Example 2
Decision View Type Allocate Separately
Recall from the introduction of Media Store (see figure 2.1) in section 2.1 that the components can be deployed to different hardware nodes. The decision about the actual deployment can be subject to a discussion of different quality attributes (performance, reliability, etc.). If an architect has made a deliberate decision to allocate the business and the database components to different hardware nodes, this decision can be captured as an instance of an *Allocate Separately* decision. This decision type contains references to the components that are deployed separately.

When, after a while, the architectural model is changed, this decision can be checked by a constraint: the hardware nodes where the components are deployed must not be the same. The architect does not have to check this constraint manually.

Interface decisions: An interface is a contract between two separate components of a software system. It hides all implementation-specific details and may contain method signatures (including exception specifications) or procedures, data types, and constants. Section 3.3 has highlighted all the important aspects. The decomposition of a software system works only if the interfaces are agreed upon, implemented correctly, and used in compliance with the specification. Therefore, the interface design is a crucial aspect of component-based software engineering where many explicit and implicit decisions are made.

When focusing on business interfaces (i.e., on those interfaces that are accessed by clients or other business components), most interface decisions are triggered by a requirement or feature request. An architect working on a list of feature requests must analyze the request and make explicit at which point in the system the requested functionality shall be accessed. If an interface already exists, it can be updated. Otherwise, a new interface must be introduced. In all cases, the internals of the implementing components must be updated, and components that require the interface can be updated to use the new functionality. Typically, this is a step-by-step process and a chain of smaller decisions about the updates or implementations of parts of the system.

Some typical interface decisions can be checked automatically if applied to a system modeled in PCM. Reconsider the architecture of the Media Store (figure 3.13). Accessing the database over the network can fail at many points, throwing various kinds of exceptions. Business components, such as the MediaAccess or the UserDBAdapter, require the database interface. They provide business interfaces themselves, which have been designed by an architect. A common decision would be to wrap all exceptions that are related to calling database functionality (e.g., all SQL exceptions). Instead of re-throwing the database exception, a new exception type must be introduced, and the interface of the business component

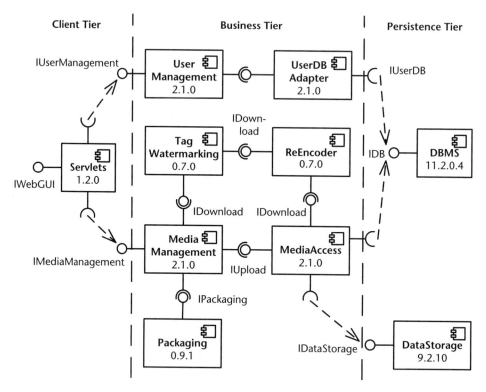

Figure 3.13
Media Store architecture enriched by several design decisions (adapted from section 2.1.3).

must throw this kind of exception. The interface decision that has been made can be summarized as follows:

- Forbid throwing of database exceptions (SQL exception, etc.).
- Define new user-defined exception type.
- Throw this exception instead of the database exception.

A design rule can be associated with the decision that checks whether all calls to database functionality possibly causing exceptions are wrapped. The interface methods must not contain database exceptions.

Inclusion or exclusion of methods, constants, and data types can be defined by decision types that are very easy to check automatically. Together with the common attributes that all decisions share, architects get the possibility to see for each attribute or method why they have been introduced (via the linkage to triggers, such as issues, feature requests, or bugs).

Component decisions: Interface definitions are a major concept of component-based engineering. Also important is the definition of which component requires or provides which interface. A facade, for example, provides a simplified interface to a large body of code. In some cases, it may be good practice to introduce the facade for higher understandability of the application code or to reduce the number of dependencies on third-party libraries. A facade component, however, can grow large very easily and account for the violation of code metrics (size of class, number of methods, etc.). Thus, it is crucial to document the rationale of such a decision.

Decisions about component hierarchies are typical structural decisions, too. Tiers are aggregations of components into hierarchical groupings. They restrict the access to inner components and introduce constraints to the possible deployment of components: if combined in a tier, components cannot be deployed separately. A tier is always assumed to reside on one (virtual) machine with access to its underlying physical or logical infrastructure. Decisions about component hierarchies (as composite component or logical grouping as a tier), if linked to the architectural model, are easy to check by constraints and therefore very well suited for the model-based approach to decision documentation.

System decisions: A system in Palladio consists of the assembly and connection of various components. A component type can be implemented by different implementations. In the Media Store example, one can see the database component DB that provides the interface JDBC, which is a generic interface to relational databases. Different types of drivers provide implementations for the interface. A system decision is taken when one of these implementations is selected and put into context in the architectural model.

Versions of components play an important role, too. The architectural model should state which is the version of the selected component. In order to be able to make common upgrades when a new version is available, the architects need to be sure which version is running. An estimate of the impact of a change can only be calculated if this information is up to date in the architectural model. Every version change is subject to a decision-making process and should be recorded as such. Even if a version is *not* updated (e.g., because of incompatibilities or costs of newer licenses or heavily changed advanced programming interface (API), it is a decision. The model-based approach allows specification of the selected choice, the rationale, and a constraint checking the architectural model for consistency of the decisions.

Deployment Decision View Types All decision types that are associated with the run-time system (physical nodes, virtual nodes, network topology) and the allocation of components to nodes are captured by deployment decision types. They can be purely related to the underlying hardware system (introduction of virtual machines, introduction of network linkages). Then, the linked model elements are from the *resource environment*.

If the deployment of components to hardware is of interest, *allocation contexts* are the prime associated elements. Allocation of two components on the same machine can be captured as an *Allocate Together* decision type, a separate allocation analogous to the *Allocate Separately* decision type. The links of these model elements go to the allocated components. The invariant must check whether the the components are deployed on the same node (allocate together) or on different nodes (allocate separately).

Logical groupings of components to tiers can affect the deployment as well: if aggregated as a tier, components must not be deployed separately. Tiers are designed for distributed allocation. They support the needed functionality of transporting parameters (including marshaling and unmarshaling) via the network. If a tier is introduced for structuring of the set of components, but not for distribution, and the different tiers are put on the same machine, this is another special type of deployment decision. Generally, if an exception from the default architectural design is chosen, it is subject to documentation with a decision model element. In later evolution stages, these exceptions are otherwise very hard to grasp.

Replication is a very specific type of deployment decision. In a symmetric replication, the same components are allocated more than once. A load balancer is usually employed to distribute the requests (via round-robin or a different strategy). It is crucial for the integrity of the architectural design that *no* changes (except parameterizations) are made to the deployed components. Otherwise, it would harm the idea of the replication—looking at one component, one can no longer know if the other replicated components behave symmetrically.

Deployment decisions are often made after a performance problem has been detected. For example, if the hardware on which an application server runs is under high load and a database is deployed on the same machine, it can violate given service-level agreements. Instead, the database can be put on a different machine, solving the load problem of the initial node. Of course, this can have ripple effects: if the network connectivity between the two nodes is very bad, the separate deployment can lead to another bottleneck. The chain of discussions and the alternatives that have been considered (and dismissed) need to be documented. This can be done by introducing the relations between decisions (e.g., conflicts or decisions that enable or override each other).

3.6.4 Extended Example (Media Store)

Figure 3.13 shows the enriched architecture of the Media Store discussed in section 2.1.3. Here, we will discuss typical decisions and several decision alternatives that can be found in the example architecture.

Interface Decisions   The UserManagement uses the interface to access users from the database. An alternative to the given design would be to implement create, read, update, and delete operations (CRUD) on the User object and have an object/relational mapper that maps the objects to database entities. In Java, this can be done by using the persistence API (JPA).

A young developer might ask why this approach has not been implemented. Explicit documentation of the decisions can help: reuse of existing code (older, not using JPA) could have been favored over reimplementing the existing functionality. Or the reason could have been the lack of knowledge about the new technology. All this information can be retrieved when the interface in question (IUserDB) is asked for linked decision elements. We can find the reasons for using the standard way to access the database (JDBC) from the required interface of UserDBAdapter.

Component Decisions   The TagWatermarking and ReEncoder components use the pipe-and-filter architectural style: they provide the same interface that they require. Using this interface design, the components can be made optional very easily. This is the central rationale for the interface design of these components.

The system design is a three-tier architecture: the client tier comprises the servlets that access the business functionality. The business tier consists of all functionality that is needed for user and media management. The sole purpose of the persistence tier is to store the data about users and media meta-data. It consists of the database only. The business tier could have been split into different tiers. But this option would have had the consequence that many interfaces needed to be capable of remote invocations. The possible benefit of more distribution to different nodes has the downside of more implementation of the components. We assume that the option has therefore been discarded. It especially allows for easy sharing of files between the components of the business tier because they share a common file system.

System Decisions   Selecting a certain database management system (DBMS) is one major system decision. According to the requirements of your system, you may have to select one concrete DBMS of a certain vendor. To get access to the DBMS, you need to select an adequate driver implementing the JDBC interface: you may select a certain version of the driver of your selected DBMS. You need to choose either a stable release of the driver that has already been used in other systems or you may choose the latest version to get the newest features.

In figure 3.13 UserManagement, MediaManagement, UserDBAdapter, and MediaAccess have the same version number for harmonization of versions. This has been a deliberate decision after a major version change of third-party components.

Deployment Decisions   The business tier and the persistence tier are put on the same physical machine in the system architecture (not depicted in figure 3.13). Although the system is prepared for distribution between these two tiers (e.g., by remote interfaces), an architect has chosen to put both tiers on the same server. First, the JDBC API is prepared for local and remote access anyway (connections are established by URLs and can access the local host if necessary without a performance penalty). So there is no special overhead to make the component a separate tier. Second, the system is designed for scalability: in the initial architecture, there is no need for a separate server (including operational costs, etc.) because the usage scenario contains very limited access. But, as the business grows and there are more accesses from the users, the system can be easily migrated to a distributed three-tier architecture. This deployment decision has been made deliberately.

3.7 Questions and Exercises

3.7.1 Questions

3.1 *: What are the view types and viewpoints that can currently be modeled and analyzed with Palladio?

3.2 **: Why should components not *have* but *provide* and *require* interfaces?

3.3 ***: Why can a component have multiple required interfaces?

3.4 **: Why do we distinguish between components, assembly contexts, and component types in Palladio? What is the difference?

3.5 *: Which abstract component types exist? What is their purpose? Can they be used within the assembly view of a system to define its architecture?

3.6 ****: Using the PCM, can connectors be defined that are independent from the interfaces they are supposed to connect? Can connectors provide functionality in addition to linking and request passing? Is there an alternative?

3.7 ***: Why is the intracomponent behavior in Palladio not modeled using UML activity diagrams but with service effect specifications? What is the difference?

3.8 ***: What is the relation of the intracomponent and the intercomponent behaviors in Palladio?

3.9 **: What are the differences between the assembly context and the allocation context? Why is this separation important?

3.10 *: What is the relation between software architecture and design decisions?

3.11 **: Why should architectural design decisions be modeled explicitly? Does this argument also apply to all design decisions that do not affect the architecture of a system but affect the implementation code?

3.7.2 Exercises

3.1 *: Using the graphical notation presented in this chapter, model a repository that features the following: the interfaces IDownload and IEncoding as well as the basic components EncodingAdapter and LameWrapper and the composite component ReEncoder. The ReEncoder and the EncodingAdapter provide and require the IDownload interface. Additionally, the EncodingAdapter also requires IEncoding. The LameWrapper provides IEncoding.

3.2 **: Using the graphical notation presented in this chapter as well as the entities defined in section 3.1, model an assembly of the ReEncoding composite component that features the following: its provided and required interface; a LameWrapper assembly context; an

EncodingAdapter assembly context whose interfaces are connected coherently to the LameWrapper and the outer interfaces of the ReEncoding component by using assembly and delegation connectors.

3.3 ***: Model a component repository and system assembly for a typical Web shopping system. This system should offer functionalities for browsing catalogs, adding goods to a shopping cart, and checking out and paying by credit card. The repository should contain components for all essential building blocks of the Web shopping system. The system assembly should connect all provided and required interfaces of the instantiated components to each other or to the system interfaces that can be accessed by its users.

3.4 ****: Recall the Web shopping system of exercise E3.3. Model a possible resource environment for the system and two different possible allocation models for it. Which quantifiable quality metrics that can be observed by end users might be affected by the different allocations? What could be the better solution, and how could that be tested?

3.5 ***: Recall the Web shopping system of exercise E3.3 and E3.4. Model the typical checkout procedure of a customer using a UML activity diagram. This function should be offered by one of the business logic components. Remember to consider possible alternatives and exceptional behavior. The procedure should be used when the customer clicks on "Proceed to checkout" after he or she added all goods to his or her shopping cart.

3.8   Further Reading

The fundamental concepts of architectural views and component-based architectures are also described in many books that do not focus on architecture-based quality predictions: *Software Architecture: Foundations, Theory, and Practice* (Taylor et al. 2009), for example, is used in many courses and is an excellent book for a first introduction but also provides guidance in the field of software architectures. Other books, such as Gorton (2011) or Bass et al. (2012), can be consulted to read more about the role of software architectures in the software engineering process or in real-world projects. Two influential books on component-based software development are the book by Szyperski et al. (2002) and the book by Cheesman and Daniels (2000). They describe component-based software development principles and offer alternative definitions of what a component is. While the book by Szyperski et al. (2002) covers many aspects from what exactly a component is to concrete technologies, Cheesman and Daniels (2000) focus on the development process.

The concept of *view-based software development* existed even before the era of object-oriented languages. It can be traced back to 1985, when Wood-Harper presented the multiview approach (Wood-Harper et al. 1985). The term *viewpoint* was coined by Finkelstein and colleagues in the early 1990s to describe the structuring of software in certain methods, languages, formalisms, and work plans (Finkelstein et al. 1992, sec. 3).

Recently, the terms *view* and *viewpoint* have been specified for software architecture engineering: the ISO 42010 standard was finalized in 2011.

The Accuracy Add-on extends the accuracy statements of Palladio with an influence analysis. The accuracy statements enable statement of the accuracy of behavior specifications in *.quality* files. Both aspects are today integrated into the simulation-based analysis of Palladio. Groenda (2011) presents the meta-model for accuracy annotation in detail. Groenda (2012a) describes the heuristic for determining the effect of inaccuracies and shows examples based on the Media Store example. The launch configuration of the simulation provides an Accuracy Influence Analysis section in the Analysis Configuration tab for enabling the analysis and providing the accuracy statements. A description and examples are provided online [21].

The PCM Coverage Add-on supports managing and presenting coverage information on behavior specifications. Coverage information for Palladio behavior models is comparable to coverage of source code but focuses on the architectural level. It allows reasoning about covered and uncovered aspects of behavior specifications. The main-use cases are quality assurance, testing, and certification of specifications. Coverage criteria for Palladio performance models are described in Groenda (2012b). The overarching concept and the required additional meta-models are presented in Groenda (2013). PCM Coverage provides extensive integrated development environment (IDE) support for all required tasks. Details on its installation and use as well as additional examples are provided online [35].

The Test-based Validation Add-on allows the automated verification and validation of implementations and hardware-independent behavior specifications. It generates a test suite tailored for covering a given specification with selected criteria. The Add-on supports the automated execution and compares the behavior of that specification and a running implementation. The validation uses the Accuracy Add-on described above for stating allowed deviations between a tested specification and a running implementation. The results of such a validation run show success or provide detailed information on deviations. The validation supports the creation of coverage information. Please refer to the PCM Coverage Add-on paragraph above for additional information on this topic. Groenda (2011) describes the application for platform-independent behavior specifications. Groenda (2012c) discusses the advantages of validated specifications for intellectual property protection. Groenda (2013) describes the application of test-based validation for the certification of behavior specifications and demonstrates the applicability and effectiveness based on the CoCoME benchmark. The Test-based Validation Add-on provides extensive IDE support. Details on its installation and use as well as additional examples are provided online [39]. The Behavior Validation Effort Estimation described online [21] extends the validation and provides estimates on the required effort for covering selected criteria for given specifications.

Each and every detail of the Palladio Component Model can be looked up in the Palladio technical report (Reussner et al. 2011). If one is interested in the rationale and scientific background of it, the main journal article (Becker et al. 2009) or the initial doctoral dissertation (Becker 2008) might be more helpful.

Enterprise information systems and business processes mutually affect each other in non-trivial ways. They are frequently not well aligned, however, meaning that business processes are designed without taking information systems impact into account and vice versa. While Palladio provides adequate means for modeling information system architectures, the approach Integrated Business IT Impact Simulation (IntBIIS; Heinrich et al. 2015a) extends Palladio by model elements to reflect business processes and their organizational environment. On the basis of a quality reference model (Heinrich 2014) for business processes, Int-BIIS models and analyzes the mutual performance impact between business processes and information systems.

3.9 Takeaways

In this chapter, we explained the architectural modeling elements of the Palladio language. The separation into views and the use of components and connectors seem to be an established standard and well known from other architectural modeling languages. There are, however, some specifics of the Palladio language that we want to point out here. Palladio has explicit first-class entities such as components and interfaces, which can exist alone, and second-class entities such as connectors, which cannot. This is in contrast to other architectural modeling approaches, which consider connectors as first-class entities such as components. Interfaces are well known to exist for themselves, but often enough, the classical lollipop notation obfuscates this fact.

The views of Palladio are motivated in particular through the information needed for further system realization and for the simulation of the system. Palladio's views enable a good separation of modeling concerns. For example, components and interfaces can be defined independently of their later use in a system (*component assembly* in the architectural view). Behavior views are mainly modeled by intracomponent behavior (i.e., what a component does when executing a provided service) and intercomponent behavior (i.e., the wiring structure of components and resulting control flows). The deployment view summarizes information on the resource environment (e.g., servers) and which component assemblies are executed in which resource environment. Decision views capture information (cross-cutting for the other view types), for example, on why a system is in a certain state and why certain architectural structures exist.

Other languages (e.g., AADL, Acme, EAST-ADL) provide other or additional views, such as the model by Hofmeister et al. (1999). The view of architectural decisions is mainly driven by concerns of system evolution. First, documented design decisions go beyond the results of the architectural design process by also documenting why this result was created. Second, they also act as a link between requirements and architectural elements.

4 Architectural Reuse

Ralf H. Reussner, Zoya Durdik, Oliver Hummel, Benjamin Klatt, Florian Meyerer,
Sebastian Lehrig, and Robert Heinrich

This chapter presents approaches for reusing different elements of software architectures.
Besides the classic reuse of software components of a component repository, reuse concepts
ranging from architectural patterns and styles via reference architectures to software product
lines are described. These concepts combine technical solutions for artifact reuse and generic
solutions for knowledge reuse. The chapter describes, for example, precise techniques for the
systematic development of products with a set of shared features, but it also demonstrates
well-proven solution patterns and styles that are applicable to general and common development challenges. All these concepts are concerned with the increase of software development
productivity through the reuse of architectural information and also need to be considered
in later model-based architecture simulations and predictions.

4.1 Terminology

Although the techniques presented in this chapter are all concerned with the reuse of architectural decisions, they differ considerably regarding their scope and the reused artifacts.
Techniques can be distinguished by their orientation toward reuse of design or code, as
depicted in figure 4.1.

Following the figure, we distinguish the reuse concepts components, interfaces, patterns
and styles, reference architectures, and product lines. We describe these concepts hereafter.

The reuse of *components* typically refers to the reuse of the implementation of the component; however, the sole reuse of component types is feasible as well (i.e., reusing the component design with its interfaces; see section 3.3.3). Note that in any case, component reuse
always includes the reuse of architectural elements; namely, the interfaces. Figure 2.1 gives
examples of components and interfaces of the Media Store.

Software quality is determined by a large extent through the software architecture as it
reflects important decisions (e.g., on structure and technology). *Design patterns* enable the
reuse of such design decisions for recurring design problems. Model-view-controller is an
example of a design pattern that could be used in Media Store to separate data presentation

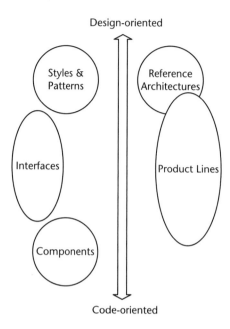

Figure 4.1
Levels of architectural element reuse.

from storage. This separation facilitates replacing a database component, for instance, without touching the components responsible for data presentation.

An *architectural pattern* represents a proven solution to balance conflicting quality requirements (e.g., performance, security, maintainability). Also, such architectural patterns enable a reuse of design decisions but with a broader scope than that of design patterns (i.e., for whole classes of recurring problems). As several quality requirements to be balanced exist, architectures often comprise several patterns.

Similar to patterns, *architectural styles* refer to reuse of quality-relevant design decisions. Architectural styles are expressed as constraints and hold system-wide. Unlike architectural patterns, however, architectural styles should not be mixed to keep integrity of design. This rule is in analogy to the word *style* in classical building architecture, where from an aesthetics perspective, buildings with mixed styles are considered as impure. Client-server is an architectural style in the Media Store used to structure the system from a high-level perspective.

A *reference architecture* comprises all the reuse of a larger set of architectural design decisions for a well-defined application domain. Reference architectures define component types through interfaces, the component assembly, and often options for deployment. But there is an implicit variability in using a reference architecture: components need only be instantiated in the actual architecture, if needed for the specific applications. Hence, not all components of a reference architecture need to be realized. For example, the Media Store architecture might serve as a reference architecture if its general structure is applied as a guideline or blueprint for other file-hosting systems.

A *software product line* adds to a reference architecture an explicit model for variability. Usually, a feature diagram shows configuration options and their inner dependencies. Imagine that variants of the Media Store system exist. Common features of these variants may be developed, managed, and evolved as a product line.

4.2   Component and Interface Reuse

As already discussed in section 3.3.1, a component is a piece of software that can be deployed in arbitrary contexts without the need to understand or even change its internals. In other words, component reuse is supposed to happen in a black-box manner. This manner in turn implies that the functionality of a component is accessible via a well-defined interface clearly stating its provided operations and required dependencies. Because interfaces in common programming languages usually contain merely syntactical and only rather limited semantic information (e.g., a method name, a list of parameter and result types), various works have aimed to enrich interfaces with additional information, such as protocol information (Nierstrasz 1993) or quality of service information (Frølund and Koisten 1998). But, "Without a precise specification attached to each reusable component ... no one can trust a supposedly reusable component," as Jézéquel and Meyer (1997) state in their closing comments of their assessment of the Ariane 5 failure. In other words, without efficiently and reliably selecting the "right" (or actually "best") software component, the potential benefits of reuse cannot be fully exploited. Consequently, Meyer's idea of *design by contract* (DbC; Meyer 1986) aims to clearly specify the responsibilities of the code calling a method and the code of the method body. From a DbC point of view, a software system consists of communicating components whose interactions are based on mutual obligations and benefits specified in the form of contracts inspired by the Hoare triple (Hoare 1969). Contracts state (a) what conditions a caller (client) has to fulfill in order to call a method (preconditions) and (b) what conditions a method (supplier) has to ensure (postconditions), given that the preconditions have been fulfilled. One of the biggest advantages of DbC is that implicit information and assumptions concerning a software component are made explicit so that obligations are clearly attributed to the responsible party. But the concept of DbC reaches its limitations whenever the definition of the contracts is approximately as complex as the implementation of the underlying functionality (cognitive complexity) or the validation of contracts at run time is as time consuming as the execution of the guarded program code (computational complexity). Moreover, the undecidability of the halting problem also puts a theoretical limitation on the ability to check by prior analysis before run time whether a component is compliant with its contract. Also, matching two contracts to search for reuse candidates could be undecidable if the logical formalism used to specify the preconditions and postconditions is beyond first-order predicate logic (Gödel 1931). Further established ideas concerning the enhancement of the expressiveness of interfaces include the use of ontologies (Braga et al. 2001) or state machines (Nierstrasz 1993; Reussner et al. 1998; Alfaro and Henzinger 2001). These approaches aim to support the identification of reuse candidates and to simplify the matching of reuse candidates to a given specification.

The "open source revolution" has made thousands of potentially reusable software projects freely available on the Internet and hence opened interesting new opportunities for researchers and practitioners alike (Hummel and Atkinson 2006). Both academia and industry have developed a number of software search engines that aim to make this vast amount of reusable material better accessible to developers. After all, these are at least supporting searches for the interfaces of indexed classes so that an application to "real" components is straightforward. But as discussed above, the match of an interface still does not guarantee the availability of the desired functionality (Hummel et al. 2007). In addition, the larger an interface, the more challenging it will be to find matching candidates for it. Two pragmatic solutions have emerged for this challenge in recent years: first, inspired by test-driven development (Beck 2003), researchers in Germany and the United States have developed the notion of test-driven reuse (Hummel and Atkinson 2004; Lazzarini Lemos et al. 2011) where test cases are used to specify the syntax and at least partially the semantics of a desired component.

The second pragmatic approach presented aims at the automatic creation of adapters (Hummel and Atkinson 2010) in order to overcome the problem of mismatching interfaces. Again, the core idea is to use test cases to identify the correct adapter from a set of generated adapters for the potentially matching component (usually called the adaptee). The adapters are created systematically by combining all possible operation mappings between the desired interface and the reusable candidate (i.e., the adaptee). Each created adapter is then executed with its corresponding adaptee and the test cases until the tests either pass or finally fail. Mismatches on the protocol or quality of service level, however, are only implicitly addressed by this approach.

Once a suitable component is found (e.g., with the approaches mentioned above), it needs to be "built in" to the architecture, and its impact on the quality of the overall system needs to be estimated. The quality of service of executing component services, however, depends on several *context factors* that are external to component specifications and implementations. These factors include usage profile, externally connected components, and the execution environment where the component is deployed. Only with information about such external context factors can software architects accurately estimate quality of service properties. For example, the software architect needs knowledge about the resource environment the Database component is allocated to so that the architect can accurately estimate the response times of Media Store's Database services.

As illustrated in figure 4.2, Palladio accounts for such external context factors by an explicit context model for components (Becker et al. 2006). The left column of figure 4.2 depicts different levels within the software life cycle; with earlier levels at the top and later levels at the bottom. Each of these levels is linked to corresponding Palladio submodels. These submodels provide the means to model the Palladio Component Model (PCM) elements illustrated in the middle column of figure 4.2. Most interesting, each level comes with a different set of unbound context factors important for quality of service analysis (right column of figure 4.2). Lower levels come with fewer unbound context factors and, thus, enable software architects to estimate quality of service more accurately.

As shown in figure 4.2, the *specification and implementation* level comes with the most unbound context factors. At this level, component developers specify and implement component types in repositories. These component types can be any type of the component type hierarchy (see section 3.3.3). Accordingly, component developers specify provided and required component roles as well as their service effects specifications; however, they have no knowledge about the resolving of external services within assembly contexts, their allocation, the state of components at run time, or about concrete usage profiles. To cope with this lack of knowledge, component developers parameterize component types by the listed context factors; they leave binding of these factors to lower levels. For example, the component developer of Media Store's Database component may specify an action that demands some CPU work units but leaves the specification of the actual CPU processing rate as an unbound context factor.

At the next lower level, the *assembly* level, software architects bind the unbound *external services* context factor for component types, thus still leaving three factors unbound. They realize this binding by specifying assembly contexts within assembly models for systems. Given such systems, software architects can already give early, manual quality of service estimates; however, these are typically inaccurate and cannot be automated because of unbound context factors. For example, the CPU processing rate from the example above is still unbound at this level.

Estimates become more accurate at the *allocation* level, where system deployers bind the *allocation* context factor. For this binding, they specify resource environments and allocate assembly contexts of systems to available resource containers within these environments. Therefore, quality of service estimates can now consider the actual resources on which components will operate (e.g., CPUs and hard disks including their scheduling). The software architect from the example with the unbound CPU processing rate can now estimate (e.g., response times) with a higher accuracy because he or she can now compute response times on the basis of demanded CPU work units and CPU processing rate. But the architect still lacks information about the workload to the Database component (i.e., its usage profile) and has again to stick to inaccurate estimates.

At the *run-time* level, system deployers instantiate components, thus making state information available (*state* context factor). This argumentation follows the classical instance

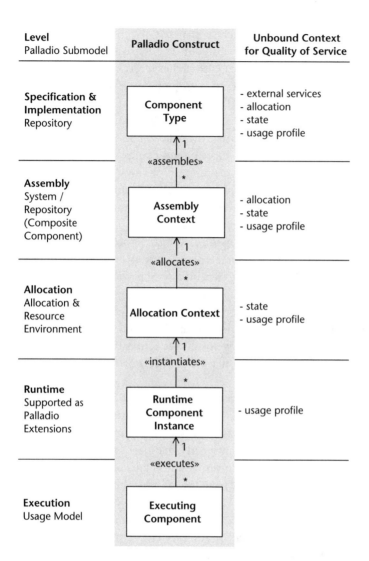

Level Palladio Submodel	Palladio Construct	Unbound Context for Quality of Service
Specification & Implementation Repository	**Component Type**	- external services - allocation - state - usage profile
	↑ 1 «assembles» *	
Assembly System / Repository (Composite Component)	**Assembly Context**	- allocation - state - usage profile
	↑ 1 «allocates» *	
Allocation Allocation & Resource Environment	**Allocation Context**	- state - usage profile
	↑ 1 «instantiates» *	
Runtime Supported as Palladio Extensions	**Runtime Component Instance**	- usage profile
	↑ 1 «executes» *	
Execution Usage Model	**Executing Component**	

Figure 4.2
Palladio submodels can be distinguished on the basis of unbound component context factors.

definition of compiler construction: as soon as a component type allocates its memory to manage state information, it becomes an instance. Palladio supports modeling such state information only using extensions such as those available at the SDQ Wiki [37] and from Kapova et al. (2010) and Happe et al. (2013). The architect of the example still cannot give accurate estimates because the usage profile of the Database component is unavailable at this level.

The lowest level, the *execution* level, comes with no remaining unbound context factors. At this level, usage profiles of components become available that set components into execution: threads arrive at components, requesting their particular functionality and potentially demanding resources and altering state information. In Palladio, domain experts use usage models to characterize such usage profiles on the system level. The concrete usage profile for a given run-time component instance can then automatically be computed within simulations according to section 5.4. Given that all context factors are bound at this level, software architects can use Palladio simulations that accurately reflect the actual execution of real-world components in terms of their quality of service. For example, the architect analyzing the Database component can now accurately estimate its performance in terms of response times.

Finally, note the cardinalities depicted at the middle column of figure 4.2. Generally, the relation between an upper and a lower Palladio construct is a one-to-many relation. Accordingly, component types can be assembled several times within assembly contexts. Assembly contexts can likewise be allocated several times (e.g., when one assembly context is replicated in a cluster). Also, the allocation context potentially involves several run-time component instances as, for example, typically used for component instance pools. Finally, a run-time component instance can have several executing components reflecting created threads for a given user.

4.3 Architectural Style Reuse

Architectural styles are a means to the reuse of architectural knowledge. The idea of architectural styles is best explained in the analogy to building architecture, where also one speaks of the style of the building (e.g., romanic, gothic, baroque, etc.). Examples for software architecture styles are object-oriented design (with its inheritance), modular design (without inheritance), and layering. In software architecture as in building architecture, styles can be seen as rules restricting the design space of the architect. Through this restriction, in software architecture the system is organized and structured in a coherent manner that is easier to understand than in the case of systems that are designed without such comprehensive rules. As styles are similar to architectural patterns, which are also sometimes expressed as constraints of the design space, the terms *architectural style* and *architectural pattern* are sometimes used interchangeably in the literature. More formally, this is expressed in the definition by Taylor et al. (2009):

Definition 9 (Architectural style) *An* architectural style *is a named collection of architectural design decisions that (1) are applicable in a given development context, (2) constrain architectural design decisions that are specific to a particular system within that context, and (3) elicit beneficial qualities in each resulting system.*

Architectural styles enable the reuse of quality-relevant design decisions, expressed as system-wide constraints (see section 4.1). We can derive four characteristics of such styles:

Coarse-grained decision: An architectural style can be seen as a large coarse-grained design decision, and it is followed by a collection of finer-grained design decisions. This coarse-grained design decision is based on the experience with similar problems in a similar context. It can be seen as a kind of "best practice" to approach the solution in a general way.

Restricted design space: This coarse-grained decision immediately limits the design space. For example, decisions for a component-based architectural style forces structuring of the subsystem parts inside of smaller reusable entities—components. It limits all kinds of following design decisions, starting from management and organizational design decisions (e.g., which developers shall work on the project), to the technological decisions (e.g., decisions on deployment and frameworks).

Warranty for quality: The use of an architectural style is, to a certain extent, a warranty that its promised quality properties are achieved. Because of its restricted design space, software architects can only select from potential design decisions that are already tied to a given problem in a given context. And although the final result still strongly depends on how architects and development teams followed a style, the architectural style creates borders for the potentially better architectural design. Therefore, the selection of style ensures qualities and properties of the to-be-built software system.

Improved maintenance and evolution: A clearly defined architectural style improves understanding of a system. Maintainers of the system know which parts or interactions of a system to expect. The style also guides and supports the system's further evolution.

Given these characteristics, architectural knowledge can be reused as styles; this means as bundled, meaningful restrictions on different parts of an architecture. Examples of such parts that are restricted by styles are system interactions, its deployment, and its structuring paradigm, which can be used to classify architectural styles.

The *interaction* restricts the way and potentially the protocols according to which components interact. For example, in the *service-oriented architecture* (SOA) style, the main architectural entities are services, which use only loosely coupled interactions with other services to implement workflows.

Other styles may restrict the *deployment*; for example, impose restrictions on the number of layers and tiers as well as the interaction among them. For example, the *client-server* architecture style implies that the system is deployed on at least two types of nodes—client and server—and that the client somehow initially knows how to access the server (but not the reverse). A *multi-tier* architecture style is based on tiers, which are physically separated logical system concerns. This means that the tiers are deployed on independent physical nodes.

A system's *structuring paradigm* restricts the structural entities of the architecture. For example, in a *layered architecture*, a layer is a logical separation of a system. Higher layers are restricted to interact only with lower layers. The most common layers are presentation (UI), business or system logic, and data access layers. This style is also used in the Media Store example. Here, the handling of data is separated from the actual (business) logic of the system, which itself is also separated from the user interaction.

In this line of classification according to the parts of the architecture that are restricted, it makes sense to limit "architectural" styles in particular to styles that restrict parts of an "architecture." Sometimes, however, the style of the programming paradigm (e.g., object oriented, functional, procedural, logical) also affects the architecture indirectly. In addition, there are software development approaches that help in architectural and object-oriented design, which can also be seen as styles according to the given definition of style. For example, in the *WAM approach* ("Tools, Automation, Materials," or as in German, "Werkzeuge, Automation und Materialien"), software components are classified by the role they are playing in analogy to real-world artifacts, as tools, materials, or automata. According the the inventors Reinhard Budde and Heinz Züllighoven, a *material* is processed with *tools*. Repetitive processes can be automated by an *automaton*. More information can be found in Züllighoven (2005).

4.4 Architectural Pattern Reuse

In this book, we use the definition by Taylor et al. (2009):

Definition 10 (Architectural pattern) *An* architectural pattern *is a named collection of architectural design decisions that are applicable to a recurring design problem and parameterized to account for different software development contexts in which that problem appears.*

There are many controversies over architectural pattern definitions and naming conventions, in particular:

Architectural patterns versus design patterns: Roughly, an architectural pattern is concerned with the organization of the whole system, while a design pattern has much more local impact only. A design pattern is strongly coupled to a well-defined problem, which it is solving. But for an architectural pattern, it is sometimes more challenging to precisely define the single problem to be solved. Therefore, Frank Buschmann and Michael Stal speak from well-balanced design forces through an architectural pattern (Buschmann et al. 1996).

Architectural patterns versus architectural styles: Compared to architectural patterns, styles are more abstract and have more degrees of freedom in the realization as they are restriction based; that is, they define restrictions but leave the constructive definition of a solution open. Opposed to this, *architectural patterns* are more concrete and explicit, as they are prescription-based; that is, they give constructive advice about what a solution should look like. Patterns can be mixed but mixing styles results in impure design that is hard to understand. This is pretty much in analogy to the term "architectural style" for buildings.

Architectural patterns only share some characteristics with architectural styles:

Fine-grained decision: Architectural patterns are a collection of prescribed architectural design decisions. Therefore, they allow refinement of the decision space opened by architectural styles.

Restricted design space: For such refinements, a decision to use an architectural pattern at the same time constrains and enables design possibilities. While some solutions get excluded, some solutions get enabled and can be used together only with the pattern.

Warranty for quality: The use of an architectural pattern is, like a style, a warranty to achieve certain qualitative properties in design. So, architectural patterns are tightly related to the quality properties, such as performance, security, and maintainability. They usually influence several properties at a time, both in a positive and negative way. Therefore, their application is often a trade-off between nonfunctional goals of the solution. So for example, a Facade pattern (a unified interface to a set of components in a subsystem) may improve the maintainability of the system component, but at the same time it could decrease its performance. The final quality influence of a pattern application, however, depends on how the pattern is implemented in the system and the actual system context.

Improved maintenance and evolution: Architectural patterns improve system comprehension as they can be seen as a common language between team members. Empirical studies from a group around Tichy (Prechelt et al. 2002) show that documented design patterns help in software evolution (even compared to the same architecture without pattern documentation). Identifying an applied pattern gives information about solved problems and provides details on its solution.

But there are also drawbacks of the pattern application. The most common problems are pattern misuse and false implementation. Such situations potentially lead to performance and maintenance problems due to worsened understandability through needless complexity and confusing implementations instead of the expected quality improvement and improved system comprehension.

As patterns are approved solutions to reoccurring problems, these solutions typically bring a better quality and are less error-prone compared to self-invented solutions. Therefore, architectural patterns allow software architects to reuse available knowledge about concrete architectural solutions.

There are many pattern catalogs available, such as by Buschmann et al. (1996), Schmidt et al. (2000), Gamma et al. (1995), Kircher and Jain (2004), Douglass (2002), Fowler et al. (2002), Erl (2009), and Schumacher et al. (2005). In catalogs, patterns are grouped by the specific topic (security patterns, SOA patterns, etc.) and goals (organizational, behavioral, etc.). These catalogs provide information on a pattern's quality goals, which problem a pattern solves, details on a pattern's structure, which set of design decisions is required, advantages and consequences of pattern application, and implementation details. Some integrated development environments (IDEs), such as Eclipse, have a built-in support for common patterns. Some famous examples of architectural patterns are Facade, Decorator, Model-View-Controller, Observer, and Factory.

4.5   Reference Architecture Reuse

As the architecture of a software system depends on the application domain, it is often possible to reuse a software architecture for different systems if they share the same domain. We define a *reference architecture* inspired by Taylor et al. (2009) as follows:

Definition 11 (Reference architecture) *A* reference architecture *is the set of principal design decisions that are simultaneously applicable to multiple related systems, typically within a single application domain, with implicitly defined points of variation, such as the presence or absence of a component.*

Accordingly, not all components of a reference architecture need to be used in the definition of an architecture for a specific system. Any component of the specific architecture, however, can typically be mapped to a component of the reference architecture. Therefore, reference architecture is a way of standardization of software architectures for a specific domain and is a template for the system design. This template contains structural elements, their types, and the relations between them and is based on the experience of system construction in the domain. The template shall be applicable for all systems of a domain.

Reference architectures help to deal with the increasing complexity of systems for a specific domain. They originate from the experience of experts in the domain and support the architectural knowledge reuse, thus improving system comprehension. Reference architectures are standardized solutions targeting an increase in system quality. Moreover, they help to reduce time-to-market and costs of systems, as the main architectural carcass is already available and allows for concentration on project-specific details. Some examples of reference architectures are *Quasar* for the business information system domain (Siedersleben 2004) and *AUTOSAR* for the automotive domain (Kindel and Friedrich 2009).

4.6   Product-Line Architectures

The concept of *software product lines* (Clements and Northrop 2001) has been introduced to explicitly target planned reuse and managed variability in software engineering. Here it is defined as follows:

Definition 12 (Software product line) *A software product line is a set of software-intensive systems that share a common, managed set of features satisfying the specific needs of a particular market segment or mission and that are developed from a common set of core assets in a prescribed way.*

Hence, a product line plays a similar role as reference architectures, but it goes beyond reference architectures through an explicit model of variability (often expressed in feature diagrams) where variation points are made explicit, variation alternatives are shown, and their dependencies are specified. Product lines ease the creation of customer-specific or domain-specific variants as instantiations from the product line. To achieve these general goals and to respect company-specific and project-specific setups, different strategies for handling reuse and variability in a software product line have been developed. These strategies are categorized according to the phases of software development in which a specific variant is chosen or the reuse is done. The categories range from reference architectures up to context-specific behaviors during run time. The subsections that follow describe product-line reuse concepts and how they are represented with Palladio.

The earliest software development phase when a product-line approach can be used is during the software architecture design. If a company develops a set of similar systems (e.g., Web-based e-commerce solutions or controller management software for the automotive industry), they do not want to design these applications from scratch every time. In addition, bringing up a new software architecture for every developed solution would result in huge maintenance efforts because developers would have to understand each solution separately. Instead, the company can develop a reference architecture during domain engineering and derive a solution-specific architecture whenever necessary.

Such an architecture-level product-line approach can be realized with Palladio by specifying the reference architecture with the PCM and starting with this architecture whenever a new solution should be designed. Here, the implicit variability of a reference architecture, whether or not a component of the reference architecture is used for a specific product, can simply be yielded through keeping or deleting component from the reference architecture. Furthermore, when the architecture model for the specific solution is adapted or extended, model comparison techniques can be applied to keep track of the modifications. This also helps to transfer improvements back into the reference architecture.

4.6.1 Product Composition

A very common approach is to assemble a product from existing components. This includes composing a component assembly from scratch as well as selecting from optional or alternative components for a base product. Many modern technologies and frameworks, such as OSGi, EJB, or .Net, provide component infrastructures to bundle and assemble them. Building a software product line based on components requires designing them as self-contained units for which provided and required interfaces are clearly specified. Furthermore, an explicit documentation of components that can be used alternatively for each other, respectively which extension points exist to develop custom components, must be provided. A more advanced management of such a product line includes configuration management that documents the products a component is used in.

In Palladio, the component repository model can be used to specify all available components. Several components providing the same interface represent alternatives to select from when assembling a product. Furthermore, when assembling a product, the assembly contexts reference the composed components in the repository. These references allow for tracing which components are used in which product variant and to plan any changes made on the product-line level. In addition, custom components developed for a specific product reference their provided interface in the central component repository. If such a custom component is decided to be published for the whole product line, it can simply be moved into the central repository.

4.6.2   Product Configuration

Product configuration makes use of component-specific variability. Specific to the applied technology, a configuration file, registry, or configuration management system is considered to parameterize the component to influence its behavior. For example, a data processing step such as filtering or compression can be turned on or off. This allows adaption of a component to custom or use-case-specific purposes and is done before the product is used. More specifically, the configuration is loaded at system initialization.

Palladio provides component parameters to parameterize an existing component without changing its internals. These parameters can be evaluated in the conditions of BranchActions or LoopActions or used in the resource demand specifications. But the component developer has to define their usage and provide the component parameters available for configuring a specific product. When configuring a product using the system model, VariableUsage elements can be added to an AssemblyContext to specify the component configuration.

4.6.3   Context Interpretation

Context interpretation means selecting for a specific product behavior or feature at run time. While this type of variability potentially requires additional resource demands for variant decisions, it also allows for the most flexible type of software product line because of the late variant binding. In particular, modern software as a service (SaaS) and multitenant systems make use of this strategy.

What is called context in general can be the user currently interacting with the system, his tenant's license, or the currently activated usage scenario.

Reflecting this type of variability in Palladio requires modeling the variability again as part of the loop and branch conditions or within the stochastic expressions of the resource demands. In contrast to the product configuration strategy, the context is not specified as component parameters but as part of the usage profile. For example, a complex parameter representing the user, respectively his context, can be modeled to influence the product's features and behavior.

4.7 Questions and Exercises

4.7.1 Questions

4.1 **: What are the differences between architectural style, architectural pattern, and reference architecture? Briefly compare these three concepts.

4.2 **: What is the fundamental difference between an architectural style and an architectural pattern?

4.3 **: What does a qualitative influence of an architectural style mean?

4.4 **: What is the essential difference between layered architectural style and multi-tier architectural style?

4.5 **: Is the application of architectural pattern always beneficial?

4.6 **: Does a specific system always utilize all of the components defined by a reference architecture?

4.7.2 Exercises

4.1 **: Your task as a software architect of a company that builds cloud-based data-analytic solutions is to design a software architecture for a cloud platform. Which concepts could you use?

4.2 *: Your task as a software architect of a company that builds mobile phones is to design a software architecture for a mobile phone platform. The software architecture should allow one to dynamically choose the functionality a certain phone model provides. The architecture should allow building of phones that provide only basic functionalities, building of phones that provide full functionality, as well as building of phones that provide functionalities between those of the first two models. Which concept would you use to enable these requirements?

4.8 Further Reading

For architectural styles and in general for good reading about software architecture, refer to Taylor et al. (2009). The same source provides a good introduction to architectural patterns. If you would like to see which patterns exist, there are many basic sources to help you. General and quite widely spread patterns are described and explained by Gamma et al. (1995) and in a series of so-called POSA books by Buschmann et al. (1996) and Schmidt et al. (2000) (for concurrent and networked objects) and by Kircher and Jain (2004) (patterns for distributed services and components). Real-time design patterns are described by Douglass (2002). Patterns of enterprise architectures can be found in a book by Fowler et al. (2002) and SOA design patterns in a book by Erl (2009). Security patterns are explained in a book by Schumacher et al. (2005). There are many more sources available, but these are sufficient for a start.

A very detailed example of a reference architecture for business information systems called Quasar is provided in a book by Siedersleben (2004). A similar example is available for the automotive domain called AUTOSAR, which is described by Kindel and Friedrich (2009).

4.9 Takeaways

The takeaways from this chapter are that there are several ways to reuse architectural knowledge. This ranges from fine-grained reuse of interfaces and components to the reuse of architectures. Often, domain knowledge is captured in reusable architecture elements, such as in reference architectures or software product lines.

Architectural elements can be reused on multiple levels. For example, components can be reused: on the level of component types (i.e., mainly described by their interfaces and roles), on the level of implementation (i.e., having a single implementation used in different contexts), on the level of deployed component (i.e., multiple deployments of the same component for redundancy or scalability), and so on. We introduced a full hierarchy of reuse levels, the so-called *contexts* (e.g., component type, assembly context, etc.). *Contexts* of Palladio's model elements make the reuse of architectural elements explicit.

We introduced software product lines as reference architectures with explicit variability. We also distinguished between architectural patterns and architectural styles. Architectural patterns provide bundled solutions of architectural knowledge to recurring problems, while architectural styles provide system-wide guidelines and best practices. Both are often formulated as restrictions (i.e., which kind of dependencies not to introduce). Styles are meant not to be mixed, while several patterns can be used in the same architecture and can even overlap.

Part III Architectural Analysis

This part describes how Palladio can be used to enrich architectural models with quality attributes and how to perform automated, quantitative analyses based on these models to predict the performance and reliability of the represented systems. It begins in chapter 5, which explains how information has to be added to architectural models in a goal-driven way in order to analyze and predict quality properties. The modeling of service effect specifications, usage profiles, resource demands, and execution environments is described, and domain-specific requirements for quality modeling are discussed.

In chapter 6, it is explained how the data can be obtained; for example, using code analysis, instrumentation, and tests. The chapter describes how quantitative information on resource demands, processing capacity, and failure rates can be retrieved using instrumentation, measurement, and estimation techniques.

Software architects can use these data and analyses in order to search, interpret, compare and choose design alternatives for specific design questions, which chapter 7 illustrates. The chapter also explains how software architects can interpret performance and reliability prediction results to identify and resolve potential problems.

Finally, chapter 8 provides insights into the simulations and transformations that are performed "under the hood." The operating principles as well as the strengths and weaknesses of the quality analysis tools are presented. This helps to select and configure the appropriate tool for specific prediction tasks.

5 Modeling Quality

Heiko Koziolek

This chapter explains how information has to be added to architectural models in order to analyze and predict quality properties and discusses why goals at the right level of abstraction are helpful when modeling quality. Along exemplary service effect specifications and usage profiles, it shows how relevant information can be expressed; for example, in the form of resource demands for individual actions. The chapter also explains which properties have to be modeled for the execution environment and presents domain-specific requirements for quality modeling, which can be indirectly addressed with domain-specific component repositories.

5.1 Quality Attributes

A well-designed software architecture achieves a good trade-off between the required quality attributes. The ISO/IEC 25010 standard (ISO/IEC 25010:2011[E] 2011) provides a standard taxonomy for common quality attributes, among them maintainability, security, usability, portability, performance, and reliability. There are several established measures for some quality attributes, such as the response time to determine a performance characteristic or mean time to failure to determine a reliability characteristic. For other quality attributes, quantified measures are harder to determine and sometimes system specific.

To predict quality characteristics for a system model, Palladio focuses on easily quantifiable quality attributes (i.e., performance, a reliability, and monetary costs). Palladio can compute system-level quality characteristics out of quality characteristics of software components, their connectors, and their deployment environment.

5.1.1 Performance

Performance in terms of timing behavior is important for many applications. While essential for the functionality of real-time critical systems, performance is also often a distinguishing feature in many less-critical systems. Web and desktop applications require short response times to avoid users selecting competing solutions. Web servers need to be able to handle load peaks so that user requests are not discarded. Video-streaming services must provide a fluid transfer of media data for thousands of users in parallel. Performance usually covers timing behavior and resource efficiency and is usually quantified with the following three measures:

Response time refers to the time between issuing a request to a system (or a service) and receiving its response. For example, a request to an Internet search engine provides a response time of 1 second for presenting the search results. The response time of a usage scenario (i.e., a sequence of interactions of the user with the system) is the time between issuing the first request until receiving the final response.

Throughput refers to the amount of requests a system can process per time unit. For example, a Web server could handle 100 requests per minute.

Utilization refers to the percentage of time a hardware resource is used per time unit. For example, during the past 5 minutes, the utilization of the main CPU was 27%.

With Palladio, one can annotate software components with parameterized execution times as detailed later. It is also possible to specify a rate of incoming requests to a system with the Palladio usage model in order to support throughput analyses. Palladio also provides means to specify the speed of hardware devices, so that one can perform an analysis of utilization.

5.1.2 Reliability

In addition to performance analysis, the Palladio Component Model provides capabilities to analyze the reliability of a modeled software system. A software system is perceived as reliable by its users if it provides an expected service without any unwanted side effects. Any deviation from the expected results is recognized as failure resulting from a fault in the system. Therefore, system reliability is defined as the probability that a system operates failure-free in a specified execution environment for a specified time interval (IEEE Std 610.12–1990 1990). Any software system can have the following failure potentials:

Software failure potentials refer to flaws in the implementation of a software system, which can lead to failures during service execution.

Hardware failure potentials refer to the limited availability of hardware resources (CPUs, HDDs), which can cause failure during service execution.

Network failure potentials refer to failed message transmission over a network link.

You can annotate failure probabilities to software components and hardware resources with Palladio. This enables calculation of, for example, the system reliability for a given usage scenario.

5.1.3 Cost

You need to trade off quality attributes against monetary costs, as a highly reliable, high-performance system is often associated with prohibitively high costs. Costs arise in multiple phases of the software development life cycle and are caused by multiple activities. Costs that are affected by the software architecture are software component costs, hardware costs, and system costs. To assess the total cost of ownership, a cost model has to take development costs, but also later costs such as maintenance, into account.

Component costs arise in various life-cycle stages (e.g., for in-house development or procurement, when adapting components, or for testing and maintenance).

Hardware costs arise from the procurement of hardware to deploy the system. This includes costs for servers as well as for infrastructure such as a network. In addition to operating costs, hardware maintenance and energy costs can be taken into account if these costs will be attributed to the developing organization, too.

System costs are related to the overall system and cannot be attributed to single components. These costs arise when assembling the system and when selecting and preparing the required middleware (such as application servers, operating systems, and messaging systems).

Palladio allows one to annotate model instances with estimated costs per component and hardware parts, so that the overall costs can be calculated and traded off against the desired quality properties. This allows assessment of different design alternatives cost-wise (e.g., the overall costs when using alternative component implementations or a higher-sized deployment environment).

5.2 Goal-Driven Approach

Any useful model has at least three properties (see section 3.2): *pragmatism*, *representation*, and *reduction*. To be *pragmatic*, a Palladio model must be tailored to answer specific quality questions (e.g., how many servers are needed to operate the Media Store flawlessly for a given workload). Pragmatism focuses the modeling activities to specific *goals* and ensures that a Palladio model fulfills its intended purpose. As a *representation* of the system under study, a Palladio model must include those parameters (e.g., the file sizes in the Media Store) having an impact on a quality measure. A prediction that is based on the model must have a meaning for the system under study under the selected pragmatism to become a valid representation. As a *reduction*, a Palladio model excludes details of the modeled system that are not relevant for the pragmatism of the quality analysis (e.g., the use of inheritance to implement the Media Store's watermarking algorithm). Reduction, also called *abstraction*, lowers the modeling effort by only looking at those attributes relevant for the decided pragmatism. It ensures that resources for modeling are not wasted and that the models can be understood and analyzed efficiently.

5.2.1 Pragmatism

Missing or limited *pragmatism*, often also called *goal orientation*, is a common mistake in quality modeling, leading to useless models and wasted modeling efforts. Without clear goals, the activity of modeling tends to the creation of general-purpose models that are complicated to handle and provide little value. Goals also drive the selection of methods and tools for quality analyses and vastly influence the whole modeling process. Thus, when using Palladio, one should state the goals for quality modeling explicitly.

The goal-question-metric (GQM) approach (Basili et al. 1994) can assist in the statement and refinement of quality goals. GQM provides a template to specify goals. It then requires one to operationalize a goal into a set of specific questions. For each question, concrete metrics must be defined that allow formulation of answers in a measurable way.

For example, for the Media Store system, one could formulate the following performance-related goal: "The system must enable users to download a music album in 90% of the cases in less than 8 seconds." A question derived from this goal could be: "Can the system adhere to the performance goal if a watermarking component for the music files is introduced?" To answer this question in a measurable way, one could state as a metric: "Response time for the Media Store 'Download Scenario' with a user arrival rate of five users per minute and negligible concurrent workloads." During modeling, one can now focus on the latencies between the components involved in the scenario and, for example, neglect unimportant details, such as the configuration of the operating system scheduler. Later, the metrics derived from the model will answer the question, and the question contributes to the achievement of the goal.

Stating quality goals that drive the creation of a Palladio model is not trivial. It requires a good understanding of the modeled system's business drivers and of the target domain of the system. In practice, a software architect often receives ambiguous statements about quality goals from system stakeholders, who can be product managers, customers, and marketing experts. For example, they may demand that "the system shall be fast and reliable." It is the software architect's responsibility to translate and break down such statements into quality requirements and metrics.

Metrics to operationalize goal-oriented questions can include ranges and percentiles (e.g., 5-second response time in 80% of the cases, 8-second response time in 99% of the cases). This is in particular helpful in systems that do not have real-time guarantees. This is the case in business information systems, which are not built on real-time operating systems and networks. Metrics should be defined with the assumed working conditions (e.g., the user workload, the involved data volume, and concurrently running processes). Metrics are often at least partly reusable across systems in the same domain. Thus, it is advisable to reuse metric definitions from older systems, competing systems, industry standards, or personal experience where possible.

Although none of these methods are specific for Palladio, some specifics need to be considered when applying these techniques in the context of component-based quality modeling. A software architect can reuse a component quality model that was created for other goals by a component developer. Thus, important details that were not relevant at the time of specification would be neglected. Some quality attributes, such as security or usability, are difficult to attribute to particular components, which complicates the task to translate and break down the quality goals. In such cases, special care needs to be taken during modeling.

5.2.2 Representation

Overlooking an important parameter can render model-based predictions useless as those predictions will not represent the modeled system suitably. But how can one differentiate between important and unimportant properties? A common approach is to start modeling with simple models and refine them iteratively as needed. The best system representation is the simplest model that answers the given quality question. Both modeling and goal formulation are usually difficult to get right from the beginning, especially for inexperienced modelers. Goals get clearer during modeling, and certain model parameters are revealed to be more or less relevant as information about a system is collected.

All developer roles involved in modeling must continually improve the models until they reach a sufficient confidence level. They must ask whether the model is a good

---

Digression 5.1

The Right Representation

Finding the right representation for a system model is crucial. Experience shows that projects become hardly manageable if one starts with a too-detailed model. A good starting point for model complexity is a total of only five to 10 components. One should avoid modeling all details of the system just because it is easy to find information on certain details of the system. Instead, focus only on those parts of the system that are likely to vary (in the past or in the future) or which are more likely to possess quality problems (e.g., a performance bottleneck). These components under study should be modeled in more detail.

It is fully acceptable to summarize dozens of components—which realize a subsystem that is not within focus but is connected to the system under study—in a single component. This single component should not have detailed quality models, but can comprise only non-parameterized measured values (e.g., for response times of provided services).

Imagine a component with 20 provided services that differ in terms of business cases but technically look the same, which means that they are identical in resource consumption, external service calls, and mutexes/passive resources. Those provided services should be summarized in a single provided service that abstracts from business cases. For example, a calculator may have more or less the same performance behavior for addition and subtraction. These two services could be combined in a single provided service to limit effort for modeling service effect specifications (SEFFs).

representation if a certain part of the system is abstracted (see the next subsection). They must question the details in the model and judge whether a detail added to the model contributes to the answering of the stated questions or whether it is merely incorporated to just let the model resemble the structure of the system.

If a system implementation or prototype is available for taking quality measurements, it is possible to calibrate the model to get a good representation reflecting the system appropriately. For example, resource demands or failure probabilities for certain components in the Media Store can be added or changed depending on further measurements. Usually, certain parameter ranges (e.g., different workload levels) are covered during calibration. The model is a good representation for these ranges if the model-based quality analysis differs from system measurements only to a limited extent. After calibration, the model can be used as a representation of the real system to perform extrapolation (e.g., exploring the system's handling of higher workload levels, different component implementations, or other resource environments).

Sensitivity analysis is another approach for validating a model and checking whether a sufficient representation has been reached. It involves altering individual model parameters by a small amount and then observing changes in the overall quality metrics derivable from the model. If a small parameter change results in a large difference of the overall quality metrics, the model cannot be considered reliable and needs further refinement.

5.2.3 Reduction

Choosing a suitable reduction and granularity level is crucial for any quality prediction model. Including too much detail into a model makes it unnecessarily complex, difficult to understand, and potentially mathematically intractable. It also wastes available resources for modeling.

A goal-oriented approach is a good method to identify system aspects that can be reduced (i.e., omitted when creating the model). Depending on the goal, certain parts of the system can be treated as black boxes, or completely neglected, because the analysis of their internals does not contribute to the achievement of the goal. The goal shifts the emphasis of modeling to the parts that contribute to the desired quality properties. For example, in the Media Store, a usage scenario for administrating user rights can be neglected when conducting a performance analysis. User administration is a less computationally intensive scenario compared to upload and download of media files. So the user administration component needs no detailed modeling to answer a throughput question.

As a challenge, iterative modeling is inherently complicated in component-based modeling approaches. A component developer must decide for a reduction without knowing all future usage contexts of the modeled component. In one usage context, a certain parameter (e.g., a caching strategy) can be irrelevant, in another one highly relevant. With higher effort, the component developer can provide multiple quality models for one component (e.g., one for each assumed typical usage context). As an alternative, one must lower the abstraction level of a reused component quality model before integrating it into an overall system model.

5.3 Component Quality

To enable model-based quality analysis with Palladio, the models introduced in chapter 3 need to be enhanced with quality annotations (e.g., for performance and reliability).

Palladio's component quality specification is based on the notion of resource demanding service effect specifications (RDSEFFs), which are an extension of the SEFF (see section 3.4) for performance prediction. Each RDSEFF provides a parameterized, behavioral abstraction and quality specification for a single component service. The set of RDSEFFs for all services of a software component forms the complete component quality specification.

Table 5.1 shows the most important elements of the RDSEFF meta-model. Some additional elements have been left out for brevity but can be used in the respective tooling. This chapter refers back to the running example Media Store from chapter 2 to explain Palladio's quality modeling language.

As a simple example, figure 5.1 shows the RDSEFF for the service Download of the Media Store's MediaManagement component. RDSEFFs are similar to annotated UML activity diagrams but provide special constructs to simulate software components. The figure uses a UML-like visualization for easy comprehension, but the actual modeling elements are not tied to UML. Instead, the stereotypes in angled brackets refer to classes in the Palladio meta-model. In the example, the control flow starts and then executes the internal action JNDI RMI Overhead, which puts the specified demand on the CPU. Next, an external call is

---

Digression 5.2

What about UML or MARTE?

Palladio provides a proprietary modeling language that is not connected to the de facto standard modeling language UML. There is also a UML profile called MARTE [28], which enhances UML models to also capture quality-related information, such as resource demands or failure probabilities. In contrast to UML and MARTE, Palladio provides a much simpler modeling language specifically designed for quality prediction of component-based software systems. Palladio's meta-model and tools do not allow users to specify ambiguous models and ensure that a model is suitable for automated quality analysis. UML was initially designed as a general-purpose modeling language mainly meant for communication, not automated quality analyses. Thus, it includes many more constructs, but also complicates creating a robust quality analysis tool chain. Palladio provides special abstractions for software components (RDSEFFs) and features a parameterized component specification that adheres to the separate roles of component developer and software architect. For example, Palladio stores the models of the component developers and software architects in separate files so that they can be distributed independently.

Table 5.1

Overview of some important RDSEFF elements

RDSEFF Element	Short Description
Internal action	Represents a part of the component service's own code and can be annotated with resource demands and failure probabilities
External call	Expresses a call to one of the component service's required services
Emit event action	Asynchronously emits events to other component services
Resource demanding behavior	Abstract entity to group a number of actions, can for example be used for RDSEFFs, branches, loops, and forks
Branch action	Splits the control flow of the RDSEFF either based on a fixed probability or based on a conditional statement depending on the component service's parameters
Loop action	Contains a loop behavior that groups a number of actions; this behavior is executed as often as defined in the loop count
Fork action	Splits the control flow into two or more concurrently executing behaviors; is used to model threads being invoked from a component service
Synchronization point	Used to joined synchronous forked behaviors, the control flow only continues if all forked behaviors have finished their execution
Start action	Starts a resource demanding behavior; an RDSEFF always has a single starting point
Stop action	Stops a resource demanding behavior
Acquire action	Models the acquisition of a passive resource, such as a semaphore or buffer; if the passive resource is not available, the control flow needs to wait until it is available
Release action	Models the release of a passive resource
Resource demand	Models the consumption of a hardware resource; e.g., CPU units or I/O units
Failure probability	Assigns a failure probability to an internal action

performed to retrieve the requested audio files from the next component. An external call is made to package the files, if more than one are requested. Then the control flow ends. The following will explain selected elements in detail.

Internal actions model computations of the component service itself. The level of detail in the model is not predefined by Palladio but depends on the component developer providing the specification. It is possible to have only one to many *internal actions* for a single component service. An *internal action* can represent a single line of code or subsume a larger number of statements if its effect on the quality properties can be abstracted to a single value accordingly. As a rule of thumb, all code between the service invocations and an external service call and between two external services should be abstracted into a single *internal action*.

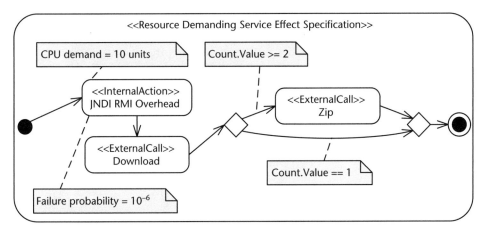

Figure 5.1
RDSEFF example for the download service of the Media Store: the RDSEFF notation resembles an anno-tated UML activity diagram but is part of the Palladio Component Model.

Resource demands specify the processing amount requested from a certain active resource, such as a CPU or hard disk. To keep the specification independent from a particular resource environment, a component developer specifies resource demands as abstract work units. Work units derive for example from the number of CPU instructions for a computation or from the size of the data read from a storage device. Once a system deployer has modeled a concrete resource environment with processing frequency for CPUs and hard disks, a tool can calculate timing values from the abstract work units. For example, if a system deployer models that a CPU can process 10,000 work units per second, the CPU demand of 10 work units in figure 5.1 yields a processing time of 0.001 second.

Component developers can also specify the interaction with passive resources in RDSEFFs. A passive resource does not execute demands, but instead provides a limited set of tokens, which a component service can acquire and release as required for a certain execution. If all tokens of a passive resource are acquired by other component services, an acquiring service is placed into a FIFO queue to wait for the next free token. Passive resources may for example be semaphores, memory buffers, or thread pools. RDSEFFs provide *acquire actions* and *release actions* to express the usage of a passive resource. For example, the Media Store's service watermark could request exclusive access to the file cache via a passive resource to avoid cache inconsistencies.

Failure probabilities on internal actions specify the likelihood of running into a defect when executing the action. They refer to the pure software reliability and do not take hard-ware reliability into account. Component developers specify these probabilities to enable a reliability prediction for an overall component-based architecture. There are different tech-niques for determining failure probabilities, which are detailed in section 6.4.

External calls model the invocation of a service specified in a component's required interface. *External calls* are synchronous requests, meaning that the invoking component blocks its execution until the required service has finished processing the request. To model asynchronous calls to required services, the PCM allows encapsulating *external calls* into *forked behaviors*. In this case, the control flow of the invoking component continues immediately after issuing the request by processing the actions following the *forked behavior*.

For event-based communication between components, Palladio RDSEFFs may also send events via the *emit event action*. In this case, the event triggers the invocations of RDSEFFs in other components, which have subscribed for the respective event type on the respective event channel.

RDSEFFs define the control flow between *internal actions* and *external actions* as sequence, branch, loop, or fork. RDSEFFs disallow backward references in the control flow to avoid tangled loops and require component developers to make the branch, loop, and fork bodies explicit using nested behaviors. For larger component services, it is important to abstract the control flow from the real code-level control flow to avoid complexity. For example, if a conditional statement has only limited performance or reliability impact, it is not needed to model a branch in the RDSEFF, but instead abstracts the conditional statement into a single *internal action*.

To be able to analyze the quality properties of a Palladio model and convert RDSEFFs into stochastic models, it is required to specify branch probabilities and loop counts. The direct specification of branch probabilities is, however, problematic in a component-based setting. The actual branch probabilities and loop counts usually result from the usage profile of a component service, which the component developer, who provides the specification, does not necessarily know in advance. Therefore, a parameterized specification is desirable as explained in section 5.4. For debugging purposes and components not meant for reuse, the PCM RDSEFF also allows direct specification of branch probabilities and loop counts.

For control flow forks in RDSEFFs, it is necessary to specify a *synchronization point*. A *fork action* may then contain multiple asynchronous and synchronous forked behaviors with included internal and external actions. Asynchronous forked behaviors execute in parallel threads and do not block the main control flow through a component service. Synchronous forked behaviors also execute in parallel threads but block the main control flow until all behaviors for the respective *synchronization point* are finished.

RDSEFFs allow the specification of numeric values, such as resource demand work units or loop counts, not only as constant values but also as probability distribution functions. A distribution of a value can occur due to insufficient or unreliable data collection for a value. For example, if an internal action executes on a complex stack of middleware and operating system layers, its execution time may vary heavily depending on surrounding context conditions. Distribution functions provide a convenient way of specifying such timing values, with uncertainty ranges then also yielding a distribution function as output of the quality analysis.

Digression 5.3

Palladio's Stochastic Expressions Language

In order to specify randomly distributed parameters, the Palladio Component Model uses a specialized language called *Stochastic Expressions* (StoEx). It is similar to other quality annotation languages such as the Value Specification Language (VSL) found in MARTE; however, it has a clear grammar and tools, which make the annotations available for easy automated processing.

One of the main features of the StoEx language is the specification of empirical distributions. For discrete random variables, the histogram has to be specified. For example, IntPMF[(1,0.2) (2,0.8)] specifies an integer random variable whose value is 1 in 20% of all cases and 2 in 80%. Such a specification might be useful to characterize the performance impact of a two-valued integer parameter. For continuous random variables such as resource demands, a specification might look like this: DoublePDF[(0.5,0.3)(1.3,0.7)]. Such a variable takes values between 0 and 0.5 in 30% of all cases. The values between 0 and 0.5 are uniform distributed. Values between 0.5 and 1.3 show up in 70% of all cases. Notice the more of such ranges that are specified, the more accurate the specification is; however, more accurate specifications might result in increased run time of quality predictions.

In addition to the specification of constants, mathematical distributions, and empirical distributions, StoEx also allows calculations (e.g., 5 * file.BYTESIZE) or comparisons (e.g., request. TYPE == "download"). Calculations are often needed to specify parametric dependencies, while comparisons are needed for the specification of guards in branch conditions.

The PCM allows normal, gamma, uniform, beta, and other distributions for numeric annotations. The component developer only needs to specify the defining parameters of the distribution (e.g., the expected value). It is also possible to define empirical probability distributions and feed measured histograms into the PCM RDSEFF annotations (see chapter 6).

5.4   Usage Profiles and Their Propagation

A software component exhibits different quality properties depending on its usage profile. If the Media Store's watermarking service adds a watermark to a 100-megabyte (MB) audio book, it has a much longer processing time than watermarking a 5-MB song. A component developer should provide a parameterized service effect specification so that the component specification can be used for quality analysis in different contexts with different usage profiles.

In Palladio, a domain expert first specifies the usage profile at the system boundaries in a *usage model*. This model specifies the order and frequency in which component services, which are exposed to the system boundaries, are called by human users or other systems (*system calls*). It also includes specifications of parameter values and input data. Each component developer provides a component specification that may be parameterized for these parameter values and input data. A tool can then propagate the domain expert's usage profile values through the component specifications and resolve the parameter dependencies.

Figure 5.2 shows an example for a Palladio usage model specified by a domain expert. First, users register a new account with a probability of 60%. They then call the Login service. After a short delay, they request a list of all available audio files. Then, after a longer delay for making a decision, the users either upload a new file or send a download request. The domain expert has additionally specified an input parameter for the Download service: each call requests two audio files. The domain expert can specify the branch probabilities and the number of requested files from experience or market research.

In case of performance analyses, the domain expert needs to provide an open or closed workload specification in the usage model. An open workload specification indicates that the usage model is executed with a specific frequency. The frequency can be defined as an arrival rate (e.g., 5 requests per minute) or as an interarrival time (e.g., every 12 seconds, a user arrives). The domain model can also express how the incoming requests are distributed in time. The domain expert defines that users arrive exactly every 12 seconds at the system (which is quite unlikely for human users, but might be relevant for other systems or sensors issuing the requests). He or she can also define that users arrive with an average interarrival time of 12 seconds and also define how these interarrival times are distributed. In the Media Store example (figure 5.2), the domain expert estimates that the interarrival time is 25 seconds and exponentially distributed. A closed workload specification models a fixed number of users circulating in the system. When using a closed workload, the domain expert must define a user population (e.g., 15 users) and a think time (e.g., 10 seconds), which models the time a user waits before reexecuting the usage model. The reason for this kind of workload specification is the fact that Palladio models are mapped to queuing networks for analysis, which use these constructs as there are standard analytical techniques to evaluate them.

A domain expert may also specify control constructs, such as branches and loops, in Palladio usage models to express complex user scenarios. Although a Palladio usage model looks similar to an RDSEFF, there are actually major differences between the two models. The usage model may not contain parameter dependencies as branch probabilities, and loop counts need to be specified as concrete values. Usage models cannot access active or passive resources. They can only call component services. A usage model has a workload specification and is provided by a domain expert, while an RDSEFF has no workload specification and is provided by a component developer.

To be able to express the quality-relevant influence of parameter data values, the PCM includes a parameter model derived from CORBA syntax [32]. It is possible to specify *primitive*, *collection*, and *composite* data types. Predefined primitive parameter types include int, string, bool, char, double, long, and byte. Collection data types model sets of parameters from the same type (e.g., a set of ints). Composite data types represent complex data types and may be composed out of primitive, collection, and other composite data types.

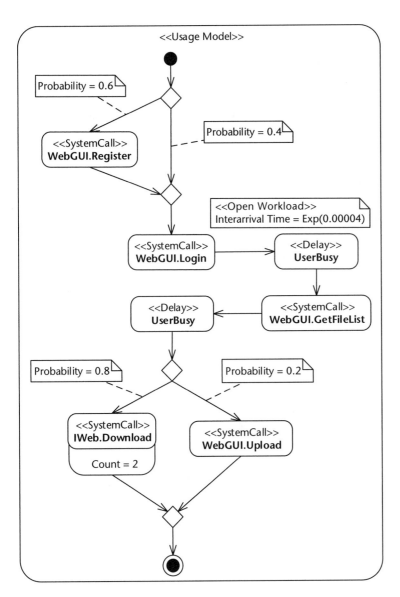

Figure 5.2
Usage model example for a user interaction with the Media Store: besides the flow of user activities, the usage model also captures transition probabilities and workload specifications.

PCM *parameter characterizations* allow specification of the concrete values for specific data types in a concrete context. Besides concrete values, it also enables characterizing the number of elements in a collection or the byte size of a binary data type. Figure 5.2 included as an example the parameter characterization of the number of files that the user requests to download.

Another example would be to specify the byte size of files uploaded to or downloaded from the Media Store, which can have a significant influence on quality properties. Besides constant values (e.g., 5-MB files), the PCM also allows specification of parameter characterization as random variables with distribution functions (e.g., 10% of files 4 MB, 90% of files 5 MB) to express uncertainty.

In RDSEFFs, component developers can specify parameter dependencies on branch transitions, loop counts, resource demands, and external calls. Figure 5.3 shows a simple RDSEFF with a parameter dependency. The branch transition probabilities now depend on the value of the parameter cacheHitProb, which must be characterized as an input parameter to the component service. In addition, the CPU and hard disk drive (HDD) demand depend on the size of the parameter file and also define a function to calculate the concrete demand. For example, if the byte size of file is specified as 1 by the calling component, the resulting CPU demand would be 8 $(2 + (6 * 1))$.

The functions including parameter references are called stochastic expressions in the PCM. Stochastic expressions can include distribution functions as parameter characterizations, and the included arithmetic operations are then calculated on these distribution functions. The stochastic expression for CPU or HDD demands are similar to the Big-O Notation (or Landau notation) used to specify the complexity of algorithms (Knuth 1997).

Component developers can also specify parameter dependencies when characterizing the input parameters of external service calls. They can propagate a parameter without change or even perform a calculation on a parameter and then use the result as the input value for the called required service. With this mechanism, the usage profile specified by the domain expert in the *usage model* can be propagated through a complete component-based architecture.

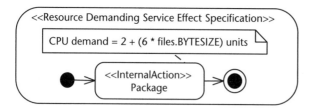

Figure 5.3

RDSEFF example with parameter dependencies for one service of the Media Store: the CPU demand depends on the size of the input file.

Digression 5.4

What Are Stochastic Expressions?

Stochastic expressions have the form of x.NumberOfElements * y.VALUE + 1 (i.e., they are mathematical expressions). Stochastic expressions are required to specify, for example, CPU and HDD demands ("calculating this action takes 10 CPU units and 3 HDD units"), the number of iterations of loop ("loop three the value of x"), when to choose the if or else branch ("if the input value of x is true, choose if branch"), or to express which data parameters are passed to another component ("pass the value of parameter x to the next component").

Besides parameters supplied as parameters during invocation of services, components can also include static configuration parameters or databases, whose content influences its quality properties. For example, the contents of the Media Store's database determine the time needed to execute a search function. To capture such data, the PCM allows component developers to specify *component parameters*. These are parameter values for a specific component, which are accessible from all of its RDSEFFs. For example, the resource demands inside an RDSEFF may depend on the component parameter value characterization. The component developer can provide default values for component parameters, which can be overridden by the software architect in the system model.

Using parameter dependencies in component quality specification has several implications. The component developer needs to define the important parameter characterization types (e.g., value, byte size, number of elements) for a component in its interfaces, so that components calling these services are aware of which characterizations they must supply. If a distribution function is used to characterize the domain of a parameter, the partitions of the domain need to be fixed in the specification so that elements of RDSEFFs (e.g., branch transitions) can also refer to these subdomains.

5.5 Execution Environments

When component developers specify the performance of their components, they cannot know the concrete resources (e.g., Intel CPU with 2 GHz) a component will be using to keep their specification independent from a specific context. Palladio supports this fact by decoupling the resource environment model from the components specifications. While component developers provide component specifications with RDSEFFs, system administrators or deployers provide resource environment specifications and component allocations to resources. Palladio stores both the resource environment models and component allocation models in separate files. Hence, for example, the resource environment model can be reused for another software architecture.

Figure 5.4 shows a simple example of a Palladio resource environment model and alloca-tion model in a single diagram. In the example, the system deployer has specified a *resource environment* consisting of an application server and a database server. Both servers contain *processing resources*, each with a processing rate and a scheduling policy. The processing rate specifies the frequency in which the resource can execute the abstract work units specified in the resource demands of an RDSEFF. For example, if a component requests 1.5×10^6 work units and the processing resource is able to execute 3.0×10^9 work units per second, the component request can be executed in 0.0005 second.

Multiple component services may compete for the processing resources in a multitask-ing system. The scheduling policy models in which order the processing resource executes the requests in this case. Palladio supports simple scheduling policies, such as first come, first serve (FCFS) and processor sharing (PS), an idealized variant of round-robin schedul-ing. Besides these scheduling policies, which allow quick simulations, Palladio also pro-vides detailed models of the scheduling policies of several mainstream general-purpose operating systems, such as Linux, Windows, and Windows Server. The system deployer

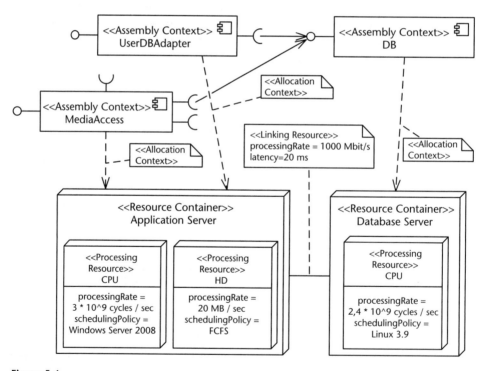

Figure 5.4

Resource environment example for the Media Store: the figure shows both the resource containers and processing resources as well as the allocation of components to the containers.

can easily select a scheduling policy without the need to understand the intricates of the scheduler.

To achieve the decoupling of components and resources desired for the reuse of components, RDSEFFs may not reference concrete resources, but must specify the required type of resources. Palladio provides a number of fixed *resource types*, such as CPU, hard disk, or LAN, in a separate repository. When creating resource demands in an RDSEFF, the component developer simply can reference these abstract resource types. The system deployer later specifies a concrete resource environment, where each processing resource in a *resource container* references a certain resource type.

The system deployer also specifies the mapping of component model instances (i.e., *assembly contexts*) to resource containers. This mapping is called *allocation context*, and one such mapping must exist for each component in a Palladio model so that the model can be analyzed. Each resource container may contain only a single concrete processing resource for a given resource type (e.g., a single CPU). Then, the Palladio tooling can resolve the references from the RDSEFFs via the abstract resources types to the concrete processing resources. With the resolved mapping, the concrete resources demands in timing values can be computed from the abstract work units.

Resource containers are connected via *linking resources*, which represent network connections. Besides a processing rate, they include a latency specification, which models the network round-trip delay for a network package (e.g., 20 milliseconds). The Palladio tooling adds the latency specification to the overall execution time of a request each time an external call over a linking resource is specified in a model. Finally, linking resources also contain a failure probability, which is incorporated by the Palladio analysis tools in case of reliability predictions.

For reliability analyses, the Palladio approach assumes that processing resources such as the CPU and HDD are either available or unavailable (alternating between these two states), and any attempt to access a currently unavailable hardware resource leads to a failure. The hardware failure potentials are thus annotated to processing resources as a probability that the processing resource is available. To express this, the system developer can specify a mean time to failure and mean time to repair for each processing resource. The values can be obtained from vendor specifications or empirical observations. From them, the Palladio tooling can compute the availability of each resource, which then is incorporated into the calculation of the probability of failure on demand for a component service call. The network failure potential is annotated to linking resources as a probability that the message transfer fails.

The Palladio resource environment model can be used to build resource libraries (e.g., for distributed or embedded systems) that are reusable for many software architectures or software product lines. For example, a hardware vendor selling servers can provide a resource environment model containing a model abstraction for each server in the portfolio. This allows software architects to quickly incorporate the performance and reliability properties of different vendors into their models and make comparisons. As another example, a company can provide a company-internal resource model capturing the available server infrastructure, so that different developer and architects can reuse these models.

To better reflect the influence of software infrastructures and operating system virtualization, Palladio includes several special constructs. Application servers and run-time environments can be modeled in Palladio as special *infrastructure components* with RDSEFFs. Software architects can compose them in the same manner as regular components. Lower-level execution layers, such as a host and guest operating system in a virtualization setup, can be modeled with Palladio *controllers*. Controllers offer *resource interfaces*, which allow a vertical composition with Palladio components. On the lowest layer of hardware abstraction, the controllers interface with actual processing resources. Using these constructs, software architects and system deployers can capture the performance and reliability impacts of middleware and virtualization layers. More detailed information is given by Hauck (2009).

5.6 Domain-Specific Quality Modeling

As a modeling language, Palladio is not tied to a specific domain of software systems, such as enterprise resource planning systems or distributed control systems. Rather, Palladio can be used for many different domains, as long as the targeted software can be reasonably partitioned into a number of software components. When it comes to simulation and prediction, Palladio is tied to systems, where the performance is mainly influenced by the architecture and not by the algorithms. This is mainly true for business information systems. But, for example, as the performance of numerical simulation software is mainly given through the algorithms used, Palladio simulations would most likely not be accurate.

Depending on the application domain, however, Palladio models may look rather diverse as the models may be created to answer vastly different questions.

In enterprise computing, distributed business information systems are often subject to performance modeling and analysis. Large business intelligence systems, enterprise resource planning systems, or customer relationship systems may be distributed onto a number of software components, which are deployed on a number of network-connected servers. Because of the complexity, only models with a limited granularity are possible, and timing values down to the range of milliseconds are prevalent. Important questions in this area are, for example, the sizing of the hardware infrastructure (e.g., how many servers are necessary) and the configuration of the communication middleware (e.g., how to configure the application servers). Databases have a major impact on the performance of such systems. Thus, these elements will be reflected with higher granularity in a Palladio model (e.g., by having detailed RDSEFFs for certain database queries).

In embedded computing, systems often use proprietary hardware and are real-time critical. Execution time and response-time requirements can easily be in the range of microseconds, although the defining element of real-time systems is their determinism, which can also be based on much longer time spans. For a controller managing a turbine in a power plant or an embedded system controlling airbags in a car, the compliance to hard real-time deadlines is important. Because of their reduced complexity, such systems can be modeled with a higher granularity than enterprise systems. Stochastic results, however, may not be sufficient in embedded concepts as hard guarantees are needed to obtain a safety certificate for a given system. Detailed modeling of scheduling can be more important in embedded systems to ensure that task deadlines are always met.

There are many other domains in which the emphasis of performance and reliability modeling may differ heavily. For single-node desktop applications, user response times below a certain threshold are important, thus the focus of modeling lies on user interaction scenarios, where short response times may be hard to achieve. Mobile applications in turn often have to deal with strict resource constraints limiting the business logic that can be executed. Database performance and reliability optimization is a separate field of study, and there are numerous modeling methods and guidelines.

Palladio does not provide special modeling constructs for different application domains. It is, however, possible to build component repositories for specific domains and then reuse such component models across different systems within the domain. In any case, a Palladio model should be designed with the formerly stated goals in mind so that the necessary abstraction level to achieve these goals can be determined.

5.7 Putting the Pieces Together

Chapter 9 will describe how the software architect needs to assemble the models from the individual developer roles to create a full Palladio model instance that is ready for analysis or simulation. Each component specification of a component developer contains a number of RDSEFFs for the component services. It is stored in a Palladio repository. Section 3.3.2 describes how the software architect can compose components to form an application called *System* in Palladio.

The system deployer's resource environment model is connected to a system via an allocation model. Finally, the software architect connects the usage model from the domain expert to the system model. At that stage, the model is complete and ready for simulation. Figure 5.5 shows a visualization of the Media Store example with assemblies, RDSEFFs, allocation, and resource environment. The usage model has been omitted for brevity.

In practice, the actual composition of the different model parts may not be equally sequential. If the detailed resource environment model from the system deployer or the usage model from the domain expert is not yet available, the software architect may rely on simplified versions to make initial predictions for quick comparisons. During the modeling process, software component models (i.e., RDSEFFs) may be subsequently refined as their design gets more detailed and more measurements from prototyping are available to achieve a higher prediction accuracy.

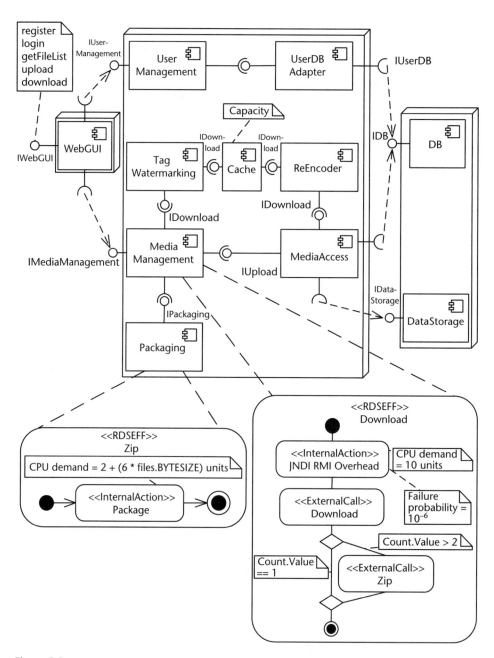

Figure 5.5
Full Media Store example model enhanced with quality annotations.

5.8   Questions and Exercises

5.8.1   Questions

5.1 *: Why is it more efficient to construct goal-oriented models instead of general-purpose models for the quality analysis of software architectures?

5.2 *: Why is it hard to formulate and refine quality goals? Name and describe three methods that can assist the quality modeler in goal formulation.

5.3 **: Why can component developers not provide simple timing or failure probability specifications for their software components? Name at least three factors influencing the quality properties of a component.

5.4 ***: Can a Palladio usage model reference a Palladio resource environment? If yes, which model constructs need to be used; if not, why?

5.5 **: Which Palladio model construct allows modeling the contents of a database?

5.6 *: How can a component developer model the required resources for a software component?

5.7 *: How does Palladio incorporate network resources into a quality prediction?

5.8.2   Exercises

5.1 ***: Model an RDSEFF for the Media Store.

5.2 ***: Create a Palladio usage model.

5.3 ***: Add a parameter dependency to the RDSEFF from exercise 5.1 and specify the concrete parameter values in the corresponding usage model from exercise 5.2.

5.4 ***: Create a Palladio resource environment model and an allocation model. The resource environment model should contain at least two servers and a linking resource. Connect the resource environment to the Media Store's system model by specifying an allocation model that assigns each component (i.e., assembly context) to a processing resource.

5.9   Further Reading

Besides GQM, there are other methods to formulate quality goals, which are beyond the scope of this section but are briefly mentioned for further reference. For example, in a one-day quality attribute workshop (QAW; Clements et al. 2001), different system stakeholders formulate, discuss, and prioritize quality goals and scenarios. The architecture trade-off analysis method (ATAM) (Clements et al. 2001) is similar to QAWs and requires the creation of a quality attribute utility tree that can be used to identify trade-offs between conflicting quality attributes. Finally, ISO-IEC 25010 provides a catalog of quality attributes with their respective definitions, which can support the formulation of quality goals.

Jain (1991) still provides one of the best introductions to the concepts of performance evaluation and modeling. Smith and Williams (2002) rather target software engineers with their software performance engineering methodology and give many hints and recommendations on proper performance modeling from years of practical experience. A literature survey by Balsamo et al. (2004) contains many academic approaches and tools for performance modeling, and another one by Koziolek (2010) focuses specifically on performance modeling approaches for component-based software systems. Woodside et al. (2007) also review a number of performance modeling approaches and highlight interesting directions for future research in software performance engineering.

For reliability analyses, Musa (2004) provides one of the most popular introductions. Lyu's handbook of software reliability engineering (Lyu 1996) is a collection of many different approaches and tools. Literature surveys on reliability prediction approaches have been created by Goseva-Popstojanova et al. (2001) and Gokhale (2007).

5.10   Takeaways

Modeling the quality of component-based software systems should follow a goal-driven approach. You should state the goals in advance to focus modeling and avoid wasted efforts. GQM provides a conceptual model useful to formulate goals and break them down into questions. Workshop-based methods such as QAW or ATAM can help to find goals and quality critical usage scenarios.

Finding an appropriate abstraction level for modeling is crucial: start with small models and iteratively refine them where needed. Construct the simplest model that answers your questions and helps you achieve your goal.

A quality model for a software component consists of a collection of annotated flowcharts (RDSEFF in Palladio), each abstractly modeling the performance and reliability properties of a particular component service. Component quality models must be parameterized for different usage profiles as the concrete usage context is not known in advance to the component developer. Palladio decouples the resource environment model from the software architecture quality model, so that both can be developed independently. Once all individual models are assembled, a performance or reliability analysis can be executed by tools.

6 Getting the Data

Jens Happe, Benjamin Klatt, Martin Küster, Fabian Brosig, Alexander Wert, Simon Spinner, and Heiko Koziolek

To predict the quality of a software system, you need information about the system's structure, its behavior, its execution environment, and its usage. In chapter 3, you learned how to model the structural and behavioral aspects of a software system using modeling concepts such as components, service effect specifications (SEFFs), assemblies, and so forth. In chapter 5, modeling of quality aspects was introduced by explaining the notion of resource demanding service effect specifications (RDSEFFs) and the propagation of usage profiles.

For all these aspects, the different Palladio developer roles need to quantify the relevant influences on the quality of the system. Component developers need to quantify resource demands and failure rates. System deployers need to quantify processing capacities and availability of hardware. Domain experts need to quantify the user behavior and estimate interarrival times. Finally, software architects might have to estimate missing values. As quantification of performance and quantification of reliability each has its specific challenges, the different developer roles mentioned above might require support by experts; namely, specialized performance analysts and specialized reliability analysts.

Enriching models with quantitative data is an essential part of the modeling process. The data must capture performance-related and reliability-related influences and reflect the usage of a software system. In addition, the data depend on the actual implementation of individual software components. The means to get quantitative data as well as its accuracy depend on the artifacts available. Typical artifacts are specification documents, prototypes, or complete implementations of software components.

The questions that arise in this context are the following: (1) Which methods exist to derive quantitative data for different available types of software development artifacts? (2) How can these methods be applied to get the data? (3) Are there any existing tools to support the derivation of quantitative data? This chapter addresses these questions. In particular, you will get to know different methods to estimate, measure, and derive quantitative data. This chapter describes techniques for instrumentation and measurement, resource demand estimation, and workload modeling, as well as corresponding tools that facilitate the execution of the mentioned tasks.

6.1 Overview

To understand how to gather the necessary, quantitative data for calibrating (see definition 13 later) an instance of the Palladio Component Model (PCM), you will first need to understand which artifacts are available in different phases of the development process. Each artifact provides different data with a certain accuracy. In the very beginning of the process, the available development artifacts are abstract and less tangible. Consequently, the data that can be derived in this phase of development are only a rough estimate. As development proceeds and the system becomes more and more concrete, additional data become available, which can increase the accuracy of performance and reliability predictions. For the purpose of this chapter, a development process can be structured in three different phases: *design*, *development*, and *operation*. During design, the application only exists on the drawing board. It comprises artifacts such as architectural diagrams, use cases, and potential deployment specifications. With the development phase, the implementation of the application has started. Parts of the system are available and can be measured. Finally, in the operation phase, the system is active, and users are working with the system. Of course, different software development processes distinguish different phases and iterations, which should not bother you here. The phases are only used to indicate which development artifacts are needed to apply a certain method.

Definition 13 (Model calibration) *In the context of this book, model calibration is the task of enriching a qualitatively specified system model with quantitative data such as resource demands, branch probabilities, and so forth. Hereby, the data may come from measurements or estimates. Model calibration is a prerequisite for conducting performance analysis (e.g., model simulation) on the system model.*

Table 6.1 summarizes the types of data that are required for a complete calibration of a Palladio model. Furthermore in table 6.1, you see a list of methods to gather or extract the necessary data from artifacts and knowledge available in different phases (with no guarantee of completeness). The required types of data are depicted at the top of the table. For the specification of a usage profile, quantitative data are required that allow derivation of different

---

Digression 6.1

Accuracy and Precision of Quantitative Data for PCM

Accuracy and precision of quantitative data for PCM denote two different aspects. *Accuracy* describes the deviation of captured data from the real values. By contrast, *precision* targets the level of detail of the data. Thus, availability of precise data means that, for instance, resource demands are available for low-level operations. High accuracy means that the captured resource demands have only a small deviation from the actual values on the real system.

Table 6.1

Overview of data to be collected and methods to retrieve the data

| | | Type of Data | | | | | | | | | | | |
| | | Usage | | | | | | | Behavior | | | Quality | |
Methods		Development Phases	Arrival Rates	Interaction Flow	Think Time	Number of Concurrent Users	Class Probabilities	Parameter Values	Parametric Dependencies	Branch Probabilities	Loop Counts	Resource Demands	Failure Rates
	Specification analysis	Design	X	X	X	X	X	X					
	Analysis of similar applications	Design	X	X	X	X	X	X				X	X
	Prototyping	Design							X	X	X	X	X
	Educated guessing	Design	X	X	X	X	X	X	X	X	X	X	X
	Beta testing	Development	X	X	X	X	X	X					
	Profiling	Development							X	X	X	X	X
	Instrumentation	Development, operation	X	X	X	X	X	X	X	X	X	X	X
	Resource demand estimation	Development, operation										X	
	Real user monitoring	Operation	X	X	X	X	X	X					
	Application performance monitoring	Operation								X	X	X	X

workload classes including their interaction flow with the software system, values of input parameters, probabilities of workload classes, as well as load intensities. Depending on the type of workload (closed or open; see section 5.4), data for the load intensity can be captured either from arrival rates (open workload) or by means of think time and number of concurrent users (closed workload). With respect to the behavioral part of a Palladio model, quantitative data are also useful to derive parameter dependencies withing a behavior specification (SEFF). Moreover, to complete a behavior specification, values for branch probabilities and loop counts need to be derived from quantitative data. Finally, with respect to performance and reliability, the quality-related parts of a Palladio model need to be calibrated with resource demands and failure rates (see chapter 5). The rows of table 6.1 show individual methods for data extraction and derivation, the development phases in which the methods are applicable, and data types that can be derived by the methods. The following paragraphs summarize the methods listed in the table.

During design time, the software system itself is not available for analyses or measurements. Instead, architects and domain experts have to rely on design documents, requirements, prototypes, similar applications, and their experience. Data derived from these artifacts can be expected to be of low accuracy and precision. As a consequence, predictions that are based on such data include a high degree of uncertainty. Domain experts can specify the usage profile on the basis of existing documentation of expected user behavior (*specification analysis*). This includes use-case models, user stories, or click-through scenarios. *Analyzing the data of similar applications* can help to determine think times or arrival rates of users, to assess the expected number of clicks before a certain activity is performed, or to estimate the total time users spend using the software system. In addition, applications from similar business domains potentially provide insights on typical workload classes and their probabilities. Apart from usage behavior, similar applications may be used to estimate quality-related data such as resource demands or failure rates. For example, for the Media Store (see chapter 2), the resource demands for reading and writing data to a database can be measured for a different application with queries and tables of similar size and structure.

While specification analysis and analysis of similar applications provide rather rough estimates of quantitative data, *prototyping* allows derivation of more accurate and more precise values. Software architects create prototypes to resemble critical parts of the system. They can integrate available third-party components to increase the accuracy of the results. Testing and measurement of prototypes using techniques from later phases (such as profiling and resource demand estimation in combination with instrumentation) generates the necessary data for calibrating the behavior-related and quality-related parts of a Palladio model. For the Media Store introduced in chapter 2, software architects can use an existing library for MP3 encoding and decoding to measure the resource demands of the encoder depending on different file sizes. If prototyping is not possible or too complex, and if similar applications are not available, software architects need to rely on estimates. These can either be based on

Digression 6.2

Instrumentation and Measurement

Instrumentation is the process of enriching the code of the target application with additional code that is responsible for taking measurements. For instance, the response time of an operation can be measured by capturing timestamps at the beginning and the end of the corresponding operation. Instrumentation can be applied either statically on source code or, in the case of managed programming languages such as Java or .NET, during execution by manipulating the byte code of the application. Measurement probes that are injected by instrumentation into the target application always entail monitoring overhead. Hence, excessive instrumentation may lead to a significant monitoring overhead that distorts the measurement data. Therefore, instrumentation should always be applied with caution, considering the potential effect of the monitoring overhead.

Digression 6.3

Application Complexity and Size

There are different concepts and measures for estimating the complexity and size of software applications. The cyclomatic complexity describes the complexity of the control flow graph of the target application. Typical metrics are Halstead complexity measures and McCabe's cyclomatic complexity metric (Leach 1990). Algorithmic complexity aims at estimating the asymptotic timing behavior of algorithms. The metric lines of code (LOC) is used to simply estimate the size of an application's source code.

Digression 6.4

Workload Classes

Even though each user behaves differently, there are classes of users that, within the class, exhibit a similar usage behavior. The set of all usage behaviors is typically divided into a set of *workload classes*. In order to derive workload classes, clustering techniques are applied to group users by the similarity of their behavior.

previous experience (*educated guessing*) or use additional information, such as algorithmic complexity or other specification, to capture the expected behavior and quantitative data of a software system.

During development, parts of the software system are already available and can be used, tested, and measured. Data that are gathered during measurements can be used to refine the prediction model software architects created in earlier phases and to increase its accuracy. If the development team follows an agile process, they may be able to ship a first version of their product to a selected group of test users very early in the process (*beta testing*). In this way, data about the actual usage of the system can be gathered including load intensities as well as potential workload classes and their probabilities. On the basis of these data, they can create more realistic usage profiles. Applying profiling during development on runnable parts of the software product allows gathering of very detailed data on the internals of an application. This includes parameter dependencies, loop counts, and branch probabilities, as well as quality-related metrics such as resource demands or failure rates. *Instrumentation* and *resource demand estimation* are core methods that are typically applied in combination with other measurement-based methods including prototyping, beta testing, profiling, real user monitoring, and application performance monitoring.

Once the application has been deployed in a productive setting and operation has started, performance analysts can collect data about the system's usage, performance, and reliability. Typical approaches for this purpose are *real user monitoring* (RUM) and *application performance monitoring* (APM). Both provide means to nonintrusively instrument an application without diminishing performance significantly. Both approaches in combination provide a major part of the required data for usage, behavior, and quality specification.

The following sections focus on the most relevant approaches for gathering the necessary data, which require (a part of) the system to be available for analysis: real user monitoring and application performance monitoring, middleware instrumentation, resource demand estimation, and estimation of failure probabilities. The different approaches are, in many cases, highly interrelated and applied in combination. The focus is on the general principles of each approach without giving too many details.

The following sections have a common structure as explained in the following. Each section starts with a general description of the method followed by an explanation of its use and applicability. You will get an idea of how the gathered data are interpreted to derive the necessary measures for the calibration of a Palladio model. The sections also provide pointers to further literature and common tools. Finally, each section is concluded by an example and a discussion.

This chapter ends with a discussion of common pitfalls in data collection for performance and reliability analysis.

6.2 Real User and Application Performance Monitoring

With respect to monitoring overhead, real user monitoring (RUM) is a lightweight technique that is mainly applied to Web-based applications to understand user behavior as well as to maintain service quality including performance and reliability. RUM provides means for nonintrusive instrumentation of the high-level services of an application. Hereby, a common method is to inject JavaScript code snippets into the application websites. RUM provides information on user behavior as well as end-user experience, such as end-to-end response times of single-user requests, conversion rates (fraction of users that complete a certain action, such as purchasing an item in an online shop), click sequences conducted by users, and so forth.

While RUM is a rather user-centric technique providing insight to the application performance from the user perspective, application performance monitoring (APM) provides performance data that focus on the internal aspects of a software system. The primary goal of APM is the identification of performance problems in order to enable quick reaction and resolution. To this end, APM provides means to monitor not only high-level services but also the behavior of single software components, their interaction, and the utilization of underlying resources.

When both RUM and APM are applied during operation, they provide precise information on the actual behavior of the application and its usage. Regarding the Palladio model of an application, RUM and APM provide the required data to calibrate the model along all three parts: usage, behavior, and quality (table 6.1). Furthermore, the data gathered from RUM and APM can be used to revise and calibrate the model and, thus, to increase prediction accuracy. As RUM and APM primarily target client-server applications, the following subsections focus on Web-based applications.

6.2.1 Usage and Applicability

RUM and APM are intended to be used in the operation phase of an application. Here, operation phase means not only the final operation phase, where real customers are using the application, but also a mode where the software product is deployed in a representative environment with a representative number and type of users. For instance, development teams may release early (and not necessarily perfect) versions of their software product to a smaller user base (e.g., internally) in order to utilize RUM and APM for refinement and revision of their development artifacts.

In order to set up RUM and APM, it is necessary to recapitulate which information needs to be captured by each of the methods. RUM aims to capture the end-user experience of Web-based applications. In particular, this comprises client-side timings, server-side service times, as well as network latencies. While client-side instrumentation may capture metrics such as network times, browser rendering times, and end-to-end response times, server-side instrumentation of provided services offers an insight to pure server timings. To this end, most Web servers (e.g., the Apache HTTP server) provide logging mechanisms that capture information on which services have been called, their response times, session IDs, and so forth.

In contrast to RUM, APM requires a more fine-grained monitoring of server-side processes. APM may apply middleware instrumentation in order to capture resource demands of component services. Sampling the utilization of resources such as the CPU, memory, hard disk, network, and so forth, allows evaluation of the status of the resource landscape. In the context of business information systems, the software layer between the operating system and the application is called *middleware*. The middleware typically provides infrastructure services to the application layer, so that the application layer can focus on the business logic. Middleware-monitoring facilities can be used to measure service response times at the component boundary-level as well as response times of the infrastructure services; however, in particular when tracking response times, the monitoring overhead has to be low to measure representative times.

There are some commercial as well as open source tools for RUM and APM, which are described in section 6.2.3. Setting up RUM or APM is basically a matter of properly installing and configuring the corresponding tools and is essentially a one-time task during a software project. In order to take advantage of RUM and APM, gathering monitoring data, aggregating it, and analyzing the data should, however, be a continual task. Moreover, as application and usage behavior as well as resource landscape and configurations may change over time, it is important to keep the model of the software system always up to date.

Users of RUM and APM have to overcome two obstacles in order to successfully apply the methods. The first is a technical constraint: instrumentation of the system under test in general introduces an overhead in performance. In test environments, measurement overhead might be acceptable. In a productive environment, however, it is essential that the overhead be negligible in the sense that the customers' perception of the software performance is not affected by the measurements. As measurement overhead depends on the level of detail of the measurements, tackling that problem requires an adequate trade-off between the acceptable impact on performance and the desired level of detail. The second constraint for RUM and APM comes from a legal perspective: both methods (especially RUM) come with excessive monitoring of the behavior of individual users. In many countries, privacy rules prohibit software service providers from storing any user information that can be correlated to individuals. Thus, RUM and APM need to be applied with care, and the users must be informed about the fact that their usage behavior is monitored by the service provider.

6.2.2 Data Interpretation

RUM and APM provide information on usage and behavior and quality data of a software system. The following paragraphs describe the basic steps how to leverage the data provided by RUM and APM to derive a representative Palladio usage model and how to provide precise data on resource demands for calibrating the Palladio model.

RUM provides information on typical usage patterns of the application, including typical request sequences, user think times, average and peak load intensities, as well as seasonal load behavior. A workload model that is derived from such information is more representative than one that is based on estimates. Usually, these data are composed of information on single requests (such as timestamps, session IDs, response times, etc.), which is persisted in an unstructured way as a list of single log entries. A usage model is defined by a set of workload classes and their intensities (see section 5.4). To derive a usage model from the log entries provided by RUM, the data need to be aggregated, correlated, and interpreted.

First, single requests can be grouped to user sessions by correlating single requests using session IDs, IP addresses, and timestamps. Based on the sessions, clustering algorithms (e.g., k-means, hierarchical clustering, etc. [Xu and Wunsch 2008]) can be applied to derive workload classes. Here, the purpose is to find user sessions with similar user behavior. For the clustering algorithms, a similarity metric based on input data characteristics and similarity of click sequences can be used. For each workload class, one representative request sequence needs to be selected for modeling this class.

Figure 6.1 illustrates the workload characterization steps by means of a simple example. The frame at the left shows a list of log entries as provided by most Web servers. In this example, the log entries provide information on the IP address and the requested URL of each user request. Utilizing the IP addresses (assuming that IP addresses identify single users), user sessions can be derived as depicted in the middle frame. Finally, clustering algorithms are applied to group similar user sessions to workload classes.

Load intensities (i.e., think-time distributions and arrival rates) for individual workload classes can be derived by analyzing the timestamps of individual requests. On the basis of the derived workload classes and corresponding load intensities, a usage model can be specified as described in section 5.4.

Considering resource demands, APM provides response times for whole requests and individual system parts as well as utilization of resources. These data can be used to derive resource demands for single actions using resource demand estimation techniques, as described in section 6.3.

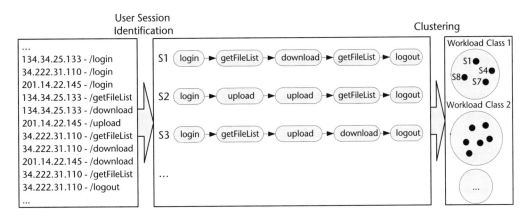

Figure 6.1
Deriving workload classes from RUM data.

6.2.3 Common Tools

There are commercial as well as open source tools that provide APM and RUM functionality. Google Analytics [1] is a commercial tool providing advanced RUM functionality with a focus on business metrics. It allows analysis of user behavior with respect to different aspects such as social interactions, conversions, advertisement effect, and so forth. For this purpose, Google Analytics users need to inject a JavaScript code snippet into their own site. Using the instrumentation snippet, Google Analytics collects client-side data, which is collected for further analyses on a Google server.

Using log entries provided by the Web server is a simple way to get minimal information to conduct real user analysis. It requires much more manual effort, however, to compute, aggregate, and interpret the raw data than in the case with advanced tools. Furthermore, pure server-side instrumentation does not provide insights to client-side and network performance, such as browser rendering times or data transmission times.

For APM, there is a large body of commercial tools available (e.g., New Relic [2], App Dynamics [3], Dynatrace [4], Scout [5], Nagios [6], Dotcom-Monitor [7], etc.), offering deep-dive analysis of performance issues. Users provide similar services and provide similar services and features. For instance, New Relic [2] is a service-based solution for features. Users of New Relic need to install a lightweight client on their system. The client collects necessary performance data and periodically transmits them to the New Relic server. Besides a REST-based interface for performance data retrieval, New Relic provides a web-based user interface for examination and analysis of performance data.

Kieker [8] is an open source tool for APM. Kieker comes with an extensible framework for performance data gathering and analysis, which allows one to provide own plug-ins for custom data gathering or data analysis steps. Furthermore, Kieker provides a mechanism (based on aspect-oriented programming) to instrument application code, to get performance insights from the deep internals of an application. This way, performance analysts may capture more detailed performance data to refine their models. The Adaptable Instrumentation and Monitoring (AIM) tool [9] is similar to Kieker, but in addition provides means for dynamically adaptable instrumentation. This means that instrumentation instructions can be adopted at run time of the application without the need to restart the target application. This feature is especially useful for automated measurement of resource demands as it allows reduction of the monitoring overhead that otherwise would distort the measurement data.

Examples of monitoring frameworks for Java EE application servers are the Oracle Web-Logic Diagnostics Framework (WLDF) [10] for the Oracle WebLogic Application Server or IBM Tivoli for the IBM WebSphere Application Server.

Digression 6.5
Aspect-Oriented Programming
Aspect-oriented programming (AOP; Kiselev 2003) is a programming paradigm that allows development of cross-cutting concerns of an application in a modular way. Typical cross-cutting aspects are logging, data validation, monitoring, and instrumentation. The AOP paradigm provides the notion of an aspect that encapsulates one cross-cutting concern. In managed programming languages such as Java or .NET, AOP can be combined with byte-code manipulation to weave the cross-cutting concerns dynamically at run time into the byte code of the target application. This technique is often used by instrumentation tools to enrich the target application with measurement probes.

6.2.4 Example (Media Store)

RUM and APM can help to refine the models for the Media Store example. Assume that all model parts of the Media Store are complete and the models have been simulated. Comparing simulation results with actual measurements shows significant deviations in performance due to inaccurate model calibration. Assume the estimated distribution of the file sizes downloaded by users does not fit to the actual usage pattern, which leads to the inaccurate prediction results. Applying workload characterization techniques on the data provided by RUM may help to derive a more representative usage model. Configuring RUM in a way that it captures the sizes of files users download, the gathered information can be easily analyzed to derive an accurate distribution of the file sizes for the usage model.

Considering the question of which impact the re-encoding component has on the overall performance of the Media Store (see figure 2.1), APM may help to capture the actual performance behavior of the re-encoding process. Assume that APM is configured to capture the response times of the ReEncoder component and the CPU utilization in the running example. Performance analysts can apply resource demand estimation techniques (see section 6.3) to derive resource demands. The results can be used to validate or refine the resource demands of the internal actions of the ReEncoder component.

6.2.5 Discussion

Although RUM and APM are methods that cannot be applied during early development stages, they can significantly contribute to increase the prediction accuracy of models by leveraging the provided data for model refinement. These models can be used for further analysis (e.g., extrapolation and sensitivity analysis) or reused in similar contexts. Moreover, RUM and APM provide precise data for model building in reverse engineering scenarios.

6.3 Resource Demand Estimation

Resource demands describe the resources required to execute an internal action of a software component (see chapter 5). Software components can require active resources (e.g., CPUs and hard disks) and passive resources (e.g., thread pools). In the following, you will learn how to estimate the resource demands for active resources based on monitoring data obtained during system development and operation.

6.3.1 Usage and Applicability

Resource demand estimation works on aggregated monitoring data that can be obtained from monitoring tools provided by the operating system or from application log files. Examples of such aggregate metrics are average response time, total resource utilization, and average throughput. Given that measurements from an executable implementation of the software architecture are necessary, resource demand estimation cannot be used at early stages of system design. Once a first working prototype of the application is available, however, resource demand estimation is a viable alternative if instrumentation of the application code is not possible or only to a very limited extent.

Fundamentally, there are two different approaches for collecting the required measurements:

• The application of interest is executed in a test environment with a configurable load driver. This offers a fine-grained control over the workload of the system (e.g., you can send only requests of the same type to the system) and simplifies the data interpretation. But certain workload behaviors (e.g., interactions between requests of different types), which can be observed on production systems, may not be captured in the estimates of the resource demands. This may have a negative impact on the accuracy of performance predictions using Palladio.

• The monitoring data required for resource demand estimation is collected during operation on production systems. In production systems, usually a complex mixture of all types of requests can be observed, which makes the estimation of resource demands more challenging.

6.3.2 Data Interpretation

There are different methods you can use to estimate resource demands. The approximation of resource demands with measured response times is a simple technique: Single requests of a workload class are issued to the system of interest, and the response time of each request is observed. Then, you can approximate the resource demand of a resource with the average observed response time, if the following assumptions hold:

• The resource for which resource demands are estimated dominates the observed response time. If a request spends significant time at other resources, the part of the processing time will be attributed to the wrong resource.

Digression 6.6

Mapping Between Palladio and Workload Classes

Most techniques of resource demand estimation use the term *workload class* to cluster requests to a resource with similar characteristics regarding their resource consumption. The mapping of workload classes to Palladio depends on the granularity of the RDSEFFs. On the architecture level, a workload class corresponds either to one or more internal actions in an RDSEFF or to component services:

• If an RDSEFF of a service is modeled rather coarse grained, and all accesses to a resource within a component are combined in one internal action, workload classes can be mapped to component services.

• If an RDSEFF contains a fine-grained description of the control flow where several internal actions model individual resources accesses, workload classes have to be mapped to internal actions within the RDSEFF. For instance, if an RDSEFF contains internal actions I_A, I_B, and I_C, where I_A and I_B have similar resource requirements, it is possible to define two workload classes, $W_1 = \{I_A, I_B\}$ and $W_2 = \{I_C\}$. In this case, more fine-grained instrumentation of the application is needed to obtain call frequencies of each internal action.

Digression 6.7

Queuing Theory

The core concept of queuing theory is a *queue*. A queue consists of a waiting line and one or multiple servers. Jobs (e.g., requests or transactions) arriving at the queue are either served immediately if at least one server is currently not occupied or put into the waiting line until a server becomes free. After service completion, the job leaves the queue. You can represent active resources (such as CPU or hard disk) by queues. Then, you can use different equations and solution algorithms from queuing theory to predict the waiting times, response times, and utilization for a given workload.

Operational laws are simple equations describing the average service behavior of a queue. In contrast to other equations and solution algorithms from queuing theory, these equations do not make assumptions on the scheduling and the distribution of the interarrival times and service times. Therefore, you can apply them to many different types of systems. You can find more information about operational laws in Menascé et al. (2004).

• The system should only be utilized lightly. If a system experiences significant resource contention during the observation period, the observed response times also include waiting times due to requests being delayed when a resource is blocked by other requests.

If the assumptions listed above do not hold, resource demands can be estimated using techniques based on operational laws from queuing theory.

One such operational law is the *service demand law*. This operational law states that the resource demand D of workload class c at resource i can be derived from the utilization U of resource i due to workload class c and the throughput X of workload class c (Menascé et al. 2004):

$$D_{i,c} = \frac{U_{i,c}}{X_c} \qquad\qquad\qquad (6.1)$$

The term *service demand* can be considered as an equivalent to *resource demand* in equation 6.1. In order to apply the service demand law, you need to obtain measurements of the utilization for each workload class at each resource; however, monitoring tools commonly used are limited to observe the total utilization of a system or the utilization of individual processes (e.g., the sar utility under Linux). Given that in many applications the same process can serve requests of different workload classes, utilization cannot be monitored directly for individual workload classes. In order to cope with this limitation, you have two options:

• Ensure that only requests of one workload class arrive at the system during an observation interval. Utilization can then be approximated for a workload class with the total utilization of the resource.
• In cases where requests of different services arrive at the system simultaneously during an observation interval, the observed total utilization needs to be partitioned between the different workload classes appropriately.

A possible approach to partition the total utilization U_i of resource i is based on weighted response-time ratios. The per-class utilization can be estimated from the total utilization with the following relationship (Brosig et al. 2009):

$$U_{i,c} = U_i \frac{R_c \lambda_c}{\sum_{d=1}^{C} R_d \lambda_d} \qquad\qquad\qquad (6.2)$$

where C is the number of workload classes, and R_c and λ_c are the average response time and the arrival rate of workload class c. Implicitly, it is assumed that the measured average response time R_c of workload class c is approximately proportional to the corresponding resource demands of this workload class; that is, the response time R_c does not include any significant time spent at other resources than the one considered. Other partitioning approaches are described in Lazowska et al. (1984) and Menascé et al. (1994, 2001, 2004).

6.3.3 Common Tools
Resource demand estimation consists of the following two activities, which require tool support: data collection and data analysis. For data collection, you can use monitoring and instrumentation tools as described in section 6.2.

For simple data analysis tasks, you may use standard statistical software (e.g., the R language [11], SPSS [12], or Matlab[13]). If you want to use more sophisticated estimation techniques, however, the implementation effort can be rather high.

Therefore, the Eclipse-based tooling LibReDE supports estimate of resource demands based on monitoring data. LibReDE implements a variety of different estimation approaches proposed in the literature (including the ones described in this section) and assists you in selecting an appropriate estimation approach depending on the available monitoring data. Furthermore, it provides mechanisms for cross-validation of the the resulting resource demands. More information on LibReDE can be found on its project website at http://descartes.tools/librede/.

6.3.4 Example (Media Store)

In a typical resource allocation in the Media Store example, several components may be deployed on the same application server, thus sharing hardware resources. In this example, assume that the components MediaManagement and Packaging of the Media Store application are deployed on the same application server, and that you want to estimate the CPU demand of the individual service operations provided by these components. For the sake of simplicity, it is possible to distinguish between the following three workload classes: $C1$ (MediaManagement#upload), $C2$ (MediaManagement#downloadCollection), and $C3$ (Packaging#zip). If the observed mean response times of these operations are $R_{C1} = 26$ ms, $R_{C2} = 53$ ms, and $R_{C3} = 40$ ms, you can use the response-time approximation approach to come up with the estimated mean resource demands $D_{C1} = 26$ ms, $D_{C2} = 13$ ms (the response time R_{C2} includes one call to $C3$), and $D_{C3} = 40$ ms in the example. Given a total CPU utilization of $U_i = 0.25$ and invocation rates for each operation $\lambda_{C1} = 2.5$ calls/s, $\lambda_{C2} = 5$ calls/s, and $\lambda_{C3} = 5$ calls/s, you can estimate the utilizations due to each workload class based on equation 6.2: $U_{C1} = 0.05$, $U_{C2} = 0.05$, $U_{C3} = 0.15$. Using the service demand law equation 6.1, it is possible to estimate the mean resource demands $D_{C1} = 20$ ms, $D_{C2} = 10$ ms, and $D_{C3} = 30$ ms. The second approach based on the service demand law provides more accurate estimates as it also considers the time an invocation is delayed due to CPU scheduling.

6.3.5 Discussion

Resource demand estimation offers the derivation of resource demands required for performance prediction from easily available performance metrics, such as overall response time, throughput, and resource utilization. Therefore, it can be applied in scenarios where detailed application instrumentation is not possible or only at a coarse-grained level (e.g., component boundaries). It can also be used to derive resource demands based on observations from a production system during operation. When reconstructing a Palladio model from an existing system, expensive and time-consuming experiments in a dedicated test environment can be avoided using resource demand estimation. It is important to mention that the techniques described above only provide platform-dependent resource demands. When switching the software or hardware platforms, the estimated resource demands are obsolete and need to be estimated again. If platform-independent resource demands are necessary, it would be necessary to count program code instructions of internal actions to determine the processing time of each instruction for a given platform. To count each instruction, a very fine-grained instrumentation is required, resulting in a high run-time overhead.

6.4 Estimating Failure Probabilities

The following paragraphs deal with the problem of estimating the failure probabilities of internal actions of Palladio RDSEFF models. For a complete reliability analysis (see section 5.3), additional data are needed, such as hardware availability specifications from vendors.

A failure probability of an internal action quantifies the reliability of a software component, so that a software architect can make an overall prediction of system reliability. In practice, these failure probabilities are usually coarse-grained estimations and will not really be experienced in practice by a particular user. They merely quantify the knowledge about the failure behavior of the system at the time of analysis. Such failure probabilities should not be overrated within a development team or communicated to customers, as they only serve to identify improvement potential for the software system under analysis.

During *design*, there are only limited possibilities to specify failure probabilities. The system cannot be tested for failures as no source code is available. The design documents may lack detail to quantify the reliability of individual components or services. One approach is to estimate components sizes (in lines of code) based on experience and then assign higher failure probabilities to the larger components. Another approach is to let experienced developers estimate upper and lower bounds for failure probabilities given a specific component and then narrow these bounds as more information becomes available. These approaches are, however, hardly seen in the literature.

If no other information is available, a viable option during design is to apply methods for failure probability estimation during development and operation on similar systems to the one currently being designed. Similar systems should have a comparable complexity and come from a related business domain. This approach is useful if the system being designed has a rather standard functionality and uses widely adopted technologies. Nevertheless, a mapping from such a similar system to the system under design needs to be made manually, which is currently not supported by any methods and tools.

During *development*, several options for estimating failure probabilities become available. Developers can use code metrics quantifying the complexity (e.g., LOC, Halstead, McCabe) of the already implemented component source code. Such complexity metrics can give an indicator, not a precise measure, of the expected component failure probability. This approach, however, is debated in the scientific literature as studies have found that in many cases, code complexity is not correlated with actual failure rates.

Another approach is to exploit test cases that become available during development. Using the test cases, code coverage for a particular software component can be determined and used as a measure for its failure probability. As all test cases may pass in properly tested

---

Digression 6.8

Software Reliability Growth Model

These models provide a statistical extrapolation of the number of detected faults in a system using mathematical functions. As the number of defects found per time unit during testing and system operation usually decreases, it is possible to fit a curve to the data and make predictions for future failure rates or for the number of still existing faults in the source code. There are many SRGMs proposed in the literature using different representations of the fault detection rate and various assumptions. Because there is no consensus in the literature which model works best, usually a number of different SRGMs need to be tested in a given context.

---

systems, it is possible to manually or automatically inject faults into the source code to get a better picture of the actual reliability. It is also possible to generate and execute random test cases to get another indicator for the software reliability. Static code analysis tools can identify faults to a certain extent, thus giving another input for estimating a component failure probability.

Finally, during *operation*, many users have executed the software for a given time and provided bug reports. In this case, a statistical analysis of the bug tracker databases provides an approach to estimate failure probabilities. This approach relies on the (practically validated) assumption that software reliability grows over time, as more and more bugs are found and fixed. In this case, it is possible to fit a so-called software reliability growth model (SRGM) to the bug report data and extrapolate curves to determine the reliability at the point of analysis. Such SRGMs require a number of assumptions (e.g., static usage profile) but are then the most sophisticated predictors of component failure probabilities.

6.4.1 Usage and Applicability

Approaches analyzing the source code for reliability data are usually straightforward to execute due to comprehensive tool support. Static code analysis tools provide basic code metrics and information about potential issues as part of their standard functionality. Often, such tools are already integrated into common integrated development environments (IDEs). This method is of course only applicable if a significant amount of source code is available. For some of the static code analysis tools, the code also needs to be compiled.

Approaches executing test cases require a nontrivial amount of test cases available for the code under analysis. Some test cases can even be created automatically using test case generators. Using testing frameworks, developers can obtain the required code coverage metrics.

Approaches analyzing bug databases can only be used after a significant usage period of the software under analysis. The reliability analyst needs to filter the bug reports, for example to exclude nonissues or minor defects. A critical step for Palladio reliability predictions is the mapping of bug reports to individual components, which can be a complicated task. Bug reports are usually classified according to the component of a system where the failure occurred. This may, however, mask the origin of the failure (i.e., the fault), which may reside in another component and was only propagated to the component exposed to the user.

The number of bugs reported for a given software component can then be aggregated for time periods (e.g., bugs per months), so that a decreasing curve should result (e.g., 10 defects in January, 8 defects in February, etc.) that can be fitted to software reliability growth models from the literature.

6.4.2   Data Interpretation

For static code analysis, code complexity metrics need to be transformed into component failure probabilities. For example, if size metrics are used, rules of thumb can be referred to, such as four defects per 1,000 lines of code as an indicator.

With this assumption, the failure probability of a 1,000-lines-of-code component would be 0.004. There are no general guidelines on how to transform code complexity metrics into component failure probabilities. In most cases, a normalization of the metric value between zero and one should already provide a first estimation.

For code coverage metrics, it is possible to directly derive a failure probability. For example, if a software component has a test coverage of 80%, a failure probability of 0.2 can be assigned as a coarse-grained estimate. As for the code metrics, in this case the estimated failure probability does not express the actual failure probability to be expected by a user. It merely reflects the uncertainty concerning the component reliability due to its insufficient testing. In a system-wide, model-based software reliability prediction, it can thus help to identify the components that need more testing.

For applying SRGMs, the current failure statistics need to be extrapolated. Tools supporting SRGMs usually provide means to interpret the data and compute the necessary failure probabilities.

6.4.3   Common Tools

There is a plethora of commercial and open source tools for static code analysis. Popular commercial tools are Understand [14] and Klocwork [15], while Findbugs [16] and SonarQube [17] are examples for open source tools. Many modern IDEs, such as Visual Studio [18] and Eclipse [19], have some rudimentary support for static code analysis.

Code coverage tools compute the degree to which the source code of a program is executed by a given test suite. JaCoCo and Clover are examples for Java-based tools, while Visual Studio and CppUnit provide support for C++.

In the area of SRGMs, many reliability analysts use standard statistics tools such as R, SPSS, or even Microsoft Excel. CASRE (Computer-Aided Software Reliability Estimation) is a specific software reliability measurement tool for nonspecialists.

6.4.4 Example

Palladio models have been involved in a number of reliability prediction studies. From these studies, examples for failure probability estimations can be extracted. For example, in Koziolek et al. (2010), a Palladio reliability model for an industrial control system was created, where the component failure probabilities were estimated from bug tracker statistics. In Brosch et al. (2012), failure probabilities for the components were simply assumed to be equal, and then a sensitivity analysis on individual failure probabilities was applied to identify critical components in the system.

For the Palladio Media Store system, there are only limited source code, test cases, and bug reports available, which are not sufficient to reasonably estimate component failure probabilities. One option is thus to leverage similar systems to estimate failure probabilities. For example, for re-encoding audio files as in the Media Store, algorithms and components can be accessed from open source websites, where code metrics are readily available. Using this information, the size of a fully implemented re-encoding component can be estimated and set in relation to the other components. On the basis of the size, a rough failure probability estimation can be made.

6.4.5 Discussion

In summary, estimating failure probabilities for software components today is still a craftsmanship approach and not an engineering approach. There are still limited empirical validations and engineering experience with many approaches proposed in the scientific literature. Existing approaches as described above often stem from different contexts than model-driven reliability prediction. For example, SRGMs are usually used on complete systems, but not on individual software components. The constraints and assumptions under which such approaches operate might not hold in a given prediction scenario and need to be thoroughly examined.

As for other modeling activities, for estimating failure probabilities it is helpful to start with simple estimations in a given model, which can be refined as more information becomes available over the course of the development. Often, sophisticated methods, such as SRGM, are worthwhile only in specific situations (e.g., for safety-critical systems). For less critical applications, it is advisable to work with less reliable estimations and instead strongly restrict the required level of detail based on the modeling goals.

6.5 Common Pitfalls

Creating and maintaining useful prediction models is a challenging task. In many cases, software architects, developers, and domain experts have only limited information to build accurate prediction models upon which design decisions can be based. The following subsections contain a discussion of common pitfalls when modeling a software system for performance and reliability prediction.

6.5.1   Wrong Resource Demands

Wrongly estimated resource demands are a typical source of inaccurate and misleading predictions. Often, the time passed between two points during execution is taken as an approximation of the consumed resources; however, these time intervals include many other influences and delays that do not reflect resource consumption correctly. Section 6.3 provides alternative solutions for estimating resource demands correctly. Load-dependent resource demands are another common source of prediction errors. In such cases, the resource demand changes with increasing load. This can be, for example, caused by optimizations of the run-time environment such as compilation of otherwise interpreted code or due to additional overheads and thrashing. Identifying load-dependent resource demands requires load tests with different numbers of users and a direct comparison of estimated resource demands.

6.5.2   Inaccurate Timers

Measuring timing behavior correctly is challenging. Many disturbances and inaccuracies can affect the results. For example, the resolution of the operating system timer is limited by the interval of the timer interrupt. Other timers might provide higher accuracy but are subject to other disturbances. For example, timers that rely on the number of clock ticks provided by the CPU, such as System.nanotime() in Java, can be misleading in a multiprocessor environment where the process may be moved to another CPU between two measurements. More details about the correct use of timers may be found in Kuperberg et al. (2011).

6.5.3   Missing Resources

Some resources are obvious and seldom go unnoticed, such as the CPU and hard disks. Other resources are harder to identify but can affect performance nonetheless; for example, passive resources, such as thread pools, connection pools, or mutexes. These resources can have a significant impact on throughput and response times, but they may be hidden deeply in third-party services and components and are thus hard to identify. Furthermore, other physical resources, such as main memory, are usually not reflected in prediction models but can also affect system performance and reliability. Static code analysis and code inspection can help to identify missing resources. But the most efficient way to identify missing elements in the model is to compare its predictions to measurements, as discussed in the following.

6.5.4   No Validation

Performance models are abstractions of the real system. As such, performance models are always based on the current knowledge of the modeler. Each model contains various assumptions about the importance, influence, and behavior of different components and services. Without comparing predictions to measurements, it is impossible to decide whether the model describes the performance of the system accurately (isomorphism of the model). In this case, predictions are always attached to a high degree of uncertainty that limits their benefits.

6.5.5 Too Many Details

While all the described risks and pitfalls mainly addressed the issues arising from missing details, it is important to find the right level of abstraction. Including too many details in a model increases the complexity of collecting all needed information and of creating and maintaining the model. It is much harder to isolate the root cause of deviations between predictions and measurements in complex and detailed models. So, it is wise to follow Einstein's advice: "As simple as possible, but not simpler."

6.6 Questions and Exercises

6.6.1 Questions

6.1 *: What are the central assumptions that you have to make for measurement-based collection of quantitative data?

6.2 *: What are the limitations of middleware instrumentation?

6.3 *: What is the main difference between real user monitoring and application performance monitoring?

6.4 **: What are the benefits of real user monitoring and application performance monitoring for architectural model building (e.g., a Palladio model)?

6.5 **: Which trade-off has to be considered when setting up application performance monitoring?

6.6 ***: Virtualization is a very common practice to save hardware costs and to run several applications on one execution node. Why does this make data collection for performance modeling more difficult? How can you still provide valuable data in a virtualized setting?

6.6.2 Exercises

6.1 ***: Imagine you would like to monitor each method of the code snippet in listing 6.1. Let us assume that the execution time of method doWork(n) is n^2 ms, and the overhead of a single instrumentation probe is 10 ms.

(a) Calculate the execution time of method doService() without instrumentation code.

(b) Assume that an instrumentation probe is injected into each method. Calculate the overhead (expressed as a percentage) of the instrumentation code to the execution time of method doService().

(c) Which methods need to be instrumented in order to have as much monitoring detail as possible without exceeding a monitoring overhead of 10% for method doService() ?

Listing 6.1

Code snippet for exercise 6.1

```
doService(){

    methodA()

    methodB()

}

methodA(){

    doWork(4)

    fori=1to10

        methodC()

}

methodB(){

    fori=1to10

        methodD()

    doWork(10)

}

methodC(){

    doWork(30)

}

methodD(){

    doWork(2)

    doWork(5)

}

doWork(n){

...

}

...
```

6.2 ****: Assume a system consisting of three components A, B, and C. Component A is the system entry point and calls components B and C. Components A and B are deployed on host $H1$ and component C on host $H2$. Each component implements one operation that uses the CPU and I/O resources of the host it is deployed on. For the resource demands of components A and B the following relationship holds: $\frac{D_A^{CPU}}{D_A^{I/O}} = \frac{D_B^{CPU}}{D_B^{I/O}}$ (i.e., the amount of I/O work is proportional to the processing time at the CPU). You observe the response times $R_A = 304.76$ ms, $R_B = 175$ ms, and $R_C = 71.43$ ms at the component boundaries. The system throughput at the system entry point is $\lambda = 20$ req/s. In each host, you monitor the resource utilizations:

$$U_{H1}^{CPU} = 0.8 \, U_{H1}^{I/O} = 0.4 \, U_{H2}^{CPU} = 0.3 \, U_{H2}^{I/O} = 0.5$$

(a) Why can you not use the response-time approximation approach to estimate the resource demands in this system?

(b) Estimate the resource demands for each component and all resources using the service demand law. Derive the per-class utilization using equation 6.2.

(c) Why is the additional relationship for the resource demands of A and B to be proportional necessary in order to obtain accurate estimates?

6.7 Further Reading

Measuring performance is a difficult and challenging task. Georges et al. (2007) summarized the common obstacles, mistakes, and problems when measuring the performance of Java applications. They also provide solutions and best practices for common issues. Kuperberg et al. (2011) provide additional details about timers and their accuracy for performance measurements. Jain (1991) also offers good hints about the collection and analysis of data for performance modeling in his guide to software performance engineering. Menascé (2003) provides a good introduction into workload characterization. Willnecker et al. (2015) introduce an approach to use the data provided by Dynatrace to derive Palladio models for Java EE applications. More details on the use of static code analysis for deriving Palladio models can be found in chapter 11 and in Krogmann et al. (2010).

6.8 Takeaways

It is a challenging task to create accurate prediction models for the performance and reliability of a software system; however, software architects, developers, domain experts, and performance experts can use various sources of information to increase the accuracy of a model and refine it throughout the development process of their software system.

In the beginning, when only little information about the system is available, prototypes, data from similar applications, estimates, and information from architectural specifications can be used to create initial rough performance and reliability estimates. As the development proceeds, more information becomes available. Techniques such as resource demand estimation, real user monitoring, and application performance monitoring help refine the model as well as the modeled user behavior. A continual comparison of predictions to actual measurements is essential to create a reliable and accurate prediction model. The combination of different techniques for data collection, analysis, and modeling is essential to build useful prediction models that support software architects and developers in making good design decisions.

In this chapter, you learned which quantitative data are required to calibrate a system model for performance and reliability analysis. Furthermore, this chapter outlined a set of methods for derivation of quantitative data depending on the artifacts that are available in different development phases. You learned some basic methods for collecting data by measurements including application performance monitoring, real user monitoring, middleware instrumentation, resource demand estimation, and estimation of failure probabilities. For each of the methods, you were referred to open source and commercial tools that are commonly used to accomplish the corresponding tasks. Finally, this chapter listed a set of common pitfalls in conducting measurements.

7 Answering Design Questions

Anne Koziolek, Qais Noorshams, and Christoph Heger

All effort invested in quality modeling and architectural analysis is meant to support decisions and improve the software design. Consequently, the predicted quality needs to be interpreted and related back to the original design questions.

This chapter begins with a review of the central design questions related to performance and reliability to discuss the typical questions that software architects face. Then, an explanation of how to interpret performance and reliability prediction results and how to use this information to identify and resolve potential problems follows. The chapter closes with a general discussion about how to choose design alternatives and touches on automated approaches to explore the design space.

7.1 Design Questions

Palladio was designed to answer typical design questions related to performance and reliability on a model basis. The following subsections discuss such questions.

7.1.1 General Quality Design Questions
Among general quality-related design questions that affect both performance and reliability are the following.

What Is the Best Design Alternative? Software architects usually come up with different alternatives of how to solve a given design problem. They can invent these design alternatives or derive them from common knowledge, such as architectural styles or patterns (see section 3.6 and chapter 4). The effect of different design alternatives on all relevant quality characteristics is usually not straightforward, as improving one quality characteristic can easily lead to drawbacks for another quality attribute. Additionally, design alternatives may influence each other (e.g., selecting an implementation technology can affect many design questions) and may often span a large design space. It would often be impossible to evaluate such a design space efficiently if every alternative had to be implemented and deployed first.

Examples of questions regarding design alternatives are: Which component should I choose to obtain optimal system quality? What is the impact of reusing a component instead of redeveloping it? Is it possible to improve the quality of the system by investing in a certain component; for example, by enhancing algorithms or caching strategies? Which architectural style or patterns should be applied? Which variant of a selected style or pattern should be used?

What Is an Optimal Configuration for the System?   Nowadays, many software systems have a large configuration space spanned by dozens to hundreds of configuration options, ranging from possible deployment options of the components over constants in the code to configuration parameters in XML files. These configuration options and their combination can be systematically evaluated on a model basis with respect to their impact on the quality of service of the system. Postponing this activity after system deployment might cause many redeployment, recompile, or restart cycles of the software system, with associated costs.

Typical software configuration questions are: Which parameters are significant for the quality of the system and are sensitive to changes? What are the most suitable parameter values for a given usage scenario? How do which parameters relate to each other, and what mutual dependencies exist?

How to Extend a Legacy Software System?   Finally, extending legacy software systems (i.e., existing software systems) is challenging because new components can affect the performance and reliability of existing software systems. Even if a legacy system is extended by adding wrappers or adapter components, its performance and reliability can change unexpectedly due to changed usage profiles for the legacy system. Modifying the legacy system to add new features can also change its performance and reliability. Both cases can lead to performance bottlenecks or introduce additional load that the legacy software is not able to process.

Consequently, typical questions when extending existing software systems include: How can legacy software be integrated into a software system? What is the impact on the quality when extending legacy systems? What quality implications arise?

7.1.2   Additional Performance Design Questions
Specific performance design questions are related to capacity planning, scalability analysis, and load balancing, as detailed in the following.

How to Optimally Size the System?   Capacity planning (or sizing) is the estimation of required hardware resources to support a certain number of users (the workload intensity). This activity is fundamental to set up an efficiently running software system. The main goal is to avoid wasting resources while at the same time preventing performance bottlenecks due to insufficient hardware capacity.

Typical capacity planning questions are: How many resources are needed to support the users during average or peak periods? How does the application perform when migrating or upgrading to new servers? Does the application perform better on a WebSphere or Glassfish application server?

How Scalable Is the System?   Scalability analysis is aligned with capacity planning and is the specific analysis and identification of bottlenecks in the software architecture. It allows the identification of the maximum workload intensity that the system is able to process, given a certain amount of software and hardware resources. Once the bottlenecks and their causes are identified, the goal is to efficiently resolve these issues by adding resources only where needed.

Typical questions related to scalability include: How many users does the system support? Where is the bottleneck if the workload intensity is high? How can I resolve the bottleneck without wasting resources?

How to Balance the Load on the System Resources?   Load balancing is a key factor for avoiding the aforementioned problem, with the specific goal being to utilize the available resources evenly.

The most frequent questions regarding load balancing are the following: How to cluster the requests such that they can be individually processed? How to distribute the requests such that the resources are evenly utilized? How to change the system if it evolves and becomes imbalanced?

7.1.3   Additional Reliability Design Questions

Specific reliability design questions at the software architecture level include where to use fault tolerance mechanisms, such as redundancy and design diversity; how to deal with physical failure; and how to decide on the amount of testing effort.

Which Fault Tolerance Mechanisms Shall the System Exhibit?   All software systems contain faults and produce errors, be it based on bugs in the software or physical failure. What makes software systems reliable is how well they can tolerate faults and/or errors and how well they avoid actual system failures. Fault tolerance mechanisms are added to the system to allow it to compensate for errors, to recover from errors, or to treat faults. A design question for reliability is where to place such mechanisms in a cost-effective manner for the greatest effect (Avizienis et al. 2004).

How Much Redundancy Shall the System Exhibit?   For system elements that can fail, having a backup element ready that can take over the failed system element's responsibilities can improve reliability. Redundancy is only meaningful if the redundant elements fail independently. For example, if certain parameter values trigger a bug within a software component, it does not help to have this software component be instantiated twice, as both copies will fail together. By contrast, hardware elements usually fail independently of each other if their failure is not due to a common physical cause such as a power outage. Adding redundant elements to the system, however, increases costs, so it should be used only where needed. Thus, the design question here is how much redundancy to add and what system elements to make redundant.

Is It Useful to Introduce Design Diversity?   As mentioned above, instantiating multiple instances of the same software component does not help against the effects of software bugs triggered by certain parameter values. To have two software component instances that fail independently (and thus reduce the probability that both fail at the same time), one needs to instantiate two different software components. To avoid a situation where the same team of developers makes the same mistakes in multiple versions of the software component, these different components should be implemented by different teams (thus the term *design diversity*). A design question for architecture-level reliability analysis is to determine whether there are software components that are so critical for the overall system's reliability that design diversity pays off.

How to Deal with Physical Failures?   Software is executed on hardware resources and thus may also depend on physical failure of this hardware. Architecture-level reliability analysis helps to assess the effect of hardware failure rates on the reliability of the overall system. Design questions include how to distribute software components to multiple servers so that failures of single servers have the least effect.

Which Components Contribute Most to the Reliability of the System?   While quality assurance is not part of architectural design, architecture-level reliability analysis can help to identify components that are most critical for the overall system reliability and may be used to direct quality assurance efforts, such as testing efforts and reviews, to where they pay off the most.

7.2   Understanding the Results

To address the design questions discussed in the previous section, the software architecture of the system can be modeled using the Palladio Component Model as described in previous chapters. Subsequently, the architecture is analyzed using simulation or one of the analytic solutions. This section uses the Media Store example (see figure 2.1 and sections 5.3 to 5.5) to explain how you as a software architect can interpret the analysis results to assess the performance and reliability of a system and how to compare design alternatives. The results can also be used to identify and solve performance problems as well as reliability problems.

7.2.1 Understanding Performance Results

Using one of the many analysis approaches (see chapter 8), the software architecture model can be analytically solved or simulated to obtain the performance characteristics. This section deals with the interpretation of performance simulation results.

Analysis Results   A performance simulation in Palladio provides results for services and for resources.

Service Results   Services are located at the system boundary (*system calls*) or within the system internals. For each service in the system, the *response time* of each individual simulated request is stored. Additionally, the response time experienced by each user in each *usage scenario* is logged.

Because of the stochastic nature of the performance of most systems, the response time of individual requests varies. For example, in the *usage scenario* of the Media Store (described in section 2.1.1), an exponential distribution of interarrival times is expected. Thus, the results contain a response-time distribution for each service and usage scenario. Table 7.1 shows the descriptive statistics of the response-time distribution. The lowest observed response time of the usage scenario during the simulation run was 3.5 seconds and the highest was 1,200.6 seconds. Note that these are the results of a simulation, so these are most likely not the theoretically possible minimum and maximum values. The observed mean response time was 137.3 seconds.

Graphically, the distribution can be visualized as a histogram or as a cumulative distribution function (CDF) as shown respectively in figure 7.1 and figure 7.2 for the overall usage scenario of the Media Store example. For each bucket, the histogram shows the probability that the response time lies within the range of this bucket. For example, the probability that the response time is between 0 and 20 seconds is about 20%.

The histogram has two peaks. To find the root cause behind these peaks, you as the software architect can additionally inspect the response-time results of the single Media Store services that are used in the usage scenario. Table 7.2 shows the minimum and maximum response times of the upload service and the download service. The response times of the other services called during the usage scenario are lower than the response time of the upload service. As there are no loops in this usage scenario, you can deduce that the second peak of the histogram in figure 7.1 is caused by the download service, while the first peak represents requests that used the upload service.

Table 7.1

Descriptive statistics of the response time of the media store usage scenario

Minimum (s)	25% Quantile (s)	Median (s)	75% Quantile (s)	Maximum (s)	Mean (s)
3.5	51.8	100.4	187.3	1,200.6	137.3

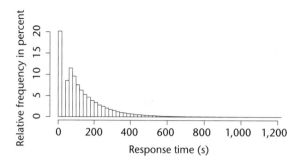

Figure 7.1
Response-time distribution of the Media Store usage scenario as a histogram (bucket width is 20 seconds).

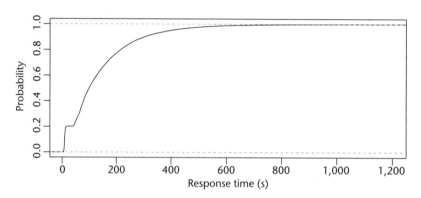

Figure 7.2
Response-time distribution of the Media Store usage scenario as a cumulative density function.

Table 7.2
Descriptive statistics of the response time of the upload service and the download service

Service	Minimum (s)	25% Quantile (s)	Median (s)	75% Quantile (s)	Maximum (s)	Mean (s)
Upload	34.5	70.9	119.4	206.7	1,194.9	160.6
Download	0.076	0.084	0.192	0.309	1.525	0.240

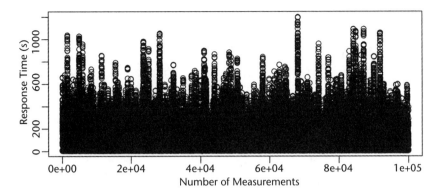

Figure 7.3
Response-time time series of the Media Store usage scenario.

The CDF shows a smooth representation of the response-time distribution. It shows the probability (on the y axis) that the response time is equal to or less than a certain value (on the x axis). For example, it shows that the response time is less than 200 seconds in about 80% of all cases.

The distributions in figure 7.1 and figure 7.2 show a relative probability. To see how the exact values develop over time, figure 7.3 shows a time-series diagram of the response time. Here, the x axis plots the sequence of the simulated requests, and the y axis plots each request's response time. On first sight, the diagram looks like arbitrarily scattered noise. The interesting aspect is, however, that the data are similarly scattered over time (x axis). This shows that the system is in a steady state and the workload intensity is not overloading the system. If it was overloading the system, there would be a trend of increasing response time over time. You will see later that this kind of diagram is helpful to identify an overload of the system (see figure 7.5 later in text).

Resource Results   Resources refer to *processing resources*, such as CPU and hard disk drives (HDD), or *passive resources*. For all types of resources, the *utilization* is stored. For multicore CPUs, this utilization is the average utilization of the single cores (i.e., an overall utilization of 100% means that all cores are fully utilized). For processing resources, the *demanded time* per request is stored additionally. For passive resources, the *waiting time* is stored, which describes the time span that each request has to wait before acquiring the passive resource. Furthermore, the *holding time* is stored, which describes how long the request holds the passive resource.

The utilization of the resources is an important indicator for bottlenecks or potentially for performance improvement. The processing resource in the Media Store is the CPU with a utilization of 82.9%. When there are several resources in the system, it is often advisable to analyze the ones with high utilization first to see the absolute time a request is processed by each resource and thus to determine if and how much a hardware upgrade could improve the performance of the system. There is no passive resource and no linking resource in the Media Store example, but if they existed, their results would be interpreted similarly.

Comparing Design Alternatives   There are usually many possible software architectures that fulfill the functional requirements. Those different software architectures differ primarily in the quality attributes, such as performance, reliability, security, or maintainability, but also in their costs.

When designing the software architecture for a system, you as the software architect usually start with a reference architecture and successively refine it for the system and requirements at hand. While doing so, one activity is to suggest design alternatives to improve some quality characteristic of the current version of the software architecture. When a design alternative has been suggested, the Palladio approach can be used to assess the design alternative's impact on performance, reliability, and costs quantitatively and thus to help decide for or against the alternative.

Using the Media Store example, this section describes how the impact of design alternatives on performance can be assessed. Recall that you as the software architect considered use of a cache for already encoded audio files, as described in section 2.5.2.

First, table 7.3 lists the descriptive statistics for the initial Media Store alternative and the alternative with a cache. You see that not only the mean response time of the download service has improved (as mentioned in section 2.5.2), but also the overall response time of the usage scenario has improved. Here, the mean response time has improved by almost 80% from 137.3 seconds down to 28.1 seconds. All quantiles listed in table 7.3 have improved as well.

The cumulative response-time distributions of the two alternatives are shown in figure 7.4. The curve for the cache alternative is always higher than or the same as the initial alternative's curves. This means that the cache is able to consistently reduce the response time for this *usage scenario*. For example, the 0.9 quantile of the response time was reduced from 304

Table 7.3
Descriptive statistics of the response time of the usage scenario in the initial media store alternative and for the cache alternative

Alternative	Minimum (s)	25% Quantile (s)	Median (s)	75% Quantile (s)	Maximum (s)	Mean (s)
Initial	3.5	51.8	100.4	187.3	1,200.6	137.3
Cache	2.9	22.7	29.4	35.5	114.5	28.1

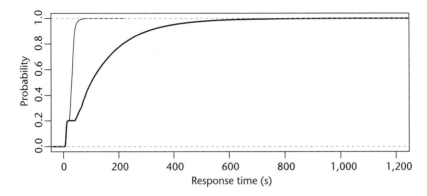

Figure 7.4
Response Time CDF of the Media Store Usage Scenario, with Cache (thin line) and without Cache (thick line)

seconds to 41 seconds. Looking at the resource results, the utilization of the CPU of server 1 has been reduced to 66.4%.

Thus, with the assumed cache hit rate of 60%, the cache design alternative is able to improve the performance of the system very well. Note, however, that the improvement might be different for other *usage scenarios* and in particular for different cache hit rates. Furthermore, introducing a cache also costs money. Thus, you have to make a trade-off decision whether the improvement in response time is worth the costs and the development effort.

Identifying and Resolving Problems   A system has performance problems if it does not fulfill its performance requirements. The software architect might only detect this late when measuring the system in load tests or even in operation, which might cause high costs as the architecture might need redesign, the implementation of some components might need to be changed, and test cycles and deployment have to be repeated. Thus, as argued throughout this book, it is desirable to notice performance problems early using architecture-based performance predictions. In the following, we first discuss an example of how to resolve a performance problem in the Media Store and then describe the core causes of performance problems in general.

Problems in the Media Store Example   As an example of how to resolve performance problems, here we consider the secure AudioWatermarking component introduced in section 2.5.3. Recall that you as the software architect considered replacing the TagWatermarking and the ReEncoder components with a more secure AudioWatermarking component, which embeds inaudible information about the user who downloads the file into the audio file. You

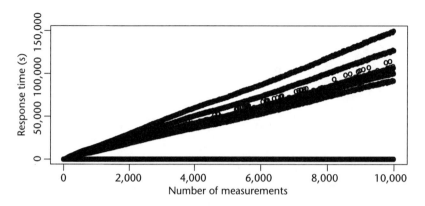

Figure 7.5
Response-time time series of the Media Store usage scenario for the AudioWatermarking alternative.

have found out in section 2.5.3 that using this AudioWatermarking component overloads the system. Now, assuming that you decide you need the additional security of the AudioWatermarking component, how can you solve the performance problem and achieve both more security and sufficient performance?

You must now *identify the problem*, then *locate the problem*, and finally *solve the problem*.

Identify the problem: After including the AudioWatermarking component, the first guess is that the system is not able to handle the load. To identify the problem, look at the time series of the response time shown in figure 7.5. The diagram confirms the assumption: the response time increases steadily over time, which is a clear indication that the system is clogged. In this case, the mean response time values and all other descriptive statistics of the run are meaningless, as the values would become higher and higher the longer the simulation run is.

Locate the root cause: During such an overload, one or more resources are probably overloaded and cause a bottleneck. To locate the root cause, you need to check the different resource utilization results. In this example, there is only the CPU of server 1. Indeed, the simulation results report a utilization of 100%. Thus, too much demand is put on this resource.

Solve the problem: Because you now know the reason for the performance problem, you can use different strategies to solve the problem. In case the system is overloaded and a single resource (here the CPU) has a high utilization, this resource is the clear bottleneck of the system. Thus, you either need to reduce the resource demand or to increase the available processing power. Note that the cache discussed in section 2.5.2 cannot be used because the AudioWatermarking component adds an individual watermark to the files (i.e., the cache hit rate would be almost zero, because a hit would only happen if the same user downloads the same file with the same encoding again). As you want to explore the more expensive (in terms of resource demand) AudioWatermarking component, you decide to add more processing power to the system and see whether that solves the problem.

Assuming that the server itself cannot be made faster, you decide for a second server. A straightforward way to use the second server is to reallocate the most demanding component (i.e., the component with the highest resource demand) to that new server, as shown in figure 7.6. After modeling this change and making the predictions, however, the situation does not improve: Similar to the design alternative to reallocate the ReEncoder discussed in section 2.5.1, also in this case the second server is overloaded while the first is only lightly used. The simulation reports a utilization of 100% for server 2 while server 1 only has a utilization of 0.8%. The response-time time series still looks similar to that of figure 7.5 without a second server.

Thus, you need to spread the load of the AudioWatermarking component better to the available hardware. You decide to add a second assembly context for the AudioWatermarking to the system. Now you have two assembly contexts instantiating the

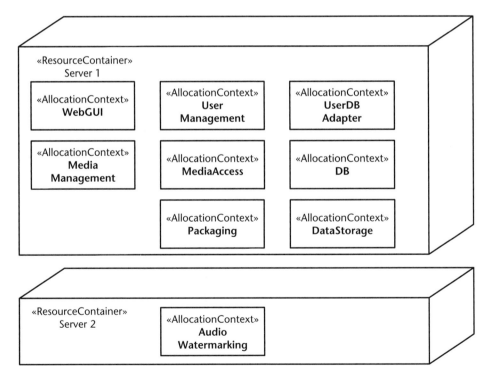

Figure 7.6
The Media Store *allocation* after reallocating the AudioWatermarking to a second server. The stereotypes in angled brackets refer to classes in the Palladio metamodel.

AudioWatermarking component from the repository, so you call one of them AudioWatermarkingReplica1 and the other one AudioWatermarkingReplica2. Additionally, you define a new component in the repository, named DownloadLoadBalancer, that provides the IDownload interface and just randomly distributes the incoming requests to one of its two IDownload required roles, as shown in figure 7.7 and figure 7.8. You assemble DownloadLoadBalancer in the system as shown in figure 7.9. Then, you allocate AudioWatermarkingReplica1 to the first server and AudioWatermarkingReplica2 to the second server. Figure 7.10 shows the resulting allocation view.

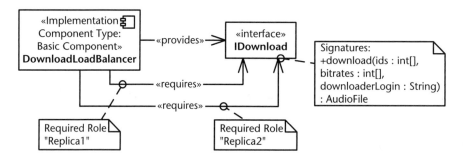

Figure 7.7
The new DownloadLoadBalancer in the *repository*. The stereotypes in angled brackets refer to classes in the Palladio metamodel.

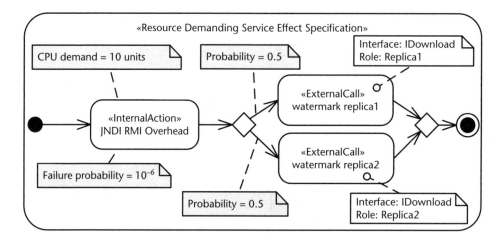

Figure 7.8
The resource demanding service effect specification (RDSEFF) of the *download service* of the DownloadLoadBalancer component. The stereotypes in angled brackets refer to classes in the Palladio metamodel.

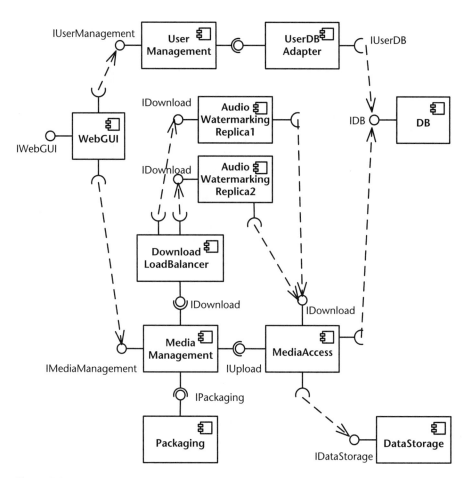

Figure 7.9
The Media Store *system* after adding a load balancer.

After simulating this new alternative with the load balancer, you get the results in figure 7.11. The figure shows the resulting CDF (thin line) next to the CDF of the initial Media Store design from section 2.1.3 as shown in figure 2.1. Table 7.4 provides the descriptive statistics. The CDFs overlap each other: while the initial design is faster when looking at the region around the 25% percentile, the load balancer alternative is faster in the other regions and even has a lower mean response time.

As a result, you have successfully solved the performance problem that occurred when using a more secure watermarking component. You now face the trade-off between costs and security: you can either procure a second server (higher costs) and use the more secure Audio-Watermarking component or keep the initial design, potentially also using the cache.

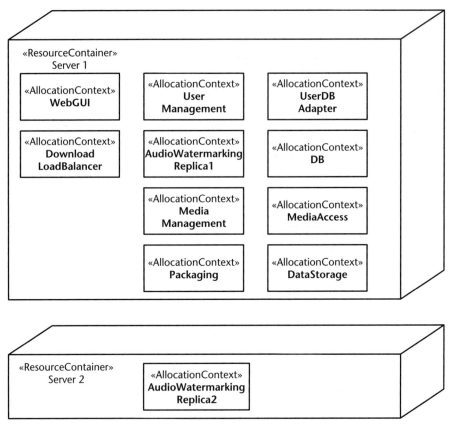

Figure 7.10
The Media Store *allocation* after adding a load balancer. The stereotypes in angled brackets refer to classes in the Palladio metamodel.

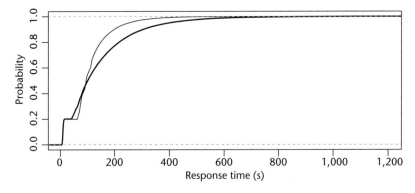

Figure 7.11
Response-time CDF of the Media Store usage scenario with two *assembly contexts* for AudioWatermarking and two servers (thin line) compared to the initial alternative (thick line).

Table 7.4

Descriptive statistics of the response time of the initial Media Store alternative ("initial") and for the alternative with a load balancer and two *assembly contexts* for the AudioWatermarking ("load balancer")

	Minimum (s)	25% Quantile (s)	Median (s)	75% Quantile (s)	Maximum (s)	Mean (s)
Initial	3.5	51.8	100.4	187.3	1,200.6	137.3
Load balancer	3.3	69.3	94.6	134.2	752.3	105.1

Core Causes: Bottlenecks and Long Paths In general, the main cause of performance problems at the architecture level are bottlenecks (as described above for a hardware bottleneck) and long paths.

Bottlenecks as described above can appear at processing resources (as described above for the HDD) and at passive resources, which cause a high utilization of the passive resource. Bottlenecks at passive resources that represent software resources, such as thread pools, are also called software bottlenecks. Together, hardware bottlenecks and software bottlenecks are common causes of performance problems. At the same time, they are easy to identify by checking the utilization of the different resources.

Solving software bottlenecks, however, can be more difficult. Usually, the capacity of a passive resource cannot be readily increased as is often possible for hardware resources (be it by using a faster resource or by starting to use replication). Especially if passive resources are used for mutual exclusion, it is impossible to change the capacity. In such cases, you need to investigate the holding time of the passive resource and try to reduce the time it is held. This requires digging into the service effect specifications (SEFFs) and understanding the dynamics of the system. For example, you can check whether calculations or calls to other components can be moved outside the protected regions to minimize holding times. Possibly, a relaxation of the mutual exclusion (e.g., by using transactions and optimistic locking) has to be used.

Note that memory, a special type of passive resource, is usually not modeled with Palladio. Palladio mainly targets business information systems, where memory is usually not an issue (except for unexpected memory leaks, which, however, are not analyzable at the architectural level but need to be detected in later steps). For other types of systems, you might consider modeling memory as a passive resource or complement a Palladio analysis with other analyses focusing on memory.

The other main class of performance problems is long paths. It may happen that the performance of a software system is not satisfactory even if all resources are not highly utilized. This means that the path contains a sequence of actions and calculations that are simply too long. To mitigate long paths, you can consider reducing the required processing within the path, or making parts of the processing asynchronous or on parallel, or reducing network latencies (if involved) by reducing the amount of required remote communication. All these mitigation strategies require a detailed understanding of the system at hand and thus cannot be used without deep analysis of the system.

7.2.2 Understanding Reliability Results

As the reliability aspects of the Media Store model were not discussed in chapter 2 for sake of brevity, the following sections explain these aspects before a discussion of the results.

Reliability Model of the Media Store   Recall from section 5.1.2 that Palladio supports modeling and analyzing software failure potentials, hardware failure potentials, and system-external failure potentials. For the Media Store, two types of failures can occur during upload and download of media files.

Software failures can occur during processing of user requests due to software faults. The cause can be bugs in components developed for the Media Store or in third-party components used, such as the database.
Hardware failures occur if a CPU is unavailable while being accessed during service execution. In our model, hardware failures are only caused by the CPU, as memory is not modeled and the disk is not directly used.

The component developers have estimated a failure probability of 10^{-5} for each component service in the Media Store model, which is modeled as a failure probability of one of each service's *internal actions*. An exception is the database: As it is a third-party component that is used by many projects, they assumed a lower failure probability of 5×10^{-6}. The assumed mean time to failure (MTTF) is 12 years, and the mean time to repair (MTTR) is 2 hours for the CPU resources resulting in a steady-state availability of 99.989% [MTTF / (MTTF + MTTR)].

Analysis Results   The reliability analysis can be used to determine the probability of success for the given *usage scenario*. For the above-described Media Store model and the usage scenario from section 2.1.1, the analysis reports 99.9882% as the total probability of success (i.e., the probability of failure is 1.18×10^{-4}). Figure 7.12 breaks the overall Media Store execution failure probability down to the single services in the model. You can inspect the failure probability of a single service, which is the probability that this service causes a failure given that a user executes the usage scenario. Because not every service is called in each usage scenario execution and some services may also be called multiple times, the failure probability not only depends on the failure probabilities of internal actions but also is strongly affected by how the usage scenario is propagated through the system. Additionally, figure 7.12 shows the contribution of the service to the overall failure probability in percent.

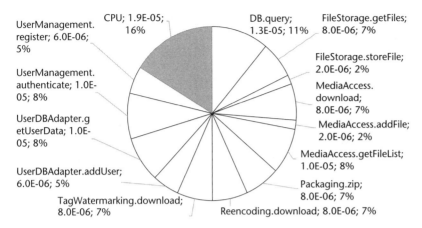

Figure 7.12
Predicted probability of failure of Media Store services.

Comparing Design Alternatives   As mentioned above for performance, design alternatives are usually suggested to improve some quality characteristic of the system, such as performance, reliability, or maintainability. Using the Media Store example, in the following we describe how the impact of design alternatives on reliability can be assessed.

Three design alternatives for the Media Store have been discussed in section 2.1.4. As an example, consider the cache alternative in the following. You as the software architect have already found out that using a cache will improve performance. Now, what is the effect on reliability? One might speculate that reliability will decrease as another software components with failure potential will be added to the system. Alternatively, one might speculate that reliability will be improved because requests that can be answered from the cache will not have to be handled by subsequent components; namely, ReEncoder, MediaAccess, DB, and DataStorage.

To assess the effect of the cache on reliability with Palladio, you first need to estimate the failure probability of the cache implementation itself. Here, you again assume the same failure probability of 10^{-5} as you have already estimated for the other component services.

After running the reliability solver for the design alternative, the analysis reports 99.9874% as the total probability of success. The probability of failure is 1.24×10^{-4}, which is 6% higher than before. Thus, the results predict that the cache design alternative reduces reliability.

Inspecting the results, you notice that the failure probability of the subsequent components has only been reduced by less than 10^{-10} and thus is negligible; however, the cache itself has a failure probability of 8×10^{-6}. Thus, the prediction results confirm the first speculation that the additional component adds failure potential.

To conclude, the Palladio approach helped you as the software architect to find out that introducing the cache will slightly increase the overall probability of failure. Now, you can make a trade-off decision whether the improvement in performance is worth the reduction of reliability.

Improving Reliability   Identifying and resolving reliability problems is mainly concerned with identifying the points in the architecture that have the highest contribution to the overall failure probability and devising means to reduce this contribution.

As mentioned above, figure 7.12 breaks the overall Media Store execution failure probability down to the single services in the model. With 1.3×10^{-5}, the query service of the DB has the highest probability of failure and makes up 11% of the overall failure probability. Even though the DB has the lowest internal action failure probability, its contribution to the overall probability of failure is highest. The reason is that the DB is used in every request to the system, both from the user-management components and from the components that handle the music files. Together, all software failures have a joint probability of failure of 9.9×10^{-5} (84% of the overall failure probability). In addition to the software failures shown in figure 7.12, the hardware failure probability of the CPU is 1.9×10^{-5}.

Looking more closely at the software side, the results show that the service DB.query contributes the most to the overall probability of failure (11%). Aggregating over components, the MediaAccess component contributes the most with 17% (with its three considered services MediaAccess.download, MediaAccess.addFile, and MediaAccess.getFileList).

To improve reliability, there are two main approaches. First, you can try to reduce the underlying probability that a failure occurs in an internal action. This can be achieved, for example, by increased testing effort or by reusing well-proven components and algorithms. Second, means to tolerate failures can be added to the system (e.g., by redundancy or by retry mechanisms). Note, however, that whether such means help to reduce failures depends on the failures at hand. For example, failures that are caused by reproducible bugs (also called *bohrbugs*) in the software will be repeated when a request is simply retried with the same input data.

Palladio jointly considers software and hardware failure potentials, so that possible investments into more reliable or redundant hardware can be compared to efforts to reduce software failure potentials.

7.3   Tactics for Improving Quality

Architectural tactics for quality attribute improvement of software architectures include design knowledge and rules of thumb (Bass et al. 2003). They are intuitively applied by experienced architects when designing an architecture.

7.3.1 Performance Tactics

The list of performance tactics in table 7.5 have been aggregated from multiple sources about performance improvement at the architectural level. The SPE book (Smith and Williams 2002) highlights technology-independent performance principles, patterns, and antipatterns. Further rules have been integrated from Microsoft's performance improvement guide (Microsoft Corporation 2004) and literature on architectural tactics (Bass et al. 2003; Bachmann et al. 2005; Rozanski and Woods 2005; Taylor et al. 2009).

7.3.2 Reliability Tactics

Several authors have described architectural tactics for reliability (Bass et al. 2003; Rozanski and Woods 2005; Taylor et al. 2009). From these sources, table 7.6 aggregates several reliability tactics (Brosch et al. 2011). The terms mean time to failure (MTTF) and mean time to repair (MTTR) are properties of hardware resources, which are often specified by hardware vendors and which can be used to calculate the overall system's reliability (Brosch et al. 2011). In practice, a common tactic for reliability-critical systems is to introduce redundant hardware (e.g., stand-by nodes, RAID discs, etc.). Some safety-critical systems use design diversity to increase reliability, which, however, introduces high development costs.

The table shows in the third column, which is specific to Palladio, how the reliability tactics can be applied on Palladio instances. Most of them require the identification of reliability-critical components. This identification can be done by a sensitivity analysis, where component failure probabilities are varied in the model to find out the influence of these probabilities on the reliability of the system.

7.4 Automatically Searching for Better Architectures

Usually, it is not easy to find good combinations of design alternatives manually. The architectural design needs to be analyzed to iteratively improve the quality properties, which requires time and expertise. To optimize the efficiency of this process, the search can be automated if it is formulated as a search problem. An example of applying such automated design space exploration in an industrial project is provided in chapter 14.

7.4.1 Evaluation Criteria

First, it is important to define an evaluation criterion to compare design alternatives objectively.

A priori methods aggregate the quality properties to a single value based on the stakeholders' preferences so that they can be easily compared. For example, priorities obtained by using the analytic hierarchy process (AHP) by Saaty (1980) can be used to weigh the quality property values; however, it is difficult to find out the stakeholders' preferences and define the priorities.

Table 7.5
Performance improvement tactics

	Name	Rule or Principle	Modeling in Palladio
Software	Asynchronous communication	Let components exchange data asynchronously to avoid synchronization delays ("parallel processing principle")	Change components: change interfaces and RDSEFFs of blocked components to support asynchronous communication; adds cost
	Caching	Keep the most frequently used data in a cache in main memory to allow quick access ("centering principle")	Create a cache component either immediately serving a request with a cache hit probability or delegating the request; adds cost
	Concurrency/ parallelization	Introduce parallelism using multithreading or multiple processes ("parallel processing principle")	Change components: use fork actions in RDSEFFs and reduce resource demand per thread; adds cost
	Coupling and cohesion	Ensure a loosely coupled design that exhibits an appropriate degree of cohesion ("locality principle")	Change components: merge components with a high interaction rate; build subsystems; adds cost
	Internal data structures and algorithms	Use appropriate data structures and algorithms within the components ("centering principle")	Identify components with the highest resource demand and exchange them with different component implementations
	Fast pathing	Find long processing paths and reduce the number of processing steps ("centering principle")	Introduce additional components to serve the most frequently used functionality in a dedicated way; adds cost
	Locking granularity	Acquire passive resources late and release early; minimize locking ("shared resources principle")	Change components: change RDSEFFs and minimize the time between acquire and release actions; adds cost
	Prioritization	Partition the workload and prioritize the partitions so that they can be efficiently queued ("centering principle")	Not yet supported
	Resource pooling	Ensure effective use of pooling mechanisms (objects, threads, database connections, etc.) ("fixing-point principle")	Identify passive resources with the highest waiting delay and adjust their capacity
	State management	Use stateless components where possible to keep them decoupled and allow scalability ("shared resources principle")	Not yet supported

Table 7.5 (continued)

	Name	Rule or Principle	Modeling in Palladio
Hardware	Component reallocation	Allocate software components from saturated resources to underutilized resources ("centering principle")	Identify resources with U>=maxThreshold and reallocate components to resources with U<=minThreshold
	Component replication	Start multiple instances of the same component and spread the load on multiple servers ("spread-the-load principle")	Identify components accessed by many users, create multiple component instances, and introduce a load balancer component
	Faster hardware	Buy faster hardware to decrease the node utilization and response times ("centering principle")	Increase the processing rate of bottlenecked processing resources; increases hardware cost
	More hardware	Buy additional servers and spread the load among them ("spread-the-load principle")	Increase the number of processing resources, introduce a load balancer (including costs); increases hardware cost
Network	Batching	Avoid network accesses by bundling remote requests ("processing versus frequency principle")	Insert messaging components that bundle remote requests to batches and unpack them at the receiver side; adds cost
	Localization	Allocate frequently interacting components to the same hardware devices ("locality principle")	Identify components with a high interaction rate and reallocate them to the same resources
	Remote data exchange streamlining	Decrease the amount of data to be sent across networks (e.g., using compression) ("centering principle")	Create a compression component that shrinks the size of the data transferred but adds a resource demand to the CPU

Source: Koziolek et al. (2011a).

For *a posteriori methods*, the (predicted or measured) quality properties of design alternatives are compared pairwise, and a design alternative is only better than another if it is better in at least one and not worse in every other quality attribute. This concept is called *Pareto dominance*, and a design alternative is called *Pareto optimal* if it is not dominated by (i.e., worse than) another design alternative. As an example, consider three design alternatives with the respective performance (mean response time), reliability (probability of failure on demand), and costs:

$$a = \begin{pmatrix} 10 \text{ s} \\ 0.01\% \\ \$9\text{k} \end{pmatrix}, \quad b = \begin{pmatrix} 15 \text{ s} \\ 0.03\% \\ \$8\text{k} \end{pmatrix}, \quad c = \begin{pmatrix} 20 \text{ s} \\ 0.05\% \\ \$9\text{k} \end{pmatrix} \qquad (7.1)$$

Table 7.6
Reliability improvement tactics

	Name	Rule	Modeling in Palladio
Software	Design diversity	Realize one algorithm in different ways; apply a voting algorithm that chooses a result (e.g., majority voting)	Change components: decrease internal action failure probability; increases cost and resource demands
	Heartbeat/ ping	Periodically test the availability of components; initiate immediate repair upon failures	Decrease the MTTR of resources; adds monitoring cost and resource demands
	Highly reliable software components	Apply a high-quality development process to software components for high reliability	Change components: decrease internal action failure probability; increases cost
	Rejuvenation	Automatically restart components after failures or periodically.	Change components: decrease internal action failure probability; increases resource demands and cost for restarts/monitoring
Hardware	Dependency-aware reallocation	Allocate components together that depend on each other, so that hardware failures affect a smaller set of components	Reallocate components based on the execution paths; allocate components together that fail together anyway
	Highly available hardware	Operate the system on hardware with low failure rates and low service times in case of failure	Increase resource MTTF, decrease MTTR; increases hardware cost and servicing cost
	Redundant hardware	Buy additional servers and replicate components to them	Increase resource MTTF, decrease MTTR; increases hardware cost and resource demands; add overhead for fail-over
	Sensitive component reallocation	Allocate reliability-sensitive software components to high-availability resources	Identify processing resources with A>=maxThreshold and reallocate critical components to them

Source: Brosch et al. (2011).

In this example, both *a* and *b* dominate *c*, because they are both better than *c* in, for example, performance and not worse in the other attributes. Alternative *a* and *b* are not dominated by one another, because *a* is better in performance and reliability than *b*, and *b* is better in costs than *a*. Therefore, the alternatives *a* and *b* are two Pareto-optimal design alternatives.

7.4.2   Degrees of Freedom

Next, to make an automated search possible, it is required to define *what* can be varied, meaning how the architecture can be changed in the search to find a *valid* design alternative. For component-based software architecture, it is possible to identify typical ways of how the architecture can be changed, called degree of freedom types. For example, the

degree of freedom type "component allocation" describes how components may be reallo-
cated to different servers that provide the required resources. To do so, degree of freedom
types are defined on the architecture meta-model level (such as Palladio); they refer to
changeable meta-model elements and prescribe rules how the architecture may be changed
(Koziolek et al. 2011).

The degree of freedom types can be instantiated in a given software architecture model.
Consider the Media Store running example shown in figure 2.1. The system consists of 10
components. Assume that the system now faces a higher load, so that you expect it should
be distributed to more than two servers. You can assume there are up to five servers available
called S1 to S5. Additionally, assume there is another alternative implementation of the
watermarking available, which is named QuickWatermarking, costs twice as much as TagWatermarking, but is faster due to internal optimizations. Also, assume that the servers can have
different processor types; for example, with higher clock rate.

Then, in this system there may be several change options. Five options how to allocate a
component exist in this example for each component. Thus, each component has a *degree of
freedom instance* with five *design options* each. Overall, this example features 16 degree of freedom instances, each with specific design options:

• Allocation of WebGUI
• Allocation of MediaManagement
• Allocation of TagWatermarking
• Allocation of Packaging
• Allocation of UserManagement
• Allocation of UserDBAdapter
• Allocation of ReEncoder
• Allocation of MediaAccess
• Allocation of DB
• Allocation of DataStorage
• Select processor for S1
• Select processor for S2
• Select processor for S3
• Select processor for S4
• Select processor for S5
• Select component to provide watermarking functionality

In combination, the degree of freedom instances and their options define the set of possible architectural models. Each of these possible architectural models is defined by choosing
one design option for each degree of freedom instance. In addition, there can be certain *constraints* for the design options; for example, that two components cannot be deployed on the
same machine to guarantee availability. The set of possible architectural models is the *design
space*. The quality attributes of interest form the *solution space*. Then, the *search problem*

formulation is as follows: Find the Pareto-optimal design alternatives from the design space that adhere to the constraints.

Now, the Pareto-optimal architectural candidates can be found automatically using, for example, *meta-heuristic* search techniques in an *optimization process*.

7.4.3   PerOpteryx: Automated Exploration

The PerOpteryx tool is an automatic design-space exploration tool for Palladio models (Martens et al. 2010; Koziolek et al. 2011a). PerOpteryx applies a meta-heuristic search process on a given Palladio model to find new architectural candidates with improved performance or costs. It is an *a posteriori* tool; that is, its goal is to determine the Pareto-optimal candidates. Figure 7.13 shows a high-level overview of PerOpteryx's search process.

In step 1, the search space for the given initial candidate performance model is modeled as a set of degree of freedom instances to explore, as described above. As mentioned above, each degree of freedom instance has a set of design options (e.g., a set of CPU clock frequencies between 2 and 4 GHz, or a set of servers a component may be allocated to). Each possible architectural candidate in the search space can be represented relative to the initial Palladio model as a set of decisions. This set of decisions—one for each degree instance—is called the genome of the candidate.

Furthermore, the *optimization goal and requirements* are modeled in step 1. For example, it is possible to define that the response time of a certain system service and the costs should be optimized, while a given minimum throughput requirement and a given maximum utilization requirement must be fulfilled.

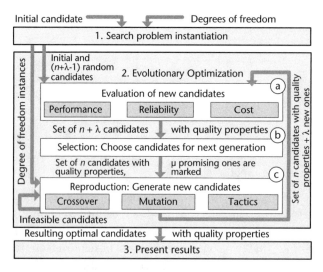

Figure 7.13
PerOpteryx process model. From Koziolek et al. 2011a.

If multiple quality metrics should be optimized, PerOpteryx searches for Pareto-optimal candidates: a candidate is Pareto optimal if there exists no other candidate that is better in all quality metrics. The result of such an optimization is a Pareto front: a set of candidates that are Pareto optimal with respect to other candidates evaluated so far, and which should approximate the set of globally Pareto-optimal candidates well. If only a single quality metric should be optimized, the minimum or maximum value (depending on the metric) is searched.

In step 2, PerOpteryx applies evolutionary optimization based on the genomes. This step is fully automated. It uses the NSGA-II algorithm (Deb et al. 2000), which is an advanced elitist multiobjective evolutionary algorithm. Its configuration parameters are the size of the population n, the number of new candidates generated in each iteration λ, and the number of candidates selected for reproduction μ, as explained below. In addition to the initial Palladio model genome, PerOpteryx generates additional candidate genomes randomly based on the degree of freedom instances to get a starting population of size $n + \lambda$. Then, iteratively, the main steps of evaluation (step 2a), selection (step 2b), and reproduction (step 2c) are applied.

First, each candidate is evaluated by generating the Palladio model from the genome and then predicting the quality attributes of interest, such as mean response time, probability of failure, or costs (step 2a). The μ most promising candidates (i.e., close to the current Pareto front, fulfilling the requirements, and well spread) are selected for further manipulation, while the λ least promising candidates are discarded (step 2b). During reproduction (step 2c), PerOpteryx creates λ new candidates based on the selected candidate genomes using crossover, mutation, or tactics (Koziolek et al. 2011a) and creates a number of new candidates.

With crossover, the genotypes of two selected candidate solutions are merged into one; for example, by combining the processing rates from one candidate with the allocation by another candidate. With mutation, PerOpteryx varies one or more design options. For example, PerOpteryx might change the component deployment to allocate all components on one server or increase the processing rate of another server. With tactics, the genome is changed based on general rules of how to improve the system's performance; for example, components are removed from overutilized servers or highly utilized servers are replicated (Koziolek et al. 2011a). Before exiting step 2, tactics are again applied to the resulting optimal candidates.

From the results (step 3), you as the software architect can identify interesting solutions in the Pareto front fulfilling the user requirements and make well-informed trade-off decisions. To support this task, researchers have developed a number of multicriteria decision analysis methods, such as multiattribute utility theory, analytic hierarchy process, weighting methods, outranking methods, and fuzzy methods (Kornyshova and Salinesi 2007).

An example of how PerOpteryx was used to improve an architectural design of an industrial system is provided in chapter 14.

7.5   Questions and Exercises

7.5.1   Questions

7.1 *: What are typical design questions for performance and reliability? What design questions are independent from a quality characteristic or affect multiple quality characteristics?

7.2 **: What percentage of the requests is completed in less than 200 seconds according to figure 7.2?

7.3 ***: What is the most likely response time of the Media Store in its initial configuration according to figure 7.1? Is this observation reliable?

7.4 **: With respect to figure 4.2, what Palladio elements are shown in the boxes in figure 7.9 and figure 7.10? How do these boxes relate to the actual implementation of the components? How many AudioWatermarking components are there?

7.5 *: What type of failure potentials are considered in Palladio?

7.6 *: How can failure potentials be incorporated and predicted in Palladio?

7.7 **: How can the system part with the highest failure potential be identified?

7.5.2   Exercises

For these exercises, download the Palladio model of the Media Store from the companion website to this book.

7.1 ***: For the initial design of the Media Store, what is the maximum number of users the model is able to serve? Identify the first encountered performance bottleneck.

7.2 ****: Consider the design alternative with a load balancer and two AudioWatermarking components from section 7.2.1. You see in the model that both servers have two CPU cores. What can be done to further improve the response time of the system? Come up with potential solutions and investigate them using the Palladio bench.

7.3 **: Analyze the reliability of the design alternative with a load balancer and two AudioWatermarking components from section 7.2.1. Does the probability of failure change, and if yes, how much? What causes this change?

7.6   Further Reading

A wide variety of performance analysis publications is available by Menascé and colleagues; for example, Menascé et al. (1994, 2004). Tactics for improving performance are discussed in the SPE book (Smith et al. 2002) and in Microsoft's performance improvement guide (Microsoft Corporation 2004). A recent book on performance analysis has been published by Bondi (2014). Xu (2010) provides a more detailed discussion of the most common performance problems on the model level, namely bottlenecks and long paths, and discusses mitigation options.

Details on reliability concepts, including definition of concepts such as error, fault, and failure, are provided by Laprie (1985). Goseva-Popstojanova et al. (2001) discuss architecture-based software reliability prediction approaches and survey several early approaches.

While Palladio targets performance and reliability, there are other analysis methods for other quality characteristics. For maintainability, the architecture-level modifiability analysis (ALMA) has been suggested by Bengtsson et al. (2004). For security, several approaches for attack tree analysis have been suggested, among them the approach by Grunske and Joyce (2008) that explicitly considers the software architecture as a set of components and builds a modular attack tree.

Literature on architectural tactics in general (Bass et al. 2003; Bachmann et al. 2005; Rozanski and Woods 2005; Taylor et al. 2009) also lists tactics for both performance and reliability improvement.

Different approaches to automatically search for optimal software architectures are surveyed by Aleti et al. (2013). A more comprehensive background on automated search for optimal architectural candidates is presented in the thesis of one of the authors of this book (Koziolek 2013).

While Palladio provides adequate means for analyzing information system architectures, IntBIIS (Heinrich et al. 2015a) extends Palladio by simulation behavior to analyze business processes and their organizational environment. IntBIIS enables holistic simulation that combines performance prediction on the software architecture level and business process level. In this way, the alignment of business process designs and information system architectures can be supported by comparing the performance impact of design alternatives and verifying them against requirements.

7.7 Takeaways

Palladio operates on a model basis. Hence, design questions and comparisons of design alternatives are supported during early phases in the development process. Other typical application scenarios of such model-based analyses are the identification of optimal configurations (e.g., tuning the size of a connection pool and available CPU power) and the extension of legacy systems (i.e., how are legacy systems affected by adding new functionality or changing other parts of the system context).

This chapter discussed typical design questions for performance, reliability, and quality in general. On the basis of the Media Store example, it showed how to analyze performance results and reliability results to answer typical design questions. Several known architectural tactics of how to improve performance and reliability were briefly presented. These tactics are a core learning goal to enable readers to manually derive and design alternatives.

The typical results of quality analysis approaches such as Palladio have no unique origin. Hence, interpreting the results and deriving the right clues from the results is crucial. Histograms, CDFs, and time series were therefore introduced.

The chapter also showed that searching for architectural candidates can be simplified by quickly exploring changes on a model basis. While finding good architectural candidates is not necessarily straightforward, the overall process can be automated using meta-heuristic techniques to find the best set of alternatives the decision maker can choose from.

8 Under the Hood

Philipp Merkle, Jörg Henss, Sebastian Lehrig, and Anne Koziolek

The Palladio-Bench offers an assortment of quality analysis tools. The main focus is on performance analysis, for which a range of tools, each with strengths and weaknesses, is available. Additionally, Palladio offers a reliability analysis and a simple cost analysis.

This chapter provides details about the available performance and reliability analyses in Palladio. This detailed knowledge is particularly important for specialized performance analysts or reliability analysts, who support other developer roles in modeling and interpreting the results. But although internal analysis techniques are not exposed to software architects using Palladio's quality analysis tools, a basic understanding of their operating principle can help architects, too, to interpret quality estimates.

This chapter starts with an overview of different Palladio tools for performance analyses. For performance, this chapter introduces important quality analysis tools for Palladio models, explains their operating principle, and discusses strengths and weaknesses. The individual characteristics of the different performance analysis tools arise from different analysis techniques employed "under the hood," ranging from discrete-event simulation to numerical approximation of queuing network models. Building on this, the chapter introduces a decision process for selecting an appropriate performance analysis tool. The chapter provides an overview of important configuration parameters and their influence on the credibility of performance simulation results.

Additionally, the chapter describes the Palladio reliability analysis on the basis of discrete-time Markov chains and the Palladio cost analysis on the basis of the Palladio cost model that can be used to annotate Palladio models.

8.1 Quality Analysis Tools

The tools presented throughout this chapter make analysis models, along with appropriate analysis techniques, available to software architects.

An *analysis tool* in the context of Palladio is a piece of software that implements one or more *analysis techniques* for solving a specific type of *analysis model*. Solving refers to the process of gathering quality metrics for the system represented by the analysis model. Analysis model types are often also called formalism. They include queuing networks, Petri nets, and queuing Petri nets, for example.

Analysis tools can be considered black boxes because software architects can use them without in-depth knowledge of how they work internally. After the system has been modeled with Palladio, you select an analysis tool. The analysis tool takes care of predicting quality metrics of interest, without requiring you to understand how exactly this was achieved. So there must be another role responsible for providing analysis tools. We call this role the quality methodologist. With detailed knowledge of both Palladio and of quality modeling formalisms along with analysis techniques, the quality methodologist builds analysis tools that encapsulate this knowledge.

For each quality metric of interest, there is a large variety of analysis techniques and analysis models. For example, there is already a wide range of analysis models for queuing network models to predict performance. Some queuing network models can be solved analytically (i.e., there is formula that can be solved exactly); this is also called a closed-form solution. For some classes of queuing network, no analytical solution is known or viable. Analysis of these

---

Digression 8.1

Discrete-Event Simulation

The Palladio simulators are *discrete-event simulators*. Such a discrete-event simulator (or simulation) is a piece of software that, when executed, resembles a discrete system such as a cash desk at which customers line up. *Discrete systems* differ from continuous systems in that their state changes stepwise rather than continuously; when customers line up, the queue length increases step by step, customer by customer—not in indefinitely small amounts that sum up to one eventually. The latter characteristic would instead apply to a continuous system such as weather where temperature, for example, is a continuous quantity.

The central ingredient of each discrete-event simulation is the *timeline* (technically speaking, the list of future events) on which *events* are placed. The *simulation procedure* scans the timeline from left to right (assuming that simulation time increases to the right). For each encountered event, the simulation procedure executes the corresponding *event routine*. The event routine is an integral part of each event. It tells the simulation how this specific event influences the state of the system under simulation. The event routine of a CustomerArrivalEvent, for instance, increments the number of waiting customers by one. The occurrence of an event usually entails one or more future events. A customer lining up needs to be served in the near future or will leave the waiting line otherwise. Therefore, an event routine usually places one or more future events on the timeline. Placing an event on the timeline is called the *scheduling* of an event.

Unlike wall-clock time, simulated time (embodied by the timeline) usually advances at an uneven pace and as fast as possible. It leaps from event to event in the order of their occurrence time. If there is no event scheduled at a certain point in time, the simulation skips to the time of the most imminent event. The chain of event routines executed this way yields the system behavior that is to be observed by the simulation.

classes of queuing networks can still be done using simulation as an alternative solution technique. The same argumentation applies to most types of performance models, which is why there are plenty of solution techniques that can be employed by the tools.

The different tools developed for the quality analysis of Palladio models are shown in figure 8.1. The performance tools (highlighted with the gray box labeled "performance" in figure 8.1) differ mainly in their range of functions, their result accuracy, and the analysis speed at which they yield the desired quality metrics.

This chapter provides an overview of the alternative tools and aims to provide decision support in deciding for the right tool in a given context.

8.2   Performance Simulation of Palladio Models

So far, you might have a basic understanding of what a software performance simulation is—a piece of software that resembles the performance characteristics of a system under

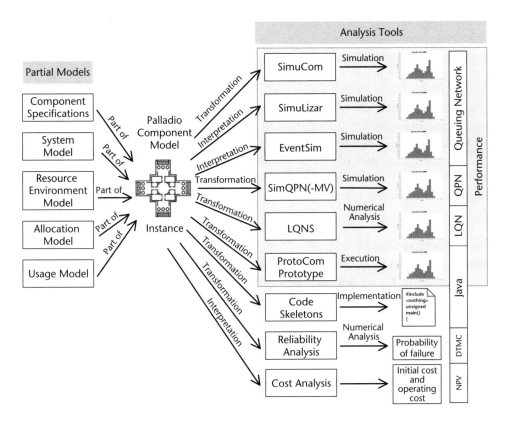

Figure 8.1
Multiple partial models constitute an instance of the Palladio Component Model (PCM), for which Palladio provides transformations to different analysis models.

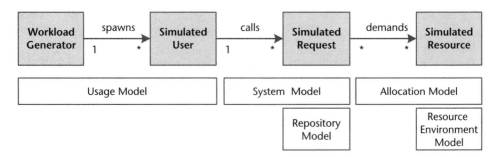

Figure 8.2
Important simulation entities and corresponding models they operate on.

study, including response times and resource utilization, for instance. If you are wondering how a Palladio simulation produces these performance characteristics from instances of the Palladio Component Model (PCM), keep reading. This section covers the main ingredients of a Palladio simulation, their interrelation, and their relation to the input models.

To understand how Palladio simulators produce performance metrics, it helps to think of the simulation as an assembly of four central entities that work together. They are depicted in figure 8.2. Each entity operates on one or more Palladio partial models displayed below the entities. A simulated request, for example, draws its information from two partial models: the system model and the repository model.

Over the course of a simulation run, the *workload generator* continuously spawns *simulated users* who put the simulated system under load by sending *simulated requests* to the system services. To process the request of a simulated user, these simulated systems services consume *simulated resources*—say a certain number of CPU cycles. Multiple concurrent system calls face limited *simulated resources* so that calls compete for resource accesses. This competition for scarce resources is usually referred to as resource contention.

8.2.1 Workload Generator

The workload generator is responsible for applying load to the simulated system. It continuously creates simulated users according to a Palladio *usage model*. The creation frequency is determined by the type of the workload and how the workload is parameterized. For a closed workload parameterized with think time being zero, the workload generator sustains a constant amount of simulated users. The workload generator will not spawn a simulated user before another user reaches the end of its lifetime. This keeps the user population at a constant size. For an open workload, the workload generator spawns a simulated user whenever the specified interarrival time elapsed. The amount of simulated users may therefore vary over the course of a simulation run. In particular, simulated users pile up if they arrive faster than the simulated system is capable of serving them.

8.2.2   Simulated Users

Simulated users (in short, "users") complement the workload generator. The workload generator merely determines when to spawn a new simulated user, but it is not concerned with the user's behavior. Instead, it is the simulated user's responsibility to simulate how a user interacts with the system. When interacting with the system, a user basically invokes a sequence of system services, each called with certain parameters. With Palladio, such an invocation sequence is expressed as part of the *usage model*, via an action chain called a *usage scenario* (figure 8.3, left).

Now the task of a simulated user is to traverse this chain from the start action through to the stop action. For each action encountered on the path, its effect on the simulated system is simulated. There is, however, no single path, but usually a multitude of possible paths. Consider, for example, the *download* usage scenario of the Media Store. With a specified probability, a user needs to register with the Media Store before being able to log in. The usage scenario reflects this fact by a *branch* action. Whenever a simulated user comes across that branch, the user draws a random number that determines if the user takes the left or the right branch transition. Let us assume the model specifies a probability of 20% for the left transition. The simulated user then takes the left transition when drawing a number from the interval [0, 0.2]; drawing a number in the range (0.2, 1] lets the user take the right transition. In the long run, with many simulated users traversing the usage scenario, the fraction between "left" and "right" users reflects the probability specified for the branch action. Whenever a simulated user encounters an *entry level system call*, the system call is simulated before the simulated user moves on to the call action's successor.

8.2.3   Simulated System Requests

A simulated system request (in short, "request") simulates the behavior of a system call issued by a user. For this, a request starts at the system's provided interface, follows the delegation connector toward the providing component, and simulates the component behavior relating to the requested service. The component behavior is modeled by a chain of actions contained in a resource demanding service effect specification.

Simulating a request means to traverse the chain of actions as introduced for the simulated users above. In addition, whenever a request encounters an *external call action*, it simulates the behavior of the called component service before continuing to traverse the calling service. Hence, the chain of actions traversed by a request is not restricted to a single *resource demanding service effect specification*. The control flow simulated by a request may span multiple components as can be seen in figure 8.3.

Once a request discovers an *internal action*, it looks up the resource demand specified for that action and issues the resource demand accordingly. The request is blocked until the processing resource has served the demand. A request behaves in the same manner when running across an *acquire action* (i.e., when a passive resource is to be acquired). The traversal will not continue until the requested number of instances has been granted.

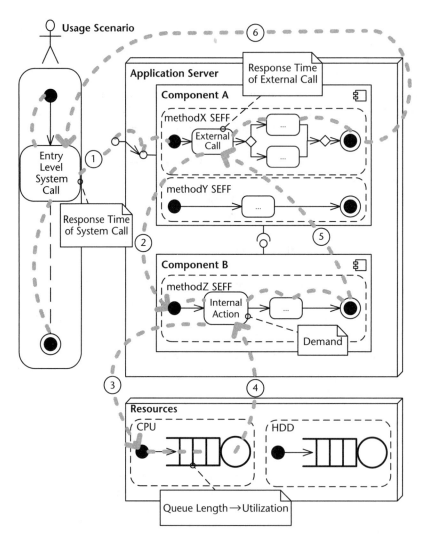

Figure 8.3
Path of a simulated user request through the simulated system.

8.2.4 Simulated Resources

The performance simulation is centered around the two kinds of resources in Palladio; namely, *processing resources* such as a CPU, hard disk drive (HDD), or solid state disk (SSD) and *passive resources* such as database connection pools or semaphores, as explained in section 5.5. A property that all resources have in common is that they are a scarce commodity. Processing resources can only process a limited number of tasks simultaneously (depending on the number of physical or logical cores) while all other tasks must wait. Passive resources are likewise limited by the number of instances—say database connections—they provide to clients: if connections are acquired faster than they are released to the pool, the resource gets exhausted eventually. Clients must then wait for the release of an instance. Waiting for a resource makes the contention for scarce resources visible. The presence of multiple concurrent requests in the simulated system, each issuing demands to shared resources, leads to the overall system behavior that the simulation aims to imitate. Observing the involved entities over the course of a simulation run yields the simulation results. These are, for instance, resource utilization over simulation time as well as response times of system calls and calls to component services.

8.2.5 Simulated Scheduling Policies

These principles of having a system captured by resources and links between them are simulated using the concepts of queuing theory (Lazowska et al. 1984); that is, a resource demand is a job that is enqueued in the waiting line of a server representing the corresponding resource (e.g., the CPU or HDD). The duration required for servicing a resource demand is calculated from the processing rate of the resource and the scheduling strategy. In Palladio, the First come, First served (FCFS) and Processor Pharing (PS) strategies are commonly used; additionally, more complex strategies are available.

In figure 8.4, an example for a resource queue with the FCFS scheduling strategy is shown. At the point in time $t = 0$, two resource demands reside in the queue of the resource, the first with a demand of 30, and the second with a demand of 25. When proceeding one time unit, the first job in the queue is served, resulting in reduction of demand by the rate of the resource (10). Moreover, a third resource demand arrives and is enqueued in the waiting line. At the point in time $t = 3$, the first resource demand is finished, and the processing of the second resource demand starts. At 2.5 time units later, the second resource demand can also leave the queue. The FCFS scheduling strategy is used to simulate an in-order processing of resource demand jobs. Thus, this kind of resource scheduling is commonly applied for exclusively used resources, such as HDDs. Oftentimes, FCFS scheduling is used as an abstraction for all kinds of network and batch processing resources.

Figure 8.5 shows a similar sequence of resource demands, which are, however, serviced using the PS scheduling strategy. The server is shared among the resource demands in the queue. Because the server has no higher processing rate, the time for finishing an individual resource demand can increase. In the example, this leads to the situation that the second

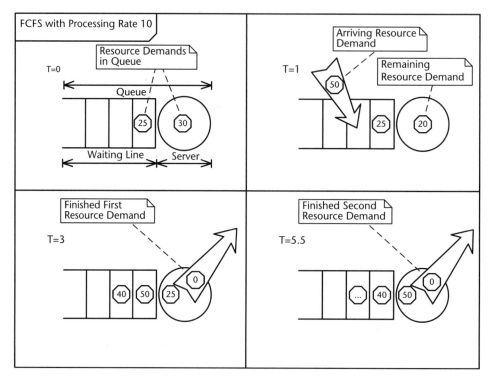

Figure 8.4
Resource demand processing using the FCFS scheduling strategy.

resource demand even finishes before the first demand has been finished completely. In total, both demands take longer to finish than with the FCFS strategy. Please note that the third resource demand would finish at the same time in both strategies, showing that the PS strategy is not slower, but shares the processing capacity among the enqueued demands. The PS scheduling strategy can be used for all resources where parallelism in processing is present. It is commonly used for representing CPUs and other time-shared resources.

Passive resources are a concept to limit the degree of parallelism in the processing of requests. They are acquired by requests, then held for a certain amount of time and are finally released. Passive resources have a limited capacity that decreases whenever a request is being granted a resource instance. Conversely, the available capacity increases when a request releases a passive resource instance. If a request tries to acquire a resource instance although no instances are available, it has to wait until a free instance becomes available for it. The waiting time is reflected by an advance in simulated time. In the Palladio simulation, passive resources are implemented using counting semaphores. They can be used to represent resources such as thread pools, database connections, or locking mechanisms.

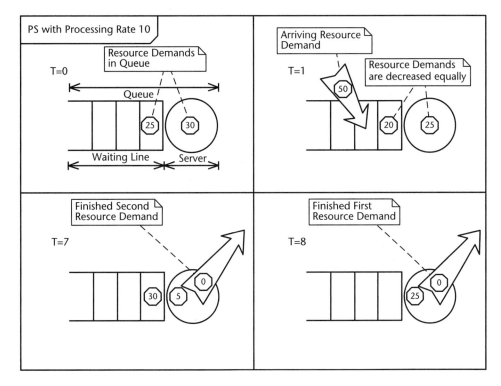

Figure 8.5
Resource demand processing using the PS scheduling strategy.

8.2.6 Gathering Measurements

To gather measurements from different analysis tools, Palladio uses the Quality Analysis Lab (QuAL), a framework for conducting, storing, and visualizing metric measurements. Figure 8.6 gives a high-level overview of the corresponding data flow through QuAL. The lower part illustrates the parts of QuAL that are responsible for data specification, while the upper part illustrates how QuAL uses these data for metric measurements in Palladio analyses.

The following descriptions contain material from the technical documentation of QuAL (Lehrig 2014b). The second of the two following subsections particularly includes detailed descriptions for each QuAL component.

Data Specification: Metrics and Measurements   The data specification of QuAL (lower part of figure 8.6) includes the following main components:

Metric descriptions: *Metric descriptions* characterize metrics to be measured. For example, a *point in time* metric represents the point in time when a measurement value is taken and can

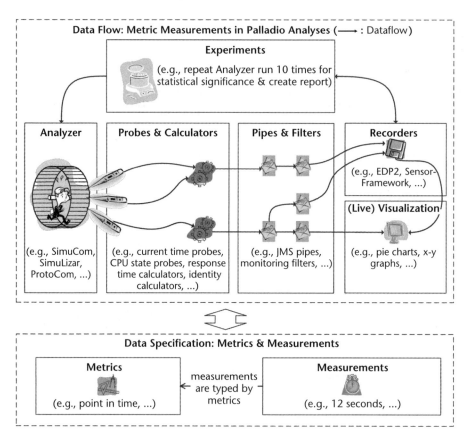

Figure 8.6
Overview of Palladio's Quality Analysis Lab (Lehrig 2014b).

Digression 8.2

Steady State

Palladio simulations are designed to analyze the *steady state* of a system; that is, a state where all resources show a steady behavior, opposed to the ramp-up phase during which, for example, queues of simulated resources are filled. Hence, a behavior that is changing over time for a single simulation run is not what Palladio is designed for. To analyze changing system behavior over time, multiple discrete (intermediate) states have to be simulated individually. This can, for example, be automated by means of changing model parameters over multiple simulation runs.

To approach dynamic system changes (e.g., horizontal scaling by adding resources, as targeted by SimuLizar; see section 8.3.3), one can seek time boxes with steady-state behavior in an overall analysis run. Within those time boxes, the steady-state assumption holds. Changes to the system are then performed after reaching a steady state.

be measured with real numbers (capture type) and in seconds (unit). Another example is response times: the response-time metric represents the duration between the start of an operation call and its end; it can be measured with real numbers (capture type) and in seconds (unit). In Palladio, *metric descriptions* are realized in the *metric specification framework*. The *metric specification framework* comes with a library of commonly used *metric descriptions*. Moreover, it offers the specification of custom *metric descriptions*.

Measurements: *Measurements* specify data objects for storing *measuring values* at a given *measuring point*, typed by a corresponding *metric description*. For example, "12 seconds wall-clock time of an analysis" is a valid measuring value/point combination corresponding to the *point in time* metric. An example measurement for the response-time metric of the Media Store example is "12 seconds for a download operation call." In Palladio, *measurements* are realized in the *measurement framework*. The *measurement framework* provides a library to measure *basic measurements* (one value) or *measurement sets* (set of basic measurements). These two types of *measurements* should generically cover all measurement needs; thus, the framework does not provide extension points for custom *measurements*.

Data Flow: Metric Measurements in Palladio Analyses   The data flow of metrics and measurements within Palladio analyses (upper part of figure 8.6) involves the following main components:

Analyzer: An *analyzer* runs the environment to be measured (e.g., a simulation or a performance prototype of the Media Store example). At the time of writing, typical Palladio simulators are SimuCom, SimuLizar, and EventSim; a typical performance prototype is provided by ProtoCom (see section 8.3). In Palladio, *analyzers* are realized in the *analyzer framework*. The *analyzer framework* provides interfaces and abstract classes serving as a starting point for custom *analyzers*. The above-mentioned concrete *analyzers* are examples for such custom *analyzers*.

Probes: *Probes* know how to measure values (e.g., "current analysis time" or "CPU state/queue size") for a given *analyzer* (i.e., they come with a suitable, *analyzer*-specific implementation). Once implemented, *probes* can be placed all over the analyzer to steadily probe. In Palladio, *probes* are realized in the *probe framework*. The *probe framework* comes with an analyzer-independent library of abstract *probes*. These abstract *probes* allow one to easily specify custom, analyzer-specific *probes*.

Calculators: *Calculators* attach themselves to a set of probes to enrich their *measurements* by the investigated metric (e.g., response time) and the measuring point (e.g., the Media Store's download operation). *Calculators* can then be used further (e.g., for visualization or recording). Therefore, *calculators* specify which *measurements* are of interest outside of the *analyzer*. For example, the response-time *calculator* provides response-time *measurements* that are calculated on the basis of current time *probes* for start and end time (response time = end − start time). Another example is the identity *calculator* that directly lets *probe measurements* pass through, without changing the measured value. In Palladio, *calculators* are part of the *probe framework* (due to their strong dependency on *probes*). The *probe framework* comes with a factory for commonly used *calculators*. Moreover, it offers the addition of custom *calculators*.

Pipes and Filters: *Pipes and filters* offer the transfer and filtering of *measurements* by *calculators* to data sinks, such as *recorders* and *live visualization*. For example, *measurements* can be transferred via java message service (JMS) to dedicated servers for measurement storage. In Palladio, *pipes and filters* are realized via the push-based, third-party framework *Kieker* (Hoorn et al. 2012) (elements are pushed through the pipeline, not pulled). *Kieker* provides an easy way to create custom filters.

Recorders: *Recorders* offer the storage of *measurements* received via the *pipes and filters framework* (e.g., in a database, an XML file, or a binary file). In Palladio, *recorders* are realized in the *recorder framework*, which offers the specification of custom *recorders*. Currently, two of such custom recorders exist: The *SensorFramework* and the *Experiment Data Persistency & Presentation (EDP2)*. At the time of writing, *EDP2* is the preferred *recorder* and is supposed to fully replace the *SensorFramework*.

(Live) Visualization: A *visualization* presents *measurements* in graphical form. For example, CPU utilization can be visualized via a pie chart or the response times of the Media Store example can be visualized in a *x-y* graph. Such a visualization can either be based on recorded *measurements* (*recorders* provide data input) or based on live monitoring data (*pipes and filters framework* provides data input). In Palladio, visualization is realized in the *UI framework*. For recorder-based visualization, the *UI framework* provides a pull-based pipes and filters framework to request data from *recorders*. For live visualization, the *UI framework* provides suitable listener interfaces.

Experiments: *Experiments* are used to conduct a series of *analyzer* runs and to aggregate recorded *measurements* to new *measurements* (so-called *experiment reports*). For example, an *experiment* can repeat an *analyzer* run for 10 times. The variance over these runs can be reported, indicating the statistical significance of these *analyzer* runs. Another example is to conduct the same analysis using different *analyzers* and to report on the analysis time per *analyzer*. In Palladio, experiments are realized in the *experiment automation framework*. With the *experiment automation framework*, performance analysts may specify *analyzer* configurations, run *analyzers*, and store *experiment reports* based on investigating *analyzer measurements* within *recorders*. In particular, the framework provides extension points for adding custom *analyzers*.

Digression 8.3
Credible Performance Simulation
Probabilistic simulations as commonly used in the Palladio approach are stochastic experiments and as such require proper treatment to yield trustworthy results. Unlike analytical solution techniques, a probabilistic simulation cannot provide an exact solution, but instead approximates the true solution. The achieved accuracy can strongly benefit from setting up the simulation experiment carefully—or suffer from a careless setup. Just like a single opinion in a poll is not

representative of the entire underlying population, one cannot regard a single short simulation run as representative of the true characteristic to be predicted. This is illustrated in figure 8.7. The figure summarizes the outcomes of five different simulation runs. You could feel tempted to claim that observations from run 1 must come from a system faster than the one represented by run 3: while the probability for a response time lower than 20 seconds is roughly 60% for run 1, it is merely 35% for run 3. In fact, however, there is no difference at all: the figure shows the results of five repeated but otherwise identical simulation runs. What you could perceive as a difference in system performance is rather caused by the small number of observations. These observations are not representative of the true outcome you would observe for a very long simulation run.

To make the sample more representative, performance analysts can combine measurements from repeated runs or let a single run simulate for a longer time. This can be seen in figure 8.8. The more measurements from repeated runs that are combined, the more stable and representative the simulation result becomes.

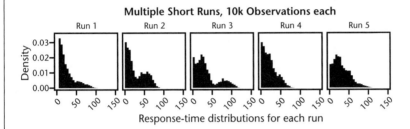

Figure 8.7
Short simulation runs yield unstable results that cannot be trusted.

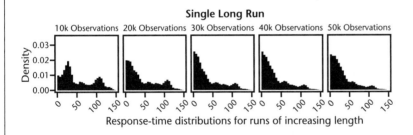

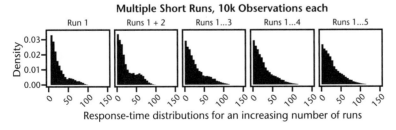

Figure 8.8
Simulation results become more stable and trustworthy with longer simulation runs (top) or additional replications (bottom).

8.3   Performance Analysis Tools

Palladio provides multiple tools to analyze the performance of a modeled system. This section discusses their particular features, their strengths, and their limitations. The section closes with a decision process that helps in selecting an analysis tool best suited to the given context.

8.3.1   SimuCom: Generative Simulation

SimuCom is a discrete-event software performance simulator for Palladio models. Supplied with a Palladio model, SimuCom computes various performance characteristics for the modeled system. These include response times of both system-level and component-level services, as well as utilization of resources. As the most feature-rich simulator available for Palladio models, SimuCom is often considered Palladio's reference simulator.

From a technical point of view, SimuCom is interesting because of its extensive use of model-driven software development techniques. For a given Palladio model, SimuCom generates simulation code tailored to this model using model-to-code transformations. The generated simulation code essentially consists of Java classes and interfaces packaged in an OSGi bundle. For each element in the Palladio model, there is a counterpart in the generated Java artifacts. Each *service effect specification*, for example, is mapped to a Java method, whereas Java classes and interfaces reflect components and interfaces modeled in Palladio. The simulation bundle plugs into the SimuCom platform providing the execution environment for generated simulation code. The SimuCom platform factors out common simulation code that would otherwise be repeated in every generated bundle. This includes especially the simulation engine and a pseudo-random number generator. Together, bundle and platform form the actual simulator.

The simulator resembles the modeled system in terms of performance, meaning that both ideally show the same behavior when supplied with the same input. Upon completion of a simulation run, the gathered results are made available in the Palladio-Bench. Note that generation, compilation, and execution of simulation code is an automated process. No user interaction is required after launching the simulation.

SimuCom follows the process-interaction simulation technique. Thus, SimuCom maps each simulated user to a dedicated thread of execution provided by the operating system. Simulated requests of the same user are executed in the context of the user's thread. Having a native thread for each simulated user is beneficial because threads can easily be suspended to reflect that the corresponding simulated user is blocked (e.g., while waiting for service in a resource queue). The one-to-one mapping between simulated users and native threads also comes with a drawback: the number of users simulated concurrently in SimuCom is limited by the maximum number of threads provided by the operating system. A common misconception relating to the use of threads in SimuCom is that multiple simulated users could run concurrently, even exploiting multicore processors. In fact, however, exactly one of the user

---

Digression 8.4
Simulation Techniques: Process Interaction versus Event Scheduling
Similar to programming languages, where different programming techniques (such as structural or object-oriented programming) can be used alternatively, a simulation modeler can choose from a number of simulation techniques. The choice for a simulation technique mainly determines the manner in which the simulation is modeled, just as writing machine code feels quite different from coding in a high-level object-oriented language. The *event-scheduling technique* could be considered the machine code of simulations. Here, the modeler creates fine-grained event types, each associated with an event routine that encapsulates simulation logic and ensures that events are scheduled at the right time. The *process-interaction technique*, by contrast, abstracts from events; the modeler creates coarse-grained processes from which events are derived automatically. Similar to events, processes contain simulation logic (i.e., they cause state changes of the simulated system). While events encapsulate simulation logic for a time instant, processes define simulation logic that spans periods of time—potentially the entire simulation run. It is often argued that this type of modeling feels more natural. Notice that the terms *world-view* and *conceptual framework* are (rather historical) synonyms for the term *simulation technique*, which is used in this book. Sometimes, simulation techniques are also referred to as *simulation paradigms*.

---

threads is active at the same time from the operating system's perspective. There is no real concurrency between simulated users in SimuCom; only simulated concurrency, meaning more than one user runnning at the same point in simulation time, but never at the same point in wall-clock time.

In section 11.2.1, we describe how each Palladio construct is mapped to simulation code generated by SimuCom.

8.3.2 EventSim: Interpreting Simulation

EventSim is a discrete-event simulator for performance analyses of Palladio models. EventSim aims at complementing SimuCom in that it is primarily geared toward highly complex simulation models, where SimuCom might suffer from scalability and performance issues. As the name might suggest, EventSim relies on the event-scheduling simulation technique. This relieves the costly one-to-one mapping between a simulated process and a native thread of control and allows EventSim to scale well with increasing workload intensities and with increasing simulated concurrency in general. It must be noted, however, that EventSim does only support a subset of the most import Palladio modeling constructs.

From a technical point of view, EventSim is a set of Eclipse plug-ins that provide an additional analysis tool to the Palladio-Bench. Unlike SimuCom, no simulation code is generated and no model transformations are used. EventSim instead interprets the loaded Palladio model at simulation run time. The interpreter simulates the behavior of system users and the system requests issued by them. The behavior of system users is captured by usage scenarios in the usage model. The behavior of system requests is captured by one or more Resource Demanding Service Effect Specifications (RDSEFFs) depending on the number of components involved in the system-provided service. Simulating a user means to follow a path from the scenario's start action through to its stop action while executing the simulation logic associated with each action encountered on the path. The same applies to the simulation of system requests. For each type of action, the interpreter looks up a simulation strategy that contains the actual simulation behavior. Passing through action chains this way while executing the simulation behavior for each type of action yields the overall simulation.

8.3.3 SimuLizar: Self-Adaptions in Simulations

SimuLizar extends Palladio to support modeling and analysis of self-adaptations (Becker et al. 2012, 2013) . Such adaptations commonly occur in cloud-computing environments, for example, when scaling-out components by replicating a component and adding it to a corresponding load balancer.

For modeling adaptations, SimuLizar enriches the PCM to specify monitoring annotations as well as adaptation rules. Monitoring annotations mark PCM elements (e.g., an operation of a component) to be monitored during analysis using a metric such as response time. Adaptation rules can then react on changes of monitored values. For example, when a certain response-time threshold is exceeded, an adaptation rule could trigger a scaling-out of bottleneck components.

For analyzing adaptations, SimuLizar comes with a simulation-based solver that interprets involved models (PCM, monitoring annotations, and adaptation rules). Such an interpreter approach can monitor values of interest during simulation time and trigger adaptation rules when feasible. These rules can subsequently adapt involved models; the interpreter considers updates directly during simulation time.

8.3.4 ProtoCom: Performance Prototyping

Performance prototypes mimic demands to different types of hardware resources to evaluate their performance in a realistic environment (Hu and Gorton 1997; Becker 2008). ProtoCom (Becker 2008; Lehrig and Zolynski 2011; Giacinto and Lehrig 2013; Klaussner and Lehrig 2014) is an approach to this performance prototyping. ProtoCom transforms Palladio models into executable performance prototypes. Such performance prototypes can operate in different target environments and take performance measurements for an early assessment of the modeled software system within a real environment.

Each target environment potentially requires a different target technology. Supported target technologies of ProtoCom are based on Java SE and Java EE with EJBs (Enterprise Java Beans) and Servlets (as of the time of writing). For Java SE and EE, ProtoCom supports the following intercomponent communication technologies:

Remote Method Invocation (RMI), Java's base class library for remote procedure calls (RPCs).

RMI over IIOP (RMI-IIOP), a commonly supported technology by Java EE application servers where RMI calls are sent over the Internet Inter-Orb Protocol (IIOP) for distributed intercomponent communication.

RPC via HTTP, implemented via sockets and a custom JSON-based communication protocol.

When running a generated performance prototype, an external HTTP load generator (e.g., JMeter for RPC over HTTP) is used to simulate users interacting with the system according to the usage scenario specified in the model. While executing, the performance prototype collects several measurements for metrics such as response times that allow for a subsequent analysis of the software architecture's performance in a real environment. Section 11.2.2 describes the mapping of each Palladio construct to implementation artifacts generated by ProtoCom.

8.3.5 Further Analysis Tools

Besides the aforementioned simulation-based approaches, Palladio users can employ further analysis tools to obtain performance estimates for modeled systems. Most of these approaches rely on transforming Palladio models to independent formalisms that are also commonly used for software performance predictions. In the following, two formalisms will be briefly introduced.

Layered Queuing Networks (LQN) are an extension of queuing networks with a layered structure. The formalism introduces some additional elements (e.g., for conditional branching or fork/join semantics). Using LQNs, numerical mean-value approximation methods can be applied efficiently to calculate the performance estimates. For LQNs with no numerical solution, a simulation can be performed as well.

Queuing Petri Nets (QPN) are an extension of colored Petri nets that use special queuing places for representing queuing semantics. QPNs can be solved numerically using a Markov chain analysis. Because of the state-space explosion problem, however, a simulation-based approach is often used when analyzing large models.

While these formalisms are often used when time for getting performance estimates is limited, users should be aware that accuracy of results can be degraded due to restrictions in these formalisms. Moreover, these approaches are only feasible for calculating steady-state probabilities and cannot be used for transient analyses.

8.3.6 Deciding for a Performance Analysis Tool

Deciding for an analysis tool is not easy and requires weighing up different criteria. No general recommendation can be made because a tool's intended use determines the weight given

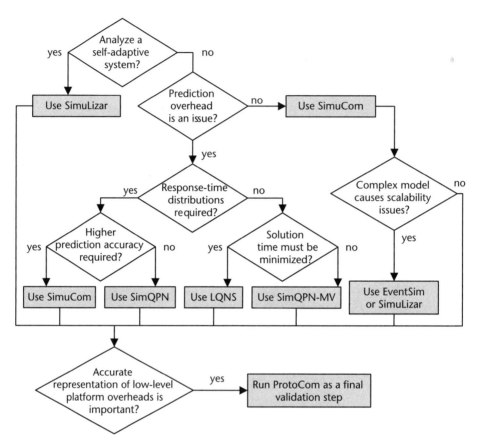

Figure 8.9
Decision process for selecting an appropriate analysis tool (Brosig et al. 2015).

to each criterion. The following therefore introduces different criteria and discusses how they steer the decision-making process. Figure 8.9 summarizes the key factors driving the analysis tool selection.

The first criterion is the type of system to be simulated. Is the modeled system supposed to adapt itself to variations in usage intensity? Then SimuLizar is the analysis tool of your choice. Among competing analysis tools, SimuLizar stands out for its ability to adapt the modeled system throughout simulation. Once the current simulation state triggers an adaption rule—when a resource is overloaded, for example—SimuLizar modifies the supplied Palladio model according to the adaption rule. The simulation then continues on the adapted model. At the time of writing, no other Palladio analysis is able to do so.

For analyzing nonadaptive systems, the choice for an analysis tool is less clear. You can afford higher analysis run times? Then SimuCom is the first choice. SimuCom covers virtually every modeling element provided by Palladio, whereas other analyses usually focus on a subset of modeling elements. Using SimuCom, you can expect the results to be more accurate and more expressive, as described later. In rare cases, when trying to simulate highly complex models with thousands of simulated users, you might run into scalability limits of SimuCom. Using EventSim or SimuLizar can help to work around these limits.

Let us come back to the analysis run-time criterion. If low analysis run time is crucial, better choices are SimQPN, SimQPN-MV, or LQNs. There are situations where the mean value of a characteristic—the response time of a service, for example—is completely sufficient. Then you decide for SimQPN-MV or LQNs. Notice the MV suffix that stands for *mean value* and denotes a SimQPN operation mode where no probability distributions are stored for results. Storing only mean values will accelerate the analysis substantially. The high level of aggregation, however, tends to discard essential information. You lose what has been called expressivity above. Take for example a bimodal probability distribution, indicating you actually have two different groups in your results. The first group could be the requests served from cache, whereas requests in the second group encountered a cache miss. Using a single aggregate like the mean value, you would lose this information.

If mean values are not sufficient, you would choose either SimuCom or SimQPN. SimQPN provides a better balance between prediction accuracy and overhead. By contrast, when accuracy is more important, SimuCom should be chosen, at the cost of higher prediction overhead.

Where feasible, ProtoCom is recommended as a final validation step after sufficient results have been gained through the model solvers. It requires much more time to set up and run (i.e., up to several hours in contrast to several minutes for the model solvers). ProtoCom, however, is able to provide insight about realistic scheduling overheads, memory contention impacts, realistic I/O delays, network overheads, or virtualization impacts. In cases where the magnitude of response times is very low, platform overheads are more likely to distort the results, thus ProtoCom is especially recommended for such systems. It also allows refinement of the generated prototype application (e.g., by including realistic database queries or using real external services).

8.4   Reliability Analysis

For predicting reliability, the Palladio model can be annotated with software failure potentials (failure probabilities annotated to internal actions) and hardware failure potentials (mean time to failure and mean time to repair of active resources as well as failure probabilities for communication links), as described in chapter 5. On the basis of this information, the Palladio reliability solver (PCM-REL) can predict the probability of failure on demand of a usage scenario by transforming the Palladio model into a discrete-time Markov chain (DTMC) as explained in the following.

The prediction process has the following four steps: (1) solve parameter dependencies (section 8.4.1), (2) determine possible physical system states (PSSs) and their probabilities (section 8.4.2), (3) generate a DTMC for a single PSS (section 8.4.3), and (4) evaluate the DTMC and aggregate the results (section 8.4.4) (Brosch et al. 2011).

8.4.1 Solve Parameter Dependencies

As described in chapter 5, component developers use parameters to make their RDSEFFs applicable to varying resource environments, assembly contexts, and usage profiles. Only after other developer roles have provided the usage profile, the assembly model, and the allocation can you use the Palladio reliability analysis to predict the reliability of the resulting system under the given usage profile.

As a first step in the analytical prediction of reliability, the parameter dependencies need to be resolved (see, e.g., "Count.Value >= 2" in figure 5.1).

The Palladio dependency solver (Koziolek 2008) is a tool that propagates the parameter values of the usage profile through all elements of a Palladio model and inserts them into guard specifications, parametric loop iterations, parametric resource demands, and parameter usages specified by the component developer. While traversing the model, the solver uses the assembly model and the allocation model to determine called components and used resources. Then, it solves the resulting stochastic expressions, so that they become constant values or probability distributions, and stores them, so that they can be used for a transformation into a performance model.

8.4.2 Determine Possible Physical System States and Their Probabilities

Next, the hardware failure potential is taken into account by enumerating the possible physical system states and determining their probabilities.

At any point in time, each resource r in the set of resources R can be either available (ok) or unavailable due to hardware failure (na). Let $S_r = \{ok, na\}$ denote the these two possible states. On the basis of the mean time to failure ($MTTF_r$) and mean time to repair ($MTTR_r$), PCM-REL calculates the probability $P(r, ok)$ that a resource r is available as

$$P(r, ok) = MTTF_r / MTTF_r + MTTR_r$$

On the basis of these availability values, PCM-REL calculates the probability of each resource state combination. The overall physical system state PSS of a system with resources $r_1, ..., r_n$ is an element of the Cartesian product of the individual state spaces:

$$PSS \in S_{r_1} \times ... \times S_{r_n}$$

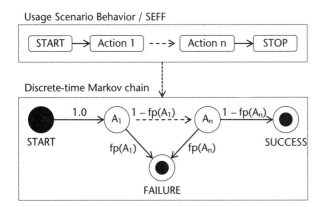

Figure 8.10
Markov chain generation (Brosch et al. 2011).

As each resource has two possible states, there are 2^n physical system states. Assuming independent resource failures the probability of the system being in a physical system state $P(PSS)$ is the product of the individual resource-state probabilities.

8.4.3 Generate a DTMC for a Single PSS
Next, PCM-REL generates a DTMC that describes the failure possibilities of the combined software and hardware system for each PSS. This example is a simple case without fault tolerance mechanisms (Brosch 2012). There is one start, one failure, and one success state. Furthermore, there are two intermediate states that potentially lead to the failure state. You can see the absence of fault tolerance mechanisms as there are no alternative paths from start to success that represent failure recovery states.

Under the assumption of a given PSS, PCM-REL traverses the resolved Palladio model (i.e., without parameters) starting from the usage scenario, for which a start state is generated. For internal actions that access a resource that is unavailable in the current PSS, it generates a transition to a failure state. Additionally, it generates a behavior state in the Markov chain for every internal action A_i with a failure probability $fp(A_i) > 0$. From this state, a transition to a failure state is generated with probability $fp(A_i)$, and a transition to the next behavior state is generated with probability $1 - fp(A_i)$. Finally, a success state is connected to the final internal actions of each path. Figure 8.10 illustrates the DTMC generation.

Additionally, each branch action is translated into a state with outgoing transitions with the probability of each branch. Loops, which have finite iteration count in the PCM, are unrolled and converted into branches, which are then handled as described above.

8.4.4   Evaluate the DTMC and Aggregate Results

The generated DTMC is acyclic (due to the unrolled loops) and absorbing. To determine the probability of successful execution of a usage scenario for each PSS, PCM-REL calculates the probability to reach the success state. Additionally, PCM-REL calculates the probability of different failure types by determining the probability to reach the respective failure state.

The result of this step is the probability of success P(ok | PSS) and the probabilities of the modeled types of failures of a usage scenario for a given PSS.

To determine the overall probability of success P(ok) of a usage scenario, the results are aggregated over all PSS.

$$P\,(\mathrm{ok}) = P`(\mathrm{ok} \mid P\,SS)P\,(P\,SS)$$

8.4.5   Summary

PCM-REL analyzes a Palladio model annotated with failure probabilities of internal actions or hardware reliability (MTTF and MTTR) and determines the probability of success of a given usage scenario as well as the probability of different types of failure.

This approach is based on several assumptions:

• Resources are assumed to fail independently.
• The response time of requests is considerably smaller than the time between physical system state changes. Thus, the assumption is that the physical system state does not change while answering one request.
• Software and communication link failures are transient and have no side effects on subsequent calls.
• Each failure propagates to the system boundary (unless explicit fault tolerance mechanisms have been modeled).

8.5   Cost Analysis

A simple cost model can be used to specify the types of costs for a Palladio model discussed in chapter 5. Software architects can use it to express the cost differences of different design options and to assess the cost differences between architectural candidates. The model offers annotation of software architecture with cost estimations. Similar to models of other cost optimization approaches, such as by Cortellessa et al. (2008), it does not provide means to estimate the costs, as this is a different research field. The advantage of the independent costs annotation model is that it can either be created on the basis of rough estimations or it can be created on the basis of results from more sophisticated cost estimation approaches, such as COCOMO II (Boehm et al. 2000) and its relatives (Boehm and Valerdi 2008), or project-specific or organization-specific approaches.

With the used cost model, developers can assign costs to components and to hardware. It distinguishes initial costs and operating costs, so that the software architecture effects on the total cost of ownership can be assessed. Users can either calculate total costs, for example calculating the current value of the costs based on an assumed interest rate, or they can treat the two types of costs as separate criteria to improve and to trade off. Thus, component costs reflect all relevant costs induced by that component's implementation and later life-cycle phases. Different options for a component can be modeled as different available components and then be annotated with component costs.

Hardware costs annotate servers or processing resources. Here, selection of fixed hardware entities can be annotated with fixed costs each. For example, a server of type A with certain reliability and performance properties costs $1,000, while a server of type B with different properties costs $1,500. Alternatively, a cost function can be specified to map parameters of the hardware to a price to reflect a wider range of options. For example, a cost function can map clock speed of CPUs to costs on the basis of the price tables of CPU producers. Again, the model allows specification of both initial costs and operating costs.

The Palladio cost solver determines the overall cost for a model annotated as described above. It relies on a static analysis of a Palladio model annotated with the presented cost model. It calculates the cost for each component and resource on the basis of the annotations specified in the Palladio model and then adds these costs to derive the overall expected cost for the architecture. If a server specified in the model is not used (i.e., no components are allocated to it), its costs do not add to the overall cost.

The cost model and cost solver are simple, because the main challenge of cost prediction is the estimation of costs. If the initial costs and operating costs of the single parts of the architecture are known, it is straightforward to calculate the overall cost.

8.6   Questions and Exercises

8.6.1   Questions
8.1 **: What is the difference between the different quality analysis tools for Palladio?
8.2 *: What parts constitute a typical Palladio simulator?
8.3 *: How can the confidence of simulation results be increased?
8.4 ***: Why are pseudo-random numbers used to conduct the simulations?
8.5 ***: What differentiates ProtoCom from SimuCom and EventSim?
8.6 ***: Which statistical means can be used to decide simulations have run "long enough"?

8.6.2   Exercises
8.1 ***: Imagine you are asked to build an automated design space exploration tool for Palladio models that works similar to PerOpteryx introduced in section 7.4.3. Let us assume your tool is already capable of creating new architectural candidates, but these candidates cannot yet be evaluated and compared to each other automatically. To avoid reinventing the

wheel, you plan to reuse an existing Palladio analysis tool to evaluate candidates. Consider the specific requirements of this scenario and decide on a suitable analysis tool.

8.2 **: Consider the scheduling examples from figure 8.5 and figure 8.4. If in time step $t = 1$ an additional resource demand of 5 arrives right after the demand of 50, when can we expect this job to be finished under a processor sharing policy? When is the newly arriving job finished when using an FCFS policy instead?

8.7 Further Reading

For an introduction to the foundations and principles of modeling and simulation, refer to Law and Kelton (2000) and Banks et al. (2000). Both books provide in-depth explanations on queuing systems, performance simulations, and statistical properties of results.

The Palladio reliability analysis is described in more detail by Brosch et al. (2011) and Brosch (2012). In general, reliability prediction at the software architecture level has been studied since the mid-1990s (Gokhale 2007). Surveys are presented by Goseva-Popstojanova et al. (2001), Gokhale (2007), and Immonen and Niemelä (2008). The "blue book" by Trivedi (2001) explains the basics of probability theory and statistics as needed for analyzing reliability and also queuing behavior of software systems. In particular, it explains Markov chains and presents numerous numerical solution techniques. Heinrich et al. (2015b) establish a relation between business process simulation and information system simulation by extending Palladio.

8.8 Takeaways

This chapter gives an overview of the basic principles used for the analysis of Palladio models. You should know that there are several solution methods available for analyzing the performance of Palladio models that have differing properties concerning accuracy, speed, and the range of supported features.

Palladio maps requests from the usage profile to individual user requests in the simulated system. All control flow and data flow defined in the Palladio model is executed by the simulated users. Whenever the control flow hits resource demands or the network, simulated resources are loaded by the requests to account for the resource load. Every time consumption of a simulation in Palladio originates from simulated resources. Control flow and data flow are executed by the simulated users as specified in the Palladio SEFF model.

Basically, there are three different classes for Palladio analysis: one based on generated source code (SimuCom), one based on interpreted model (SimuLizar and EventSim), and one based on real hardware (Protocom). SimuCom generates source code for workload, the modeled system (including components, interface, etc.), and resources. SimuLizar and EventSim interpret input models without creating source code. ProtoCom generates so-called performance prototypes that run on a physical target hardware platform and put actual load onto hardware. In these cases, simulated resources (e.g., queue) are replaced by actual resources (e.g., CPU). The chapter introduced a decision tree to support the selection of appropriate analysis methods.

For reliability, Palladio offers a transformation into discrete-time Markov chains, which combines software faults and hardware faults and can be used to determine probability of success for a usage scenario. Additionally, the Palladio cost analysis calculates initial costs and operating costs on the basis of cost annotations of software components and hardware.

Part IV Embedding into the Software Engineering Process

Part IV puts the architectural modeling and analysis discussion of the previous parts in relation to other important steps in the software development process that have not yet been discussed. This part is structured as follows.

Chapter 9 describes how the Palladio approach fits into different software development processes. It first presents the idealized Palladio development process, which is strongly influenced by component-based software engineering principles. Then, the approach is relaxed and aligned with existing, popular development processes, such as the Unified Process (Kruchten 2003) or agile development.

Chapter 10 specifically discusses the relation of software architecture and requirements. While it is common knowledge that existing requirements should drive the software architecture design and evaluation, it is less known that software architecture evaluation can also give insight to requirements decisions and even inspire new requirements. Finally, the chapter discusses how software architecture can help to continuously validate requirements throughout the system life cycle, first on the basis of evaluation models and later on the basis of tests and measurements.

Chapter 11 addresses the relation of software architecture to implementation artifacts, such as source code and deployment descriptors. This chapter deals with forward engineering (i.e., getting from Palladio models to source code), reverse engineering (getting from source code or running instances to Palladio models), and options to establish round-trip cycles between model and source code. At the end, the chapter presents a brief summary of recommended tools.

9 Software Engineering Processes

Lucia Happe, Oliver Hummel, Anne Koziolek, Klaus Krogmann, and Ralf H. Reussner

This chapter describes how Palladio-based modeling and accompanying tools fit into various software development process models. First, it introduces dimensions of a cost-benefit analysis for model-based performance prediction approaches in general and specifically for Palladio. After that, it presents an idealized Palladio development process, which is strongly influenced by established component-based software engineering principles and approaches. The approach is then relaxed and aligned with existing, popular development processes such as the Unified Process (UP) or agile development methodologies. The chapter closes with a discussion of the impact of the engineering principles in Palladio on common software development challenges, such as distributed development and schedule pressure.

As a reader, you will learn how the Palladio approach can be used in your development process and what advantages you will gain, but also what pitfalls may appear. To do so, this chapter describes the relation of architectural modeling and simulation to other phases of different development processes. The subsequent two chapters will provide additional details about the relation of software architecture and requirements engineering (chapter 10) and the relation of software architecture and implementation (chapter 11).

9.1 When (Not) to Use Model-Driven Quality Prediction

Before discussing the inclusion of Palladio in the software engineering process, it is advantageous to step back and consider whether application of a model-driven quality prediction approach (such as Palladio) is worthwhile. Obviously, the cost-benefit ratio depends on the costs and the benefits. These two dimensions are discussed below.

9.1.1 Costs of Model-Driven Quality Prediction
Architectural Modeling The creation of service effect specifications always creates the highest fraction of the overall modeling costs. Additional costs through architectural structural views and deployment views depend strongly on the current state of architectural modeling in a software engineering process. If architectural models and deployments are already modeled, Palladio creates virtually no additional overheads. On the contrary, the costs of service

effect specification are always in addition to those of a standard modeling practice, but these costs can be spread across several projects if the component implementation where the service effect specification belongs is reused.

Usage Profile Efforts to get realistic data on the usage profile depend on the method of acquiring these data. Such methods range from structured stakeholder interviews, to estimations, to logging activities on precursor or similar systems.

Model Calibration   As discussed in chapter 6, quality characteristics of resources need to be included in quality prediction models. Here in particular, expertise with use of monitoring frameworks and low-level performance measurement tools strongly influences the costs to be expected. Often, "educated guesses" (rational estimates) and existing documentation can help to get rough but useful data without high investment.

9.1.2   Benefits of Model-Driven Quality Prediction

Avoidance of Performance Failures The more costly the consequences of performance failures are, the more should be invested into model-driven performance prediction. On the contrary, if performance is uncritical, as easily acceptable levels can be achieved or consequences of failures are low, the up-front investment in the above-mentioned cost dimensions is questionable.

Avoidance of Costs through Trial and Error   One of the main arguments for *model*-driven quality prediction is that through automated analysis and the use of models instead of code, the design space can be explored much cheaper than with costly trial-and-error cycles. However, this is not true for all projects. In small systems, well refactorable, with low load, implementations, and accompanying performance benchmarks can also be an option, in particular, if only a low number of design space options are to be explored.

9.1.3   Indicators for the Application of Palladio

In a software engineering project, there are many indicators for the application of Palladio. Depending on the project setup, there are varying project risks with respect to external software quality that recommend use of Palladio. Whenever there are high risks of low performance, low reliability, or high costs, they should be mitigated using software engineering tools, such as Palladio.

When looking at the Media Store example, adding the feature of video file handling, in contrast to handling just MP3 files, can be a huge risk for a productive platform. Videos imply much higher data volume, which must be handled by storage and network bandwidth. Recoding such videos has much higher CPU load than that of processing a single audio file. Furthermore, a new service, such as exchanging videos, can attract a large number of new users. Imagine a press release that announces the new video feature and an accompanying expensive marketing campaign. If the advertised audio and video platform becomes unavailable during the launch (e.g., overload, unavailability, no scaling), potential new users will hardly give the platform a second chance. Consequently, business risks also arise from technical uncertainties.

From the authors' experience, there are multiple indicators to recommend the application of Palladio in software projects:

• **Project risks from a quality perspective** exist (performance, reliability, costs). For example, there may be no experience with certain load situations or the deployment in cloud resource environments. In such cases, scalability of a system is unknown.

• **New technologies or architectural concepts** are used in a project. The power and pitfalls of new technologies are typically not known to developers. Before shifting efforts and using a new technology (e.g., moving from Enterprise JavaBeans [EJBs] to Spring-based setups), these can be evaluated using Palladio. New architectures are another example. When changing, for example, from a thick client-server architecture to a cloud-based, browser-based client-server architecture, huge impacts for the server infrastructure occur.

• **A new domain** is targeted. The domain can be new to the developing companies or the client. For example, a cloud-based pet Web shop is new to people only experienced with the development of Linux administration tools.

• **New user groups** are approached. For example there can simply be more users to be expected or users that upload videos instead of only MP3 audio files. Also, offers for previously non-targeted power users can affect how users challenge a software system. Another example is a change between expert users (individual people per company) to mass-market users (millions of potential users) and vice versa.

• **Assurance of service-level agreements** is required. For example, a new customer claims a new stricter service-level agreement (SLA) that previous customers never forced. If high availability is claimed (e.g., 99.999% availability), looking at the past year's availability and extrapolating these value will not help, because 99.999% means rare events with a total unavailability of just 5 minutes per year. Such low downtimes cannot be reliably monitored and extrapolated from a period of just a few years. Another example for the assurance of SLAs is a need to reduce operational costs for an IT system. Using new hardware, fewer resources can potentially save money and hold a given SLA. Yet, before migrating to the new hardware, it should be checked how likely the previous SLA can still be held.

Derived from experience, Palladio is especially helpful if one of the following technical application scenarios occur:

• Comparison of design alternatives (e.g., using a database cache or deploying a database on a separate server)
• Sizing (e.g., finding a resource configuration to support 1,000 concurrent users)
• Scalability (e.g., checking whether a software system can scale up for 100,000 concurrent users)

• Optimized resource usage (e.g., fulfill a given SLA with less resource effort in terms of servers used)
• Realization of new major features (e.g., introduce support for real-time data analytics of business data for a software product)
• Extension of legacy software systems (e.g., connect a new web-based self-service to the existing Enterprise-Resource-Planning [ERP] planning system)

Using Palladio, some advantages are typically perceived when engineering software. These effects either are caused by the actual use of Palladio or are some side effects that become visible because of prerequisites for the application of Palladio.

For example, when predicting an existing software system, one first needs to gather up-to-date measurement data on the running system. Having up-to-date data is not granted for all systems. These data are the foundation for becoming aware of the actual state of the software system and beginning to reflect on the system behavior (as discussed in chapter 6). Means such as automated log file analysis and system monitoring enable automated supervision of systems. Hence, ad hoc quality assurance can be replaced by permanent integrated quality assurance, which, for example, is able to detect performance degradations at early stages.

Through use of Palladio, fewer trial-and-error cycles are needed during engineering. Because Palladio enables lightweight model-based evaluation of, for example, design alternatives (i.e., model-based fast-feedback cycles), only one major design alternative has to be exploited during implementation. Palladio is the foundation on which to replace "code first" and observe the impact of changes on running systems via systematic design with estimation of effects before the actual implementation.

9.1.4 Embedding into Software Engineering Activities

Palladio can be used in multiple types of software engineering activities. The more activities Palladio is used for, the less overhead Palladio has for modeling and keeping the model up to date, because the costs to create the base model are incurred only once. For example, models can already be present from a design phase to evaluate different options during a planning phase and later propagate to the implementation phase. In such cases, models from design are reused and refined for implementation.

The application of Palladio for common development activities will be detailed in the following. In all of these phases, an explicitly modeled architecture helps in communication, as it shapes a terminology for components, interfaces, and other architectural elements.

Requirements During requirement engineering, Palladio, or quality modeling in general, can help to capture desired component features in terms of the quality expected by the different stakeholders. It is valuable to make explicit and to solve conflicts between different quality expectations. Feedback that describes the consequences of specific quality requirements on software development or operation costs is most valuable. Palladio aims to give quantitative feedback as early as possible. In addition, the need to explicitly model the usage profile helps to clarify the expected interaction of users with the system. The use of service signatures as a base of the usage profile specification helps in communication between stakeholders and software architects, thus the terminology used for the description of the outer interfaces is close to the problem domain of the stakeholders. Hence, questions such as "How often will this activity be performed?" and "Which value of this parameter is most likely?" can be discussed. Service signatures are also still formalized enough for later use in quality prediction and for generation of component implementation.

Design   Palladio can document architectural design decisions. It offers the possibility to flexibly combine components for new architectures and assists during architectural planning. Furthermore, all techniques for explicit reuse of architectural knowledge (see chapter 4) can be applied.

Planning   Explicitly modeled software architectures are also useful for planning tasks, such as risk identification and cost estimation.

On the basis of the architectural design, Palladio is able to predict quality of service properties and can be used to estimate, for example, deployment considerations or operation costs before the actual implementation of the code is completed. Depending on the results, software architects can decide to change the architecture, renegotiate requirements and contracts on quality properties, or start implementing the design if it successfully fulfills the requirements.

Concerning performance risks, software architects can identify whether response time or throughput requirements can be fulfilled or whether indicated performance optimizations would be too costly. For reliability threats, missing fail-over capabilities, which would threaten required availability levels, can be identified. For costs, overly high resource requirements (and implied operation costs) to fulfill, for example, a certain scalability can be estimated using Palladio.

Digression 9.1
Time and Cost Estimation
Time and cost estimation for software development is easier if the costs of smaller single components are estimated separately, in contrast to estimating the costs of software on the basis of the requirements (i.e., the not-decomposed system). Cost estimations based on software architectures can take software reuse and even information on the productivity of developers into account, as single components can already be assigned to developers or teams. In this sense, software architectures can serve as *staff assignments*. Further details can be found in Paulish (2001) and Rostami et al. (2015).

Several studies in the past decades have shown that early feedback on costs is particularly valuable because early changes of the software are most often several orders of magnitude cheaper than later changes in a software development project (Fagan 1976; Boehm 1984; Humphrey et al. 1991; Leffingwell 1997; Boehm and Turner 2004).

Implementation   The ability to generate prototypes and implementation stubs of the source code on the basis of an architectural model can speed up the initial development. Palladio can be used to generate the initial implementation, which is then refined in integrated development environments (IDEs) such as Eclipse. When using these forward engineering features, the codification of the architecture in Java is automatically generated by Palladio. Of course, as information of the execution is (intentionally) omitted in architectural diagrams, stubs of provided services have to be filled with source code. This automated generation has three benefits: First, it is convenient for developers, as they do not need to manually create code stubs. Second, and even more important from a quality perspective, it ensures consistency with the architectural models and hence also the results of the quality predictions based on these architectural models. Third, it ensures that architectural concepts are consistently mapped to code structures (e.g., how composed components are mapped to flat middleware component models such as EJB). This supports understandability of the code, for example, in software evolution.

Integration activities are part of the implementation. Palladio can be used to estimate the effects of integrating components with respect to unwanted side effects on quality properties. For example, a well-running system is integrated with a new component that puts load on the existing system. The potential side effect of a slowing down overall application can be foreseen by Palladio using its prediction capabilities.

Testing and Validation   During testing and validation, Palladio can help to discover unwanted deviations between the as-is state of the implementation and predictions based on the architectural design. This can reveal unknown waste of resources, unknown bottlenecks, or contention effects. Besides, it points to broken assumptions of properties for the implementation of an architecture.

In doing so, Palladio provides an implicit comparison of the as-is architecture with the intended architecture. Both the static architecture (e.g., components are present in an as-is architecture but not in the intended architecture) and system behavior (e.g., response times of 1 second are expected with 10% CPU utilization, but CPU load is almost 80% due to unexpected resource consumption) can be compared.

If deviations between the as-is state of the implementation and predictions are discovered, architects need to decide how to handle these discrepancies. As one option, they may decide to try to adjust the implementation to conform to the indented architecture (e.g., by removing a performance flaw from the implementation). As another option, they may update the intended architectural models so that they better reflect the as-is architecture of the implementation and redo predictions to see whether all requirements are still met. Possibly, they may also combine these two options.

Performance prototypes (such as ProtoCom described in section 8.3.4) are another means to use during testing and validation. Performance prototypes behave like real software systems with respect to performance properties but do not actually implement the full business logic. If allocated to an execution environment, they put real load onto resources such as the CPU, hard disk, and network. Using a performance prototype, software architects can test the performance behavior of a full system without fully implementing it. Performance prototypes are thus able to reveal, for example, bottlenecks in the execution environment. During testing, they assist in validating assumptions on the interaction between execution environment and software system.

Maintenance and Evolution During maintenance and evolution, Palladio helps software architects to optimize the quality of service and resource efficiency. The modeled architecture can be used in comparison with the implemented architecture. Performance regressions (i.e., trending of performance over time) on either side point to deficits in the model or the implementation, which become visible over time.

Another direction for the application of Palladio are system optimizations after initially shipping a version. Because user expectations change over time (e.g., users expect better responsiveness or lower cost), systems have to adapt to stay useful. This is stated by the first of Lehman's laws (Lehman 1979–1980; Lehman and Ramil 2001).

For example, users may initially be satisfied with the response-time behavior of the Media Store, as its responsiveness is comparable to that of other systems that the clients are using, such as search engines, e-mail clients, and mobile phones. If the responsiveness of other systems improves over the months and years, but the Media Store remains unchanged, the users may eventually perceive the Media Store responsiveness as unsatisfactory.

When targeting response-time improvements, analyses with Palladio help to understand where the potential for improvement exists in a software architecture. The same applies to reliability (e.g., where to add extra hardware and fail-over behavior to increase system availability) and cost (e.g., cost pressure could force the architect to save hardware or move to more modern and more efficient hardware, i.e., to improve resource efficiency).

Besides enabling quality predictions, Palladio captures the static architecture of a system. In software evolution, such static architectures can serve as high-level guides (e.g., in which

---

Digression 9.2
Lehman's Law of Software Evolution: "Continuing Change"
"[A system] must be continually adapted or it becomes progressively less satisfactory in use" (Lehman and Ramil 2001).

component to place new functionality or understanding dependencies) or as a reference architecture (i.e., what a system should look like). Thus, Palladio helps to avoid architectural drifts due to its explicit notion of the software architecture and support dependency analysis among components. In evolution scenarios, the static architecture can be reverse engineered (see section 11.3).

Central Role of Software Architecture   These purposes of software architecture show that architectural engineering plays a central role in software development. Software architecture is influenced by various factors:

Requirements: Obviously, the architecture should be a step forward toward the realization of requirements. Note that for many systems, the architecture is the main means to realize nonfunctional requirements, such as performance, reliability, or maintainability. In principle, functional requirements are much less a driver for architectural decisions, as any functional requirement could be realized by any architecture, even if only has one single big component.

Make/buy/reuse decisions: If the reuse of own or bought components is of high concern, then the interfaces of preexisting components need to be considered early in architectural design to avoid later adaptation costs.

Conway's law: The third influence factor may sound irritating but is backed up by such anecdotal evidence that it received a name, like a physical law. Although it is a more general statement on design, it also holds for software architectures: size, complexity, and number of components will resemble the team structure (or the structure of several teams), as well as their experience. Decisions on how functionality is mapped to components are made not only on the basis of technical concerns, but also according to the competence of teams or team members and the communication structure of the project. A star topology in a team (main communication to and from a leader) will most likely result in a similar software architecture.

Given these influence factors, various developer roles using various architectural views (see chapter 3) are involved in the creation of architectural models. Very often, the role of the software architect is challenging, as it needs to reconcile concerns from stakeholders, such as clients, users, managers, external experts, and so forth. Even beyond the role of the architect, however, other roles are involved in the documentation of software architectures.

Digression 9.3
Conway's Law
"Organizations which design systems ... are constrained to produce designs which are copies of the communication structures of these organizations" (Conway 1968).

9.2   A Quality-Aware, Component-Based Development Process

Early quality analysis can be included in any software engineering process that has architectural planning activities. As a reference process for applying Palladio, we describe a quality-aware, component-based development process in this section. It is based on the component-based software architecture process introduced by Cheesman and Daniels (2000), which is itself based on the Unified Process (Kruchten 2003). The process is focused on development rather than concurrent management activities, such as scheduling human resources or defining milestones. This chapter gives hints on how to include quality analysis into this process, which combines both of the development directions top-down (starting from requirements) and bottom-up (starting from existing components).

The perhaps most specific property of component-based software engineering is the strict separation of component development (development of components) and system development (development with components). These two activities are dedicated to the special developer roles *component developer* and *software architect*. The question of how these two activities relate depends strongly on project characteristics, such as intended reuse of existing code, planned reusability for the future, application domain, and others.

But even more developer roles participate in quality modeling and analyses, as the software architects and component developers do not have all necessary information by themselves. For the additional information, it is necessary to clearly define where the data come from and to name the developers responsible for data integration. For all the involved roles, the software architecture is a central source of necessary information.

In the following, the different developer roles are explained before both component development and system development are explained. For the latter, the system development process is described, and the two most relevant workflows for the purpose of this book, namely specification and quality analysis, are further detailed. In the description of the specification workflow, the interface specification is emphasized, and several best practices or interface specifications are presented.

9.2.1   Developer Roles

In the following, the developer roles in the Palladio development process will be discussed.

The *software architect* drives the design of the software architecture. Here, the architecture is modeled structurally (i.e., as an assembly of components; see section 3.3). All information provided by the other roles is integrated by the software architect, who also has to estimate missing values. For example, the software architect might have to specify a parameter distribution for external services that influence the performance or might have to estimate the resource demand of components that have been provided without extra-functional specifications. Potentially, a dedicated communication with stakeholders is required for such estimations. In addition to driving the development process, architects collect and integrate all information to perform quality analysis and assemble the complete system from its parts.

One of the information sources for software architects is the *domain experts*, who are involved in the requirements analysis, as they have special knowledge of the business domain. They are also familiar with the users' work habits and, thus, are responsible for describing the user behavior (see section 5.4). Domain experts are responsible for specifying all information closely related to the users of the system. This includes specifying workloads with user arrival rates or user populations and think times. In some cases, these values are already part of the requirement documents. If method parameter values have an influence on the quality properties of the system, the domain experts may assist the software architect in characterizing these values.

On a more technical side, the *component developers* are responsible for the specification and implementation of components. They develop components for a market as well as on request. Component developers specify the performance or reliability of their components in a highly parameterized manner, as they do not have knowledge of where the components will be deployed. Parameterized performance descriptions, such as the service effect specification in Palladio (see section 3.4.1), enable independent third-party performance analysis (see section 5.3). First, they need to characterize the execution demands on the resources of the system in a platform independent way; for example, by specifying the number of processor or byte-code instructions their services execute (see section 6.3). Second, component developers have to specify how provided services call required services (see section 3.4). On the basis of this specification, the software architect is able to follow the control flow through the architecture. The component developer can obtain such information by code analysis or by evaluating the design documents of the components. For performance analysis, transition probabilities and the number of loop iterations are required for calls from provided to required services. These values cannot be fully determined by the component developer, in case they are not fixed in the source code. Influences on these values may come from external sources; for example, from the parameter values the service is called with or the results of external services. If such an influence exists, the component developer has to state this dependency in the component specification explicitly, so that the software architect can specify probability distributions for parameter values or exploit the postconditions of required services for this service (see section 5.4).

The *system deployer* will use the component specification and values provided by component developers to parameterize them for the environment under analysis. Software architects may design architectures that can be deployed in various differing resource environments (i.e., which are reusable in different deployment contexts). Sometimes, the actual deployment context is not determined until the late development stages, especially if the software is developed for general markets. System deployers are responsible for specifying concrete execution environments with resources and connections (see section 3.5). They also allocate components to resources. During the deployment stage of the development process, they are responsible for the installation, configuration, and start-up of the application. The system deployer provides information about the resources of the system (e.g., hardware-related such as processing devices or software-related such as thread pools). Further attributes are scheduling policies, processing rates, or context switch times and must be specified by the system deployer. The system deployer is also responsible for adapting the platform-independent resource demand specifications of the component developer to the properties of the system under analysis.

Finally, modeling and predicting each quality attribute has its specific challenges. For example, when making performance predictions, one should be aware of the different assumptions of the analysis techniques and choose the right one (as discussed in chapter 8). Similarly, when estimating reliability data using reliability growth models (as described in section 6.4), the assumptions and limitations of the growth models have to be taken into account. Therefore, system architects, domain experts, component developers, and system deployers might require support by experts for a given quality attribute. In the Palladio process, this is reflected by the special role of the *quality analyst* (e.g., performance analyst, reliability analyst, or security analyst), who provides expert knowledge to the stakeholders in the process and supports them by extraction of quality-relevant information. Quality analysts collect and integrate information from the other roles, provide support by extraction of quality information from the requirements (e.g., maximum response times for use cases), and perform quality analyses by using mathematical models or simulation. Furthermore, quality analysts estimate missing values that are not provided by the other roles. For example, in the case of an incomplete component specification, the resource demand of this component has to be estimated. Finally, the most important task quality analysts have is to assist the software architects to interpret the results of the quality analyses. The correct interpretation of the results of the analysis is crucial to answer design questions and to extract the consequences these have for the software architecture (as discussed in chapter 7).

9.2.2 Development of Components

The development of a software component actually differs only slightly from development of modules: In modules, interfaces are already fixed and the big task of translating customer requirements into developer requirements has usually already been completed in the system development process. If this is not the case, the component developer needs to make assumptions about meaningful properties of a component.

Besides, all established processes from software engineering (briefly discussed in section 9.3), ranging from agile methods to waterfall models, can be used to develop components.

It is specific to component-based development that any release of the component is put into a component repository. When doing so, component developers can refer to interfaces that already exist in the repository or define new interfaces. If additional interfaces need to be added to the repository, the component developer either defines such interfaces and adds them to the repository or needs to communicate with the software architect, who then defines and adds the interfaces. The latter case needs an already established relation between component developer and software architect (e.g., through a contractor relation). For this interaction between software architect and component developer, the Palladio component type hierarchy (see section 3.3.3) can be used. (A discussion of the information needed to be documented in the interfaces is given in digression 3.4.)

Besides general software engineering knowledge of best practices, the component developer needs to understand the impact of the granularity of the component. Experience shows that large-grained components (e.g., WebGUI component in the Media Store example of chapter 2) tend to be more oriented toward the implementation of specific user functionality. Hence, in comparison to fine-grained components (e.g., ReEncoder component in the Media Store example of chapter 2), their reuse is usually restricted by a specific application domain.

9.2.3   Development with Components

The process for the system development (development with components) is illustrated in figure 9.1. Each box represents a workflow. The thick arrows between boxes represent a change of activity, while the thin arrows characterize the flow of artifacts between the workflows. The workflows do not have to be traversed linearly (i.e., no waterfall model). Backward steps into former workflows are allowed. The model also allows an incremental or iterative development based on prototypes.

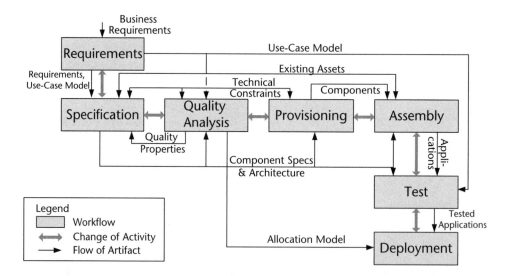

Figure 9.1
Component-based development process model with quality analysis. Adapted from Koziolek and Happe (2006) and Cheesman and Daniels (2000).

Requirements: The business requirements coming from customers are formalized and analyzed during this workflow. It produces the system requirements and a use-case model. The use-case model describes the interaction between users (or other external actors) and the system. It establishes the system boundaries and a set of use cases that define the functional requirements. The system requirements include quality requirements for the use cases, and overall quality requirements are elicited and specified in this workflow as well.

Specification: Requirements and the use-case model are input from the requirements workflow to this workflow. Additionally, technical constraints, which might have been revealed during provisioning, and quality properties from already performed quality analyses can be input to the specification workflow after initial iterations of the process model. During specification, the component-based software architecture is designed. Components and their interaction are identified and specified. The software architect usually interacts with component developers during this workflow.

Quality analysis: Component specifications, the architecture, and use-case models are input to the quality analysis workflow. During this workflow, deployers provide models of the resource environment of the architecture, which contain specifications of extra-functional properties. The domain expert takes the use-case models, refines them, and adds quality-relevant information, thereby creating a Palladio Component Model (PCM) usage model. Finally, the software architect combines all of the models, estimates missing values, checks the validity of the models, feeds them into quality analysis tools, and interprets the quality analysis results, which is targeted at supporting the design decisions of the software architect. Outputs of the quality analysis are the predicted quality properties, which can be used during specification to adjust the architecture, and allocation models that can be used during deployment.

Provisioning: Compared to classical development processes, the provisioning workflow resembles the classical implementation workflow; however, one of the assets of component-based development is reuse (i.e., the incorporation of components developed by third parties). During the provisioning workflow, "make-or-buy" decisions are made for individual components. Components that cannot be purchased from third parties have to be implemented according to the specifications from the corresponding workflow. Consequently, the provisioning workflow receives the component specifications and architecture as well as technical constraints as inputs. The outputs of this workflow are implemented software components.

Assembly: Components from the provisioning workflow are used in the assembly workflow. Additionally, this workflow builds up on the component architecture. The component implementations are assembled according to the assembly model during this workflow. This might involve configuring them for specific component containers or frameworks. Furthermore, for integrating legacy components, it might be necessary to write adapters to bridge unfitting interfaces. The assembled components and the complete application code are the outputs of this workflow.

Test: The complete component-based application is tested according to the use-case models in this workflow in a test environment. Testing must check not only functional properties but also quality properties. Thus, it also includes measuring the actual quality properties of the application and their comparison with the results of analysis. This is needed, as simulation and analysis models can only find a subset of all quality issues. Only testing can demonstrate that the quality requirements can be met by the final system. To ensure a constant quality, monitoring might be applied during the system's lifetime. This allows reaction to quality degradation caused by a change of external influences, such as user behavior. Once the functional properties have been tested and the quality properties are satisfiable in the test environment, the application is ready for deployment in the actual customer environment.

Deployment: During deployment, the tested application is installed in its actual customer environment. The term *deployment* is also used to denote the process of putting components into component containers, but here the term refers to a broader task. Besides the installation, it might be necessary to adopt the resource environment at the customer's facilities or to instruct future users of the system. For the mapping of components to hardware resources, the allocation model from the quality analysis workflow can be used.

9.2.4 Specification Workflow

In the specification workflow, the software architecture is defined: this means the definition of interfaces and the assembly of components (i.e., the dependencies between interfaces). This can happen either top-down (definition of the architecture and then searching for or commissioning components to realize the interfaces defined before) or bottom-up (assembling existing components taken from component repositories). These pure processes are followed rarely in practice. Usually, a mix between top-down and bottom-up is used.

The main difference between a top-down approach and a bottom-up approach lies in the point of time at which interfaces are defined and which role is concerned with this.

The tasks belonging to specification workflow are component identification from the repository, followed by component interaction and component specification, as already described by Cheesman and Daniels (2000). In the component identification task, an initial set of business components and interfaces is identified to fulfill the requirements. Architectural styles as discussed in section 4.1 and section 4.3 are selected in this task as well. In the component interaction task, the software architect designs how the components interact to realize the required operations at the system boundary. From these interactions, more detail about the interfaces is derived, such as which operations they have. Architectural patterns as discussed in section 4.1 and section 4.4 are often applied in this task. Finally, component specification is the detailed definition of the interfaces, including all operations and parameters but also contracts and protocols.

In case the system is built on existing components (e.g., from a repository), the specification of these components has an impact on the component identification and further specification, as the software architect can reuse existing interfaces and existing specifications by the component developer. Vice versa, newly specified components by the software architect are input for the component developers, who design and implement these new components.

As the specification of interfaces is crucial in this workflow, the next subsection provides more information on interface specification and the second subsection lists best practices for interface design. Then, this discussion of the specification workflow ends with a subsection on issues when reusing components.

Interface Specification   Interface specification is influenced by

1. the functionality assigned to the component in terms of provided methods;
2. assembly connections to other components (i.e., the needed control and data flow);
3. assumptions on externally available services (or to be realized functionality); and
4. the potential distribution of components to resources.

Any interface defined by the software architect is defined during system development, and any interface defined by the component developer is defined during component development. In the mixed approach, however, some interfaces are defined by the software architect and some by the component developer.

Ideally, these roles do not need to interact for interface definition. In practice, if only one role is concerned with interface design, the interface tends to be biased: if only the software architect (as user of the interface) is involved in the design of the interface, the interface might be hard to implement; partially redundant functionality might be included; artificial dependencies might be introduced through missing method parameters, omitted for reasons of convenience for the user; and project-specific names might be used for methods and parameters. On the contrary, if the component developer as implementer of the interface is solely concerned with its definition, the interface can be potentially hard to use: too many responsibilities are delegated to the caller of methods of the interface, and the interfaces are too generic. In particular, the latter is interesting: reusability does not necessarily imply usability for a specific context.

Therefore, an interaction between software architect and component developer during interface definition is desirable if the project setting allows it. Principally, it would only be hard to realize in a strict bottom-up approach.

Best Practices for Interface Specification   As discussed above, interface definition can be done through the component developer or the software architect. This dedicated subsection lists some collected design guidelines as best practices for this crucial task.

```
@Remote

public interface IMediaManager extends Serializable {

    public long upload(AudioFile file) throws FailedUploadException, NamingException,
    RemoteException;

    public int getFileFrom(byte[] file, InetAddress address, int port);

    public List<AudioFileInfo> getFileList() throws NamingException;

    public byte[] download(List<Long> requestedAudioIDs, List<Integer> bitrates, String
    downloaderLogin) throws FailedDownloadException, NamingException;

}
```

Listing 9.1
Media manager interface of the Media Store example.

Consistent Abstraction Levels   Methods in an interface should be all at a similar level of abstraction. This means, among other aspects, technical methods should not be mixed with user-specific methods. For example, consider the media manager interface from the Media Store example in listing 9.1.

In this case, the getFileFrom method operates at a different level of technical abstraction with its parameters byte[] file and its low-level adressing via InetAddress address, int port. The remaining methods are less technical and more user-centric. In this case, the extraction of the getFileFrom method in a separate interface would be a cleaner design.

Naming Conventions   Various general or company-specific naming conventions exist. These conventions offer a scheme for method names that makes them easier to understand and to memorize. A specific aspect of such naming conventions is established names for opposite methods, such as get/set, read/write, upload/download, lock/unlock, and so forth (McConnell 2004, p. 172). Beyond such conventions, it is important to link programming entities to concepts of the application domain. Hence, names like doComputation are less informative than calculateOverallFileLength. As a specific consequence of this, names with numbers as a differentiation should be avoided completely, such as uploadFile and uploadFile2. Similarly, one character difference between identifiers should be avoided, as there is a chance that a typo results in a legal identifier and hence is not detected during compilation.

Design for Maintainability   The oldest rule of interface design stems from the defining idea of a model and an interface: Design an interface as an abstraction of the module's code, so that a design decision that is likely to change does not affect the users of the interface in case of its change (Parnas 1972a).

Design for Reuse   The interface is most often intended for reuse, once the effort is made to define an interface instead of using concrete or even abstract classes. This should be reflected in the ease of reusing the interface in different contexts. This has basically two implications to interface design: First, choose general types for method parameters and return types where possible. For example, ArrayList<AudioFileInfo> getFileList() is an unnecessary restriction for the user, but also for the implementer. The more general List<AudioFileInfo> getFileList() leaves the decision how to store the results to the user of the method. Second, try to avoid dependencies in interfaces to specific other frameworks, libraries, or middleware products, if this is possible. As in our example above, we restrict ourselves to standard Java types and JDK classes and interfaces.

Optimized for Distribution   In principle, deployment decisions should not influence interface design; however, whether methods are called locally or remotely can have a severe impact on the overall performance. In the case that remote calls are likely, the developer may offer additional methods that are particularly suitable for remote invocation. Such methods reflect the costs of remote invocations through three techniques:

1. *Reduction of number of method calls:* Instead of calling the same method many times (e.g., in a loop) or the same sequence of several methods many times, methods that are optimized for remote invocation try to offer the same semantics in a single call. Imagine that instead of using the method getFileList(), the developer would have to iterate for each file with calls of a next() iterator method. Obviously, the result (a list of files) would be the same, but with the iterator solution, there would not be one method call, but as many as there are files in the list.

2. *Reduction of costs of method calls:* Try to pass only parameters that are really needed for the operation, and try to locally filter large data sets before invocation. Usually, this only affects the method signature, if the filtering was originally foreseen at the remote side and filter criteria were passed as a parameter.

3. *Latency hiding:* In case remote method calls cannot be avoided and their costs cannot be reduced, the developer could exploit the implicit potential parallelism of remote method invocations through splitting a method into two methods: a very fast (and thus nearly non-blocking) part initiating a costly operation at the remote side, and a blocking part collecting the results.

Hence, the method byte[] download(List<Long> requestedAudioIDs, List<Integer> bitrates, String downloaderLogin) would be split into DownloadHandle downloadInit-(List<Long> requestedAudioIDs, List<Integer> bitrates, String downloaderLogin) and byte[] downloadFinalize(DownloadHandle handle). Here, the downloadInit method just initiates the computation at the server side (e.g., in a thread) and returns to the calling client as fast as possible, leaving the work in a concurrently running job at the server side. The returned handle can then be used in the second call (i.e., downloadFinalize) to identify the corresponding job on the server side. The handle is needed to establish the correspondence between all related init and finalize calls, as several init methods could be called without the corresponding finalize methods in between. It is important that other work can be done on the client side (the caller side) between the init method invocation and the finalize method invocation. Although there are now two method calls instead of one (a clear contradiction to the first guideline of this list), the overall performance improves. Note that exceptions of the original method are usually attached to the finalize method. The init method usually only has a remote method invocation failed exception, as none of the original work is actually done in this invocation.

Specification with Reuse   When reusing components in a bottom-up or mixed process, the tasks described above for the top-down process are required in a similar way, always taking existing components and interfaces into account. Additionally, the following activities might be required.

Component Composition   A specific way to implement a component is to compose it from other components. As components are black-box entities (i.e., their internals do not need to be understood for using them), it is of no concern for the component user whether a component is implemented through, for example, an object-oriented code or by composing a component from more basic ones.

Component Adaptation   If a software component is intended for reuse, but one or several of its interfaces do not fit to the assembly context of the component, the interface(s) need to be adapted. According to the black-box nature of a software component, the adaptation mechanism should not rely on manual work of adapting code inside of the component. In practice, components are adapted mostly with adapters (i.e., an additional component that fits to the interfaces of the component and to the interfaces of the assembly context). Internally, the adapter bridges the mismatch between the interfaces of the component and its assembly context. In specific cases, the code for the adapter can be generated automatically; in the general case, however, a semantic understanding of the interfaces is needed, which requires human programming activities.

Note that in Palladio, there are two ways of component composition; namely, the creation of a composite component and the creation of a system (as discussed in section 3.3).

A *composite component* is an implementation technique for components where already defined componnts are used to define a new one. Through the black-box nature of components, a component deployment instance can only be deployed as one unit, and consequently only to one resource. This also holds for composite components. There are situations, however, where inner components should be deployed to different resources (e.g., the developer would like to create a pipeline of different servers, with each server having one inner

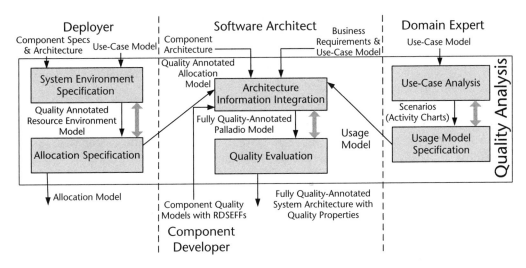

Figure 9.2
Quality analysis workflow in the quality-aware component development process with Palladio.

component deployed for performance reasons). With a composite component, this is not feasible, as it would violate the black-box nature.

To allow the exploitation of the inner assembly of a composite component, Palladio features the concept of a *system*. A system is a way to bundle components, mainly to ease future reuse, without hiding their composition. Systems again can be composed, resulting in systems with subsystems.

9.2.5 Quality Analysis Workflow
During quality analysis, the software architecture is refined with information about the deployment context, the usage model, and the internal structure of components.

Quality Analysis Workflow   Figure 9.2 shows the activities of this workflow.

The system deployer starts with the resource environment specification based on the software architecture and use-case models. Given this information, the required hardware resources and their interconnections are derived. As a result, this workflow yields a *resource environment* model that describes only the resource environment without allocated components. The system deployer can also create a description of existing hardware resources. Moreover, a set of representative resource environments can be designed if the deployment context is still unknown. During the allocation, the system deployer specifies the mapping of components to resources. The resulting *allocation* model is annotated with a detailed quality attribute specification of the deployment environment. These specifications provide input parameters for the quality analysis models used later. The resulting fully annotated allocation model, as described in section 3.5, is passed to the software architect.

The domain expert refines the use-case models from the requirements during the use-case analysis. A description of the scenarios for the users is created on the basis of an external view of the current software architecture. The scenarios describe how users interact with the system and what dependencies exist in the process. For example, activity charts can be used to describe such scenarios. The scenario descriptions are input to the *usage model* specification, as described in section 5.4. The domain expert annotates the specification with, for example, branching probabilities, expected size of different user groups, expected workload, and user think times.

As described above, the component developers provide a model of their component (as described in section 3.3.1) with quality annotations in the form of resource demanding service effect specifications (RDSEFFs; as described in section 5.3).

As the central role in the quality analysis workflow, the software architect integrates the quality-relevant information, performs the evaluation, and delivers the feedback to all involved parties.

During architecture information integration, the software architect checks whether the models provided by the component developers, system deployers, and domain experts as well as his or her own component assembly model (as described in section 3.3.2) are complete. If values are missing, he or she estimates them or communicates with the responsible role. The result of this activity is an overall quality-annotated model of the system, which can be transformed into a quality analysis model (as described in chapter 8).

The quality evaluation then either yields an analytical solution or the results of a simulation. Quality evaluation aims, for example, at testing the scalability of the architecture, at identifying bottlenecks, or at comparing design alternatives (as described in chapter 7). If the results show that the quality requirements cannot be fulfilled with the current architecture, the software architect has to modify the specifications or renegotiate the requirements.

9.2.6 Interactions when Modeling Quality

When modeling quality-related information, there is interaction among developer roles. In a scenario of the performance analysis, a component model captures the behavior of one component service including calls to required services and abstractions of their internal executions. This information, particularly the mapping from provided to required interfaces, has to be provided by the component developer, because it is a part of the inner structure of the component. Three ways are possible to determine this information:

1. A static code analysis may be performed on the existing component implementation to yield the mapping from provided to required services.

2. Design documents (e.g., sequence or activity diagrams) of the component itself can be utilized for this purpose. Possibly, XML Metadata Interchange (XMI) files of existing diagrams that were created using the Unified Modeling Language (UML) can be evaluated automatically to retrieve the information.

3. The component developers can specify this information manually, simply because they know the inner structure of the component.

As the environment in which the component will be used is unknown to component developers, they have to provide the demand for the internal actions of the component in an abstract, environment-independent way. For example, they can specify the number of byte-code or processor instructions or the number of bytes used by storage devices. The dependencies of these values to input parameter values of the component have to be made explicit by the component developer. With the abstract specification, the system deployer has to calculate the resulting demand for the actual environment of the component. The software architect has to provide information about influencing parameter values. If no abstract specification is given by the component developer, the system deployer and software architect have to estimate the values.

The probabilities of taking different branches in the control flow between components or the number of loop iterations in cycles of the intercomponent control flow are influenced by several factors, leading to the fact that component developer, software architect, and system deployer have to interact by defining these values:

Code: The number of loop iterations may be fixed in the source code; for example, by specifying a constant breaking condition in the head of a for-loop or while-loop. In this case, the number of loop iterations can be determined via a static code analysis by the component developer.

Parameter values: Characterization of parameter values is the responsibility of the domain experts (for parameters of services provided to users) and the component developer (for parameters of calls to required services). For example, influences on transition probabilities and loop iteration numbers by a service's input parameters can be considered common. The number of loop iterations may depend on the number of elements in an array that are passed to the service as an input parameter. If such an influence exists, the component developer has to make this explicit in the specification; however, the component developer cannot know which parameters are passed to component services, because he or she does not know in which context the component will be used. Thus, information about the parameter values has to be provided by domain experts. They have to provide expected distributions of the input parameter values, based, for example, on the requirements documents. The distribution of parameter values only has to be modeled if it influences the performance or control flow propagation. Parameters may be characterized not only by their values but also by their size or type. Often, this information is already sufficient to derive transition probabilities or loop iteration number, so the value distribution does not have to be specified.

Internal state: Parameter values may also influence the control and data flow propagation indirectly by altering the internal state of a component. During later executions of the component services, these values may impact the behavior of the component. Other sources, such as configuration files or system properties, may also influence the internal state of a component. The dependencies have to be made explicit by the component developer and then evaluated by the software architect.

Results of external services: The Boolean expressions responsible for altering the intercomponent control flow in an if-clause or for-/while-loop may be calculated by an external service. This case involves the semantic of that external service. The postconditions of external services specified in service contracts may be used to derive the values in this case. The component developer has to explicitly state the dependency between results of required services and changes in the control flow, so that the software architect can retrieve the information from the specification of the required services.

Availability of external services: In some cases, components may not be available at a given point during run time, resulting in a redirect of the control flow to other components. The availability specifications of those components influence the transition probabilities in this case. The dependency on these values has to be given by the component developer, while the values themselves will be determined by the software architect by evaluating the component specifications. A component may call different required services with the same functionality, depending on their availability at a given point in time. For example, in Java such a call might be embedded in a try/catch block, where the exception handling would try to call another, functional equivalent service. In this case, the transition probability in the service effect specification for the external service would be the availability of that service, which is the probability of being able to access a service at a given point in time. Therefore, this value also depends on the deployment environment of the external service and has to be specified either by the system deployer or by the component developer of that component, who specify the availability of each provided service of the component. In any case, the component developer has to make explicit the dependency of the transition probability in the service effect specification on the availability of external services.

Deployment environment: For the deployment environment, processing resources can be specified. These values and additional attributes, such as a scheduling policy, have to be provided by the system deployer prior to the actual deployment to make early performance predictions possible.

This section has presented the ideal use of Palladio in a component-based development process. In section 9.3, we discuss the application of Palladio to other types of development processes.

9.3   Application in Development Processes

Although Palladio cannot deny its origins in component-based development approaches, it has evolved and matured significantly in recent years and, as various case studies (see part V) have demonstrated, can be used on legacy (i.e., non-component-based) systems for simulation purposes as well. Hence, the integration of Palladio modeling and simulation techniques has become a serious possibility even for today's "mainstream" software development projects, which will be discussed in more detail in this section. After illustrating how the application of Palladio modeling and simulation techniques fits seamlessly into a classic waterfall-style software development approach, in this section we will also discuss how Palladio can be integrated into an agile variant of the Unified Process as it has been popularized over the past decade through the influential books on so-called agile modeling; for example, by Larman (2005) and Ambler (2002).

Moreover, we will illustrate that a potentially perceived incompatibility with agile values and practices is only superficial so that the use of Palladio can be beneficial even within purely agile development processes.

For this discussion, we distinguish three characteristics of development processes (Larman 2005). Figure 9.3 shows an example process that has all three characteristics.

Iterative: In iterative processes, the development is organized into a series of repeated cycles. The outcome is used for feedback (be it a tested, integrated, and executable partial system or prototype). Figure 9.3 shows three iterations.

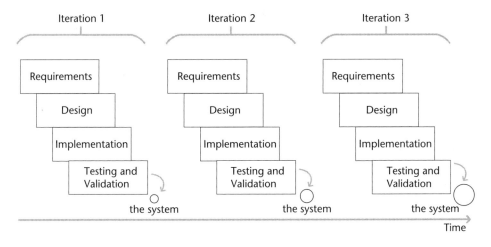

Figure 9.3
An iterative, incremental, and evolutionary development process. Adapted from Larman (2005).

Incremental: In incremental processes, the system grows incrementally over time. In figure 9.3, the system (visualized as a circle) grows after each increment.

Evolutionary: In evolutionary processes, feedback and adaptation evolve the requirements and design as well. Thus, in evolutionary processes, all steps of the waterfall are repeated in different iterations. Figure 9.3 shows how requirements and design are revisited in each of the three iterations. The requirements do not have to be changed in every iteration for the process to be evolutionary, but it has to be possible if required.

To give some examples, a development process in which a series of throwaway prototypes are built in several iterations before the final system is built is iterative, but it is not incremental and not evolutionary. Another example is a project where the requirements are defined upfront (e.g., in a contract), and then the system is built in a series of iterations, where an executable system is delivered after each iteration. Such an example is an iterative and incremental process, but it is not evolutionary. Finally, in the agile variant of the Unified Process mentioned earlier, the requirements and design are revisited in each development iteration, and the system grows in increments. Thus, the agile variant of the Unified Process (as explained below) is iterative, incremental, and evolutionary.

9.3.1   Sequential Process Models

Pure waterfall-like software development projects are losing ground in practice today for good reasons: practical experience gained over a couple of decades has shown that software requirements are often changing faster than they can be implemented, and hence software development is too unpredictable for potentially years-long planning. But the simple underlying structure of the waterfall model still forms an ideal setting that can be used to illustrate how the Palladio simulation approach can best be integrated with common software engineering activities and to show its key benefits. Moreover, under the—certainly somewhat simplifying—assumption that iterative and evolutionary (I&E) development processes are "merely" a sequence of "mini-waterfalls" (as visualized in figure 9.3 where the system incrementally grows over time), it also offers a first orientation how to embed the PCM into common I&E development approaches.

The traditional waterfall model usually prescribes software development activities in a couple of separate phases ranging from project planning over requirements elicitation, to architecture and package design, to implementation and testing, as well as the final acceptance and deployment of the system.

As implied by a waterfall, a new phase can only be started when the immediately previous phase has been successfully completed. The enormous risks and challenges arising in this approach from the need to plan for all possibilities of a software project running perhaps a couple of years should be obvious and has led to the application of the more agile process models to be addressed later.

In contrast to the waterfall metaphor, at least returning to earlier phases to resolve problems and errors in earlier phases is foreseen in the waterfall model but is nevertheless supposed to remain the exception, as uncovering and fixing problems in a later phase often implies that all previous phases also need to be revised. Some sorts of problems, such as misunderstood functional as well as not reachable, nonfunctional requirements may even put the whole project at risk. In a waterfall context, performance testing can obviously be carried out only rather late in the process, long after the core architecture has been thought out and implemented. Now imagine that the architecture turns out as unsuitable for the given hardware resources so that a totally new backbone for the system is needed.

Avoiding such situations was one of the main motivations to develop the Palladio tool suite, and various points where the PCM could be hooked into the general software development phases are apparent at a first glance: first and foremost, the Palladio modeling environment can be used during architectural and component design as a computer-aided software engineering (CASE) tool that supports the software architect in carving out the coarse-grained structure of the system under development. Because the Palladio tool suite provides various mechanisms to generate stubs out of the component models created with it, it is also able to simplify the transition to the coding phase of a project.

Moreover, the benefits of Palladio's simulation capabilities are also most obvious in the context of a waterfall-based process: because implementation is deferred until rather late in the process (e.g., for a medium-length project of about 2 years, coding might only start after around 10 months [Boehm 1984]), checking whether quality requirements are fulfilled by the implementation of the system can obviously happen only even later. Being able to simulate the performance properties of a system under development early (i.e., during architectural design after a few months) will greatly mitigate the risk of building a system that is not able to satisfy its service-level agreements after installation at a customer's site. There is, however, a price to pay, not only that the core architecture of the system needs to be well thought out (which of course might turn out as a benefit as well), but in order to be able to perform a proper simulation of the system under development, a usage profile is required, which will cause additional effort in the requirements analysis phase. Again, this aspect can even be seen as an advantage of the Palladio approach, because if performance is actually an issue, stakeholders can never be forced early enough to determine the constraints under which the system should operate.

Nevertheless, an early prediction of nonfunctional properties tends to be relatively imprecise, and hence the Palladio models should be continuously adjusted during the development process. Even assuming that a strict waterfall approach with little or no feedback into earlier phases can be implemented, the implementation will almost certainly deviate from its models. Moreover, experience has shown that it is very important to keep models in sync with code, as merely small changes to the code base may have a significant impact on performance. Although there is some support for reengineering models from a given (legacy) code base, automatically tracing changes in newly created code back to its blueprints is not supported by the PCM tool suite yet, so that this needs to be done manually where required.

Furthermore, whenever the code for an existing Palladio model is fully implemented and can be performance tested, it should be used to better calibrate Palladio's prediction capabilities for the concrete case. Hardware changes, for instance, can be simulated *in silicio* with relative ease, while it might require much more effort to set up a system on a distributed cluster of various machines, for example. In general, such "what-if" analyses are much better suited for execution in a simulation and allow almost as effective conclusions as real performance tests, provided that the model and the actual code in its development configuration are in sync.

9.3.2 Iterative Process Models

As hinted at earlier, from an abstract perspective iterative and evolutionary process models can be seen as a repeated stringing together of "mini-waterfalls" ideally exercising all waterfall activities. This is, of course, somewhat oversimplified. The famous illustration of the Unified Process (UP), as shown in figure 9.4, nicely illustrates that different phases of an iterative and evolutionary project still require the developers to focus on different activities. For instance, the UP suggests that in the beginning of a project, there is more effort invested in requirements and planning activities than in implementation and testing.

Nevertheless, this does not indicate that all requirements must be elicited before the coding can begin. In the first iteration, it is usually merely required that more requirements are documented than can be implemented, so that implementation can seamlessly

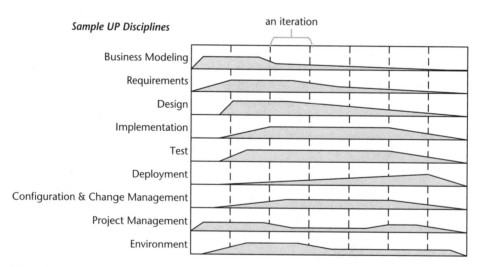

Figure 9.4

An example instantiation of the Unified Process. Adapted from Larman (2005).

continue in the second iteration. This habit of identifying more requirements than can be implemented is usually continued over a reasonable number of iterations, until most requirements (more than 90%) are understood and documented, so that better project planning becomes possible over time. It is only logical to prioritize all requirements according to business value and/or architectural impact in order to tackle the most important features first and be able to quickly deliver a usable piece of software to the user. The user, in turn, is then able to provide feedback for the delivered functionality quickly. It should be obvious that investing more effort in early requirements elicitation potentially makes better project planning possible but comes with the risk that changing requirements might render some of this effort useless later.

The industrial practice of the recent decade has basically yielded two strands of iterative approaches that will be more closely investigated for their compatibility with the PCM in the two following subsections. In the first subsection, PCM is discussed from the perspective of model-centric iterative processes, such as the Unified Process (UP), and its slightly more agile variants that are commonly dubbed "agile modeling" (Ambler 2002; Larman 2005). The second subsection then turns attention toward those process models that are usually called agile, lean, or lightweight and do not place so much emphasis on modeling activities and the upfront creation of an architecture. Common instances of such models are Scrum (Schwaber and Beedle 2002) or Extreme Programming (Beck 2005), for example.

Model-Centric Iterative Development Approaches Common model-centric development approaches have one decisive advantage that makes them more compatible with Palladio and simplifies embedding the PCM into them: as the name implies, they are model-centric. In other words, as described earlier, the Palladio tool suite can be used as a CASE tool that directly offers many of the required modeling capabilities. And again, an additional benefit in this context is the possibility to run simulations on the fundamental performance properties of the system soon after an architectural baseline has been modeled. Consequently, simulations and what-if analyses can be executed as another task under the responsibility of a software architect. Through the code generation capabilities of the Palladio tool suite, it is even possible to generate stubs for the main architectural elements, such as components and so forth, so that no time will be lost in comparison to classic CASE tools without simulation capabilities.

The relatively quick implementation of central aspects of a system within I&E approaches then also makes a calibration of models possible, using actual insights and measurements from the source. In other words, improving the precision of performance predictions can help software architects to identify potentially wrong assumptions and estimates early. Thus, it is recommended to repeat such calibrations through a comparison of simulation results and measured values at least before every intermediate release. On the basis of these findings, the simulation has an additional advantage: aspects that have to be implemented later can still be simulated in order to provide a prediction of the system's final quality of service after each milestone. As also hinted previously, a simulation always has the advantage that it is easier to systematically analyze system behavior for various workloads and configurations, so that it is not necessary to reconfigure an expensive testing environment for every different scenario.

Lightweight and Agile Iterative Development Approaches At a first glance, the utilization of the Palladio tool suite in an agile development process appears challenging. A purist might refuse the use of an architectural respectively model-centric approach, such as Palladio, in the context of an agile project right away. On the surface, Palladio's model-driven approach indeed seems largely incompatible with the rather code-centric practices of agile development approaches such as Scrum, Extreme Programming, and others. In this context, it is often circulated that a well-thought-out architecture in agile projects merely emerges through a series of refactoring steps (as, e.g., discussed by Atkinson and Hummel [2012]), which is certainly true to a certain extent. (This can be seen as one of the major weaknesses of agile approaches, as it leads to a significant refactoring overhead.) Refactoring, however, typically targets rather small design aspects instead of genuine architectural decisions that have an impact on the overall system. In other words, even agile projects need to spend some time on architecture selection early and typically implement a so-called architectural spike (Ambler 2002) to validate that the architecture is sustainably able to grow with the system.

The motivation is similar to waterfall projects: architectural decisions are typically hard to change and hence need to be done early and properly. Fowler's suggestion that these decisions can be removed by removing irreversibility from software projects (Fowler 2003) is certainly consequent, but unfortunately not yet practical in all aspects. Assume you decide to change from a JEE-based n-tier architecture to ASP.NET: this would basically mean to redo all programming efforts. If extensive (architectural) modeling is declined in such a context, as may be the case for smaller projects in well-known and understood domains, the use of Palladio would most likely impose superfluous overhead on the developers and create understandable reservations. Furthermore, such a scenario usually also implies that there is experience with various similar systems, so that a good understanding of their performance behavior should be available, and simulations may not be necessary to gain it.

Nevertheless, as discussed before, it may still be helpful to model (or to reverse engineer) software architectures with the PCM. Thus, it is possible to analyze system performance on different hardware configurations with less effort than needed for the actual performance testing of system increments. This is especially the case when predicting the whole system's behavior on the basis of a partial implementation. Furthermore, although agile development is often test-driven (i.e., it aims to create test cases before production code), there is no natural fit with those test cases required for performance testing; the former are usually too small to provoke the desired effects (although some insights can be won [Heger et al. 2013]), and hence dedicated performance testing normally requires a dedicated effort.

On the contrary, if the domain and typical architectural solutions for a system are not well understood, especially regarding quality of service, agile approaches recommend the use of throwaway prototypes in order to try out potential solutions and prepare the ground for an informed decision. Obviously, such prototyping often requires a significant amount of effort with only limited significance and reliability for quality of service aspects. Clearly, the PCM can help again as it is exactly optimized for this challenge and can provide relatively reliable simulation results in order to support architectural design decisions. In contrast to a throwaway prototype, a finally selected Palladio model even offers the derivation of stubs, from which the architectural spike can at least be partially generated. From the point of view of an agile methodology, Palladio simulations would simply become a backlog entry in their own right, similar to prototyping or refactoring activities, which the development team can prioritize and schedule at their convenience. It is unavoidable, though, that at least one of the team members be sufficiently trained and experienced to create the required models and to execute the simulations and interpret their impact on the architecture, which might still fit nicely with the idea of having specialized generalists in agile teams.

9.4   Questions and Exercises

9.4.1   Questions

9.1 *: What are the software development phases of a waterfall process in which Palladio supports engineering practices, and in which way does Palladio support these engineering activities?

9.2 **: Why must existing assets be considered during specification in the component-based development process model?

9.3 ***: Why are reusable components meaningful in iterative modeling activities?

9.4.2   Exercises

9.1 **: Instantiate a waterfall process model for a university course management system. Give example artifacts involved in each development phase and name domain-specifics that are important from the perspective of Palladio.

9.5   Further Reading

Clements et al. (2003) provide a thorough discussion of the role and use of software architecture documentation in software development. A Palladio model provides a documentation in software development and can provide many of the mentioned benefits.

The reference process for applying Palladio is based on the component-development process originally described by Cheesman and Daniels (2000). Their book explains how to use UML for requirements definition, component identification, component interaction, component specification, and provisioning and assembly. For details about the component-based software architecture process and a description of workflows and artifacts exchanged among them, we refer the interested reader to the mentioned book. Additionally, Szyperski et al. (2002) also provide insightful information about the relation of component-based development and both architecture and process.

A model-centric iterative development approach using object-oriented technology is described in Craig Larman's textbook (Larman 2005). As a starting point on more lightweight agile approaches, we recommend Beck (2005) on Extreme Programming. The combination of iterative and evolutionary development processes and component-based software development is discussed in detail by Atkinson and Hummel (2012). They discuss the opposite strengths and weaknesses of iterative and evolutionary development processes on the one hand and component-based software development on the other hand and make some suggestions for merging the principles.

For sound decision making in the software engineering process, it is important to understand the consequences of the decisions on the various development artifacts, such as architecture, code, test cases, builds, or deployments, when analyzing the impact of changes. The tool-supported approach Karlsruhe architectural maintainability prediction (KAMP; Rostami et al. [2015]) analyzes the change propagation caused by a given change request in a software system on the basis of the architectural model. Using context information annotated on the architecture, KAMP enables assessment of the effects of a change request on various technical and organizational artifacts and tasks during the software life cycle. KAMP is novel with respect to the fact that it is concerned not only with the design phase of software but basically with all software life-cycle phases. KAMP is implemented as an extension of the Palladio Component Model.

9.6 Takeaways

Palladio does not operate in a single phase of a software development process, but accompanies the development process of software systems. Palladio has strong support during system design (i.e., modeling, analyses/predictions), but cannot be meaningfully used without connection to other phases (e.g., user performance demands from the requirements engineering phase).

Palladio is neither specific to nor tied to a certain kind of software engineering process. A component-based software development process (see section 9.2) serves as a best practice to apply Palladio. Nevertheless, Palladio supports waterfall-like processes but also iterative or agile development processes (see section 9.3).

It is specific to Palladio, from the process perspective, that it emphasizes planning activities, early design stages, and explicit risk handling. As a consequence, Palladio shifts efforts to early software engineering phases to avoid efforts and risks in later phases. The goal is to reduce the total effort and costs for software engineering projects.

Palladio has support for evolution and benefits from iterative processes. The advantages when evolving a software system arise from reduced modeling efforts. Because of the option to reuse components and utilize the same component in different contexts (see section 4.2), the efforts of Palladio modeling are reduced for later iterations. Already existing components and interfaces that reside in the repository reduce efforts in later iterations.

10 Relation to Requirements Engineering

Zoya Durdik, and Anne Koziolek

Requirements are a crucial input for any architecture-related activity and thus have a tight relation to the architectural modeling and simulation phase. At the same time, although less well known, the architecture of a system can also influence the requirements engineering (RE) activities.

This chapter explains in more detail how Palladio activities relate to requirements engineering activities. After presenting some RE foundations in section 10.1, the order and dependencies between architectural activities and RE activities is discussed in section 10.2. Subsections 10.2.1 and 10.2.2 then describe in more detail how RE relates to architectural modeling and architectural analysis, respectively. Section 10.3 concludes by giving an overview of how RE results and architectural models can be used in later phases of the development process to continually check that a project is on track.

10.1 Requirements Engineering Foundations

The International Requirements Engineering Board (IREB) defines requirements engineering as follows:

Definition 14 (Requirements engineering) *Requirements engineering (RE) is "a systematic and disciplined approach to the specification and management of requirements with the following goals:*

1. knowing the relevant requirements, achieving a consensus among the stakeholders about these requirements, documenting them according to given standards, and managing them systematically,
2. understanding and documenting the stakeholders' desires and needs,
3. specifying and managing requirements to minimize the risk of delivering a system that does not meet the stakeholders' desires and needs" (Glinz 2011).

These three goals address important aspects of RE; namely, (1) process orientation, (2) stakeholder focus, and (3) importance of risk and value considerations (Glinz 2011).

Describing all requirements engineering activities is out of scope for this book. Still, in the context of the relation between requirements engineering and software architecture design, two aspects deserve more discussion in the following. First, understanding where requirements come from is relevant for understanding the different situations in which requirements and architecture interact. Second, architects encounter different types of requirements in a software project and need to be able to distinguish them to not misinterpret them.

10.1.1 Sources of Requirements

Requirements for a software system come from different sources and at different points of the development life cycle.

All persons and organizations taking an interest in the system to be developed are called *stakeholders* of the system. Stakeholder groups range from end customers and company internal users to developers and testers to managers and persons with a legal interest, such as data protection officers. Persons from each of these groups may state requirements for the system, which may need to be taken into account when designing the architecture. Additionally, requirements may be derived from documents such as laws, standards, or technical documentation of involved hardware subsystems, of third-party software systems used, or of legacy systems.

An initial set of requirements is typically collected at the beginning of a software project. Depending on the employed software development process, however, this set does not have to be complete. Even if it was, in most cases requirements will change or be added later during the project or development process.

10.1.2 Types of Requirements

Figure 10.1 shows the different types of requirements encountered during RE activities.

Definition 15 (System requirements) *System requirements (sometimes also called product requirements) are requirements that describe capabilities or properties of the software system to be created or extended.*

Definition 16 (Project requirements) *Project requirements describe requirements for projects related to this system, such as release dates of a development project, development team structures, or project budget.*

Definition 17 (Process requirements) *Process requirements describe requirements of the processes affected by the system, such as business processes or technical processes.*

In the context of architectural modeling and analysis, requirements of all mentioned types are important. Project requirements, such as development team structures, may influence how a system is decomposed into components (an observation also called Conway's law [Yourdon and Constantine 1979]). Process requirements, such as the description of a business process, may influence system requirements to achieve overall satisfactory processes. Still,

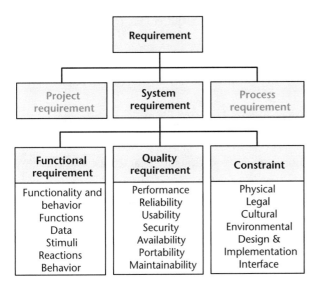

Figure 10.1
Types of requirements. Adapted from Glinz (2007) according to Glinz (2011).

the system requirements are usually the focus of architectural design activities and thus are the focus of this chapter.

System requirements can be divided into functional and nonfunctional requirements. The notion of what are functional and what are nonfunctional requirements has been debated in the requirements engineering community and is still a major source of misunderstanding. This is partly due to confusion about the kind of requirement (i.e., the matter it mainly concerns) and its representation, as detailed in the following.

In this book, we mainly follow the definitions by Glinz (2007, 2011), which are based on the underlying *concern* of a requirement.

Definition 18 (Functional or behavioral concern) *A "concern is a* functional or behavioral concern *if its matter of interest is primarily the expected behavior of a system or system component in terms of its reaction to given input stimuli and the functions and data required for processing the stimuli and producing the reaction" (Glinz 2007).*

Definition 19 (Quality concern) *A "concern is a* quality concern *if its matter of interest is a quality of the kind enumerated in [a quality model]" (Glinz 2007).*

For example, the ISO/IEC 25010 standard (ISO/IEC 25010:2011(E) 2011) enumerates quality characteristics, such as "reliability," "usability," or "performance efficiency" (we call the latter simply "performance" in this book).

Then, the *kind* of requirement is defined on the basis of the underlying concerns.

Definition 20 (Functional requirement) *A* "functional requirement *is a requirement that pertains to a functional concern" (Glinz 2007).*

All other kinds of requirements are collectively called non-functional requirements. Within the non-functional requirements, Glinz distinguishes between quality requirements and constraints:

Definition 21 (Quality requirement) *A* quality requirement *is "a requirement that pertains to a quality concern that is not covered by functional requirements" (Glinz 2011).*

Performance requirements and requirements for other quality characteristics are quality requirements.

Definition 22 (Constraint) *A* constraint *is "a requirement that limits the solution space beyond what is necessary for meeting the given functional requirements and quality requirements" (Glinz 2011).*

An example for a constraint is a legal constraint for handling private data.

Example 3
Requirement Kind for the Media Store
As an example of different kinds and quality aspects of requirements, consider some of the non-functional requirements of the Media Store from section 2.1.1. The example uses the quality terms of ISO/IEC 25010.

• "The response time shall be as low as possible, but less than 60 seconds for 95% of all requests for the expected workload, as introduced below." This is a quality requirement, as it pertains to performance in terms of the timing behavior of the system.
• "The components of the Media Store shall be loosely coupled to facilitate evolution. They should communicate with each other only using interfaces." This is a quality requirement, as it pertains to the maintainability of the system.
• "Components that are developed from scratch for the Media Store shall be reusable in future projects, if appropriate." This is a quality requirement, as it pertains to reusability.
• "The Media Store shall be, if possible, implemented using reused components from third parties to save development costs and future maintenance effort." This is a constraint, as it does not affect system quality but constrains the solution space.
• "Only authenticated users should access the system and thus audio files." This is a quality requirement, as it pertains to security.
• "Copyright is an important concern, and the Media Store shall comply with respective laws and regulations. Therefore, any copyright violation shall be detected." This is a quality requirement, as it pertains to compliance.

Example 4
Requirement Representation for the Media Store
To understand the distinction of requirement kind and requirement representation, let us assume some of the previous Media Store requirements and some potential Media Store requirements.

• "The mean response time of the Media Store upload shall be less than 5 seconds." This is a performance requirement, as it pertains to the timing behavior of the system. It is represented quantitatively.
• "The Media Store shall be easy to evolve when the operating system version changes." This is a maintainability requirement. It is represented qualitatively.
• "The Media Store shall be run in a Java EE environment." This is a constraint and is represented declaratively.
• "Users can log in by providing user name and password." This is a security requirement and thus a quality requirement, as its underlying concern is the security of the system and the protection against unauthorized access. It is represented operationally.
• "When the user selects 'Show files,' the Media Store shall provide a list of files a user can download." This is a functional requirement, pertaining primarily to the expected behavior of the Media Store in terms of its reaction to a given input. Like most functional requirements, it is represented operationally.

The representation of requirements is somewhat independent of their kind. Requirements can be defined quantitatively, qualitatively, operationally, or declaratively. The representation determines how the requirement fulfillment can be checked later in the development process. *Quantitative* requirements are expressed in a measurable way (e.g., by referring to the response time of a system). *Qualitative* requirements cannot be verified directly, but stakeholders have to subjectively judge whether it is fulfilled. *Operational* requirements define what the system is supposed to do in terms of actions to be performed, data to be provided, or states to be entered. Such requirements can be checked by reviewing, testing, or formal specification. *Declarative* requirements describe a required situation.

10.1.3 Refining Quality Requirements
When quality requirements are elicited from stakeholders, they are often in a qualitative form (Glinz 2008), which makes them difficult to check later. To make them easier to check, qualitative requirements can be refined to quantitative, operational, or declarative requirements.

If a way to measure the system's quality can be conceived, the quality requirement can be refined to a quantitative one. Requirements for some quality characteristics, such as performance or reliability, can be readily quantified. For other quality characteristics, however, such as usability or security, quantification is less straightforward.

When stakeholders, architects, and developers agree on ways to achieve a qualitative requirement, they may refine it to an operational or declarative requirement. Note, however, that they make design decisions in this process and that they make assumptions about how these design decisions affect the quality characteristics.

The refinement is an additional effort that incurs cost. Thus, whether or not to refine a qualitative requirement should depend on the risk of the system not fulfilling it (Glinz 2008). As usual, risk is the ratio of the probability of undesired events (here: of the final system not fulfilling the requirements) and their severity.

Probability of not fulfilling requirements: The probability of not fulfilling requirements is related to factors such as shared understanding, experience, and even customer-supplier relationship. For example, when stakeholders, architects, and developers already have a shared understanding about a qualitative requirement as well as a positive and supportive work relationship, there may be no benefit of refining it further. As another example, if architects and developers have no experience with the kind of system to be developed or the project context is a strict contract-based one where later additions can be billed extra, the probability of getting requirements wrong, be it by mistake or on purpose, is higher.

Severity of not fulfilling requirements: The cost of not fulfilling requirements should be considered. Here, requirements that are highly critical for the system's success usually should be refined further, because not fulfilling these will result in high cost. For other, less important requirements, the effort of refinement may not pay off.

10.1.4 Software Quality Terminology

When speaking about and specifying quality requirements, it is important to use a common terminology so that all stakeholders have the same understanding. This concerns the different quality characteristics, but also the notions of quality measures, quality scenarios, quality requirement, and quality property. Figure 10.2 illustrates the terms to describe quantitative qualities used in this book. The terms are mainly based on ISO/IEC 25030:2007(E) (2007). Recall, however, that it is not always prudent or possible to specify a quality requirement quantitatively, as discussed above. Requirements that all stakeholders have a common understanding of can be defined qualitatively. Additionally, quality requirements where stakeholders agree about how to achieve them can be formulated as declarative or operational quality requirements.

General Quality Terms *Software quality*, according to ISO/IEC 25030:2007(E) (2007), is the "capability of software product to satisfy stated and implied needs when used under specified conditions." Developing high-quality software products is a goal in many development projects. *Quality*, however, is a highly subjective term and depends on the goals and perceptions

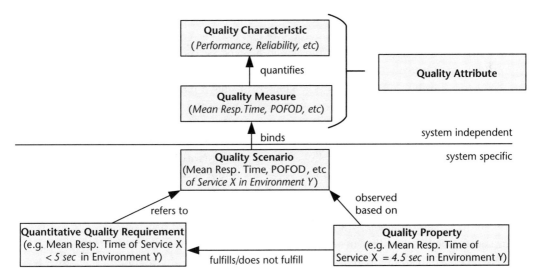

Figure 10.2
Software quality terms related to quantitative quality requirements. POFOD, probability of failure on demand.

of stakeholders. To better reason about software product quality, software quality models have been suggested to describe and measure software quality (e.g., ISO/IEC 25010:2011(E) [2011]; Boehm et al. [1976]; McCall et al. [1977]). Quality models define a "set of characteristics, and of relationships between them, which provides a framework for specifying quality requirements and evaluating quality" (ISO/IEC 25030:2007(E) [2007]).

Quality characteristics provide the basis for evaluating the quality of software systems. When designing software architecture, relevant software quality characteristics contain reliability, modifiability, performance, security, testability, and usability (Bass et al. 2003). Depending on the goals of the system to be developed, additional software quality characteristics may be relevant, such as portability or interoperability.

Additionally, economic considerations are a major driver of software development. Business qualities are, for example, costs, monetary benefit, and time to market (Bass et al. 2003). These business qualities, however, are not just characteristics of the software product itself, but are also influenced by the project and the process (see figure 10.1).

The commonly used term *quality attribute* is broader and includes both quality characteristics and quality measures (see later). The ISO/IEC SQuaRE standards family defines a quality attribute as an "inherent property or characteristic of an entity that can be distinguished quantitatively or qualitatively by human or automated means" (e.g., in ISO/IEC 25030:2007(E) [2007]).

Quantification Terms   Quality characteristics are abstract notions of quality and do not directly provide means to quantify the quality of a system. To quantify quality characteristics, quality measures (also often called quality metrics), such as mean response time or probability of failure on demand (POFOD), have been introduced.

Different research areas for quality characteristics have proposed different quality measures to describe their quality characteristics. Performance and reliability are readily quantifiable. The measures for performance, such as response time and utilization, and the measures for reliability, namely probability of failure on demand and failure rate, have been described in section 1.4.1. For some of the quality characteristics, quantification is not as obvious, but still possible. For example, two usability measures might be either the average amount of training time a user needs to be able to use a function without assistance or the average time a user needs to execute a system function after being trained.

Note that quality characteristics that can be quantified are not necessarily easy to measure and verify. Here, verifiability of requirements is "the degree to which the fulfillment of a requirement by an implemented system can be checked, e.g., by defining acceptance test cases, measurements, or inspection procedures" (Glinz 2011) and is not to be confused with the notion of formal verification in other software engineering fields.

The same quality measure can be relevant for multiple functions of the system. For example, the mean response times of the three most important services of a system can be considered separately. Additionally, the same quality measure can be relevant in multiple environmental conditions. For example, the response time of a service at normal workload conditions may be considered as well as the response time of this service at peak workload times. *Environmental conditions* are relevant conditions of the system and its environment for which the quality measure is to be collected (e.g., workload conditions for performance, already observed failure states of the system for reliability, or expected types of change requests for modifiability). Aspects of environmental conditions are also called "operational profile" or "context of use" in ISO/IEC 25030. Thus, a quality scenario in this book is defined as the collection of a quality measure for one or several functions of the software system under certain environmental conditions. While a quality measure only defines quantification, a quality scenario binds a quality measure to a concrete function of a software system under defined environmental conditions. Thus, a quality scenario is defined specifically for a system.

Throughout the book, if the mean response time or the POFOD of a software system is mentioned, there is only one relevant quality scenario for these quality measures.

For quality scenarios, quality requirements can be specified. These requirements express which values have to be achieved to satisfy the stakeholder's needs for this quality dimension. For example, a quality requirement may state that a service of a system must respond in less than 5 seconds in the given scenario. Thus, a quality requirement adds a value to achieve a quality scenario. All values that are better than the requirement satisfy the stakeholder's needs.

This notion of a quality scenario and quality requirement are related to quality attribute scenarios (QASs) of the architecture trade-off analysis method (ATAM; Bass et al. 2003). A QAS defines which quality measure to collect at which place in the system (called artifact in QAS) in which scenario (called stimulus and environment in QAS) and defines which value of the measure is required to be observed for this scenario (called response measure in QAS). Thus, in the terminology used in this book, a QAS is the combination of a quality scenario and a quality requirement for it.

Finally, we can observe a certain value for the quality scenario at a certain point in time. Note that different observations can be made for different versions of the system over time or different configurations of the system for different customers. For example, a service X of a version of the system deployed at customer Y has a mean response time of 5 seconds when called with a defined workload. This value is called a quality property in this book.

10.2   Relation of Requirements and Architectural Activities

As discussed in the previous chapter, the Palladio approach is aligned with continuous software development process models, such as agile process models (Scrum, Extreme Programming, etc.), extended V-models, the Unified Process, and others similar to these. The important feature of these models is that they do not assume that there is a sequential process, where each phase is expected to be complete before proceeding to the next one, as for example in a classical waterfall process. Thus, it is expected that requirements engineering or design phases are not happening just once, but they are rather continuously distributed along the development process. Once there is a first, usually incomplete, set of requirements available, an architect proceeds to the architectural design. And even though the requirements are known to be not final, the available design is then implemented. Implementation of new requirements and design changes is possible and is usually done incrementally and iteratively.

An even tighter integration of requirements engineering and architectural activities is suggested in the twin peaks process model (Nuseibeh 2001). While requirements engineering phases and architectural activities phases alternate in traditional incremental processes, the twin peaks model emphasizes that these two activities should be executed in parallel to support immediate feedback from one to the other (figure 10.3). The goal of this process is that requirements analysts and software architects better understand problems by being aware of requirements and their prioritization on the one hand and architecture and in particular architectural constraints on the other hand. Additionally, being able to quickly switch back and forth between the problem to solve (the requirements) and its solution (the architecture) can help to more clearly distinguish the two and to avoid mixing up problem and solution already in the requirements engineering phase.

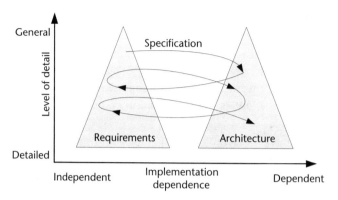

Figure 10.3
The twin peaks model (Nuseibeh 2001) showing the interplay of requirements and architecture.

In the Palladio process, requirements engineering and architectural design activities are repeated throughout the development process and can be tightly integrated. The following describes in detail how requirements engineering activities relate to architectural design in general (subsection 10.2.1) and how quality requirements relate to architectural analysis in particular (subsection 10.2.2).

10.2.1 Relation to Architectural Design
Requirements and architecture are related in two ways, as depicted in figure 10.4.

First, requirements drive the architectural design and architectural design decisions. Architects strive to design the architecture so that it fulfills the stated requirements. Whether the architecture conforms to the requirements will be evaluated at design time and will be monitored at run time and reevaluated during system evolution.

Second, already-taken design decisions, which were involved in the software architecture design, influence further architectural choices and decisions. Thus, they influence the requirements engineering process and trigger new requirements.

The following subsections explain these relations in more detail.

Requirements Drive Architectural Design   The classic understanding is that requirements engineering precedes architectural design and that known requirements are the drivers of the design. In this relation, the software architect systematically designs the architecture to fulfill requirements.

As mentioned throughout this book, software architecture of a system is critical to achieve quality (Bass et al. 2003). Thus, nonfunctional requirements and especially quality requirements should be the main drivers when designing software architecture.

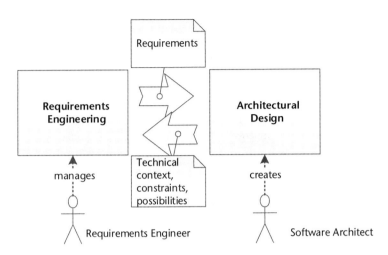

Figure 10.4
A round-trip between requirements engineering and architectural design.

The functional requirements are then realized in the architecture's components, which "encapsulate a subset of the system's functionality and/or data" (Taylor et al. 2009).

In order to address the requirements in the design, software architects usually rely on their experience, and, ideally, on design best-practices. Additionally, methods have been suggested to design software architectures on the basis of identified relevant quality attributes. For example, attribute-driven design (ADD; Bass et al. 2003) is a recursive decomposition process to identify the structural organization of a software architecture driven by relevant quality attributes. The system is structured on the basis of known architectural tactics and architectural patterns. The result is a high-level organization of the system, which is refined in further architectural design steps.

Architectural Design Drives Requirements Engineering   The lesser known relation between requirements and architecture is that design of software architecture can also drive requirements engineering. Woods and Rozanski (2011) have coined the phrase that software architecture "frames, constrains, and inspires" requirements. More generally, architectural design can provide various ways of feedback into the requirements engineering process. For example, this feedback relation might manifest in the following situations.

Very often during system design, there is insufficient information about certain expected properties, features, and behavior of the system. Thus, an architect often has to ask a requirements analyst to clarify and provide additional information about the missing features, thus driving requirements engineering.

Example 5

Clarification Example for the Media Store

In our Media Store example, the software architect, while working on the interface of the TagWatermarking component, might need details on what information will be included in the watermarks. Assume that after requirements analysts consult legal experts, they clarify that the user's full name and birth date need to be included to make the user liable for misuse of the files. Consequently, the architect might include a connector between the TagWatermarking component and the UserManagement component.

Example 6

Framing Example for the Media Store

An initial Media Store requirement might have stated that the system shall have a maximum downtime of 1 hour per year. Software architects have, however, reasoned that the combined downtime of a single server is expected to be higher than 1 hour per year due to security updates, maintenance activities, and hardware failures. Thus, achieving such a low downtime would require replication of the Media Store servers. Being confronted with the incurred high costs, stakeholders have reprioritized and decided that a higher downtime of a day per year is acceptable to reduce costs.

Example 7

Constraint Example for the Media Store

For example, currently available communication technology and Internet bandwidth forbid the requirement that a complete video file shall be downloaded within milliseconds.

A relation discussed throughout the book is that architecture design and analysis shows the costs and trade-offs required to reach certain quality properties. Here, the architecture frames the achievable quality by providing insight to the associated difficulty, risk, and cost.

Moreover, some requirements might be unfulfillable by any architecture the architects can devise or at least by any architecture that has reasonable cost, risks, and development time.

In another case, a desired architectural design solution cannot be implemented without violating an existing design decision. If such decision has to be withdrawn, the requirements that were implemented through such decision have to be revisited and possibly reprioritized, revised, or even also withdrawn.

Finally, architectural design does not just limit and constrain requirements. Architectural solutions might also inspire new possibilities and functionality and thus new

Example 8
Conflict Example for the Media Store
The above clarification example might violate a previous decision that user data is exclusively used in the UserManagement component to comply with legal privacy requirements. Now, with the above watermarking clarification, this design decision needs to be withdrawn. The requirements analysts revisit the underlying requirement that privacy law requires minimal use of personal data. In this example, they conclude that this basic requirement remains valid, as the watermarking functionality is required to provide the Media Store functionality.

Example 9
Inspiration Example for the Media Store
Assume that in an earlier stage of the Media Store design, the Media Store was intended to serve music files only. The software architect, when exploring components to reuse for the ReEncoder component, realized that several encoding libraries provide video encoding functionality as well. This inspired the requirement that uploading and downloading video files should be possible as well.

requirements. For example, deciding to use a certain technology (such as wireless communication) might enable new use cases that requirements analysts and stakeholders have not yet considered.

10.2.2   Relation to Architectural Analysis

Architectural analysis aims to study the quality attributes of a software system. Palladio's main focus is the quantitative prediction of performance and reliability, as presented in part III. Other approaches for architectural analysis, such as ATAM, Quality Attribute Workshop (QAW), or the cost-benefit analysis method (CBAM), rather aim at a qualitative analysis of quality characteristics. With these qualitative approaches, the effect of design decisions on quality characteristics is mainly assessed manually. They are complementary to quantitative approaches, which are used to quantitatively assess selected quality measures if needed. As architectural analysis activities are concerned with the quality attributes of a system, they relate to quality requirements on the requirements engineering side. In particular, Palladio activities are related to performance requirements and reliability requirements.

As mentioned before, quality attributes of the system are often pervasive properties influenced by multiple decisions throughout the architectural design. Thus, the corresponding quality requirements relate to the system as a whole and cannot necessarily be located to be implemented in certain components.

Example 10
Quality Requirement Checks for the Media Store
As an example, consider the performance requirement of the Media Store: the response time shall be less than 60 seconds for 95% of all requests for the expected workload. To check whether the designed architecture fulfills this requirement, Palladio can be used as described in part III. If the results show that for all expected usage scenarios, the response time is lower than 60 seconds in 95% of all cases, the software architect can expect that this requirement will be fulfilled by the system. If higher response times are predicted for some usage scenarios, the software architect may want to improve and update the architectural design to meet the requirements.

Quality Requirements Checks   In analogy to the previously discussed relation (requirements drive architectural design), the most straightforward relation between quality requirements and architectural analysis is the following: quality requirements define the levels of quality expected from the system, and architectural analysis is used to check whether these levels can be fulfilled by the designed architecture.

This evaluation can be done early (i.e., at design time), in contrast to late in testing or even later. As discussed before, this early evaluation helps to avoid expensive redesign and reimplementation later in the development process.

Thus, once the initial version of an architectural design is complete, it is important to evaluate if existing quality requirements are met. The evaluation process depends on the type of the quality requirements. For quantitative types of quality requirements, such as reliability and performance, evaluation of the architecture with the Palladio approach can be used. For qualitative types, such as maintainability or security, we suggest using methods such as the architecture-level modifiability analysis (ALMA) or attack tree analysis or reviews by the experts. See the resources in section 10.5 for more details.

After the analysis, the software architect compares the results of the evaluation and the requirements set. If the requirements are not met by the current design, a decision has to be taken either to make changes to the design or to redefine the quality requirements (e.g., to relax the quality requirements).

Note, however, that even a well-designed software architecture is no guarantee that the resulting software system will indeed have the envisioned qualities. Instead, it provides only a foundation for achieving these qualities. Throughout the further design and implementation of the software system, further decisions that may deteriorate the qualities are made. Thus, additional checks in later life-cycle stages need to be planned for as well, as discussed in section 10.3.

Avoiding Gold Plating and Considering Trade-offs   While an early consideration of quality attributes is desirable, collecting *quality requirements* early from stakeholders may also often lead to a long wish list of quality properties because the effects of quality demands for software are not well understood. In other engineering disciplines, such as the construction of trains, it is common understanding that, for example, demanding a high-speed train will lead to higher costs than demanding a local train with a maximum speed of 70 km/h. The consequences of demanding a software system that answers requests within 100 microseconds, is available 365 days a year, and is secured against any type of conceivable attack, however, are not necessarily known to stakeholders. Fulfilling all requirements from such a list may lead to an expensive and overengineered solution (also called a "gold-plated" solution). The costs of quality requirements is difficult to assess at an early development stage, so that quality requirements, even if stated, are often dismissed later (Berntsson Svensson et al. 2011). Thus, while quality attributes need to be considered early, the actual quality requirements must be questioned and negotiated during the software development process.

Architectural analysis also helps in this scenario by enabling software architects and other stakeholders to understand the consequences of quality requirements early via the necessary design decisions. In particular, trade-offs need to be made between different quality attributes, in particular with costs.

When designing software architectures, single software quality attributes cannot be considered in isolation, because improving a system with respect to one software quality attribute may have an effect on other software quality attributes (Bass et al. 2003). Often, architectural design decisions imply a trade-off between software quality characteristics (i.e., there is a conflict of quality characteristics for this decision). For example, security and reliability may conflict for architectural decisions regarding data storage: while a system is secure if it offers few places that keep sensitive data, such an organization may lead to single points of failure and decreased reliability. Similarly, many architectural decisions made to improve software quality characteristics have potential to conflict with performance due to additional required calculation and with costs due to increased development effort. Thus, when designing an architecture, trade-off decisions must be made.

10.3   Requirement Checks in Later Life-Cycle Stages

Work with requirements does not end with the system design. During the design implementation, various misinterpretations and wrong implementation of the design may occur, and functional and quality requirements might be violated. Thus, requirements monitoring is needed also during implementation. While during system design, evaluation of requirements is done on the basis of models and design analysis methods, evaluation of requirements during system implementation is done with measurements. An ongoing measurement of system parameters contributes to the conformance of the system with quality requirements. Conformance with the functional requirements is typically checked through the comparison of planned design (architectural design models) and of the is-state of the design restored from the implementation (reverse engineering of architectural models).

As requirements are subject to change, they most probably would also change during the implementation. When changing the system, it is important to update all artifacts, including architectural design models and requirements specifications.

Even once the system is developed and running, requirements monitoring is still needed. Especially quality requirements are easily violated. For example, a usage behavior of a system might change, and more service requests than expected would be done to the system. Such increased load might cause violation of response-time constraints. Hardware, for example, ages and becomes less reliable with time. Natural growth of the database or cache can slow down the processing time and lead to the requirements violation.

On the functional side, violations can be caused through software updates. For example, an updated third-party library might offer slightly changed functionality and thus violate a functional requirement.

Not only conformance checks are important, but also regular checks of requirement prioritization (especially for the quality requirements) and trade-off decisions. Insights won in later life-cycle stages may even lead to revision to requirements or to some of them being discarded. Therefore, a regular check of conformance to the existing requirements (both quality and functional) and reevaluation of the existing requirements must be an ongoing activity.

10.4 Questions and Exercises

10.4.1 Questions

10.1 *: What are the different types of requirements for software systems? Which type is the main driver for architectural design?

10.2 *: What is a quality requirement? What is its difference with the term *nonfunctional requirement*?

10.3 **: What is the difference between a quality characteristic and a quality measure?

10.4 *: How are requirements and architecture related?

10.5 *: What does "software architecture frames, constrains, and inspires requirements" mean?

10.6 *: What software quality characteristics can be analyzed with Palladio?

10.4.2 Exercises

10.1 ***: Consider the following requirements. What kind of requirement does each requirement represent, and what is the representation of each?

(a) "The Media Store shall be easy to use by a casual user."

(b) "The utilization of the servers shall never be higher than 95% for more than 10 seconds."

(c) "When the user selects a single file to download, the Media Store shall return the requested file."

(d) "Every page shall show a link leading to a page where users can change the user interface language."

10.5 Further Reading

Please refer to the requirements engineering textbook by Klaus Pohl for a detailed description of all requirements engineering activities and a discussion of different stakeholder groups (Pohl 2010). The software architecture textbook by Bass et al. (2003) contains a detailed discussion about how stakeholders are relevant for architectural design.

The definition of quality requirements and the different representations of requirements are explained in more detail by Glinz (2007). A risk-based, value-oriented approach to quality requirements has been suggested by Glinz (2008). In a later work, Glinz and Fricker (2014) provide a more detailed and insightful discussion on shared understanding.

For defining quality requirements, quality models provide a set of possibly relevant quality characteristics. A popular quality model is defined in ISO/IEC 25030:2007(E) (2007), but other quality models such as the ones suggested by Boehm et al. (1976) or by McCall et al. (1977) can be used as well.

For each quality characteristic, there are challenges to writing sound and meaningful requirements. Bondi's book on performance engineering is a particularly good source for information about how to define performance requirements (Bondi 2014).

Different topics regarding the relationship between requirements and architecture are discussed in a book edited by Avgeriou et al. (2011). In one of the chapters of that book, Woods and Rozanski (2011) describe an interesting case study on how software architecture can frame, constrain, and inspire requirements.

For the classical direction of designing architecture on the basis of requirements, various methods and techniques such as ATAM (Bass et al. 2003), QAWs (Barbacci et al. 2003), or CBAM (Clements et al. 2001) have been suggested.

10.6 Takeaways

Requirements engineering activities are crucial for the success of a software development process. System requirements are divided into functional and quality requirements as well as constraints. Quality requirements can be defined quantitatively, qualitatively, operationally, or declaratively. To make qualitatively defined requirements verifiable, they are transformed into other representations, which involves additional time and costs. Introducing and using quantification terms such as response time or probability of failure on demand supports the quantification of qualitative requirements. In general, a shared terminology of software quality among stakeholders and developers helps them to elicit and reason about quality requirements.

A tight integration of requirements engineering and design activities is important. Design-time feedback from architectural design back to requirements engineering not only helps to clarify system quality goals and to prevent later expensive redesigns but often also supports better understanding of the desired functional properties.

After an initial version of the software architecture has been designed, it can be used to analyze what qualities can be achieved when realizing the system. Evaluating the quality attributes early can help to identify wrong decisions, which are expensive to revert later in the process. Early architectural evaluation is reported to save costs later in development processes.

11 Relation to Implementation

Steffen Becker, Benjamin Klatt, Klaus Krogmann, Michael Langhammer, and Sebastian Lehrig

Palladio models can represent either systems under development or existing systems. These models cover all aspects of a system including deployment or system usage. Some parts of a Palladio model represent the system's implementation, especially its source code. Hence, Palladio models can be used in two scenarios related to source code: first, creation of matching source code for existing models; and second, analysis of existing systems in order to create a Palladio model. The latter helps software architects to accompany the evolution of a software system with models and quality analyses.

In case software architects have already modeled a system but there exists no code yet, they could ask themselves: *How can I generate this code from my modeled architecture to allow detailed performance analyses and to reduce the implementation effort?*

In the case where code already exists, models help software architects in planning the next development steps. A Palladio model of a system can serve as qualitative and quantitative justification for picking one or another design alternative. Such models have to be up to date and should be a good system representation (relevant with respect to the design decision to be met, cf. section 5.2.2). If no up-to-date model of the system is available, questions arise such as: *How can I get an up-to-date model from source code?*

The content of this chapter will answer the above-mentioned questions by guiding you through the forward engineering of a component-based system and through the extraction of component structures (components, interfaces, and composite structures), component behavior (service effect specification; SEFF), and control and data flow parameterization. Potential sources of information are highlighted to gather architectural information. Possible mappings between Palladio constructs (e.g., components) and source code (e.g., Java classes) will be introduced. This mapping information will ease interpretation of existing applications in a Palladio-specific way. In addition, this chapter briefly describes available tools to support forward and reverse engineering.

In the end, you will understand the relation between Palladio models and implementation such as source code, deployment descriptors, and plug-in manifests. Section 11.6 provides a brief summary of the essential takeaways.

11.1   Forward and Reverse Engineering Overview

This chapter discusses forward and reverse engineering approaches developed in the Palladio environment. The forward engineering approaches of Palladio enable code generation from a Palladio model. The code generation has two purposes: The first purpose is to enable code generation for simulation code. When executed, this code can be used to predict the performance of a software system. The second purpose is to generate prototypes from an architectural model. These prototypes can be used for further development of the software system. The forward engineering part of this chapter outlines the approach of coupled transformations, which can be used to translate Palladio artifacts, such as interfaces, components, and roles, to source code.

The reverse engineering approaches of Palladio offer the generation of an architectural model from object-oriented source code. The approaches are called Software Model Extractor (SoMoX) and Archimetrix. These approaches use heuristics and software metrics to extract Palladio *repository* and *system* views as well as the *SEFF* behavior view from source code. The effort of manually creating an architectural model from source code is reduced by this approach, so that software architects can get an overview about huge software projects very quickly and acquire an up-to-date architectural model from the extraction.

Numerous complementing tools, including forward and reverse engineering tools, have been developed for Palladio. These tools speed up the work of daily life. All so-called Palladio add-ons are accessible from the Palladio bench website [33].

Forward engineering tools for Palladio include the following:

SimuCom creates executable Java source code and Eclipse plug-ins from Palladio models. The source code's "payload" is control flow instructions from Palladio models and resource simulation utilization (more details can be found in section 8.3.1).

ProtoCom creates executable Java source code from Palladio models. The source code's payload is instructions that utilize real resources (e.g., CPU, hard disk, and network). Control flow is directly derived from Palladio's component and SEFF structure (more details can be found in section 8.3.4).

Code stub generators for Enterprise JavaBeans (EJBs) and Plain Old Java Objects (POJOs) create EJB-based components and components described in pure Java classes, respectively. Control flow is not generated and must be manually implemented. Such stubs serve as starting points for the implementation of architectures described in Palladio.

Reverse engineering for Palladio is supported by the following:

SoMoX extracts a system model consisting of hierarchical components and component control flow from Java source code (one version also supports C/C++).

Digression 11.1

Reengineering Terminology

Evolution tools can be mainly distinguished into forward engineering, reverse engineering, round-trip engineering, and restructuring tools. Figure 11.1 relates these reengineering terms, which go back to Chikofsky and Cross (1990). Forward engineering is followed in all development processes by deriving, for example, an implementation from requirements. Reverse engineering tools derive high-level abstractions (for example, Palladio model, center of the figure) from low-level abstractions (for example source code; right-hand side). Restructuring, at the same abstraction level, changes artifacts (e.g., clean up component design). Round-trip engineering tools keep multiple abstraction levels tightly synchronized.

Of these categories, forward and reverse engineering tools exist for Palladio. Work on round-trip engineering is currently under research.

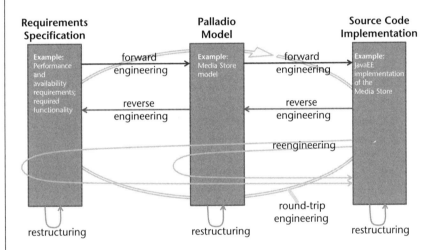

Figure 11.1

Relation among reverse engineering related terms. After Chikofsky et al. (1990).

Beagle derives parametric dependencies (i.e., *stochastic expressions*) from running instances of software systems.

ByCounter derives resources demands for individual *internal actions* from Java byte code. It counts executed byte-code instruction for running software systems.

Archimetrix allows for an iterative reengineering process. It aims at detecting and removing design deficiencies that influence the architectural reconstruction and thereby enable the recovery of more accurate architectural models.

The remainder of this chapter details these approaches.

11.2   Forward Engineering

Forward engineering concerns the translation of parts of a Palladio model into source code. It could be done manually by software developers or automatically via model transformations. In order to ensure that the quality analyses the software architect has done using the Palladio model represent the implemented system, care has to be taken that the system is implemented according to the model. The following discusses the manual approach and explains how automated transformations can be exploited to overcome the identified issues.

The quality of service of a software system is a property of the system in execution, in which all context factors are completely bound (context factors are discussed in section 4.2). Therefore, architectural analyses can only be accurate if the corresponding implementation of the software system actually matches the model that is used for analysis (i.e., is a good representation as introduced in section 5.2.2). While in forward engineering, implementation teams can theoretically achieve such a matching when they implement the software system, they typically do not achieve a good match in practice. Common reasons for this are different interpretations of model constructs, variations in design decisions, and/or neglecting the model as a blueprint. Especially software developers suffer from such issues when they have to implement a system in source code according to an architectural description. Therefore, developers optimally need guidance when translating Palladio's repository and systems models—the relevant models of source code—to source code.

Palladio employs the concept of coupled model transformations, which has been introduced by Becker (2008), to help these developers in forward engineering. The basic idea of coupled model transformations is that automated model transformations generate both the quality-relevant part of the implementation source code and the analysis model. This coupled generation of implementation and analysis model ensures that analysis results reflect the quality of service in the actual system. It can even take implementation decisions such as the communication protocols used into account. Coupled generation by definition only works for artifacts that can actually be generated automatically. Today, this is only the case for source code artifacts. Operation teams still have to ensure manually that the hardware resources match the resource environment model.

For example, the software architect of the Media Store so far has not specified a concrete communication protocol between WebGUI and MediaManagement. Feasible options for concrete protocols are Remote Method Invocation (RMI) or Simple Object Access Protocol (SOAP). For coupled model transformations, the architect therefore introduces a simple annotation model for the model transformations that specifies the concretely chosen protocol (figure 11.2). Transformations for both implementation source code and analysis models are configured via this annotation model and generate a corresponding output. In figure 11.2, such a configuration and corresponding output is shown for the case of the

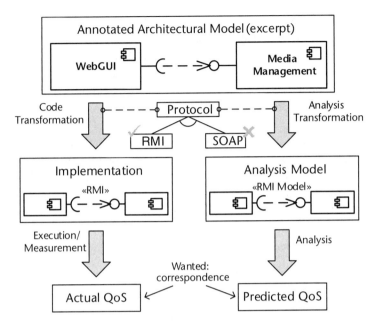

Figure 11.2
Coupled model transformation for the Media Store (stereotypes in angled brackets). Based on Becker (2008).

RMI protocol. These transformations particularly ensure that the (source code of the) system has the quality of service characteristics that correspond to the ones predicted by the analysis model.

Note that developers will typically extend the generated implementation manually. Therefore, the generated implementation should provide suitable extension points that still ensure the correspondence to analysis models when being extended. Employed transformations have to be engineered accordingly with such extension points in mind. Moreover, Palladio provides many such transformations. All types of analysis models as discussed in section 8.1 generally have to be covered (simulation code, prototype code, etc.; see figure 8.1). Different types of implementations also have to be covered (e.g., based on Java SE, Java EE, C#, etc. [Langhammer et al. 2013]).

This section outlines the concepts used for these different types of transformations. SimuCom simulations and ProtoCom performance prototypes fall into the category of analysis models. Subections 11.2.1 and 11.2.2 describe mappings to SimuCom's simulation and ProtoCom's prototype code, respectively. The mapping to implementations is explained by the example of technological mappings to Java SE and Java EE code stubs (subsection 11.2.3) and to the service component architecture (SCA; subsection 11.2.4).

11.2.1 Simulation Mapping for SimuCom

This subsection introduces the mapping of Palladio models to Java simulation code for the SimuCom solver. The simulation mapping of SimuCom is realized as depicted in table 11.1. The table lists the concerned Palladio model (models for repository, system, allocation, resource environment, and usage model) in the first column. The second column gives the concerned PCM concept within such a model, and the third column states how this concept is mapped in SimuCom.

For the Palladio repository model, transformations map PCM concepts to Java interfaces and classes of the simulation code. Such interfaces and classes represent the implementation of components based on Java SE. As an example, listing 11.1 shows how SimuCom translates the IWebGUI interface from the Media Store example into code.

For parameters, component implementations use a context variable that allows the implementation to access parameter characterizations, specified via stochastic expressions. Moreover, different software design patterns offer the implementation of *provided* and *required roles* and of *composite components*.

Provided roles are realized by so-called port classes that act as proxies, delegating operation calls to the corresponding component class that provides the concrete implementation of the operation. An example of a port class is shown in listing 11.2. This idea follows the proxy software design pattern (Gamma et al. 1995). Use of proxies allows developers to develop components where multiple operations have the same signature (Becker 2008). In listing 11.2, you can see the realization of the port class from the IWebGUI interface to the WebGUI component.

Required roles are realized in so-called context classes, which can be used by requiring components via dependency injection. This idea follows the context software design pattern

Table 11.1

Overview of the simulation mapping (SimuCom)

Palladio Model	PCM Concept	SimuCom
Repository	Interfaces	Java interface
	Data types	—
	Provided roles	Port classes
	Required roles	Context classes
	Provides/complete component types	Classes with fixed delays
	Basic components	Classes with simulated SEFF
	Composite components	Facade class
System	Assembly contexts	Instance of component class
	Assembly connectors	(a) Dependency injection
		(b) Connector completion
Allocation	Allocation contexts	Mapping to simulated resources
Resource environment	Resources	Simulated resources
Usage model	Usage scenarios	Workload driver

```
package defaultrepository;

public interface IWebGUI {

    String getComponentAssemblyContextID();


    SimulatedStackframe<Object> upload0(Context ctx);


    SimulatedStackframe<Object> getFileList1(Context ctx);


    SimulatedStackframe<Object> register2(Context ctx);


    SimulatedStackframe<Object> login3(Context ctx);


    SimulatedStackframe<Object> download4(Context ctx);
}
```

Listing 11.1
The Java SE interface IWebGUI specifies the operation signatures given in a repository and a signature for requesting IDs of assembly contexts.

(Stahl and Völter 2006). Therefore, *systems* can appropriately assemble *assembly contexts* (Becker 2008).

Composite components use so-called facade classes to delegate their calls to inner components. This idea follows the facade software design pattern (Gamma et al. 1995).

Concrete resource-demanding behavior is realized within *complete component types* and *basic components. Provides/complete component types* are realized in classes with fixed delays because their implementation is unavailable—such delays represent the requirement of a software architect to the component to be developed by component developers. In the case of *basic components*, the implementation is available in the form of *service effect specifications*. Therefore, basic components are realized by classes that simulate their *service effect specifications*. Listing 11.3 shows how the WebGUI basic component is translated into code by SimuCom.

For the Palladio system model, transformations map *assembly contexts* to classes that instantiate the classes of associated *components* and *component types. Assembly connectors* are configured via the dependency injection mechanism used for realizing *required roles* (see above). Moreover, *assembly connectors* potentially include a so-called connector completion to model the communication overhead. Such completions annotate connectors with concrete configurations (e.g., for modeling the quality impact of RMI communication). A

```
package defaultrepository.impl.ports;


// Port class for IWebGUI_WebGUI

public class IWebGUI_WebGUI implements defaultrepository.IWebGUI,

       java.io.Serializable {

  protected defaultrepository.impl.IWebGUI myComponent = null;


  public IWebGUI_WebGUI(defaultrepository.impl.IWebGUI myComponent) {

     this.myComponent = myComponent;

  }


  public SimulatedStackframe<Object> upload0(Context ctx) {

     return myComponent.iFacade_upload0(ctx);

  }


}
```

Listing 11.2
Port class for the role IWebGUI of the WebGUI component. The method upload0 delegates all calls
to the component of the port.

transformation realizes such a completion by mapping the annotated connector to semanti-
cally equivalent PCM constructs that model the quality impact of the configuration. For
example, RMI communication for a connector can be modeled by a connector-component-
connector-component-connector construct, where the first component models the serializa-
tion, and the second component models the deserialization of RMI objects.

For the Palladio allocation model, transformations map *allocation contexts* to configuration classes, which state which *assembly contexts* map to which simulated resources. This
configuration is important when SimuCom simulates resource demands.

For the Palladio resource environment model, transformations accordingly map
resources to simulated resources. Such simulated resources are realized in dedicated framework classes of the SimuCom framework (e.g., reflecting a CPU scheduled by a Linux
scheduler).

For the Palladio usage model, transformations map *usage scenarios* to dedicated workload
drivers that simulate the behavior of users. These drivers spawn threads for each simulated

```
package defaultrepository.impl;


public class WebGUI implements defaultrepository.impl.IWebGUI {


  public WebGUI(String assemblyContextID, SimuComModel model) {

    // ...

  }


  //Pseudo-code: simulate demands to resource


  public SimulatedStackframe<Object> iFacade_upload0(dContext ctx){

    AbstractSimulatedResourceContainer resource = ctx.findResource(assemblyContex
tID);

    double demand = ctx.evaluate(DoublePDF[ (1.0; 0.25) (2.0; 0.50) (3.0; 0.25) ],
Double.class);


    resource.simulate(demand);

}
```

Listing 11.3
WebGUI component class. The upload method simulates its performance while the constructor initializes required roles via dependency injection.

user. Each thread executes the behavior as specified within the corresponding *usage scenario*. SimuCom particularly uses these workload drivers to take measurements of the overall response time.

11.2.2 Java SE and EE Prototyping Mapping

While SimuCom simulates environments on the basis of Palladio's resource model, performance prototypes allow software architects to assess their designs in more realistic environments than simulations can provide. Because simulations can be conducted more easily than performance prototyping experiments, it is suggested to validate only those models with performance prototypes for which simulations already indicated that they reflect good designs. In Palladio, the ProtoCom transformation can be used to generate performance prototypes, thus reducing effort.

ProtoCom allows software architects to map Palladio models to performance prototypes on the basis of Java SE (Becker 2008; Lehrig and Zolynski 2011) and Java EE (Giacinto and

Lehrig 2013; Klaussner and Lehrig 2014). Subection 8.3.4 gives a conceptual description of ProtoCom performance prototypes. Prototypes can be configured; for example, the technology to be used for intercomponent communication can be varied. The corresponding Java SE and EE performance prototype mapping is realized as depicted in table 11.2. The table is structured analogously to the table for SimuCom (see section 11.2.1). The differences between the ProtoCom mapping and the SimuCom mapping are highlighted and are discussed in this subsection.

Five differences affect Palladio's repository model:

• ProtoCom supports Java EE business interfaces as a special kind of *interface* (Giacinto and Lehrig 2013). At run time, Java EE application servers can automatically make such interfaces externally visible to clients and link them to corresponding assembly contexts. In contrast, the ProtoCom SE framework populates normal Java interfaces via an RMI registry.

Table 11.2

Overview of the performance prototype mapping for Java SE and Java EE (ProtoCom)

Palladio Model Model	PCM Concept	ProtoCom
Repository	Interfaces	(a) Java interface
		(b) Java EE business interface
	Data types	— (not mapped)
	Provided roles	Port classes
	Required roles	(a) Context classes
		(b) Annotation
	Provides/complete component types	— (not mapped)
	Basic components	(a) Classes with simulated SEFF
		(b) Same as (a) but bundled in an EJB module, which is packed into an EAR module
	Composite components	(a) Facade class
		(b) EJB modules bundled in an EAR module
System	Assembly contexts	(a) Instance of component class
		(b) Instance of an EAR module
	Assembly connectors	(a) Dependency injection
		(b) Use of selected feature (supported: RMI, RMI-IIOP, and RPC over HTTP)
Allocation	Allocation contexts	(a) Deployment scripts (b) Allocation class
Resource environment	Resources	Calibrated resources
Usage model	Usage scenarios	Workload driver

Note: Gray cells highlight differences with the SimuCom mapping.

- ProtoCom can use annotations at methods that refer to *required roles*. Java EE application servers support such annotations to link to known business interfaces (Giacinto and Lehrig 2013). This mechanism is an alternative to the dependency injection variant implemented in context classes and needs less generated code.
- *Provides/complete component types* are unsupported by ProtoCom. The reason for this lack of support is that prototypes such as ProtoCom rely on already existing behavior specifications to put load on resources. Otherwise, prototypes cannot provide reliable performance measurements.
- A *basic component* can be realized as a Java EE Enterprise Archive (EAR) module that wraps an EJB module (Giacinto and Lehrig 2013). EARs package Java EE components—so-called Enterprise JavaBeans (EJBs)—into deployable archives. The latter includes the Java classes that implement the *basic component*. Such a packaging into EAR modules eases deployment and distribution tasks. In the Java SE variant, system deployers can manually package generated Java code into Java Archive (JAR) files.
- *Composite components* are also packed into EAR modules (Giacinto and Lehrig 2013), similar to *basic components* described earlier. Inside such EAR modules, EJB modules are composed. This mechanism is an alternative to using facade classes and needs less generated code.

Two differences affect Palladio's system model:

- *Assembly contexts* can also be instantiated EAR modules. This addition is the natural consequence of enabling *basic* and *composite components* implemented as EAR modules. Again, this variant needs less generated code.
- Transformations can map *assembly contexts*—linked by an annotation model—to implementations that directly use the annotated feature (in contrast, SimuCom uses connector completions). For example, ProtoCom can directly use the RMI API for intercomponent communication if connectors are configured to use RMI.

In Java EE, application servers commonly support Remote Method Invocation over the Internet Inter-Orb Protocol (RMI-IIOP) (Giacinto and Lehrig 2013). If RMI-IIOP is unsuited or unavailable (e.g., in the SAP HANA Cloud), RPC over HTTP can be used as well (Klaussner and Lehrig 2014). Generally, directly using the desired feature instead of modeling it with connector completions improves the accuracy and reliability of quality analyses.

One difference affects Palladio's allocation model: Transformations map *allocation contexts* to deployment scripts and/or allocation classes. These scripts and classes allow software architects to easily deploy generated performance prototypes in target environments. For example, ProtoCom can generate simple bash scripts that deploy performance prototypes using secure shell (SSH) and secure copy (SCP) (Lehrig and Zolynski 2011). ProtoCom can also generate simple deployment classes that directly allow deployment of prototypes to the SAP HANA Cloud (Klaussner and Lehrig 2014).

One difference also affects Palladio's resource environment model: ProtoCom uses calibrated resources of the target environment to measure performance (SimuCom simulates such resources). Calibrating a resource means that a scaling factor is determined that gives the linear relationship between the actual physical resource processing rate and the modeled processing rate. In order to establish the relationship between the modeled and actual system, all resource demands are scaled according to this scalar. ProtoCom uses a CPU calibration table of the CPU in the target environment storing such scalars. This table gives ProtoCom the information needed to accurately demand CPU work units as stated in the model from an actual CPU. Lehrig and Zolynski (2011) provide further details on this calibration.

11.2.3 Technological Code Stub Java SE and EE Mapping

The code stub mapping for Java SE and EE generates code skeletons that implementation teams can use as a basis for actual implementations of Palladio models. The code stub mapping generally reuses the mappings of ProtoCom (see subsection 11.2.2). This reuse is convenient because ProtoCom is already close to the implementation, and it is technology-aware. For example, ProtoCom provides RMI support.

The only difference for code stubs is that they do not use SEFFs for simulating component behavior. Instead, an abstract class with abstract template methods is generated for *basic components*. These classes mark extension points from which subclasses have to inherit. Implementation teams can then implement the concerned abstract methods within subclasses without having to alter generated classes.

Moreover, *resources* of the *resource environment* correspond to the actually used resources and are neither simulated nor calibrated. In such situations, the coupled model transformation cannot help ensuring the correspondence between implementation and analysis model. Instead, the development team has to manually ensure that the code they provide matches the modeled resource demanding service effect specifications (RDSEFFs) or report any model discrepancies.

Note, however, that the generated workload drivers (see the description of SimuCom) for usage scenarios can still be used by implementation teams. For example, they can run the workload drivers to test their implementation (code coverage, performance measurements, etc.).

11.2.4 Technological SCA Mapping

Despite the mapping of Palladio models to Java SE or Java EE, there is also a mapping to the service component architecture (SCA; Marino and Rowley 2009). SCA provides a conceptual component model that matches the concepts from the PCM much more closely than Java SE or Java EE. Hence, the SCA mapping is interesting to study as the technological differences are small.

SCA is an industrial component model with a focus on enabling an easy implementation of large component-based and distributed systems that potentially utilize several distinct technologies. To enable and ease the use of SCA after engineering a Palladio model, a

Table 11.3
Overview of the technological SCA mapping

Palladio Model	PCM Concept	SCA
Repository	Interfaces	Interface (+ Java interface)
	Data types	—
	Provided roles	Service (+ Java interface implementation)
	Required roles	Reference (+ Java attribute)
	Provides/complete composite types	—
	Basic components	Component (+ Java class)
	Composite components	Composite
System	Assembly contexts	—
	Assembly connectors	Wire
Allocation	Allocation contexts	Actual allocation
Resource environment	Resources	Actual resources
Usage model	Usage scenarios	JUnit-test

mapping from PCM to SCA translates PCM representations into SCA models. This techno-logical SCA mapping is realized as depicted in table 11.3. The table is structured analogously to the table for SimuCom (see section 11.2.1).

SCA distinguishes between a technology-independent SCA architectural model and a technology-specific SCA implementation (e.g., in Java). Therefore, a complete SCA mapping involves a mapping to the SCA architectural model as well as to at least one concrete SCA implementation. The SCA column of table 11.3 accordingly shows elements of the SCA's architectural model plus their implementation as Java elements where feasible (in brackets).

Most PCM concepts of the *repository* can directly be mapped to corresponding elements of the SCA architectural model. Some of these SCA elements require appropriate Java elements in addition. For example, *provided roles* directly map to (SCA) services. The concrete behavior of these services has to be implemented within an additional Java class; the SCA architectural model does not allow modeling of behavior directly.

Because SCA is used for implementing systems (opposed to analyzing these), the SCA mapping uses actual resources and allocations to these for setting the system in operation. Once such a system is in operation, JUnit-tests generated from *usage scenarios* can be used to test the system and to measure its performance properties.

11.2.5 Mapping Summary

Palladio supports forward engineering by providing coupled model transformations. Palladio's coupled model transformations come with mappings to simulations (e.g.,

SimuCom), performance prototypes (e.g., ProtoCom), and code stubs for different technologies (e.g., Java SE, Java EE, and SCA). Such mappings allow development teams to automatically ensure that their code implementation matches Palladio's analysis results. Therefore, the risks of deviating from the planned architecture are lowered; only a few correspondences to the planned architecture have to be implemented manually. For instance, operation teams still have to ensure manually that the actual hardware resources correspond to the modeled resource environment.

11.3 Reverse Engineering

For the analysis of existing systems, for example, to plan refactorings or investigate quality issues, an up-to-date model of the system is required. Often, such a model is not available at all or it does not match the current implementation. Manually modeling an architectural model from scratch requires a lot of effort and knowledge about the system. A reasonable alternative is to apply reverse engineering techniques to extract a partial model from the existing implementation.

Such an extraction commonly requires the execution of three steps in the following sequence: first, extract the component structure (i.e., components, interfaces, connectors, etc.; see section 11.3.1); second, add the control flow specification to these components as SEFFs (see section 11.3.2); third, convert these SEFFs into RDSEFFs by adding resource demand specifications to them (see section 11.3.3). Each of these steps is affected by design problems in the reverse-engineered artifacts. Archimetrix is an approach that enhances the three steps by taking nonideal source code explicitly into account (see section 11.3.4).

11.3.1 Component Structure Detection

An architecture's component structure consists of *components*, their *assembly*, *composite structures* (i.e., which components contain which other components), *provided* and *required roles*, and *connectors* (*assembly* and *delegation*). Component *interfaces* are referenced by *roles* and comprise *signatures*, which describe possible component services.

Digression 11.2

Ambiguities in Reverse Engineering

The reverse engineering of architectural models is always ambiguous because correct results strongly depend on the chosen mapping from architecture to source code, which is often implicit and exists only in the minds of developers. In many cases, architectural erosion and drifts make it impossible to retrieve clear architectural information from source code. In addition, due to the fact that an architecture also covers aspects not included in the source code at all (e.g., deployment or usage), reverse engineering will never result in a perfect model when using source code as input alone.

To get all this information from an existing implementation, the source code can be statically extracted and analyzed. Extracting a source code structure is a typical reverse engineering technique, which is done by discovering an abstract syntax tree of the implementation. The Object Management Group (OMG) has standardized the knowledge discovery model (KDM) as part of the model-driven software modernization initiative. The Eclipse MoDisco [30] project (Bruneliere et al. 2014) provides a standard implementation for the OMG specification and comes with a discoverer for Java applications. The resulting model of a MoDisco run contains all elements of the analyzed Java code such as classes, interfaces, packages, and so forth. Another approach to discover Java applications is Java Model Parser and Printer (JaMoPP; Heidenreich et al. 2010). Similar to MoDisco, JaMoPP can be used to get a model representation from Java source code.

SoMoX, Palladio's reverse engineering approach, allows one to detect components and uses MoDisco or JaMoPP to retrieve a model representation of the source code. SoMoX then analyzes this model, using metrics to retrieve a component-based model from the source code (model). During this analysis of the code structures, first an initial component model is derived from the source model. This is done by mapping every class to a basic component and interpreting all its public methods as provided interface signatures. By analyzing the usage dependencies between these elements, SoMoX derives assembly connections between the so-defined basic components. After this initial step, an iterative analysis of this structure is used to cluster the basic components to a more coarse-grained and manageable component structure. More specifically, clustering either merges multiple components into a single, larger component or composes several components into a composite component. The decision on clustering components is based on a set of metrics. For these metrics, system-specific configurations have to be specified.

Discovering components, interfaces, and their relations results in a mapping between those elements and the source code elements they result from. This mapping is persisted into the *source code decorator model*, a trace model that provides added value during reverse engineering of component behavior, which is discussed in the following.

The analysis of an existing system always follows a specific purpose (cf. section 5.2); for example, to improve or refactor the system or to predict the performance of the system by reverse engineering the behavior of the components. As soon as the aspects of interest are studied and design decisions are made, the system has to be changed. To map the design decisions back to the code to change, the trace model built as part of the reverse engineering can be used to plan the code changes.

You can learn about the trace model's second purpose—to reverse engineer the components behavior—in subsection 11.3.2.

Component Detection Metrics   In the following, the detection metrics that are used to detect the component structure of a software system are explained briefly. During each step of the reverse engineering run, the metrics are applied to source code. The metrics were originally presented in Krogmann (2012), where more details about the metrics are provided.

Basic Metrics   In the following, you will learn the basic metrics that are used by the SoMoX approach for reverse engineering. Before the extraction starts, the user of SoMoX has to weight each metric with a number between 0 and 100. According to the weight, the metrics are used to calculate an initial component architecture from the source code.

Package and directory mapping: The package and directory mapping metric is a simple metric. As the name indicates, it assumes that classes within the same package or directory belong to the same component. The package mapping is used for programming languages that use packages (e.g., Java), whereas the directory mapping is used for programming languages without a package language construct (e.g., C++).

Coupling: Coupling was first introduced in Martin (1994) for object-oriented code and has been adapted to components within SoMoX. The coupling of a component is the ratio between the component's internal accesses and the component's external accesses. An internal access is an access from a class to a method or field of another class within the same component, while an external access is an access to a different component. The lower the coupling between two classes or two components, the higher their independence. A low coupling between two classes also indicates that the two classes are not in the same component.

Distance from main sequence (DMS):   The DMS metric and the terms abstractness and instability have been introduced by Martin (1994) for OO code and have been adapted for components in SoMoX. The DMS metric indicates the balance between abstractness and instability of a component. Abstractness is the ratio between abstract (e.g., interfaces, abstract classes) and nonabstract elements in a component. The instability metric indicates the probability that a component has to be changed in the future. The metric is higher if the classes that implement a component have a high number of external dependencies. Because a component has to be adapted when one of its external dependencies changes, a high instability ratio indicates that a component may have to be changed more frequently. The more abstract and the more stable a component candidate is, the more likely it is that it is identified as a component in the final architecture.

Interface violation: The interface violation metric lists the direct accesses from one class to another class. Direct access occurs if one class directly uses a method or a field from another class instead of using an interface to call the method or get the field. (An example for interface violation is given in figure 11.4 later in the chapter.) The interface violation metric is later used to figure out the communication style between different classes and components.

Name resemblance: The name resemblance metric assigns classes and interfaces with similar names to one component. The idea behind the name resemblance metric is that it is more likely that classes with similar names belong to the same component; however, the metric

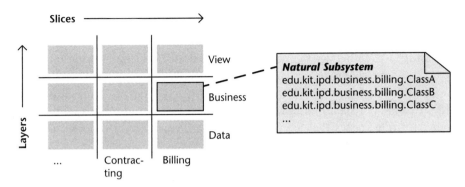

Figure 11.3
Example of slices, layers, and natural subsystems in a software system (Krogmann 2012).

also has a mechanism to avoid a situation where classes that accidentally have similar names become assigned to the same component. Only classes with similar names are considered if they are already coupled at the code level.

Sliced layer architecture quality (SLAQ):   The SLAQ metric can be applied for software systems that use different layers. A slice in such a software system realizes a specific service part in one layer (figure 11.3). As an example, take the envisioned software system from figure 11.3, which consists of several layers and slices. The SLAQ metric assumes that slices and layers are encoded in packages (i.e., each layer is in a package that contains slices in subpackages). The SLAQ is used by the natural subsystem metric to identify possible subsystems of a software system.

Natural subsystem metric: The subsystem component metric uses the SLAQ metric to determine whether a component represents at least a natural subsystem that has been identified during the SLAQ run. Again, consider the example in figure 11.3: Each of the gray boxes could be a subsystem; however, in case of a nonlayered and nonsliced software system, the natural subsystem metric is not able to find any subsystem.

Blacklisting: All of the above metrics can be combined with a blacklisting approach. Using blacklisting allows a user to define classes or namespaces that should not be considered as architecturally relevant during the reverse engineering. For example, usually when reverse engineering a Java application, the basic language classes like java.lang.* or other external frameworks are excluded.

Detection Strategies for Merging and Composing Components   In the following, you will learn about the actual component detection strategies. These detection strategies combine the basic metrics, allowing SoMoX to find component candidates. They are executed multiple times during the reverse engineering process in iterative steps. During each iterative step, the basic metrics are combined according to the initial weights the user configured before the SoMoX run.

Interface bypassing: The interface bypassing detection strategy is based on the interface violation metric. The underlying idea to compose components using interface bypassing is that interface violation is allowed between classes within one component. Hence, it is more likely for classes that are only communicating via well-defined interfaces to belong to separated components, while classes that are communicating directly to one another usually belong to the same component.

Consistent naming: The consistent naming detection strategy is based on the naming resemblance metric. Like the naming resemblance metric, the consistent naming is based on the idea that software developers tend to name classes that belong to one component similar. For instance, classes that are in a Database component may be named DatabaseConnection, DatabaseInitialization, and DatabaseRequest. Like the resemblance metric, it also has strategies to avoid a situation where classes that are not coupled at the code level are merged into one component.

Subsystem component: The subsystem component detection strategy is used to identify subsystems using the natural subsystem metric. Therefore, it checks whether a given component candidate can be used as a specific slice and layer of the software system.

Component composition and component merge: The component merge strategy checks whether two component candidates can be merged into one component. To decide whether two component candidates can be merged to one component, the strategy combines the results of the above-mentioned strategies according to their weight. Hence, indicators for merging two component candidates into one component are

• coupling between the component candidates;

• heavy communication between the classes of the components;

• communication between the classes is done by interface bypassing;

• consistent naming of the classes; and

• whether the classes of the component candidates are in the same package (usually, the component merging strategy is applied often in early reverse engineering iterations).

In contrast to the component merge strategy, the component composition strategy determines whether a given set of components can be used inside a composite component. To decide whether two component candidates can be composed to a composite component, the component composition strategy takes the results of the interface bypassing, the consistent naming, the DMS, the package mapping, and the subsystem component metrics into account. If it turns out that a couple of components can be used as a composite component, SoMoX creates the composite component and uses it in the next iterative steps.

11.3.2 Component Behavior Detection

The success of detecting component behavior strongly depends on the component's structure. This reverse engineering step is done per interface provided by the component under study. Component behavior is reverse engineered per signature of the provided interfaces of a component. The trace model, created by the previous component structure detection, provides a mapping between each provided signature and its implementing method in the source code. This method serves as an entry point for a control flow analysis discovering the component's behavior for the signature under study. The behavior is represented as an SEFF that is stored in the component repository.

The reverse engineering of a component's behavior starts at the method's entry. It analyzes the complete control flow up to the borders of the component, as identified by provided and required interfaces. The different types of operations on the control flow path are transformed into SEFF actions. For every code access that is not traced as part of the component under study, which means that it is a call to code of the required interface, an *external action* is created. This *external action* then references a required role for the interface representing the external access. Next, control flow statements are processed. For any iterating statement (e.g., a *for*-loop or a *while*-loop), a *LoopAction* is created in the SEFF. Similarly, for every conditional statement (e.g., *if* or *switch*) a *BranchAction* is created. All other statements are translated into *internal actions* representing this internal processing.

Especially the SEFFs discovered during the reverse engineering can become very large. Two different strategies are used to reduce the complexity through abstraction: summarizing internal actions and using more abstract components. Summarizing is done by creating only one internal action for every sequence of statements, neither influencing the control flow nor invoking external resources. Detecting more coarse-grained components during the structure detection results in fewer statements identified as invocations of external resources. This leads to larger sequences of internal statements and as a result to more statements summarized into fewer internal actions.

These concepts to reverse engineer component behaviors is implemented as the GAST-2SEFF component of the SoMoX tooling. To be able to analyze the architecture of an already implemented software with respect to aspects such as a system's performance or reliability, the reverse-engineered model must be further parameterized. The following subsection discusses how parameterizations can be reverse engineered from an existing system.

11.3.3 Control and Data Flow Parameterization

Palladio requires parameterization of resource demands, data flow, and control flow in order to predict performance. For example, the resource demand of an *internal action*, in terms of CPU or HDD cycles, has to be specified for a complete RDSEFF with actual resource consumption, such as "ten CPU units and four HDD units for every processed list item." *Set variable actions*, *input parameters*, and *output parameters* declare which data flows are allowed within a model. *Stochastic expressions* (see digression 5.4) define the actual data flow. They may, for

---

Digression 11.3

Static and Dynamic Analysis

Reverse engineering analysis techniques are mainly distinguished into *static* and *dynamic analysis*. *Static analysis* uses source code as the primary source. It extracts, for example, abstract syntax trees from source code. Abstract syntax trees help navigating over source code and derivation of information from it. *Dynamic analysis* uses observations from executed code. Data is captured and collected at run time. Dynamic analysis typically uses instrumentation and monitoring techniques to observe code execution. In order to use dynamic techniques, code must be installed and runnable, and test data or real/simulated users are required.

---

example, express that a loop is executed for every incoming list element, such as "each file retrieved from the database is processed in a loop inside MediaManagement when downloaded from the Media Store." These stochastic expressions are subject to reverse engineering.

Control flow can be expressed either probabilistically (*probabilistic branch transition*) or depending on input variables (*guarded branch transition*). In both cases, again a *stochastic expression* has to be defined that expresses the control flow decisions (e.g., when to take the first or the second branch).

All dependencies that have been described above are between one or more input variables and one output. These dependencies are each described by a stochastic expression. For example, such a *stochastic expression* can indicate the number of loop iterations by

`x.NumberOfElements` $\times$ `y.NumberOfElements`

for a *loop behavior* that iterates over independent input lists x and y.

Input variables of stochastic expressions are parameters that are passed by the data flow:

Input parameters are operation arguments that are comparable to method arguments in object-oriented languages.

Context parameters originate from the instantiation contexts defined in Palladio (e.g., a component can be configured for a specific *assembly context*).

Output parameters return variables from operations called previously in the control flow.

When looking back at the Media Store example in figure 5.1, you can find a guarded branch that depends on the parameter `Count.VALUE`. The latter is a parameter defined by the usage model. Resource demands of the internal action JNDI RMI Overhead in the example in figure 5.3 are modeled as fixed value (10 units in the example) but could also depend on other parameters such as the `files.BYTESIZE` input parameter:

`10` $\times$ `files.BYTESIZE.`

Outputs to be determined in this reverse engineering step are the following:

Resource demands define resource consumptions such as CPU, HDD, or memory (typically dynamically observed by instrumentation, such as `ByCounter`).

Branch transition conditions describe Boolean conditional branching behavior, which is statically derived from source code, or by observing the relation between input parameters and branch selection at run time.

Branch transition probabilities describe probabilistic branching behavior for unknown dependencies between inputs and behavior, which is observed by dynamic analysis by looking at the frequencies of executing branches.

Loop iteration counts describe how often a loop is traversed. This property can be derived statically for simple cases or dynamically in general.

Set variable actions specify the return values of a service described by an RDSEFF. This property can be derived statically for simple cases or dynamically in general.

Input parameters translate input variables into parameters passed to an *external call*. This property can be derived statically for simple cases or dynamically in general.

Output parameters translate return values from *external calls* into local variables. This property can be derived statically for simple cases or dynamically in general.

Learning from Observed Behavior   The so-called Beagle approach (Krogmann 2012) derives stochastic expressions from observed behavior and estimates the relation between input and output variables. Beagle is a dynamic code analysis approach. It combines (optional) source code or byte code instrumentation, monitoring, data collection using machine learning techniques with subsequent model enrichment to approximate resource demands, data flow, and control flow parameterizations, which is everything that is expressed in *stochastic expressions* in PCM.

An optional instrumentation is responsible for installing facilities for monitoring source code or byte code. A monitoring step then gathers data at run time, which is collected by the data collection facilities. Machine learning techniques (including genetic algorithms, correlation analysis, and regression analysis) extract dependencies between input and output variables. Finally, the extracted dependencies are stored in the RDSEFF.

The steps that are performed by Beagle can either be executed manually or in a tool-supported way. For example, the analysis of log files and checking for input-output relation is performed manually. The steps of Beagle are detailed in the following. Besides using pure parameter observations, it is possible to incorporate symbolic execution techniques (King 1976) to derive dependencies between inputs and outputs from source code. Such advanced techniques are not considered in this book. Details can be found in Krogmann (2012).

Source Code and Byte Code Instrumentation   Before starting instrumentation, you have to decide on the granularity level of the models that are to be reverse engineered. You can find hints in section 5.2 and chapter 6. Models can be either calibrated by timing values, which requires timestamp information, or by resource demand counts, which require detailed resource usage information. Resource demand counts need fine-grained instrumentation to count resource accesses, such as executed API calls (e.g., `math.sqrt()` in line 9 in listing 11.4), or executed byte code. When deciding to get parameter dependencies (in contrast to probabilistic estimates), you need to monitor input parameters (e.g., the value of a parameter x).

The first step is to enable the generation of measurable and trackable outputs. This can either be the configuration of log file formats (e.g., switching on detailed logging) or insertion of instrumentation statements in the source or byte code, which logs data. Typically, logged data includes parameter values (input and output parameters) and their characterizations (see figure 5.4, e.g., the actual values or the number of elements of a list). Furthermore, when aiming to characterize resource demands by timing values, you should log entry and exit timestamps (logEntry() in line 2 in the code in listing 11.4).

Detailed resource demand estimates go down to counting individual byte-code instructions that are executed for certain input parameters. In this case, input values are logged together with executed byte-code instructions. The corresponding tooling is named ByCounter.

Monitoring and Data Collection   Data from instrumented code is observed by monitoring program executions. To get a representative overview on executed functionality and representative timing and parameter values, test cases or manual program executions are required. These executions should represent typical usage scenarios of the software under study. To avoid overlapping effects, parallel program executions should be avoided when monitoring data dependencies.

```
public int myComponentService (int x, boolean y) {

    logEntry(); // get start time stamp

    logParameters(x, y); // log input parameters

    z = x + y;

    logCallParameters(z); // log parameters of component call

    int returnValue = otherComponent.service(z);

    logCallOutputParameters(returnValue); // log returned values
                                          // of component call

    returnValue = returnValu e+ math.sqrt(9);

    logReturnParameters(returnValue); // log output parameters

    logExit(); // get start time stamp

    return returnValue;

}
```

Listing 11.4
Example code to illustrate reverse engineering.

In order to ease the following machine learning step, data have to be collected centrally. Imagine the distributed execution of a software system. Different log formats have to be unified to grant uniform access. Ultimately, you need to be able to map data collected along a request as preparation for the machine learning step, for example x.value is 3, y.value is true, which results in argument z in the example.

Machine Learning Once the program execution has been monitored, the dependencies between inputs and outputs have to be reverse engineered. Three classes of techniques are especially suitable to identify the relationship between input and output:

1. Regression and correlation analysis; for example, linear regressions, multivariate adaptive regression splines (MARS; Friedman 1991)
2. Machine learning; for example, genetic algorithms, simulated annealing
3. Manual estimation: humans estimate dependencies on the basis of monitoring data

Generally, multidimensional approaches that support discontinuous functions (i.e., modeling if-else branches) should be preferred. Depending on requirements toward precision and computation time, either regression approaches (fast, good precision) or genetic algorithms (slower, higher precision) should be selected. MARS regressions are the recommended default approach. Manual derivations of *Stochastic Expressions* have the advantage of little tooling overhead and very strongly simplified expressions at the cost of increasing effort and the threat of losing precision.

A more complex combination of techniques is covered by the implementation of Beagle. For further reading, please refer to Krogmann (2012), Faber (2011), and Westermann et al. (2010).

Model Enrichment The last step is to translate machine learning output into *Stochastic Expressions* of Palladio models by annotating resource demands, control flow, and data flow. This step is straightforward by using the result representation from the previous step and translating it into the *Stochastic Expressions* language. Because the StoEx language is quite powerful, most constructs can be expressed in PCM.

Stepwise functions can be simulated by nested blocks of if-then-else expressions *a ? b: c*, for which each argument is encapsulated by brackets. For example, if the value is *y* multiplied by 3 for the interval *x* = 5 ... 10 (and 0 otherwise), the expression would be

```
(x.VALUE > 5) ?((x.VALUE < 10) ?(y.VALUE * 3):0):0.
```

More details on the StoEx language can be found in digression 5.4 or in Reussner et al. (2007).

Digression 11.4

Best Practices for Manual Reverse Engineering

You may wonder what are best practices for *manual* reverse engineering that should be kept in mind in case you ever have to reverse engineer a system. When discussing reverse engineering, one should distinguish between the following artifacts:

• The *usage model* is best retrieved from observing users and other systems interacting with a system under study. Suitable sources for this information are front-end servers with timestamps to derive frequency information for interactions.

• The *resource environment* is best gathered by talking to people who operate a system under study. Access to network latencies and throughput parameters is valuable. At least information on the physical distribution of servers and the number of CPU cores should be known to create resource environment models.

• The *static architecture* (interfaces, roles, components) can be retrieved in many ways. Analyzing source code, as introduced above, is one option. Use of manually drawn architectures is a valuable add-on. In this case, the architecture should be critically reviewed. Too often, those architectures are outdated, misleading, or just intended architectures that have little to do with the source code implementation. Hence, distinguish between as-is architecture and should-be architecture by talking to the software architects and developers.

• Capturing the *dynamic architecture* (RDSEFF, resource demands) requires substantial efforts. Keep in mind that they are performance and reliability abstractions of real source code. Leave out all internal details. Use static source code analysis to retrieve control flow information. Use back-end logs (logs at called systems) and monitoring (before and after executing either internal calculations or external service calls) to retrieve performance data.

Digression 11.5

Rules of Thumb

1. Bigger components tend to have smaller and more abstract RDSEFFs.

2. Systems should have less than 10 components to easily handle them. Carefully choose domain and nondomain interfaces. For example, when considering a logging service as domain interface, the SEFF's complexity (capturing every individual logger call as a separate external action) will grow a lot. In case logging is always performed locally and is not subject to any chance scenario, do not make this technical interface explicit. Performance effects of logging can, in this case, still be captured by means of resource demand (e.g., CPU and the hard disk to write to).

3. Automated reverse engineering models tend to be really detailed but more precise than manually created models, because every small piece of source code may have an impact on your models (including, e.g., mistakenly non-blacklisted logging functionality).

4. Reverse engineering of architecture is possible without having deep technical insights to the system under study. When supported by reverse engineering techniques, there will be guidance to extract architectures. Still, certain knowledge of the intent of a system's architecture helps to identify pitfalls and deviations. Furthermore, such knowledge helps in finding the right abstraction level and to communicate findings back to developers.

11.3.4 Archimetrix

While the aforementioned reverse engineering approaches already create useful models for strictly component-based source codes, they are severely affected by *design deficiencies*. Such deficiencies are deviations from the planned architecture in the system's code base, especially violations of the assumption that the code to be reverse engineered is component based. As long as design deficiencies are not considered explicitly in the reverse engineering process, they reduce the quality of the recovered architectural views. Despite this impact of design deficiencies on reverse engineering, no existing reverse engineering approach (e.g., SoMoX) explicitly integrates a systematic deficiency detection and removal into the recovery process.

Therefore, von Detten and colleagues have developed Archimetrix (von Detten et al. 2013), a tool-supported architectural reconstruction process. Archimetrix enhances the clustering-based reverse engineering approach SoMoX with an extensible, pattern-based deficiency detection. Archimetrix supports software architects in detecting, ranking, and removing deficiencies and provides the means to preview the architectural consequences of such a removal.

The remainder of this section introduces design deficiencies and exemplifies them, then describes the reengineering process of Archimetrix that supports addressing such design deficiencies. This discussion uses material literally taken from von Detten et al. (2013).

Influence of Deficiencies on the Architectural Reconstruction The upper part of figure 11.4 shows an architectural view with two components UI and Logic. They are connected via an interface ISearch. This could be a (very simple) architecture that the original software architect may have had in mind. The lower part of figure 11.4 shows a view of the classes implementing these components. The UI component contains the class ProductsListView that

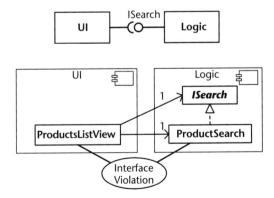

Figure 11.4
An example of the interface violation deficiency.

accesses the interface ISearch in the Logic component; however, ProductsListView also directly accesses the class ProductSearch.

This is, however, a neglect of Szyperski's principles of good object-oriented design, which state that components may only communicate via their interfaces (Szyperski et al. 2002). This *interface violation* deficiency leads to an increased coupling between the classes ProductsListView and ProductSearch (without the access between them, their coupling would be 0). Because coupling is one of the metrics that is frequently used by reverse engineering approaches, this deficiency thus influences the recovery of the system's architecture. In the example, because of the high coupling between the classes, a reverse engineering approach might reconstruct only one big component containing all three classes instead of two components.

Archimetrix Reengineering Process   Figure 11.5 visualizes the reengineering process with Archimetrix. Initially, the source code of the system is parsed into an abstract syntax graph (ASG), which represents the syntactic structure of the code (e.g., using MoDisco for Java).

In the second step, the system architecture is reconstructed from the ASG. The reconstruction is accomplished by a reverse engineering approach that measures metrics, such as coupling and name resemblance for the system's classes, and assigns them to components. Archimetrix uses the SoMoX for the architectural reconstruction. This initial clustering can be influenced by existing deficiencies in the system.

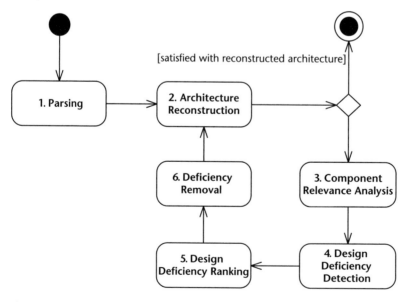

Figure 11.5
Overview of the reengineering process in Archimetrix.

The third step identifies which of the reconstructed components are worthwhile inputs for the detection of deficiencies. These are, for example, components whose modification will probably influence the recovered architecture (i.e., components that are most sensitive to the removal of design deficiencies). This relevance analysis is also helpful because the detection of deficiencies in all components does not scale well for larger systems.

In the fourth step, the detection is executed by matching predefined deficiency patterns in the ASG. The deficiency detection is accomplished by Reclipse, which is part of Archimetrix. Deficiency patterns are defined as object graphs that represent subgraphs of the ASG. The detection algorithm then tries to find occurrences of these object graphs in the ASG and annotates them accordingly. Deficiency patterns can be saved in a catalog so that they can be reused for deficiency detection in other systems. The detection yields a list of deficiency occurrences in the previously selected components.

In the fifth step, the detected deficiency occurrences are ranked according to their severity. Deficiencies that have a stronger impact on the architecture are identified as the best candidates for a removal.

Finally, after the identification of severe deficiency occurrences, the architect has to decide how the occurrences should be removed. This can be done either manually or by automated transformations that perform the reengineering in the ASG. If an automated transformation is available, the architect can also preview the architecture that would be reconstructed if the given deficiency occurrence was removed.

After the removal of one or more deficiency occurrences, a new iteration of the process can begin. The reverse engineering step may now reconstruct a different architectural view as the removed deficiency occurrences can no longer influence it. Software architects can continue this cycle of architectural reconstruction, deficiency detection, and deficiency removal until they are satisfied with the reconstructed architecture.

The presented Archimetrix reengineering process was validated in three case studies. The results of the studies show that Archimetrix is able to identify relevant deficiencies and that the removal of these deficiencies leads to an increased quality of the recovered architectures; that is, they are closer to the originally designed architectures (Platenius et al. 2012; von Detten et al. 2013).

11.4 Questions and Exercises

11.4.1 Questions

11.1 **: What are Palladio *provided roles* mapped to when using translation to SimuCom's Java source code?

11.2 **: What are SimuCom's port classes of the provided interface needed for?

11.3 *: What are the different purposes and advantages of forward engineering in Palladio?

11.4 **: How can the component detection approach SoMoX and behavior detection approach Beagle help you by evolving a software system?

11.5 **: What differences between static and dynamic source code analysis might challenge the use of dynamic analysis techniques?

11.6 *: What are possible advantages of dynamic analysis, and when should you chose dynamic analysis?

11.7 ***: Why does SoMoX account for interface violations?

11.8 *: How does Archimetrix support you by reverse engineering an architecture? Would you consider that approach as manual, semiautomatic, or automatic?

11.4.2 Exercises

11.1 ****: To understand potential source code mappings of Palladio models, imagine a component Calculator as follows. The component has one provided role ProdingRoleCalculator associating the interface ICalculator. It forms the front end of a calculator that can be switched between scientific and normal mode. Because of its mode change, two calculator back-ends can be triggered—one for normal precision and the other for high-precision calculation. Hence, the Calculator component has two required roles (RequiredRoleNormal, RequiredRoleScience), which both associate the interface ICalculatorBackend. Manually map this component, its roles, and its interfaces to Java source code. Choose a simplistic mapping that still supports the requirement to distinguish required roles.

11.2 **: Consider the UML diagram in figure 11.6. Mark the classes that can communicate with each other directly without using interfaces. Regarding the interface violation and interface bypass metrics: What can you tell about the classes?

11.3 **: Consider the Media Store system that is provided on the book's website. Use SimuCom and ProtoCom to generate (1) performance prototypes and (2) templates of the architecture.

11.4 *: Go to your Palladio installation. Find out all mappings that are currently developed for the forward engineering. What are the major differences between the different mappings?

11.5 Further Reading

Further details on forward engineering and the source code mapping of ProtoCom are provided in Becker (2008). To understand the details about reverse engineering source code with the ultimate goal to create performance models for the source code, Krogmann (2012) and Detten (2013) provide further details.

Chikofsky and Cross (1990) introduced basic terminology on engineering techniques that remains in use. A basic overview on reverse engineering at the source code level is given by Nelson (2005).

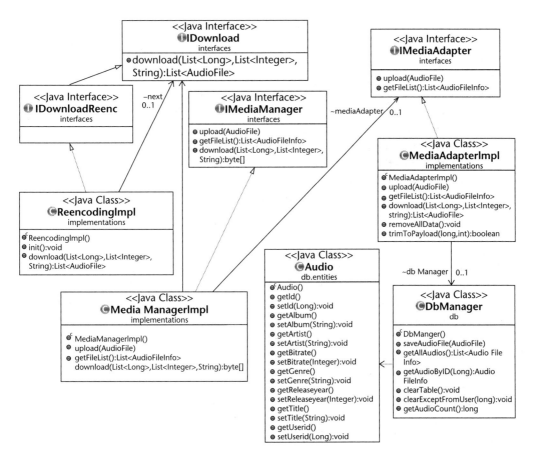

Figure 11.6
Can you figure out which classes communicate with each other directly without using interfaces?

11.6   Takeaways

This chapter gave you an insight to possible relations between Palladio models and their implementation (i.e., source code, deployment descriptors, etc.).

Therefore, you learned about *forward* and *reverse engineering* techniques that are supported within Palladio. Forward engineering assists in creation of running implementations from models. Reverse engineering supports existing systems by generating an overview and retrieving model information from source code.

Forward engineering as built into Palladio is able to speed up development. Forward engineering, from a Palladio perspective, is split into two groups: performance prototypes and performance simulation.

On the basis of initial-draft architectures and first performance annotations, Palladio can build readily deployable applications ("performance prototype"), which run on the basis of real infrastructure. Rapid prototyping enables fast round-trips between an architectural model and feedback from at least partially running applications.

Opposite to to performance prototyping, simulation-based approaches calculate performance properties directly from Palladio models. For these approaches, there is no need to actually deploy a software on real hardware. Still, because of simulation of system user interaction, architectural dynamics, and underlying resources, performance impact can be observed.

After obtaining performance specifics from either performance prototyping or performance simulation, Palladio provides a foundation for template-based generation of source code. Because Palladio aims to capture the domain architecture of an application 1:1, static structure information from Palladio models is suitable for creating initial implementations of a software architecture directly from architectural models. The generated source code of Palladio strictly follows architectural information from models.

Getting up-to-date Palladio models for evolving software systems is a challenge because of the need to match other models and implementation. Reverse engineering approaches, such as SoMoX and Archimetrix, are realized as add-ons to Palladio. The goal of these reverse engineering approaches is to allow you to rapidly get an up-to-date component-based architectural model of your system. SoMoX uses different metrics to iteratively build a component-based architecture from source code. Archimetrix helps you to find and remove deficiencies in your system.

Part V   Case Studies

This part presents three different case studies that use the Palladio approach to trade off different design decisions. The case studies contain valuable tips and tricks on how to create architectural models of IT systems, how to gather data to parameterize and calibrate a model, and finally how to analyze the results for design decision trade-offs. The goal of the following chapters is to inspire you to apply the Palladio approach in your context.

Chapter 12 demonstrates the modeling of a large and distributed system of 1&1 Internet consisting of several hundreds of servers. The main challenge of this case study is how to create a Palladio model using only monitoring data. Chapter 13 is a case study about applying the Palladio approach outside of its target domain of business information systems. In this case study, the PCM is used to compare two design alternatives for storage virtualization in IBM systems. Chapter 14 presents a case study applying the PCM in the context of a design exploration of a distributed software system from ABB. The approach shows how to determine a cost-efficient architectural solution.

12   Workload-Aware Monitoring of a 1&1 E-mail System

Ralf H. Reussner and Klaus Krogmann

Offering services on the Internet requires dependable operation of the underlying software systems with guaranteed quality of service. The workload of such systems typically significantly varies throughout a day and thus leads to changing resource utilizations. In this chapter, we present a Palladio case study for workload-aware performance monitoring. It shows how we detected performance issues before they became critical in the e-mail system operated by Germany's largest e-mail provider, 1&1 Internet AG. This case study demonstrates the applicability of Palladio for predictive monitoring scenarios and shows its accuracy in the predicted resource utilization with an error of mostly less than 10%.

The following section is based on the case study published by Rathfelder et al. (2012).

12.1   Introduction

The dependable operation of software systems with guaranteed quality of service is one of the most important aspects when hosting large and distributed systems. Because of the complexity of such systems and the distribution across several servers, the detection of potential performance problems such as overloaded resources or delayed requests is a complex but substantially important activity. To detect such potential problems and malfunctions within the system and the infrastructure as early as possible, management applications enable a centralized and automated collection and aggregation of performance indicators such as CPU and network utilization, the current length of request queues, or the processing time of requests.

In most systems, the workload intensity induced by real users varies over time. Especially in the case of systems offering services to end users over the Internet, significant variation regarding the system's usage depending on the time of day can be observed (Urdaneta et al. 2009; see also chapter 6). These changes lead to variations within the resource utilization of servers and the system's response times. These load-dependent variations complicate the detection of anomalies such as "higher CPU utilization than expected" that might be indicators for potential performance problems.

Existing monitoring and software management solutions support the definition of rules and conditions that are evaluated at run time in order to detect potential performance problems and to identify malfunctions of the system. Most of these solutions use fixed thresholds as upper or lower bounds to differentiate between normal system operation and a potentially problematic system state (Cherkasova et al. 2009). But using fixed values allows for detecting problems only when the system is under high load (i.e., the conditions are already critical or close to critical; for example, CPU resource utilization is more than 80%). In low-load situations, deviations from the expected value and potential malfunctions can hardly be detected. Some more advanced monitoring systems already support time-dependent thresholds to handle load variations. These systems are limited to fixed recurring patterns in the usage of the system and cannot handle unexpected peak loads or other variations in the user behavior, which might be caused by uncontrollable factors. Because there are no historical data on expected behavior for unexpected peak loads, no comparison can be made to what performance behavior should be considered stable for the peak (see chapter 7).

In this chapter, we present our approach to a workload-aware performance monitoring process. We apply model-based performance prediction techniques to derive the expected behavior and resource utilization induced by the current workload. Deviations between predicted and measured values serve as early indicators of performance abnormalities for all workload situations. Compared to the use of fixed threshold values, the detection of unexpected behavior can be improved, especially in the case of low-load situations. We describe the application of our method to the e-mail system operated by 1&1 Internet AG, which is one of Europe's largest e-mail providers. Additionally, this case study demonstrates and validates the applicability of our modeling and prediction approach to large and distributed systems.

12.2   Goals and Questions

The goal was to monitor a system and define alert thresholds in a scenario with varying workload. The questions that needed to be answered to achieve the goal were as follows:

- How to integrate model-based predictions into the run-time monitoring of systems?
- How to model a large and distributed system consisting of several hundred servers?
- How to calibrate the prediction model only on the basis of existing run-time monitoring data without running experiments?

12.3   System Description

1&1 Internet AG is a brand of the *United Internet AG*, which also includes the brands *Web.de*, *GMX*, *United Internet Media*, *Fasthosts*, *InternetX*, *AdLINK MEDIA*, *Affilinet*, and *Sedo*. With

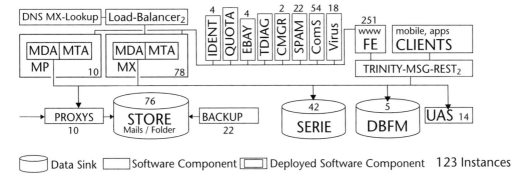

Figure 12.1
Back-end software components of the e-mail system.

more than 13 locations, the *United Internet AG* is one of the world's biggest Web hosters and leading domain registrars. The company is number 1 in e-mail services in Germany. The 1&1 e-mail system is the basis of several national and international e-mail platforms such as *GMX*, *web.de*, *mail.com*, and *india.com*. The system comprises more than 2,000 servers and provides services for more than 40 million users in Germany alone.

On the systems back-end, the core functionalities for e-mail sending, receiving, request- ing, and persistence are realized and provided through interfaces such as restful HTTP ser- vices, POP3, or IMAP. Further products such as Web clients or mobile mailers are built on top of these interfaces. The different internal software components follow the service-oriented design paradigm. The dimensioning of the system allows for an individual deployment of each component on dedicated servers that exist in redundant instances. Figure 12.1 illus- trates the components that realize the core functionality and the number of deployed instances.

In the STORE, folder structures of mailboxes and e-mails and their attachments are saved. The SERIE and DBFM databases provide fast access to information about the internal instances to which single mailboxes are dedicated. Mail delivery agents (MDAs) and mail transfer agents (MTAs) are located on the mail exchanger (MX) and mail proxy (MP) servers. They are external interfaces of the system and responsible for sending and receiving e-mails. For requesting e-mails, external clients connect to the proxy servers using IMAP and POP3 requests, which translate and forward the requests to the STORE servers. Internally managed clients such as Web-based user interfaces and mobile mailers use the restful HTTP services. Additionally, several other components for contact management, virus and spam protection, handling of quotas, trusted e-mails, and other tasks are available.

12.4 Modeling

The integration of performance predictions into a continuous system monitoring process promises several benefits compared to the use of fixed thresholds. Performance predictions consider the influence of the workload on the system's behavior and resource utilization. Thus, the predicted performance metrics (e.g., predicted response time) vary corresponding to the metrics collected on the running system (e.g., actually measured response time). If the run-time measurements correlate with the predictions, the system is in the expected state. Using workload-aware adaptations of the thresholds allows for an improved and faster detection of deviations between measured and expected values. In contrast to the use of historical data to derive the thresholds and their variation over time, the presented prediction-based approach can also be applied in situation when the workload caused by the users differs from the normal and expected one or in situations that are not covered by the historical data. Additionally, using architecture-level performance models allows us to adapt the prediction models to changes of the system's architecture or deployment without re-collecting a large set of historical data to derive the varying monitoring thresholds. The detailed prediction results support the system operator in detecting the root cause. Furthermore, the prediction model itself can be used by the operator to evaluate the performance impact and compare different possible counteractions such as, for example, adding new hardware resources (see chapter 5).

In figure 12.2, we illustrate our workload-aware continuous performance monitoring process, which consists of the main activities *model preparation*, *model calibration*, and *prediction and comparison*. The result of the first two activities is an initial performance model. This model has to be specified only once and is used within the fully automated continuous run-time monitoring represented by the *prediction and comparison* activity. Each of these main activities consists of several subactivities, which we describe in the following.

The aim of this first activity is the creation of a model describing the system. Therefore, the subprocess starts with the *system analysis* subactivity. This includes the identification of components, their interactions, and their behavior. Additionally, it is necessary to identify the available hardware resources and the deployment of the system on those resources.

On the basis of this information, the architecture of the system is described in the *architecture modeling* step using the Palladio Component Model (PCM). This architectural model consists of the specification of components including a description of their behavior as well as the provided and required interfaces and their connections to build up the complete system. In the PCM, these aspects are covered within the *Repository Model* and *System Model*.

As a final step of the model preparation activity, the available hardware resources are described; namely, the different servers including the available CPUs and storage devices and their network connections. Additionally, the *hardware modeling* includes the specification of the deployment of system components on available servers.

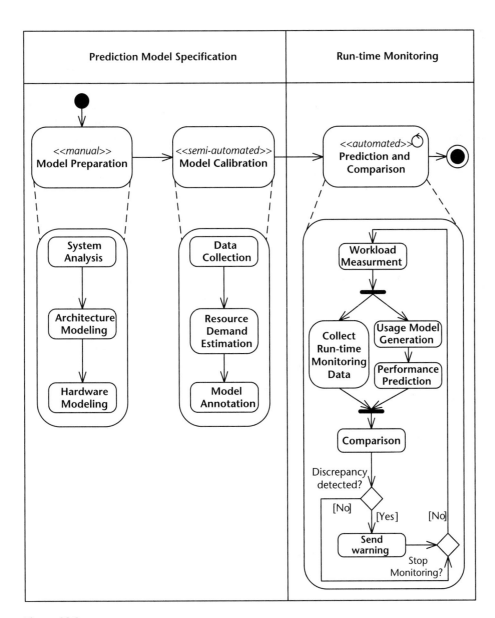

Figure 12.2
Workload-aware continuous performance monitoring process.

12.5   Data Collection

To enable the prediction of resource utilizations and response times, the behavioral specifications of the architectural model need to be annotated and calibrated with resource demands (e.g., amount of data written to disk and required CPU time), as shown in chapter 6. In our case study, we automated the data collection and analysis; however, depending on the scenario, it might be necessary to perform these activities manually. The first subactivity is the *data collection*. Systematic experiments as proposed by Westermann and Happe (2011) can be conducted to ease the derivation of dependencies between input parameters such as the size of an e-mail attachment and the resulting resource demand (i.e., CPU and hard disk in the case study). Such experiments, however, require set up of an equivalent system. For large systems such as the e-mail system of 1&1, distributed over hundreds of servers, this is quite infeasible. In such cases, the calibration of parametric resource demands needs to be done using monitoring and log data of the live system.

The collected data often only consists of aggregated values such as the mean resource utilization, the number of invocations per second, or the overall CPU time of a specific component. On the basis of the collected data, the *resource demand estimation* activity is responsible for deriving the individual resource demands for each operation provided by a service based on the collected data. Furthermore, the estimation also includes the analysis of dependencies between input parameters such as the size of an attachment or the type of request and the induced resource demand.

As part of the *model annotation* activity, the estimated resource demands including their dependencies on other parameters are integrated into the prediction model. The Stochastic Expression Language (StoEx), which is part of the PCM, allows for specifying different types of resource demands, including simple constant values, different probabilistic distribution functions, and mathematical functions reflecting the dependencies between input parameter values and the resulting resource demands.

12.6   Analysis

After the specification of the performance model in the previous activities, the performance monitoring can be started. As mentioned before, the utilization of resources often varies depending on the workload of the system. For this reason, the prediction of the expected resource utilization requires measuring the current workload, which is performed in the measurement workload activity. In most production systems, the external interfaces are already extended with interfaces to monitor the system's usage. Hence, these interfaces can be used to collect the required data.

On the basis of these data, the prediction model is completed with the specification of the system's usage within the *Usage Model generation* activity; that is, a new Palladio usage model with per-case adapted interarrival times is created for each system usage situation. This usage model specification can contain several independent usage behaviors to differentiate between the normal usage of the system by the customer and, for example, additionally data analysis or report generation processes invoked by internal users of the system. To reduce the run-time load induced by monitoring and data collection, live monitoring data often do not include as much information as the data gathered in the previous data collection step. The resulting *Usage Model* is then used as an input to the *performance prediction* activity, which in our case is a PCM-based performance simulation, to derive the expected utilization of servers and response times of operations.

After collecting the performance metrics of interest (e.g., CPU utilization, service response times) on the running system and predicting the expected values for the current workload, they are analyzed and compared. In the case of a deviation between predicted and measured values within the *comparison* activity, a warning is sent to the system's operator. The operator is then in charge to analyze the potential error and plan counteractions if required.

12.6.1   Application of the Workload-Aware Performance Monitoring Process

In the following, we present the application of our approach in the industrial context of the 1&1 e-mail system. For the sake of brevity, we focus in this case study on the STORE subsystem, which still consists of about 100 server nodes. The whole case study (Becker 2011) covers the complete incoming e-mail processing including the MX, Virus, and Spam servers as well as the SERIES and DBFM databases. After presenting further details of the STORE subsystem, we demonstrate the use of the PCM for modeling the system and the application of performance predictions.

12.6.2   STORE Subsystem

The STORE consists of several software components (figure 12.3) that are deployed on three different types of servers; namely, *Proxy*, *Store*, and *Backup* servers. The Proxy servers protect

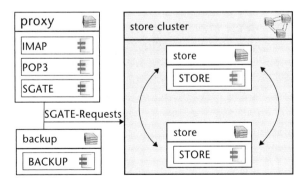

Figure 12.3
Composition of the STORE.

the Store servers from a direct access by hosts that are not part of the e-mail system. They provide access to the e-mails using IMAP and POP3 protocols by dedicated components. Additionally, the SGATE component is responsible for handling internal requests from other components of the e-mail system. The communication between Proxy and Store servers is exclusively performed by the SGATE component. Thus, the IMAP and POP3 components act as adapters that transform IMAP and POP3 requests into requests supported by SGATE and vice versa. The Store servers are responsible for storing all data related to customers' mailboxes including the folder structures, e-mail texts, and attachments.

To guarantee high availability and to prevent data loss, each Store server is running as a cluster of two servers. Each client's mailbox is associated with exactly one cluster. The responsibility for mailboxes is balanced over both hosts while the mailbox data is stored and continuously synchronized on both servers. In the case of software or hardware failures on one host, the other host automatically takes over the responsibility within seconds. The Backup servers are an additional instance to assert data persistency.

To handle the large amount of requests, multiple instances of all components are deployed on several servers to distribute the load. The SGATE, IMAP, and POP3 are running on 10 servers. The Store clusters consist of 76 servers overall. The BACKUP component is deployed on 22 servers.

12.6.3   Performance Modeling Study

After this overview of the STORE system, we will now describe the application of Palladio to obtain a performance model in the context of the workload-aware continuous performance monitoring process.

Model Preparation   The selection of an adequate abstraction layer that promises a good trade-off between prediction accuracy and modeling effort requires an analysis of the system regarding the available calibration data (i.e., data from log file analysis) and the potential performance-influencing factors. The monitoring tool running on the Store and Backup servers only measures the resource utilization of the whole server and does not allow measurement of the resource consumption of individual processes or components. For this reason, we introduce logical software components STORE and BACKUP that summarize all resource utilizations on one of these servers. Because of the missing calibration data, a more fine-grained model would not provide any improvements for the prediction results. On the Proxy servers, component-dependent resource monitoring is possible. Thus, we model the IMAP, POP3, and SGATE components as individual components as illustrated in figure 12.3.

The API of the SGATE component supports a large set of different request types. Modeling the huge amount of different possible requests would result in an infeasible modeling effort. To identify the request classes with a potentially high impact on the overall system's performance, we analyzed existing log files and performed interviews with the responsible architects and developers. The selection of the performance-relevant request types is based on two criteria. A request is categorized as potentially performance relevant if its occurrence within the overall workload is higher than 1% on average or the request is expected to be very resource intensive. Interviews with the developers were used to identify these resource-intensive requests and additionally to select requests that are known as performance irrelevant (table 12.1). In our performance model, we included all potentially performance-relevant requests that are not classified as irrelevant as well as all requests classified as expensive operations.

On the basis of this system analysis, we started system modeling by describing the different components in the Palladio Repository Model, which is shown in figure 12.4. In addition to the interfaces, components, and roles (assignment of provided and required interfaces), the Repository includes a resource demanding service effect specification (RDSEFF) for each provided interface.

As part of the Palladio System Model (figure 12.5), the different components defined within the Repository are instantiated, and the components SGATE, POP, IMAP, BACKUP, and STORE are connected to each other through the interfaces ISgate, IPop, IImap, and IBackup. Additionally, the model includes the definition of four system external interfaces that are used to connect the Usage Model, which contains the user behavior generated within the performance monitoring activity, with the System Model. The model includes three instances of the STORE component, as during the interviews, we identified that the servers hosting the Store can be clustered in three server types with identical hardware. The load balancing between the different server groups is integrated into the behavioral specifications and not modeled as an explicit load balancing component, as the modeling of load balancers as separate components would not have any impact on the prediction quality.

Palladio provides a dedicated model, called the *Resource Environment*, to describe the hardware resources of the system. Caused by the huge number of involved servers—in this subsystem more than 100—we had to find a way to abstract from modeling each individual server to reduce the size of the model and the required modeling effort. As already mentioned above, the servers can be classified on the basis of their hardware and configuration into clusters of servers with nearly identical resources and configuration. For each cluster, we modeled only one node within the *Resource Environment* (figure 12.6). All logical servers are sized with the cumulated resource capacities of the real servers they represent.

The mapping of instances of the described software components and server groups is done in the *Allocation Model* . As shown in figure 12.6, each server group contains one instance of the software component for which this group is responsible.

Model Calibration   After specifying the different components, the system's structure, and the deployment on hardware, the resource demands of the components need to be derived

Table 12.1

Performance-relevant requests

miweb::SGATE	%	p	miweb::POP	%	p	miweb::IMAP	%	p
SortMails	49		**COMPLETE**	31		**FETCH**	30	
GetMailText	16		**TOP0**	21		**STATUS**	30	
GetMails	14		**ABORTED**	16		**SEARCH**	15	
AppendMail	9		**RETR**	12		**STORE**	10	
ChangeMails	5		**DELETE**	8		**SELECT**	4	i
MoveMails	4	i	**TOPN**	8		LIST	2	i
RemoveMails	1	i				LOGIN	2	i
ReplaceMail	1	i				CAPABILITY	2	i
CreateFolder	0					ID	1	i
Subscribe	0					LOGOUT	1	i
ChangeFolder	0					CLOSE	1	i
FindMails	0					**APPEND**	0	e
RemoveFolder	0					.	0	
Unsubscribe	0					.	0	
GetFolderInfos	0					.	0	

msweb::STORE	%	p	mbweb::BACKUP	%	p
AppendMail	44		Remove expired	21	
ChangeMails	27		u-summary	17	
RemoveMails	10		sm-summary	17	
ExpungeMails	9		f-summary	17	
MoveMails	8		AppendMail	11	
CopyMails	1		Force deletion	8	
Subscribe	0		UpdateMails	3	
CreateFolder	0		Retrieve nonexpired	2	
ChangeFolder	0		RemoveMails	2	
SelectFolder	0		CopyMails	1	
Create	0		.	0	
Unsubscribe	0		.	0	
RemoveFolder	0		.	0	

Note: Boldface identifies entities considered within the model.

Abbreviations: %, portion of workload; p, interview-based characterization; i, performance irrelevant; e, expensive operation.

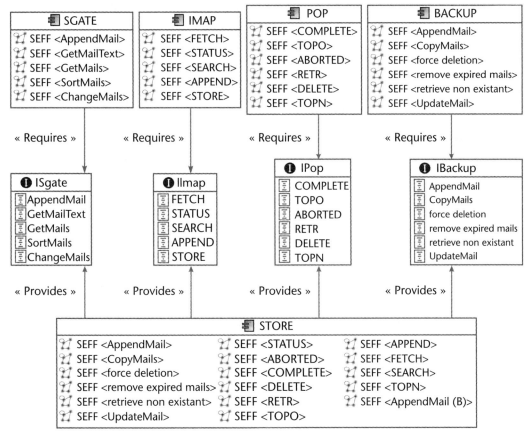

Figure 12.4
The Repository as part of the structural model.

within the model calibration activity (see chapter 6). For each server, we analyzed log files and monitoring data to derive those hardware resources (e.g., CPU, HDD, LAN) that are significantly used by the implementation of the system. In the case of the Proxy servers, these resources are CPUs and the network connection. As expected, the HDD usage is very low on these servers, because they only forward requests without any local persistence. In contrast, on the Store servers, the HDDs, CPUs, and network connections are heavily demanded resources and therefore need to be modeled.

For the sake of brevity, we now focus our description on the calibration of the Proxy servers' components and omit the Store and Backup servers. The procedure is the same for the other components. The system monitoring tools running on the Proxy servers provided us with detailed measurements of the resource utilization. Each component, namely the IMAP,

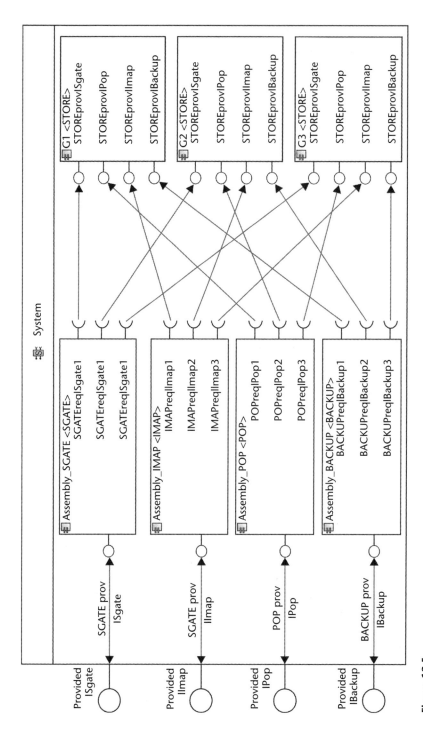

Figure 12.5

System Model of the STORE.

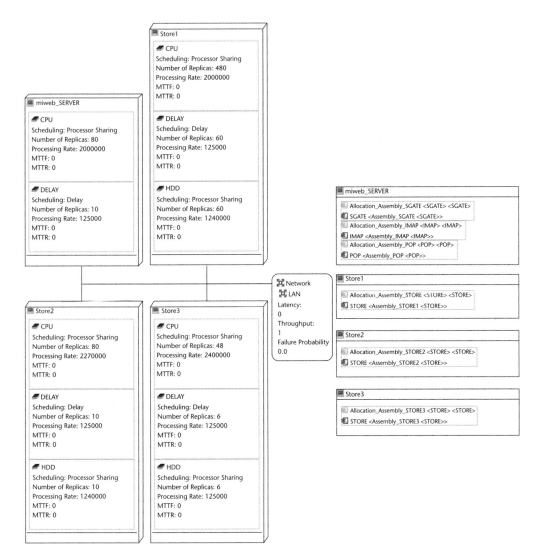

Figure 12.6
Resource Environment and Allocation Model.

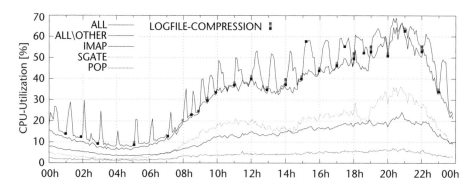

Figure 12.7
CPU utilization on a Proxy server over 24 hours.

SGATE, and POP3, are individually measured by the tool, which provides logs of the induced resource consumption every 30 seconds. Additionally, the overall CPU utilization is logged. Thus, we were able to derive the resource demands that are induced by the operating system or other monitoring activities. Figure 12.7 shows the CPU utilization on a Proxy server over 24 hours, induced by the software components SGATE, IMAP, and POP, as well as the sum of these values and the overall utilization.

Detailed analyses of the overhead peaks showed that they appear directly after the compression of request log files is initiated. To estimate the resource demand for each request type classified as performance relevant, we conducted further measurements to derive the distribution frequency of the different request types. We collected 864 sample sets covering 5 minutes each. In addition, data about the size of the requested data were collected. Table 12.2 shows the derived correlation coefficients of the request types and the resource utilizations on the different server clusters caused by them.

In order to calculate the absolute resource demands of the different request types, we had to consider the available hardware resources on the servers. Each server is equipped with two dual-core CPUs running with 2 GHz. The network connection has a capacity of 2 GBit/s. On the basis of this knowledge, we calculated our modeling functions describing the resource demand for each resource type. Table 12.3 exemplarily shows the utilization of a Proxy server's CPU resource caused by the processed requests of the POP component. We differentiate between resource demands with fixed value for each request and request demands that depend on the size of the contained data. Then, we determined the capacities of the resources to model, which are shown in table 12.4.

The knowledge of these capacities is essential to estimate the absolute resource demands based on percentage metrics stored in the resource-monitoring log files.

In a last step, the behavioral descriptions of the components are annotated with the derived resource demands. As already mentioned above, we integrated the load balancing

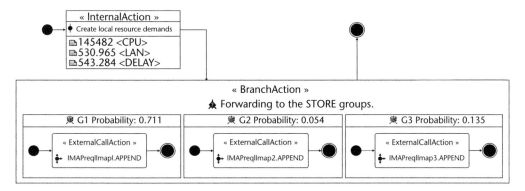

Figure 12.8
RDSEFF of the APPENDMAIL request on a Proxy server.

functionality within the proxy component. Thus, we also needed to calibrate the distribution of requests to the different groups of servers (i.e., the three Store server groups mentioned before). We modeled the load balancing behavior with a ProbabilisticBranchAction (control flow branch in the RDSEFF) on the basis of data available from individual request logs contained in the Store cluster's redirect logs. Figure 12.8 shows the annotated RDSEFF for the APPENDMAIL request on a Proxy server. It includes the resource demands for different resources of the server and the BranchAction forwarding the requests to the different server groups.

Prediction and Comparison   To consider the current workload of the running system in the performance prediction, we first have to specify the user interactions with the system. For each external interface specified in the System Model, a dedicated usage profile is defined within the Usage Model. Each usage profile is a template for the measured workload (i.e., request frequencies can be automatically integrated). Figure 12.9 illustrates the usage model of the SGATE interface.

To achieve full automation, we implemented tools that automatically collect, parse, and analyze the log files of the servers. On the basis of these data, the parameters for the usage profile are calculated. These values are then automatically integrated in the XML representation of the usage profiles by replacing the previously inserted placeholder values. The usage profiles are then used to execute the performance predictions. The relevant prediction results, namely the average resource utilizations, are compared with the measured values to identify mismatches.

Because we are working with the live system, we were not allowed to induce failures resulting in an unexpected behavior of the system. To demonstrate the detection capabilities of our process, we applied our approach during a planned software update on the live system as

Table 12.2

Correlation coefficients between requests and resource utilizations

	SGATE													
	# AppendMail	Σ AppendMail Size	# GetMailText	Σ GetMailText Length	# GetMails (+)	Σ GetMails (+) IDs	# GetMails (−)	Σ GetMails (−) IDs	# SortMails (+)	Σ SortMails (+) IDs	# SortMails (i)	# ChangeMails (+)	Σ ChangeMails (+) IDs	# ChangeMails (−)
CPU	0.79	0.83	0.86	0.7	0.86	0.74	0.84	0.86	0.86	0.86	0.85	0.58	0.34	0.86
CPU SGATE	0.82	0.87	0.97	0.78	0.97	0.86	0.96	0.97	0.97	0.97	0.97	0.71	0.45	0.96
CPU POP														
CPU IMAP														
CPU OTHER	0.27	0.27	0.24	0.2	0.23	0.18	0.22	0.24	0.23	0.24	0.23	0.12	0.05	0.24
NET-IN	0.81	0.87	0.97	0.8	0.97	0.85	0.95	0.96	0.96	0.97	0.96	0.66	0.4	0.96
NET-OUT	0.84	0.9	0.96	0.79	0.96	0.85	0.94	0.95	0.95	0.96	0.95	0.65	0.39	0.96
DISK-READ	0.05	0.05	0.09	0.08	0.09	0.06	0.09	0.09	0.09	0.09	0.09	0.06	0.04	0.09
DISK-WRITE	0.48	0.49	0.49	0.4	0.48	0.41	0.47	0.49	0.48	0.48	0.47	0.31	0.17	0.49

Abbreviations: #, amount of processed requests within one examined interval; Σ, sum of a numerical parameter over the requests of the examined interval; +, Boolean parameter indicating expensive requests; −, Boolean parameter indicating cheap requests.

Table 12.3

Average CPU demands caused by the POP component

Request	CPU Demand
ABORTED	16,134,069 cycles/request
COMPLETE	4,520,880 cycles/request
TOPN	3,267,070 cycles/request
DELETE	684,569 cycles/request
RETR	353,879 cycles/request
TOP0	4,319 cycles/request
RETR	48 cycles/byte

	POP							IMAP				
# COMPLETE	#TOPO	#ABORTED	#RETR	Σ RETR Size	# DELETE	#TOPN	ΣTOPN Lines	# FETCH	# STATUS	# SEARCH	# APPEND	# STORE
0.9	0.82	0.91	0.86	0.84	0.83	0.03	0	0.87	0.9	0.87	0.79	0.89
0.95	0.85	0.94	0.91	0.91	0.88	0.15	0.06					
								0.96	0.96	0.91	0.84	0.93
0.35	0.33	0.36	0.32	0.31	0.3	–0	–0	0.4	0.38	0.32	0.31	0.34
0.9	0.8	0.9	0.86	0.84	0.83	0.08	0	0.81	0.88	0.89	0.8	0.89
0.91	0.8	0.91	0.87	0.86	0.84	0.05	0	0.81	0.88	0.9	0.8	0.9
0.08	0.07	0.08	0.08	0.08	0.08	–0	0	0.08	0.08	0.08	0.06	0.08
0.57	0.52	0.56	0.52	0.5	0.5	0.01	0.02	0.57	0.56	0.54	0.49	0.55

Table 12.4
Resource capacities of the Proxy server

Host	CPUs	Cores	Frequency	Network Connections
miweb001–005 miweb101–105	2	4	2 GHz	2 Gbits

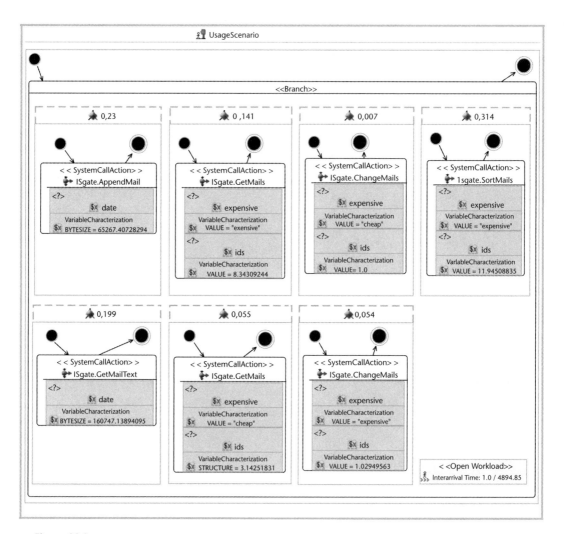

Figure 12.9
Usage model of the STORE model.

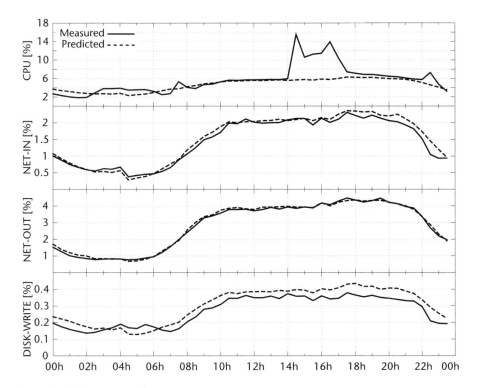

Figure 12.10
Measured and predicted resource utilizations of a STORE server.

the system administrators expected that the update induces additional load on the system resulting in deviations from the normal and expected behavior of the system. Figure 12.10 illustrates the monitored and predicted resource utilizations over the day of the scheduled update. In the time slot between 2 p.m. and 5 p.m., the measured CPU utilization was significantly higher than the predicted values. This deviations from the expected respectively predicted values started exactly at the same point, when the rollout of the update was executed. With this scenario, we could demonstrate that deviations from the expected resource utilization under the given workload can be detected using our approach.

12.7 Evaluation

With the case study presented in the previous section, we demonstrated the applicability of PCM-based performance predictions in an industrial context; however, the accuracy of the prediction results has not been discussed. Because the accuracy is an important aspect when integrating predictions in a performance monitoring process, this section presents a detailed evaluation of the prediction results. Validating performance predictions is often done by conducting benchmarks or controlled experiments and comparing measured with predicted values. Such experiments cannot be performed on the live system as they might influence the reliable operation of the system. To perform integration tests, a dedicated test system is available; however, this system is downsized and running on virtualized systems with some business logic realized as mockups. Thus, this test system cannot be used to perform representative load tests and performance measurements. Because of the cost, complexity, and size of the system, we refrained from setting up an equivalent system with identical hardware resources and a load driver inducing the workload of millions of users.

Instead, we base our evaluation on measurements on the live system using the real workload. We exploit the fact that the workload of the system significantly varies during a day of operation, which allows us to collect measurements in different load situations. Figure 12.11 illustrates the variation of CPU utilization on one of the servers over 1 week. The workload varies between low-load situations at night and high-load situations in the evening when after work, the private mailboxes are checked for new e-mails.

Within our evaluation, we analyzed one reference-day and measured the average resource utilization every 30 minutes. Additionally, we derived the 48 usage profiles of the same intervals using the existing monitoring system. This way, we gained 48 tuples of predicted and measured values representing different load situations of the system. In contrast to the calibration measurements, these measurements cover the whole workload range and thus are a valid set of measurements to perform an evaluation of the accuracy. Furthermore, we determine the resource demands for individual components running on the Proxy servers, while our evaluation is based on the resulting combined resource utilization on the server.

Figure 12.12 presents the measured (solid) and predicted (dashed) resource utilizations on the Proxy servers for 1 day. The predicted curves have the same characteristics compared to the measured ones, with small differences between predicted and measured values. They

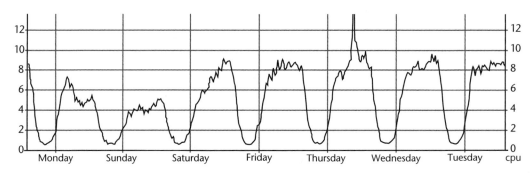

Figure 12.11
CPU utilization of a server over 1 week.

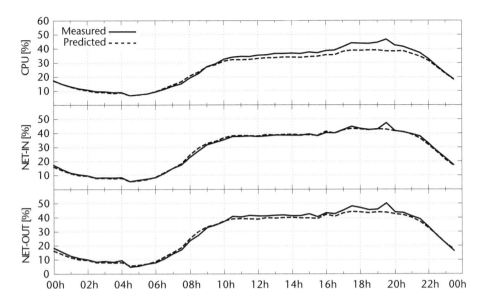

Figure 12.12
Measured and predicted resource utilization of a Proxy server.

show that the expected resource utilization based on the performance predictions fits the measured values on the live system with only small deviations. In table 12.5, we list the averaged relative error in percent, the averaged absolute error in percent points (PP), and the upper decile for the errors between measured and predicted values of the entire model and individually for the Proxy and Store servers for all observed resources. Although the percentage error exceeds 10% in few cases, the averaged absolute error is always less than 2 PP, and upper deciles never exceed 5 PP. This accuracy is acceptable for the integration in a performance monitoring process.

The graphs in figure 12.10 show the resource utilization on the Store servers and illustrate a good correspondence of predicted and measured values except from the interval between 2 p.m. and 5 p.m. In this time slot, the measured CPU utilization was significantly higher than the predicted values. Further analysis showed that a software component update took place on all Store servers at this point. The lower predicted CPU utilization values can be explained by the additional CPU usage caused by the handover mechanism. This observation conforms to the unchanged measured values of traffic and disk usage for this interval. With these measurements, we were able not only to validate the accuracy of the predictions but also to demonstrate that unexpected behavior can be detected by applying our workload-aware performance monitoring process.

Table 12.5
Error characteristics

Parameter	CPU Relative Absolute (%)	(PP)	NET-IN Relative Absolute (%)	(PP)	NET-OUT Relative Absolute (%)	(PP)	DISK-WRITE Relative Absolute (%)	(PP)
Entire model								
Average	12.94	1.32	5.99	0.25	5.92	0.5	9.64	0.027
Upper decile	36.7	2.98	13.46	0.56	12.37	1.55	20.1	0.052
Proxy server								
Average	5.9	1.91	2.93	0.67	5.92	1.48		
Upper decile	10.1	4.24	6.4	1.43	11.09	2.5		
Store server								
Average	15.29	1.13	7.01	0.12	6.01	0.18	9.64	0.027
Upper decile	42.1	2.47	16.19	0.25	13.31	0.40	20.1	0.052

12.8 Lessons Learned

During our case study, we faced several challenges when modeling the system that were caused by its size and the fact that we were not allowed to perform any experiments on the live system. But even if we had been allowed to do so, the generation of a representative workload (i.e., millions of users) would have required a lot of resources and thus makes this strategy infeasible. Because these challenges are valid for all large and distributed systems, the experiences we gained are not limited to e-mail systems and thus are considered helpful for modeling large and distributed systems in general.

Often, large-scale systems provide business-critical functionality, and therefore run-time monitoring of those systems is very detailed. Especially systems that offer services to end users over the Internet have significant variations within their workload. Combined with the detailed monitoring data, they allow for a good estimation of the required resource demands and a validation of the model accuracy. In large systems consisting of several subsystems and components, the knowledge about the architecture is often distributed among several people or even departments. This fact significantly increases the effort needed to collect information required for modeling the system's architecture. Additionally, the available architectural documentation often turns out to be outdated, and the information has to be gathered in interviews. In the case of redundant components and nearly identical servers, the approach to abstract these servers as one abstract resource with multicore scheduling for each resource can significantly reduce the modeling effort without negative influences on the prediction results.

In addition to our original aim to improve the performance monitoring, applying a model-based prediction approach such as PCM has further benefits. Because the PCM is an architectural modeling language, it can serve as architectural documentation that counteracts missing or outdated documentation. Although this prohibits the application of modeling abstraction like the one we presented in our case study, the creation of a usable architectural documentation can balance the additionally required effort. While analyzing the system and collecting monitoring data, we performed several plausibility checks of the predicted values. Even early-stage prediction models could reveal some misconfigurations of the system. On the basis of the statistics collected by our analysis tools for log files, we could, for example, detect a server with inadvertently disabled hyperthreading. When modeling a component's behavior combined with deriving the resource demands, we furthermore identified some potential performance improvements that the developers accepted to be considered in the next version of the component.

In general, the use of the prediction models is not limited to the performance monitoring aspect. They can, for instance, be used to (1) evaluate different deployment variations, (2) evaluate architectural changes caused by integrating new components, or (3) predict the system's behavior in exceptional high-workload situations. Furthermore, the performance models can be used to optimize resource sizing and deployment of the components and thereby improve the system's efficiency.

Comparing the accuracy of the predictions for the different hardware resources, it attracts attention that predictions for network traffic and CPU usage seem to be more precise than predictions made for the HDD writing rate. This larger prediction error is caused by the low main usage of this resource, which makes the accuracy of predictions more vulnerable for external disturbances.

13 Design Trade-offs in IBM Storage Virtualization

Nikolaus Huber and Max Kramer

Analysis methods and tools for performance predictions at early design stages are not yet well-established and in widespread industrial use. This chapter presents a case study applying Palladio to predict performance properties in an industrial environment at IBM Research and Development GmbH in Böblingen, Germany.

The goal of this case study was to assess the applicability of Palladio for evaluating storage hardware virtualization design alternatives for IBM systems. We used an IBM z System for our proof of concept. It is very different from the business information systems that are usually analyzed with Palladio. Therefore, this case study also conveys many ideas and examples about how to successfully apply Palladio in other domains: it gives some insights about the challenges that we identified and can support you in addressing them when applying Palladio to different domains. The results of this case study have already been published in a paper that was originally presented at the "Software Engineering in Practice Track" of the International Conference on Software Engineering (Huber et al. 2010).

In section 13.1, we explain the goal of the case study and the questions that should be answered using Palladio. In section 13.2, we describe the modeled system. Then, we present how we created a performance model of the system architecture and behavior (section 13.3) and how we derived the performance-relevant parameters (section 13.4). Our analysis using the performance model and its results are described in section 13.5, and we conclude in section 13.6 with the lessons we learned.

13.1 Goals and Questions

The case study presented in this chapter was conducted to answer the following two research questions:

• Will a different design of a potential storage virtualization layer for IBM systems improve their performance?
• Is the Palladio approach for performance modeling suitable to answer this question?

Hence, the main goal of this case study is to use the Palladio approach to create a performance model that reflects the performance behavior of a potential virtualization layer for I/O for IBM systems and to evaluate it using a proof of concept implemented on an IBM z System. The evaluation should cover different parameter configurations to answer evaluation questions such as:

- To what extent does the request size influence the system's throughput?
- How does the request type influence the throughput of the system?
- How many resources (CPUs, thread pool size) are required to achieve a certain throughput?

The results of these questions can then be used for a comparison of different design alternatives. The design alternatives explicitly evaluated in this case study are synchronous versus asynchronous virtualization layer implementation.

13.2   System Architecture

The core element of the systems under investigation is the hypervisor, depicted in the center of figure 13.1. The hypervisor abstracts and separates the hardware (processing resources, main memory, etc.) of an IBM z System into several logical partitions (LPARs). Each logical partition can be configured with an individual amount of the system's processing resources, main memory, and I/O devices. Logical partitions can either host a special operating system (e.g., z/OS) or can again be virtualized (e.g., by z/VM) to host further guest systems. These guest systems share the hardware resources of the logical partition. Both the single operating systems and the virtualized guests are users of the storage hardware. We call these users *clients* in the remainder of this chapter.

In the initial system, the hypervisor handles all client I/O requests. In this case study, we evaluated whether performance can be improved if the storage I/O request processing is migrated into a dedicated *storage virtualization layer* (VL). The VL itself is an application running in a specialized operating system and is privileged to directly access the memory of logical partitions. To access the storage hardware, the VL uses the I/O interface provided by the underlying operating system. The I/O interface is connected to the storage hardware by channels. Each channel has a bandwidth (bytes/second) and throughput (requests/second) restriction.

In this case study, we evaluated two possible design alternatives for a synchronous and an asynchronous implementation of the VL.

13.2.1   Virtualization Layer Design
The VL is situated between the request-issuing clients and the request-processing storage hardware as depicted in figure 13.1. The request handling can be accomplished in either a

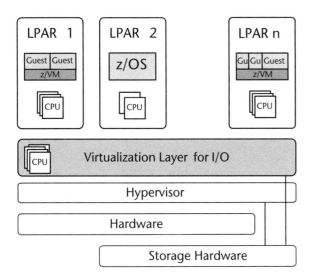

Figure 13.1
Architecture of an IBM z System with several logical partitions.

synchronous or asynchronous manner. These two design alternatives are investigated in this case study and described in the following.

Clients have separate *queues* for each attached storage device (figure 13.2). The queue is part of the client's memory to store the requests for processing. The storage hardware device is the receiver of a request. If a client wants to issue a new request to a device, it puts the request in the corresponding request queue. To process a request, it is collected by an I/O thread of the VL and forwarded to the I/O interface. Request queues, however, cannot be accessed concurrently by I/O threads of the VL. If a thread wants to access a queue, the access may be blocked if the queue is already in use by another I/O thread. I/O threads, however, cannot block client threads and vice versa. In both design alternatives, the I/O interface to the storage hardware can be accessed in parallel. The VL's behavior of forwarding the client requests can be implemented as described in the following.

13.2.2 Synchronous Design

The VL contains a theoretically unlimited number of *I/O threads*, which handle client requests. An I/O thread accesses a client's requests queue, collects a request (if available), and sends the request to the storage hardware by passing it to the I/O interface (figure 13.2). While the request is executed by the storage hardware, the thread waits for the result and signals the result back to the client after completion. Then, the I/O thread continues processing the next requests in the queue. If a request queue is empty, the thread accesses one of the remaining request queues and continues with request processing.

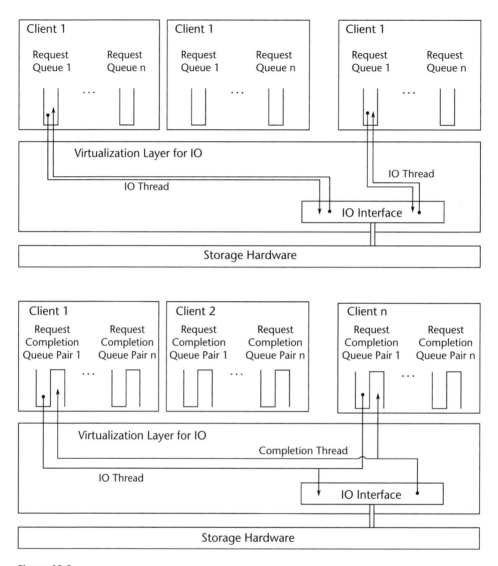

Figure 13.2
Design alternatives: synchronous (top) and asynchronous (bottom) request handling.

13.2.3 Asynchronous Design

In this case (figure 13.2), forwarding requests to the storage hardware is decoupled from sending the results back to the clients. Here, a fixed number of I/O threads works on the request queues. The I/O thread's work is completed after sending the requests to the storage hardware via the I/O interface. Instead of waiting for the result, the I/O thread processes the next request. To receive the results, the clients are equipped with an additional completion queue, where the results of requests are signaled to. The signaling is accomplished by another thread type, the *completion thread*. Such a thread is started by the VL as soon as results of the storage hardware become available. It may happen that a completion thread is blocked because another completion thread signals a result to exactly the same queue.

13.2.4 Impact of the Synchronicity Decision

The differences in the proposed design alternatives regarding their influences on the system's performance lead to the following questions: Which design alternative provides better performance; that is, provides quicker response times and higher throughput? Which design alternative is more efficient; that is, uses fewer resources (threads, memory)? How does the number of threads and queues used influence the system throughput? How many threads are necessary to handle a specific system load? How does queue blocking influence the overall performance? What VL hardware configuration is required to provide an efficient virtualization? Where are the system's performance bottlenecks? To answer these questions without having to implement each design alternative, we derived a performance model that is described in the following (for answering design decisions, see also chapter 7).

13.3   Structure and Behavior Modeling

To be able to analyze the impact of deciding for a synchronous or asynchronous VL design with Palladio, we created the necessary models (for creating the models, see chapter 3).

13.3.1   Component Interaction and Control Flow

The developed Palladio model is depicted in figure 13.3. Its illustration follows a simplified combination of the UML deployment diagram and the UML composite structure diagram. We will now explain the modeled components according to the control flow through the model.

The control flow of the VL starts at the system interface depicted on the left. A client invokes the system via this interface. This invocation is delegated to the IOThread component. Now, the IOThread calls the RequestGenerator component to get a request in return. The RequestGenerator component represents the clients and their request queues. It can be configured by several parameters such as request size, request type (READ or WRITE), number of queues, and so forth. The IOThread demands a specific amount of CPU time before passing the received request to the IOInterface. The IOInterface calls the CapacityController used

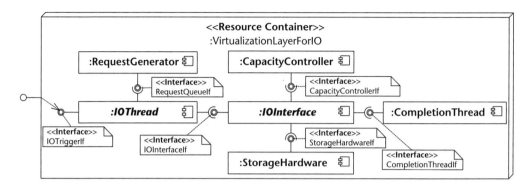

Figure 13.3
Modeled components, interfaces, and their relations in the VL.

to ensure the throughput constraint of the I/O interface. In case the maximum throughput of requests is reached, further requests will be delayed. Afterward, the IOInterface consumes some CPU time and forwards the request to the StorageHardware. This component models the request execution on the physical hardware by a delay depending on the request size and type. In the synchronous case, the control flow subsequently returns to the client. In the asynchronous case, the control flow already returned from the IOThread to the user, as the call of the IOInterface was forked. Hence, the IOInterface calls the CompletionThread, which signals the results and thereby the end of the transaction to the client. The CompletionThread also requires a specific amount of CPU time.

The behavior of the IOThread and IOInterface differs in the synchronous and asynchronous cases. Therefore, the performance model includes a synchronous version and an asynchronous version of these components as depicted in figure 13.4. This offers the flexibility to easily switch between the different design alternatives.

13.3.2   Modeling Restrictions

As already mentioned, the target domain of the PCM is business information systems. Therefore, the model could not be created as straightforwardly as it might appear. Several workarounds were required to implement a performance model equivalent to the system. One problem was that components have no active behavior. They must be invoked by either a client or other components. The modeling of the I/O thread in the virtualization system requires such active behavior. To realize this, we extended the IOThread component with a trigger interface. This interface is then called from an external workload.

Second, the PCM currently does not support automated replication of components. This is, however, required to explicitly model a varying number of one to 100 request queues. The RequestGenerator solves this issue. It is an additional component representing all request

(a)

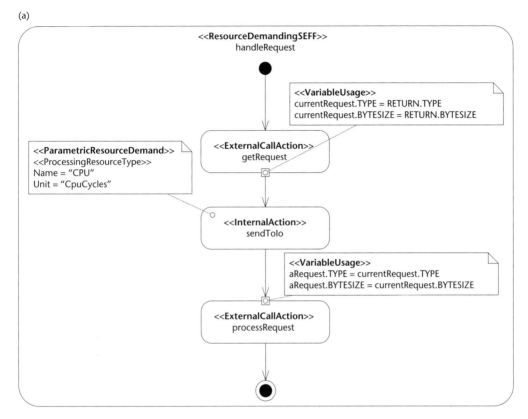

Figure 13.4
Resource demanding service effect specification (RDSEFF) of the synchronous (a) and asynchronous (b) I/O thread's handleRequest.

queues, reflecting the behavior of queue accesses and returning requests. Depending on the parameter settings of the RequestGenerator, the IOThread's call is delayed to simulate blocked queue accesses.

Third, the current version of the PCM has no direct support to model the component state. Hence, it is impossible to count and limit the throughput of a component directly. The CapacityController component encapsulates and reflects the throughput restriction by using the features PCM currently provides (forks, passive resources, and delays). A more detailed description of the model and the specific behavior implementation of each component is available (Huber 2009).

(b)

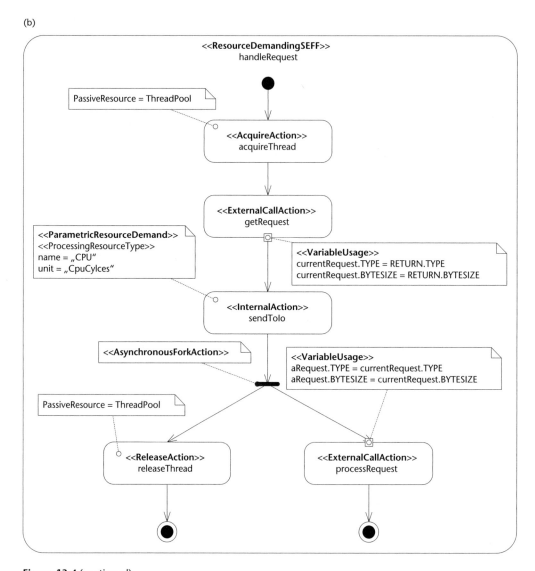

Figure 13.4 (continued)

13.4   Data Collection

In this section, we describe the experiment setup that was used to determine the model parameters (for determining model parameters, see chapter 6). The calibration and validation of the functional performance model is based on the experiment-based derivation of software performance models presented by Happe (2008). This approach is inspired by the general ideas and rules proposed by Jain (1991). It combines existing knowledge of the system under study with iterative, goal-oriented experiments. These experiments support performance analysts in identifying valid assumptions for performance modeling. They help to assess the prediction accuracy of the model. Furthermore, it is important that the performance model design is driven by a specific goal. This directs the design effort to the factors of interest, similar to the goal-question-metric (GQM) approach of Basili et al. (1994).

All experiments and measurements were executed on a System z9 with 48 processors and 128 gigabytes of main memory. The storage controller was a DS8000, connected via four 8 Gbit/s Fiber Channel Protocol (FCP) channels.

In the experiments, two different variables were observed. Response-time measurements were conducted for calibrating the resource demands of the model components. Moreover, we measured the throughput used to validate the model that we will describe in the next section. In the following, the system's throughput (X) is defined as the ratio of requests (R) per time (T); that is, $X = R/T$.

We gathered measurement data with two different tools. The first tool was used to identify the response times of different components of the request handling stack depicted in figure 13.5. The second tool generates system load and measures the overall system throughput and response time.

The generated workload was a closed workload with a configurable number of clients issuing requests to the system. Open workloads were not supported by IBM's load

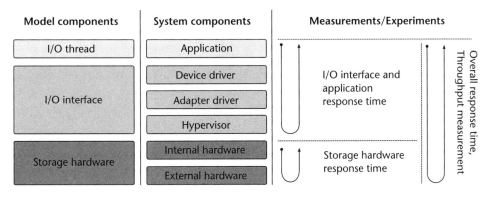

Figure 13.5

Setup to measure request handling response times of different components.

Table 13.1

I/O Interface plus I/O thread, storage hardware and overall response times, and system throughput with and without simultaneous response-time measurement

READ	4 KB	16 KB	64 KB	256 KB	1,024 KB
I/O interface + I/O thread (μs)	180	200	300	650	1,820
Storage hardware (μs)	100	160	420	1,490	5,160
Overall response time (μs)	270	360	720	2,140	6,980
Throughput (requests/second)	**4 KB**	**16 KB**	**64 KB**	**256 KB**	**1,024 KB**
With response-time measurement	3,600	2,750	1,400	470	145
Without response-time measurement	6,219	4,707	2,184	656	223
WRITE	4 KB	16 KB	64 KB	256 KB	1,024 KB
I/O interface + I/O thread (μs)	170	180	200	300	1,120
Storage hardware (μs)	250	380	890	2,180	5,830
Overall response time (μs)	420	560	1,090	2,480	6,950
Throughput (requests/second)	**4 KB**	**16 KB**	**64 KB**	**256 KB**	**1,024 KB**
With response-time measurement	2,350	1,780	915	400	145
Without response-time measurement	3,276	2,286	1,130	498	175

generator. In our experiments, we measured the throughput for a varying number of clients (1, 2, 4 , …, 256), various request sizes (4 KB, 16 KB, 64 KB, 256 KB, 1,024 KB), and different request types (READ, WRITE). Moreover, we ascertained response times for the same request size/type combinations with an additional tool. For this measurement, we restricted the number of clients to one client to avoid mutual disturbances. The results are listed in table 13.1. We chose a synthetic benchmark to calibrate the model with reasonable costs for measurements. The benchmark was, however, designed to cover different load conditions and request sizes.

13.5 Analysis and Evaluation

To validate the created performance model and to evaluate the simulation results, we used a two-step approach (for interpreting the results, see chapter 7). In the first step, we validated the synchronous performance model by comparing the simulation results with measured experimental results conducted on the prototypical synchronous design alternative.

In the second step, we compared the results of the validated synchronous model with those of the asynchronous model. Note that we use only one single model instance, which is calibrated and parameterized once, and have no separate models for the synchronous and asynchronous design alternatives. The design alternatives can be simulated by simply replacing components, which has no effect on the calibrated resource demands of the model.

13.5.1   Model Validation

To validate the performance model, we conducted two specific throughput measurement series and compared the results to the simulated throughput. In one series, the request type (a mix of 60% READ and 40% WRITE requests) differs. In a second series, we used the same mix and added an additional CPU to the VL. For both series, we measured the throughput for 1, 2, 4, ..., 256 clients (figure 13.6).

The diagrams show a qualitatively high correlation of measured and predicted throughput. The predictions are not completely accurate, but tend to the same error behavior: the initial throughput with 1 client, for example, is overestimated, whereas the maximum throughput with 256 clients is underestimated for all sizes of the plain READ/WRITE mix. On average, the relative prediction error $f = (x_{sim}/x_{meas}) - 1$ for all measurement data for the READ/WRITE mix is below 19% and below 21% for the mix with an additional CPU.

The predictions show, however, a relatively high quantitative discrepancy in some cases (e.g., for the 16-KB READ/WRITE mix). The discrepancy can have its origin in the

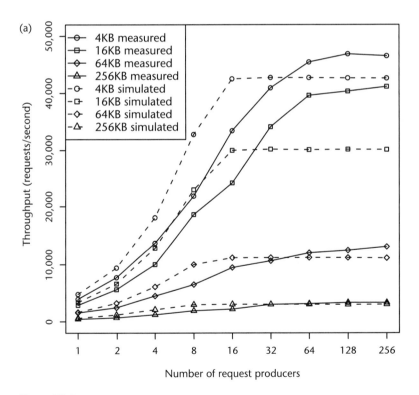

Figure 13.6
(a) Throughput comparison for READ/WRITE mixtures. (b) Throughput comparison for two CPUs.

(b)

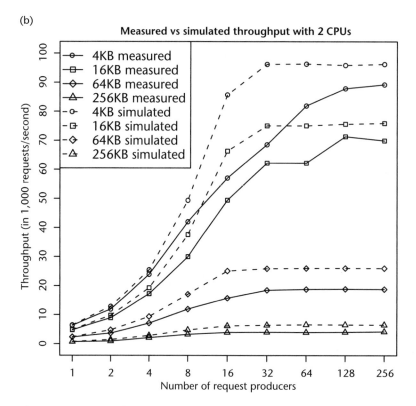

Figure 13.6 (continued)

measurements. For example, although we configured the tool to avoid caches, cache hits cannot be completely precluded, especially in case of the READ/WRITE mix. But each cache hit can cause a considerable speedup in the measured throughput. Another reason could be an absent detail in the performance model (e.g., a possible influence of a scheduling overhead for two CPUs). To test this assumption, we provisionally integrated a more detailed scheduler simulation for multicore platforms (Happe et al. 2008) into the PCM. This scheduler improved the prediction accuracy for the maximum throughput (in which case the CPU is the bottleneck) by about 7% on average.

Additional measurements would have been necessary to obtain further system details and to create a more accurate model; however, the benefits of a more accurate model have to be traded off with the cost and effort for creating the model. Therefore, despite the quantitative errors, the qualitative prediction accuracy of the model was considered to be sufficient to discern the system behavior as the trends are accurately simulated.

13.5.2 Discussion of Simulation Results

The validated model can now be used to vary parameters such as request size, request type, number of threads and queues and design alternatives such as synchronous and asynchronous components to observe their influences on the system performance. As there exists no asynchronous system prototype, the validated parameters of the synchronous model were used to parameterize the asynchronous model, too. This is feasible as the design alternatives only vary in the behavior of the I/O thread and the completion thread, respectively, not in the resource demands of the I/O interface or storage hardware components. To simulate the asynchronous performance model, the synchronous components must simply be replaced by their asynchronous counterparts.

The comparison of the simulation results of both design alternatives unveils little differences with respect to the selected metric throughput. Also, the response times in both scenarios are very similar for closed workloads. A crucial difference is, however, observable if an open workload with an exponentially distributed interarrival time is used instead of a closed workload. In this case, the asynchronous design alternative is more capable in handling peak loads. In the synchronous case, the response times were distributed relatively constant compared to the closed workload, whereas they improved in the asynchronous case (figure 13.7). The open workload also demonstrates that one to 10 asynchronous I/O threads are capable of handling the same load as synchronous I/O threads. Additional asynchronous I/O threads do not further improve the results.

In the synchronous case, there is one active I/O thread per request. In the asynchronous case, however, more than n I/O threads are active. In addition, there is one thread per request for handling the request within the I/O interface. Furthermore, completion threads are required to signal the results. Nevertheless, the model revealed that the influence of the number of I/O threads and completion threads on the throughput is negligible because their run time is insignificant compared to I/O interface and storage hardware response times.

Several conclusions can be drawn from a comparison of both models. The differences between both implementations concerning the system throughput are low. Hence, one must consider the advantages and drawbacks of the design alternatives themselves. For example, the synchronous version is easier to implement and to maintain in case of malfunctions. Moreover, it has an intrinsic overload protection as the synchronous threads must wait for the result and cannot send more requests to the I/O interface than it can process. The asynchronous implementation, however, offers higher flexibility and better responsiveness in case of peak loads. Hence, for this case study, the decision whether to use a synchronous or asynchronous approach mainly depends on factors other than performance.

13.6 Lessons Learned

Performance models must be elaborated thoroughly, and the creation of performance models can cause high initial costs. Nevertheless, this case study demonstrates that performance

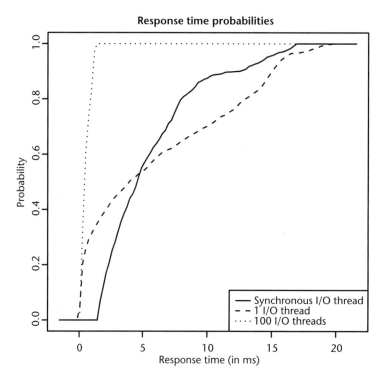

Figure 13.7
Cumulative distribution function of the response time for one and 100 asynchronous I/O threads.

models provide a quick, easy, and flexible way to compare and analyze design alternatives without implementing prototypical design alternatives in industrial settings. Hence, they provide a valuable alternative to performance prototypes or performance measurements in real systems. For example, Palladio offers the flexibility to easily switch between the modeled design alternatives and vary their parameter settings to observe the influences on the performance.

What we also experienced impressively during building the model is that performance models are abstractions of systems. Hence, the performance model can concentrate on relevant and important parts of a system. Especially for complex systems such as System z9, the focusing on relevant factors and their easy changeability offers a higher flexibility in system analysis.

When using Palladio, no experts for performance models are required, as it provides tool support to easily create and modify performance models on a very high level of abstraction.

But one must consider that there is always a trade-off between model accuracy and modeling effort. In this case study, for example, the prediction results revealed certain inaccuracy.

The reason for this could have been identified with additional, more costly measurements. The objectives were, however, already achieved with the presented model. The case study shows that performance models support the design and analysis and improve the understanding of existing systems. During the modeling and calibration, the simulation results caused revisions of measurement results and assumptions about the system behavior. For example, the model indicated a higher throughput for two CPUs than the measurements. The flaw was the bandwidth limit, which was exposed by the measurements and could be fixed by adding a channel.

The case study shows that performance modeling and analysis can replace further prototypical implementations of design alternatives. We estimate the effort of creating a calibrated and validated performance model by an inexperienced person who is not familiar with the system and the PCM to be about four man-months. The effort to implement a plain asynchronous VL running in a logical partition is at most three man-months. One would, however, still need to implement a simple and flexible configuration of the VL and the communication with other partitions. The front ends to generate traffic and the back-end drivers were already available at IBM. If all this had to be implemented, the effort to implement a full-fledged prototype, taking into consideration all the required skills, would be at least 24 man-months. Hence, in a scenario like this where knowledge of a complex system is distributed over several departments, a performance model can be created by few people with much less effort than a performance prototype. This fortifies the idea that the initial effort for creating a performance model is high, but if a model is available, it is an easy, cheap, and flexible way to investigate different alternatives.

Furthermore, the performance model has identified other performance bottlenecks than originally expected. It revealed that the influences of the number of threads and queues on blocked queue accesses on the system performance are eclipsed by the *IOInterface* and the *StorageHardware*. Besides, the model demonstrates that optimizing the storage hardware influences the initial throughput of the system (i.e., if system load is little, faster hardware can improve the throughput). In contrast, to increase the throughput for high system load, it is necessary to improve the I/O interface response time by decreasing its CPU resource demands.

Concerning the applicability of Palladio, we learned that its performance meta-model is practical and capable of modeling component-based software architectures. Workarounds had to be implemented, however, to model circumstances such as queue blocking or throughput constraint. Hence, we can show that with some creativity, PCM is applicable outside the domain of business information systems.

14 Design Space Exploration for an ABB ASP.NET Server

Heiko Koziolek and Anne Koziolek

Determining the trade-off between performance and costs of a distributed software system is important as it enables fulfillment of performance requirements in a cost-efficient way. The large number of design alternatives for such systems often leads software architects to select a suboptimal solution, which may either waste resources or cannot cope with future workloads. This chapter, which is based on Gooijer et al. (2012), presents a case study applying Palladio and PerOpteryx to explore the design space of a distributed software system from ABB. To facilitate the design exploration, we created a detailed performance and cost model, which was instrumental in determining a cost-efficient architectural solution using an evolutionary algorithm. The case study demonstrates the capabilities of various modern performance modeling tools and a design space exploration tool in an industrial setting, provides lessons learned, and helps other software architects in solving similar problems.

14.1 System under Study

The system under study is one of ABB's remote diagnostic solutions (RDSs). The RDS is used for service activities on thousands of industrial devices and records device status information, failures, and other data. The system consists of roughly 150,000 lines of code. Certain details of the system are intentionally changed to protect ABB's intellectual property.

During normal operation, the industrial devices periodically contact the RDS to upload diagnostic status information. In cases of abnormal behavior, the devices upload error information to the RDS for future analysis. Customers can track the status of their devices on a website and can generate reports, for example, showing device failures over the past year. Service engineers can troubleshoot device problems either on-site or remotely by sending commands to the device through the RDS.

Part of the RDS is illustrated in figure 14.1. The devices run device-specific software that connects to the RDS Connection Point, which runs in ABB's DMZ (perimeter network for security reasons). Here, the data enters ABB's internal network and is sent onward to the core components on the application server.

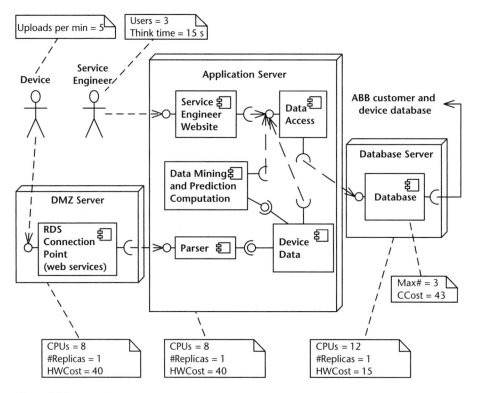

Figure 14.1
Palladio Component Model of the ABB remote diagnostic system (in mixed UML component and deployment diagram notation).

The system core components handle both the processing (Parser) and storing (Data Access) of the uploaded data, as well as the publishing of data (e.g., Service Engineer Website) and interaction with external systems. Data that are received from devices are processed and then stored in the database. Certain data uploads are mined in the component Data Mining and Prediction Computation, for example, to predict the wear of parts. The customer website is hosted outside the RDS back end and gets data from the RDS Web services via a proxy (not shown here). The Service Engineer Website is hosted within the same environment as the RDS Web services. Both websites offer access to reports that are created by a separate reporting component, which is also not shown here.

The RDS is connected to various other systems. One example is shown in the diagram in figure 14.1: the ABB customer and device database interface, which represents a Microsoft SQL Server (MS-SQL) plug-in that synchronizes the RDS database against a central ABB database recording information on which customers have what service contracts for which devices. This synchronization scheme reduces the latency for lookup of this information when a human user or device connects to the system.

14.2   Goals and Questions

ABB wanted to improve the performance of RDS by architectural redesign because its back end was operating at its performance and scalability limits. Performance tuning or short-term fixes (e.g., faster CPUs) would not sustainably solve the problems in the long term for three reasons. First, the architecture was conceived in a setting where time to market took priority over performance and scalability requirements. Hence, the current architecture has not been designed with performance and scalability in mind.

Second, the number of devices connected to the back end is expected to grow by an order of magnitude within the coming years. Finally, the amount of data that has to be processed for each device is expected to increase by an order of magnitude in the same period. Together, these dimensions of growth will significantly increase the demands on computational power and storage capacity.

The performance metric of main interest is the device upload throughput (i.e., the number of uploads the system can handle per second). It was decided that the system resources on average must not be utilized more than 50% to be able to cope with workload peaks. Considering that the speed of the target hardware resources will grow significantly in the next years, the performance goal for the system was specified as: "The system resources must not be utilized more than 50 percent for a ten times higher request arrival rate of device uploads."

The architectural redesign should manage to fulfill the performance goal while controlling cost at the same time. It was not feasible to identify the best design option by prototyping or measurements. Changes to the existing system would have been required to take measurements, but the cost and effort required to alter the system solely for performance tests were too high because of its complexity.

Furthermore, the capacity predicted by a performance model could be combined with the business growth scenario to get a timeline on the architectural road map. Thereby, starting the work too late and experiencing capacity problems or being too early and making unnecessary investments were avoided.

Therefore, the goal of this case study was to create a performance model and cost model to aid architectural and business decision making, to conduct capacity planning, and to search the design space for architectural solutions with the best performance/costs trade-off. The case study followed the steps depicted in figure 14.2.

14.3   Modeling

To construct a performance model for the ABB RDS, we first selected an appropriate modeling notation, which turned out to be the Palladio Component Model. We constructed a Palladio

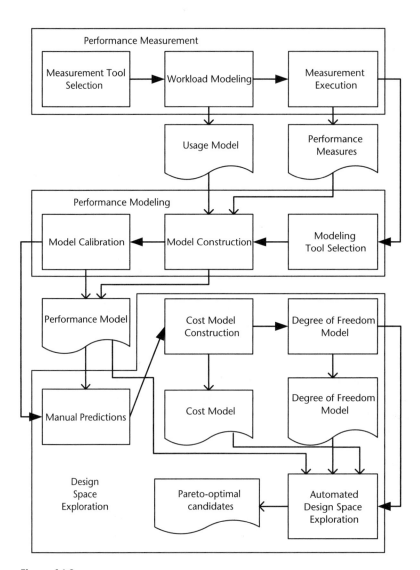

Figure 14.2
Activities executed for this case study.

model for the ABB RDS, which we calibrated until it reflected the performance of the system under study well.

14.3.1 Method and Tool Selection

We conducted a survey of performance modeling tools (Gooijer 2011) and selected initial candidates on the basis of three criteria: (1) support for performance modeling of software architectures, (2) available recent tooling, and (3) tool maturity and stability. Most mature tools do not meet the first criterion, while prototypical academic tools often fail on the latter two as described in the following. We opted to use the Palladio workbench because it supports the simulation of architectural models and because its "UML-like" interface makes it easier to construct models and communicate them to the stakeholders than it is with layered queuing networks (LQNs). The ability to reuse models and components was another useful feature (Gooijer 2011). (The reuse aspect is described in chapter 4.) Moreover, the Palladio workbench has been used in industrial case studies before (Huber 2010; Koziolek et al. 2011b), thus we assume that it is mature and sufficiently stable. Palladio's drawbacks lie in its more laborious model creation due to the complex meta-model and its weaker user documentation.

The Palladio workbench tool provided two performance solvers: SimuCom and PCM2LQN (for more information on performance analysis tools, see chapter 8). We chose PCM2LQN in combination with the LQN analytical solver because it is usually much faster than SimuCom. Automatic design space exploration requires evaluating many candidates, so run time is important. PCM2LQN maps the Palladio models to an LQN. The LQN analytical solver (Franks et al. 2009) is restricted compared to SimuCom, as it only provides mean value performance metrics and does not support arbitrary passive resources such as semaphores.

14.3.2 Model Construction

To model the RDS as a Palladio model, we studied its structure and behavior by analyzing the available documentation, talking to its developers, analyzing the source code, and performing different load tests (creating models is further described in chapter 3). Then, we constructed the model as follows.

Component Repository Using the existing architectural descriptions to create the component repository formed a major challenge because these documents were limited in detail and only provided a component-level logical view and a deployment view. We used these views to select the components to include in our Palladio component repository. Initially, the RDS repository consisted of seven components, seven interfaces, and 27 component services.

Resource Demanding Service Effect Specifications To specify the resource demanding service effect specifications (RDSEFFs) for each component service, we opted to model system behavior at the level of Web service calls between the tiers. In some cases, we added more detail to capture differences between use cases. For example, the data mining component needed to be modeled in more detail to get accurate predictions for each type of upload because the component is complex and resource intensive.

One of the complex service effect specifications (SEFFs) in the RDS Palladio model is depicted as an example in figure 14.3. While abstracting from the actual source code, it still shows a complex control flow with several resource demands to CPU and hard disk as well as several calls to other components and Web services.

System Model From the resulting Palladio component repository, we created a system model instantiating and connecting the components. It contained seven component instances and seven connectors. In this case, creating the connections of the components was straightforward (see figure 14.1).

Resource Environment This model was made up of three servers, each with a CPU and hard disk. The network capacity was assumed to always be sufficient and scaled up by the IT provider as required. The first reason for this assumption is that we expect our IT provider to be able to provide the capacity and latency required. The second reason is the limited detail offered by Palladio's network simulator and the subsequent difficulty of specifying the network subsystem in detail. One would have to determine, for a complex system running in .NET, how many latency network messages are issued in each layer.

Allocation Model We mapped the seven component instances to the three servers in the resource environment according to the allocation in our experimental setup.

Usage Model Our usage model reflects the upload service and the service engineering interaction with the system. The former was a periodic request to the system modeled with an open workload and three differently weighted upload types. The latter comprised a more complex user interaction with different branches, loops, and user think times and a closed workload.

14.4   Data Collection

14.4.1   Tool Selection
The first step in data collection to populate the Palladio model with resource demands entails finding the appropriate tools to measure the system performance:

• A load generator tool to simulate stimuli to the systems in a controlled way.
• An application performance management (APM) tool, which can measure the response time of different stimuli (called business transactions) to the system.

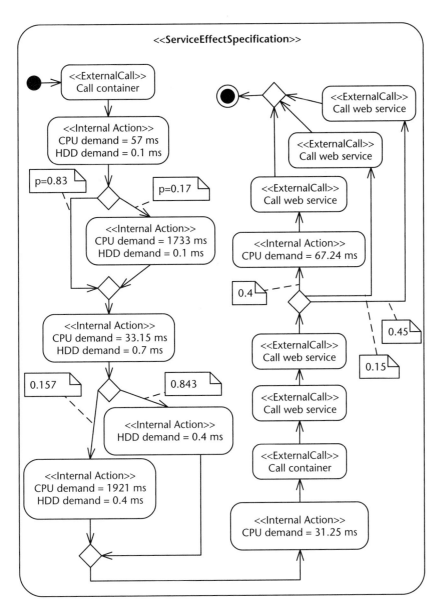

Figure 14.3

An example SEFF from the RDS Palladio model showing the inner behavior of one component service in terms of resource demands and calls to other components.

• A (distributed) profiler, which can tell us how the response time of the different stimuli is distributed. This information is vital, as we would like to understand how the performance is built up to focus our architectural redesign efforts.

We created an initial list of 58 different tools that could fulfill some of this functionality. After removing the alternatives that were no longer maintained or lacked feature completeness, the list shrunk to 17 tools. For each of these 17 tools, we classified their functionality and costs by attending online sales presentations of the various tool vendors. In the end, we settled on using the NeoLoad load generator tool (*Neotys Neoload Load Testing Tool*, 2011) in combination with the dynaTrace APM tool (*Dynatrace—Application Performance Management and Monitoring*, 2011), because the tools integrate nicely, dynaTrace makes instrumentation .Net applications easy, and NeoLoad supports MS Silverlight.

The dynaTrace tool offers normal performance measurement functionality and distributed profiling functionality. DynaTrace traces requests through all tiers in a distributed application and stores measurements on each individual request in so-called PurePaths. DynaTrace instruments the .NET application code in the Common Language Runtime (CLR) layer, thus allowing PurePaths to show timings (i.e., CPU time, execution time, latency) as deep as at the method level. The recorded measurements can be summarized and viewed in several ways. For example, dynaTrace can create sequence diagrams of PurePaths or show a breakdown of how much time was spent in various APIs.

14.4.2 Workload Modeling

The second step deals with the issue of finding out what the typical workload on the system is (for determining model parameter, see chapter 6). First, we organized a workshop with the developers to find out the actors on the system and their main-use cases. Second, we turned on the logging facilities of the IIS containers to record the stimuli to the system for a month in production. Using the Sawmill log analysis tool (*Sawmill—Universal log file analysis tool*, 2011), we determined the most frequently used use cases: the periodic uploading of diagnostic/error information by devices and the interaction of service engineers (SEs) with the system. Surprisingly enough, the customer-related use cases were relatively low in frequency. Most likely, this is due to customers being only interested in interacting with the system when the devices have considerable issues, which is not often the case.

The RDS thus executes two performance-critical usage scenarios during production: periodic uploading of diagnostic status information from devices and the interaction of SEs with the system. We approximated the uploads with an open workload having an arrival rate of 78.6 requests per minute. Furthermore, we characterized the SE interactions with a closed workload with a user population of 39.3 and a think time of 15 seconds. All values were derived from the production logs of the system.

We decided to run load tests with the system on three different workload intensities: low, medium, and high. The workloads are specified in table 14.1 as the number of sustained

Table 14.1
The model calibration workloads used

Workload	Uploads/Minute	SE Requests/Minute
Low	41.0	20.5
Medium	78.6	39.3
High	187.9	93.9

Note: Data have been altered to protect ABB's intellectual property.

uploads received from the devices per minute and the number of concurrent service engineers requesting internal Web pages from the system.

The medium workload approximates the current production load on RDS. The low workload was used as an initial calibration point for the performance model and is approximately half the production load. The advantage of the low workload is that the system behavior is more stable and consistent, making it easier to study. The high workload represents a step toward the target capacity and enables us to study how the resource demands change at increasing loads.

14.4.3 Measurement Execution

The third and final step, performing the measurements, has to deal with an important constraint to the case study: the need to minimize the impact of the study on ongoing development and operation activities of the system. To address this issue, we built a separate "experimental" copy of the system in the ABB Corporate Research labs. This copy consisted of a recently released version of the RDS, which is deployed on a large server running virtualization software. This deployment in virtual servers allows us to easily test out different deployments of the system with varying hardware resources. For the virtualization software, we chose to go with VMWare ESX, as we have local in-house IT expertise to manage such servers.

The experimental copy of the RDS runs on three virtual machines. The NeoLoad load generator runs on a separate physical machine to emulate industrial devices uploading data and service engineers generating requests to the RDS. DynaTrace data collection agents were installed on the DMZ and application server. Information on the performance of the database server was recorded by subscribing dynaTrace to its Windows performance monitor counters, as dynaTrace cannot instrument the Microsoft SQL Server (MS-SQL).

During the first load tests on our system, we verified the consistency of the performance measurements, and we gained sufficient confidence in dynaTrace's instrumentation to run all our measurements for 30 minutes. In the next tests, we stressed the system to observe its behavior under peak loads and to find its bottlenecks and capacity limits. Both test phases needed several iterations to adjust dynaTrace's instrumentation, so that requests were traced through all tiers correctly. During the stress tests, we varied the hardware configuration of the virtual machines to explore the sensitivity of the application to the amount of CPU cores and memory and several concurrency settings of the ASP.Net container.

Finally, we performed two types of structured measurements to support the performance modeling. First, we ran load tests matching our workload model, which later could be compared to model predictions for calibration of the model. We used average values from these load tests to instantiate our model. Second, we measured just a single request to get a clear picture of run-time system behavior to base the behavioral part of the performance model upon. When re-creating the workload model in NeoLoad, we needed several iterations until the generated workload matched the model.

Some data we could not gather using dynaTrace. First of all, some metrics were not easily recorded or isolated. For example, network latency measurements were more easily obtained using a ping tool, and MS-SQL's performance counters were better studied with the MS-SQL profiler tool. Second, it was difficult to interpret results. For example, significant differences between CPU and execution time were difficult to account for, because the instrumentation of the ASP.Net container itself was insufficient.

14.4.4   Model Calibration

Calibration of performance models is important to ensure that the resource demands in the model accurately reflect the resource demands in the real system. A prediction error can only be given for the calibrated model not for an altered version. After changing the model to reflect an alternative architecture, we cannot determine the error, but only assume the error remains constant. Validation of the changed model is only possible by prototypes or full implementation.

For calibration of the RDS model, we executed the Palladio performance solvers and compared the predicted utilization for each resource with the utilizations measured by their respective Windows performance counters. We conducted this comparison for each of the three workloads introduced in subsection 14.4.3 to ensure that the model was robust against different workload intensities.

Despite using the detailed resource demands measured by dynaTrace, the utilizations derived from the initial RDS Palladio model showed a moderate deviation from the actually measured utilizations. Thus, we ran additional experiments and performed code reviews to get a better understanding of the system and why the prediction was off. We focused on those parts of the model where it showed errors of more than 20% compared to the measurement results. This led to useful insight, either to refine the model or to learn more about the RDS architecture, the system behavior, and bottlenecks in the system. The utilizations derived in each calibration step were recorded in an Excel sheet to track the model accuracy and the effect of changes made to the model.

After calibration with the high workload, the model gives values up to 30% too low for the DMZ server CPU utilization. That means that for a 25% CPU utilization, the actual CPU utilization could be 32.5%. The application server utilization figures are off by a maximum of 10%, and the database server CPU utilization results are at most 30% too high. Three quarters of the response times for both internal and external calls are within 30% of the measured value.

We report the errors for our high-load scenario because this is most representative of our target workload. The errors for the other two workloads are lower. Overall, the error percentages are reasonable but not desirably small; however, both our measurements in the experimental setup and our experience during earlier work (Gooijer 2011) showed that the application server, for which our model most accurately predicts utilization, would be the most likely bottleneck. There are two main reasons it was not economical to further improve the accuracy of the model. First, the complex behavior of the ASP.Net container especially with our asynchronous application could not be understood within a reasonable time. Second, the application behavior was complex because of its size and the way it was written.

14.5 Analysis

On the basis of the created performance model, we want to find cost-efficient architectures to cope with the expected increased workload (for interpreting the results, see chapter 7). We consider three workload scenarios: Scenario 1 considers a higher workload scenario due to more connected devices. Scenarios 2 and 3 additionally consider an eightfold (scenario 2) and fourfold (scenario 3) increase of processed data per device.

Initially, we partially explored the design space by manually modifying the baseline model (Gooijer 2011), as described below in subsection 14.5.1. The potential design space for the system is prohibitively large and cannot be explored by hand. Thus, both to confirm our results and to find even better solutions, we conducted an automatic exploration of the design space with PerOpteryx. We selected PerOpteryx, described in subsection 7.4.3, because of its ability to explore many degrees of freedom, which sets it apart from similar tools. Additionally, its implementation can directly process Palladio models.

To be able to apply PerOpteryx on the RDS Palladio model, we first created a formal PerOpteryx cost model (subsection 14.5.2) and a degree of freedom instances model (subsection 14.5.3). Then, subsection 14.5.4 presents the optimization results.

14.5.1 Manual Design Space Exploration

For manual design space exploration, first, we used the AFK scale cube theory, which explains scalability in three fundamental dimensions, the axes of the cube. According to the AFK scale cube, capacity can be increased by moving the design from the origin of an imaginary cube by cloning (x axis), task-based split (y axis), and request-based split (z axis).

We created three architectural alternatives, each exploring one axis of the AFK scale cube (Abbott and Fisher 2009). Second, we combined several scalability strategies and our knowledge about hardware costs to create further alternatives to cost-effectively meet our capacity goal. Finally, we reflected several updates of the operational software in our model, because the development continued during our performance study.

The first of our alternatives inspired by the AFK scale cube scales the system by assigning each component to its own server. This complies with the y axis in the AFK scale cube (task-base split). However, some components put higher demands on system resources than others. Therefore, it is inefficient to put each component on its own server. The maximum capacity of this model variant shows that network communication would become a bottleneck.

A move along the x axis of the AFK scale cube (cloning) increases replication in a system (e.g., double the number of application servers). All replicas should be identical, which requires database replication. We achieved this by having three databases for two pipelines in the system: one shared-write database and two read-only databases. This scheme is interesting because read-only databases do not have to be updated in real time.

The AFK scale cube z axis (request-base split) also uses replication, but additionally partitions the data. Partitions are based on the data or the sender of a request. For example, processing in the RDS could be split on warning versus diagnostic messages, or the physical location, or the owner of the sending device.

All alternatives did not consider operational cost. Therefore, we also developed an informal cost model with hardware cost, software licensing cost, and hosting cost. Hardware and hosting costs are provided by ABB's IT provider. A spreadsheet cost model created by the IT provider captures these costs. For software licensing, an internal software license price list was integrated with the IT provider's spreadsheet to complete our informal cost model.

We further refined the alternatives with replication after finding a configuration with a balanced utilization of the hardware across all tiers. In the end, we settled on a configuration with one DMZ server running the connection point and parser component, one application server running the other components, and one database server only hosting the database; that is, a 1:1:1 configuration.

To scale up for the expected high workload (scenario 1), we first replicated the application server with an x split (i.e., two load-balanced application servers, a 1:2:1 configuration). For further workload increase (scenarios 2 and 3), this configuration could be replicated in its entirety for additional capacity (i.e., a 2:4:2 configuration). This resulting architecture should be able to cope with the load, yet it is conservative. For example, no tiers were introduced or removed, and there was no separation based on the request type to different pipelines (i.e., z split). Furthermore, system development continued during our manual exploration, and capacity was improved by 56%.

To improve on our results, we applied an automatic exploration of the design space with PerOpteryx, as described in the following sections.

14.5.2 Formal RDS Cost Model

For automated design space exploration, we additionally need a model to analyze the costs of different design options. The PerOpteryx cost model allows annotating both hardware resources and software components with the total cost of ownership, so that the overall costs can be derived by summing up all annotations. For our case study, we model the total costs for a multiple-year period, which is reasonable because the hosting contract has a minimum duration of several years. In total, our cost model contained seven hardware resource and six software component cost annotations. The hardware resource costs were a function depending on the number of cores used.

The cost prediction, however, cannot be fully accurate. First, prices are renegotiated every year. Second, we can only coarsely approximate the future disk storage demands. Finally, we do not have access to price information for strategic global hosting options, which means that we cannot explore the viability of replicating the RDS in various geographical locations to lower cost and latency.

Furthermore, we are unable to express between different types of leases. The IT provider offers both physical and virtual machines for lease to ABB. The two main differences are that virtual machines have a much shorter minimum lease duration and that the price for the same computational power will drop more significantly over time than for physical servers. While these aspects are not of major impact on what is the best trade-off between price and performance, it has to be kept in mind that a longer lease for physical machines that have constant capacity and price (whereas virtual machines will become cheaper for constant capacity) reduces flexibility and may hinder future expansion.

14.5.3 Degrees of Freedom and Goal

For the ABB RDS system, we identified and modeled three relevant degree of freedom types (subsection 7.4.3) for the automated design space exploration:

Component allocation may be altered by shifting components from one resource container to another. But there are restrictions to not deploy all components on the DMZ servers and to deploy database components on specific configurations recommended by the IT provider. With four additional resource containers as potential application servers in the model, PerOpteryx can explore a y-axis split with one dedicated application server per component. When instantiating this degree of freedom type, we limit the options on the basis of two constraints. First, certain components have to be deployed on a machine in the DMZ, and not all components can be moved to the DMZ. Second, the model ensures the database components are always deployed on a hardware configuration recommended for these by our IT provider.

Resource container replication clones a resource container including all contained components. In our model, all resource containers may be replicated. We defined the upper limits for replication on the basis of the experience from our manual exploration (Gooijer 2011). If database components are replicated, an additional overhead occurs between them to communicate their state. This is supported by our degree of freedom concept, as it allows us to change multiple elements of the architectural model together (Koziolek and Reussner 2011). Thus, we reflected this synchronization overhead by modeling different database component versions, one for each replication level.

Number of (CPU) cores can be varied to increase or decrease the capacity of a resource container. To support this degree of freedom type, the cost model describes the hardware cost of a resource container relative to the number of cores. For the degree of freedom instances, the options are defined by the hardware we can acquire from ABB's IT provider. The degree is not used for the database hardware configurations, however, as the options here are more limited.

The resulting design space has 18 degree of freedom instances:

• Five *component allocation* choices for the five components initially allocated to application server AS1: they may be allocated to any of the five application servers and to either the DMZ server or the database server, depending on security and compatibility considerations.
• Six *number of (CPU) cores* choices for the five available application servers and the DMZ server; each instance allows use of 1, 2, 3, 4, 6, or 8 cores as offered by our IT provider.
• Seven *resource container replication* choices for the five application servers (1 to 8 replicas), the DMZ server (1 to 8 replicas), and the database server (1 to 3 replicas). The *resource container replication* degree of freedom instance for the database server also changes the version of the database component used to reflect the synchronization overhead of different replication levels.

The size of this design space is the combination of choices within these instances and thus is 3.67×10^{15} possible architectural candidates.

The goal of the design space exploration for a given workload is to find an architectural candidate that minimizes costs while fulfilling performance requirements. Three performance requirements are relevant: First, the response time of service engineers when calling a system service should be below a given threshold. Second, the response time of the upload service called by the devices should be below a given threshold to ensure the timeliness of the data. Third, the CPU utilization of all servers used should be below 50%.

14.5.4   Automated Exploration Results
In the following, we present the exploration results for the three scenarios mentioned in subsection 14.5.1. They are motivated by stakeholder expectations of the growth of the system.

Scenario 1: Higher Workload   For the higher-workload scenario, we first ran three PerOpteryx explorations of the full design space in parallel on a quad-core machine. Each run took approximately 8 hours. Analyzing the results, we found that the system does not need many servers to cope with the load. Thus, to refine the results, we reduced the design space to use only up to three application servers and ran another three PerOpteryx explorations. Altogether, 17,857 architectural candidates were evaluated.

Figure 14.4 shows all architectural candidates evaluated during the design space exploration. They are plotted for their costs and the maximum CPU utilization, which is the highest utilized server among all used servers.

Candidates marked with an "×" have a CPU utilization that is too high (above the threshold of 50%). Overloaded candidates are plotted as having a CPU utilization of 1.

The response-time requirements are fulfilled by all architectural candidates that fulfill the utilization requirement.

Many candidates fulfilling all requirements have been found, with varying costs. The optimal candidate (i.e., the candidate with the lowest costs) is marked by a square in figure 14.4. This optimal candidate uses three servers (DMZ server, DB server, and one application server) and distributes the components to them as shown in figure 14.5. Some components are moved to the DMZ and DB server, compared to the initial candidate. No

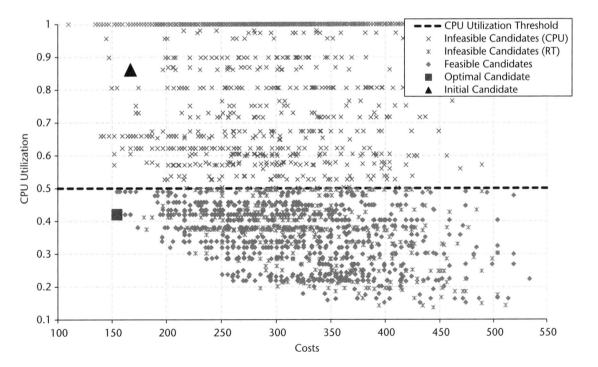

Figure 14.4

Evaluated architectural candidates for the high-workload scenario (scenario 1). The line at 50% CPU utilization separates feasible candidates (below) from infeasible ones (above).

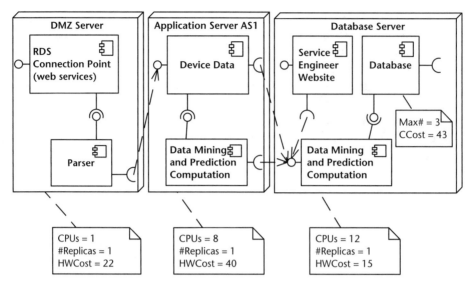

Figure 14.5
The optimal architecture discovered for high workload (scenario 1).

replication has to be introduced, which would lead to unnecessarily high costs. Furthermore, the number of cores of the DMZ server are reduced in the optimal candidate to save additional costs.

Note that we did not consider the potentially increased reliability of the system due to replication. A reliability model could be added to reflect this, so that PerOpteryx could also explore this quality dimension (e.g., as done in Martens et al. [2010]).

Scenario 2: Higher Workload and Information Growth   If each device sends more data for processing, this leads to an increased demand of some of the components per device request. Thus, the overall load of the system increases further. In this scenario 2, we assume an increase of device information by a factor of 8, which leads to higher resource demands in some components where the computation is dependent on the amount of processed data. The new demands were modeled by adding a scalar to the original demands. We defined the scalars on the basis of the theoretical complexity of the operation. For example, a database write scales linearly with the amount of data to be written.

A total of 8,436 candidates have been evaluated for this scenario in three parallel PerOpteryx runs, each running for approximately 8 hours. Figure 14.6 shows the evaluated candidates. Compared to the previous scenario, fewer candidates have been evaluated because only the full design space has been explored. More of the evaluated candidates are infeasible or even overloaded, and the feasible candidates have higher costs, as expected for the

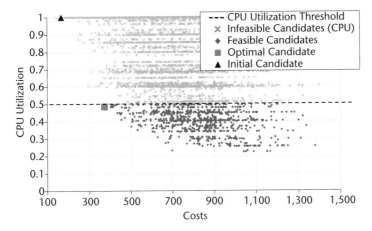

Figure 14.6
Evaluated architectural candidates for high workload and information growth 8 (scenario 2).

increased workload. The initial candidate as shown in figure 14.1 and the optimal candidate found for the previous scenario 1 are overloaded in this workload situation.

The optimal candidate is shown in figure 14.7. The components are allocated differently to the servers. Additionally, five replicas of the application server and two replicas of the database server are used. This also leads to higher component costs for the database, as two instances have to be paid for. Still, PerOpteryx found it beneficial to use the database server as well and even add components to it, because the (physical) database server is less expensive relative to computing power.

Scenario 3: Higher Workload and Intermediate Information Growth As a migration step from scenario 1 to scenario 2 with information growth, we additionally analyzed an intermediate information growth by a factor of 4. The PerOpteryx setup and run statistics are comparable to scenario 2. Figure 14.8 shows the evaluated candidates. As expected, the cloud of evaluated candidates lies in between the results of scenarios 1 and 2. For example, there are fewer feasible candidates than in scenario 1, but more than in scenario 2.

Figure 14.9 shows the resulting optimal candidate. Compared to the optimal candidate from scenario 1 (see figure 14.5), PerOpteryx has moved the Parser component to the application server as well, to be able to use only one DMZ server. The database server is unchanged. The application server has been strengthened to cope with the increased load and the additional Parser component.

But additional manual exploration shows that the candidate is not truly optimal: PerOpteryx chose to use five replicas with four cores each here. After inspecting PerOpteryx's optimal candidates, we found that an application server with three replicas and eight cores

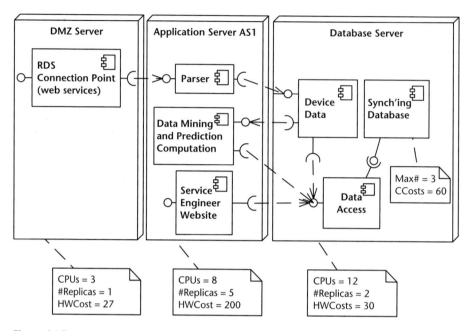

Figure 14.7
The optimal architecture discovered for high workload and information growth 8 (scenario 2).

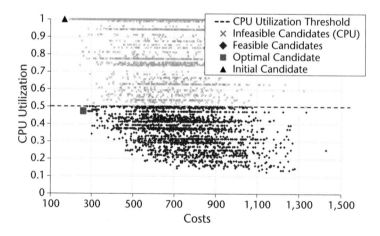

Figure 14.8
Evaluated architectural candidates for high workload and information growth 4 (scenario 3).

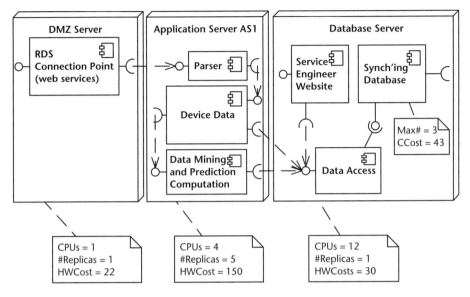

Figure 14.9
The optimal architecture discovered for high workload and information growth 4 (scenario 3).

each would actually be even slightly faster and cheaper (only costs of 120 instead of 150). Thus, a longer exploration run would be required here for a truly optimal solution. Alternatively, we could devise additional PerOpteryx tactics that first analyze the costs for replication of cores and servers and then adjust the model to achieve the cheapest configuration with equivalent processing power. Note, however, that PerOpteryx's automation still is beneficial, as it would be laborious or even impossible to come to these conclusions with manual exploration only.

Summary and Recommendations   On the basis of these results, we can recommend a road map for scaling the RDS. First, to cope with the expected workload increase (scenario 1), the system should be configured in a three-tier configuration as shown in figure 14.5. During our manual exploration, we made a similar conclusion with regard to the DMZ server; however, we did not know which components to off-load from the application server to the database server. We did consider placing both the data access and data mining predictions on the database server, but this overloaded the database server. Hence, the optimal solution for scenario 1 is a partial surprise, but is still valid.

If the workload becomes higher (e.g., because of information growth, scenario 3), the application server should host more components and should be replicated as shown in figure 14.9. Finally, a further increased workload due to more information growth (scenario 2) requires replication of all three tiers as shown in figure 14.7, while at the same time the allocation of components to application server and database server is slightly adjusted to make optimal use of the processing power. On the basis of these findings, we formulated a 5-year road map for the future development of the system. We plan to validate our evaluation after 2 years, as the first steps in the road map have been realized.

14.6   Lessons Learned

In this section, we share the lessons that we took from our study and that we consider of value to other industry practitioners. Fellow researchers may find ideas on how to improve their performance modeling techniques to meet the needs of the software industry.

14.6.1   Performance Modeling Increases Understanding

The performance modeling proved useful in itself, because it forced us to understand the system's (performance) behavior and identify the bottlenecks. It helped us to ask the right questions about the system and gave us insight that was potentially just as valuable as capacity predictions. For example, model calibration helped us to find oddities in the system behavior. The model represents a polished version of the system that should match its average behavior, but under varying loads, measurements and predictions occasionally diverge. One of the things we learned during calibration was that a lock statement was put in the code to limit the amount of concurrently running data-mining processes to free resources for the internal website that was running on the same server.

14.6.2   Predictions Shift Stakeholder Discussion

The discussion about the architectural road map with our stakeholders changed once we introduced the model predictions. The data shifted the conversation from discussion toward a situation where we explained the modeling/evaluation results and the road map was more or less taken for granted. There was no longer discussion about what the way forward should be. This means that the credibility of our study was high because we presented a detailed overview of the assumptions underlying the model, their effect on accuracy, and a list of things we did to ensure accuracy.

14.6.3   Economic Benefit Must Exist

The costs of measuring and modeling are quite high. One has to consider the costs for load generator and measurement tools, training, an experimental copy of the system, and human resources. The latter cost includes the strain on developers and product owners, in addition to the cost for the performance study team. Our study took approximately four full-time employees 6 months. Adding everything up, one can conclude this type of project is too expensive for small systems. Short-term fixes may turn out to be cheaper, despite their inefficiency. We are therefore not surprised that performance firefighting is still common practice. More support for performance modelers would be required to decrease the effort needed (e.g., by automatically creating initial performance models based on log data).

14.6.4   Performance of Performance Modeling Tools Is Limited

Even for modestly sized systems such as the RDS, the performance of the performance modeling tools may be a problem. In our earlier study, we could not use the standard distribution of the Palladio workbench because it ran out of memory (Gooijer 2011). In this study, we reverted to the LQNs to limit the run time of our design space exploration. The scalability of the modeling formalism also proved to be important. We could comfortably model the RDS and various architectural variations, but we think that the model complexity will be significant for systems that are two times bigger.

14.6.5   It Pays Off to Invest in Good Tools

It is difficult to overemphasize the convenience of having the right tools. The combination of dynaTrace and NeoLoad enabled us to take an enormous amount of measurements and to navigate these easily. In practice, this meant that we could easily study the effect of different software and hardware configurations on performance. The changing of hardware configurations was enabled by using virtual machines in our experimental setup. The repository of performance measurements, which included more than 100 load-test runs, was frequently consulted during model construction.

Future Trends

Sebastian Lehrig, Steffen Becker, Christian Stier, and Ralf H. Reussner

As the case studies with Palladio show, we simulated the quality effects of software architectures in realistic industrial contexts. We can accordingly conclude that Palladio, the world's first software architecture simulator, successfully implements the idea of an engineering discipline: in using Palladio, we can predict the properties of a software system on the basis of its design instead of actually realizing and testing it.

But that does not mean that Palladio is complete. First of all, Palladio has limitations, which offer concrete challenges for future work, as listed in the first section of this chapter. In addition, common future trends in IT offer new challenges to Palladio or, more generally, to any approach for architecture-based quality prediction. The last section of this chapter briefly discusses some of them.

Future Work on Limitations

Despite many successful projects with the Palladio Component Model (PCM), there are still limitations of the PCM modeling language or its corresponding analysis tools. Limitations of the modeling language include the following:

- **Active components:** Palladio components always require an explicit request from the outside to start execution, as it is not possible to specify proactive components. Several analyses in the past used a workaround for this. Software architects have to extend any active component with an artificial trigger interface. This interface is then configured to be called from an external workload.
- **Missing memory consumption:** For example, resource demanding service effect specifications (RDSEFFs) do not allow specification and analysis of main memory consumption. In particular, software architects cannot express how much memory internal actions require. As a consequence, scalability issues of the modeled system due to memory limits remain undetected in PCM analyses.
- **Lack of subroutines:** It is not possible to reuse RDSEFFs within the same component as a programmer would do by creating a subroutine. While there are no major conceptual issues

involved in this, the possibility to reuse component internal behavior from several external services often would significantly decrease the effort needed for a Palladio model.

• **Dynamic architectures:** There is currently limited support for dynamically changing architectures (e.g., situations where required services are replaced during run time). Such situations can be modeled when using SimuLizar and its PCM language extensions. The SimuLizar tooling, however, is still a work in progress, and only SimuLizar's simulation itself is able to read and interpret models using the new language features.

• **Stateful components:** The current version of the PCM has no direct support to model component state. Hence, it is impossible to count and limit the throughput of a component with state directly. Additionally, if the system's overall performance depends mainly on the state of such stateful components, predictions would become too inaccurate to be useful.

• **Simplistic network models:** Network modeling is rather abstract in the Palladio model. More detailed modeling of the network could lead to even more accurate prediction results. There exists an early PCM extension that allows use of the Omnet++ network simulator together with a Palladio model allowing much more realistic networking scenarios.

• **More resource types:** The resource types supported by the PCM (CPU, HDD, etc.) can be considered as a basic set, which has to be extended and refined in the future, e.g. with memory.

In addition to language extensions, other quality attributes than those available for performance, reliability, and maintainability could be developed (see the next section). Furthermore, performance measurement and modeling should become more tightly integrated (e.g., by creating Palladio models automatically from dynaTrace results). Finally, support for sensitivity analyses should be increased where model parameters such as resource demands or failure rates are varied in the model to learn their influence. This step is limited to the PCM's tooling so far. The experimental automation framework provides initial support but is not yet fully integrated into the Palladio workbench.

Future Topics

Young disciplines such as software engineering continually have to follow up on new trends. For instance, the trend to outsource resources to third-party providers is also a game-changer for software engineers. In this section, we investigate trends in this area—cloud computing, green computing, and DevOps.

Cloud Computing

A central characteristic of cloud computing (Mell and Grance 2011) is the pay-per-use business model. This is realized through the use of virtualized resources. Virtualized resources can be assigned for more or less physical resources, depending on the current workload. In case of changes of the workload, the assignment of physical resources to the virtual resource is changed, also called elasticity. Together with the pay-per-use business model for resources offered by cloud providers, elasticity therefore shifts upfront capital expenditure (e.g., for servers) to operational expenditure (e.g., for providing a Media Store service to 100 concurrent users for 1 hour). In situations where workload often varies or where workload is unpredictable, this shift saves cloud consumers cost for system operation while avoiding performance issues: in low-load situations, resources for only a few users have to be paid, and in high-load situations, more money is spent for more resources to avoid performance issues. Such a behavior is fundamentally different than classical setups, which typically align resources used with peak workloads to avoid performance issues. In low-load situations, such resources will lie idle, thus effectively wasting money compared to a cloud-computing solution. While such elastic systems seem to solve all performance problems, performance predictions still are important because the new unit of performance in the cloud era is euros or dollars. This means that any design decision leading to bottlenecks or other unrequired resource demands directly lead to increased bills from service providers. Hence, performance-optimized architectures are now even more crucial.

SimuLizar (section 8.3) is currently the only analysis tool that supports the analysis of reconfigurations such as the resources used to provision a cloud service. Analytical approaches such as layered queuing networks (LQNs; chapter 8) as well as the existing cost analysis (chapter 8) are unsuitable for such situations.

In the CloudScale project (Brataas et al. 2013), several Palladio and SimuLizar extensions have been developed, enriching SimuLizar with dedicated metrics for elasticity and costs. CloudScale also provides a customized PCM bench for cloud computing that allows detection of cloud-specific scalability antipatterns and design of cloud-computing environments on the basis of reusable architectural templates (Lehrig 2014a). These novel features are currently evaluated within the CloudScale project and potentially lead to their integration into Palladio.

Green Computing

Green computing (Murugesan 2008) aims to reduce the energy spent in provisioning ICT services. Besides reducing environmental damage, the main goal of green computing is to reduce the operational cost of software systems by cutting the energy bill. The move from dedicated hosting to cloud solutions has enabled a more efficient use of resources. Instead of dedicated hosting for each client, cloud data centers collocate the software stack ("infrastructure as a service"), applications ("platform as a service"), or provision the service requests ("software as a service") of multiple customers using the same physical server.

When deciding whether to use a cloud service, consumers focus on quality and cost with which a cloud operator offers a hosting service. The total cost of ownership (TCO) of the hosting infrastructure determines the price at which the infrastructure operator is able to offer services to customers. Energy consumption is more than 15% of the TCO of data centers

(Greenberg et al. 2008). To accurately predict the cost of a cloud service, it is thus necessary to consider energy consumption.

As part of the CACTOS project (Östberg et al. 2014), Palladio has been extended by an energy consumption analysis (Stier et al. 2014). The analysis enables data center operators and software architects to estimate the effect of architectural design and deployment decisions on the energy efficiency of a software system. The analysis is also currently being integrated with SimuLizar. This will allow architects and data center operators to reason about the effects of energy-conscious resource provisioning mechanisms on energy efficiency and other quality dimensions.

Currently, SimuLizar executes all adaptations immediately. The execution of the adaptations in itself does not affect performance or energy consumption. An open challenge is the integration of transient effects with SimuLizar's design-time analysis. Transient effects capture the performance and energy consumption impact of adaptation operations such as VM migrations or switching the power state of servers. Incorporating the transient effects would increase the accuracy of the energy efficiency analyses and enable software architects to make informed decisions about the benefits and risks of using self-adaptations in software systems.

DevOps

DevOps (Hüttermann 2012) is the trend to overcome the isolation of the different phases of the software life cycle. In particular, the strong separation of development and operation often causes avoidable costs during deployment, operation, and evolution. (Hence, the name "DevOps" as union of "Development" and "Operation.") In particular, DevOps means that specific requirements of the operation are considered systematically during design and that design-time information on software is still usable (and ideally even adaptable) during operation.

For modeling quality in software architectures, new chances arise through DevOps. Through run-time monitoring performance, relevant information can be measured with high accuracy. For example, usage profiles, resource demands, and performance and reliability properties of resources can be monitored and used to recalibrate design-time performance models. Conversely, design-time models of the software can be used for an optimized run-time resource management.

Currently, such interaction between design time and run time requires manual efforts in Palladio; however, the use of run-time monitoring data (from the Kieker monitoring framework [Hoorn et al. 2012]) is investigated in the iObserve project (Heinrich et al. 2015b). The use of Palladio-inspired design models for run-time resource management is investigated in the Descartes Project (Brosig et al. 2013).

Conclusion

This small chapter concludes our journey through an engineering approach to software design. It was a journey that started with the *introduction* of our motivation to make software design a true *engineering* discipline. This refers to the ability to predict the consequences of design decisions for the quality of the created artifact (the executing software) on the basis of analyses at the modeling level (the software architecture). For mechanical machines, Ferdinand Redtenbacher introduced this for the first time in the mid-nineteenth century. Hence, he is usually seen as the father of mechanical engineering, lifting machine creation from a craft to an—or, in fact, the first—engineering discipline. His work in Karlsruhe, Germany, acted as a role model for the Massachusetts Institute of Technology and the ETH Zurich.

Next, we climbed onto a *nutshell*; however, a nutshell tall enough to give us an overview of where our journey will take us. From there, we descended to *architectural modeling*. We saw software architecture from different view types and learned about techniques to reuse architectural knowledge accross different software development projects. The next stop of our journey was *architectural analysis*: we learned how to enrich software architecture models to perform automated quality analysis. Then, we got to know how to collect data for architectural quality analyses and how they help us to answer design decisions. Then, in a larger excursion, we glimpsed under the hood of Palladio where we saw how architectural models are transformed into analysis models and their simulation. The next stop was at the *embedding into software engineering processes*. We looked at software processes in general, at software engineering processes for component-based software development, and at processes for modeling quality aspects in software architectures. Then, we had a closer look at the relationship between requirements engineering and software architecture and, likewise, software architecture and implementation. At the end of our journey, we met three case studies, showing us the application of architectural modeling and analysis in the real world.

Everyone that travels has stories to tell. In this sense, what are the essential lessons learned from this journey? Well, this may depend on you, the reader, with your individual background, interests, and needs. But for us, the authors, it is the following:

1. It is possible to quantitatively evaluate the impact of architectural design decisions on performance and reliability, even without having an implementation of the architecture.

2. The better the models, the better the results, of course. But for deciding between different design options, most often rough estimates are sufficient. When being more concerned with resource dimensioning or exact scalability analysis, it is beneficial to take measured values into account; for example, from older versions of the system, from the usage profile, or from the vendor documentation of the hardware to be deployed.

3. Architectural performance impact analysis is best when the architecture is the main factor in the performance of the resulting system; or, in other words, if the algorithms of the system do not have a strong impact on performance. This means the approach presented in this book usually works well for business information systems and is usually not appropriate for scientific computing codes, where the properties of numerical algorithms mainly drive the overall system performance.

4. It is possible to reason about performance and reliability in a compositional way: the quality of a composite component can be predicted on the basis of the quality of its inner components. The quality of the composite component, however, does not only depend on the quality of the inner components.

And quality is not a constant property of the component. It is in fact a function of the component's internal implementation, but also of external factors, such as the usage profile, the assembly context (connected components), and the deployment context (execution environment). Hence, when predicting the quality of a composite component, these external factors also need to be taken into account. Most likely, their values differ from the values for the inner components.

Well, does this journey of software design engineering really end here? No! Some hints for further traveling can be found in the previous chapter on future trends.

Beyond this, the horizon offers a remarkable view. As known from software engineering, we need different view types on a software system: structural design, deployment, or service effect specifications were the ones discussed here. In software engineering, we know about additional view types, such as, for example, requirements or code. And code, which specifies the exact behavioral semantics, is as well only a view and not the only truth about a software system, as often believed. It does not include crucial information of the software, such as deployment, run-time configurations, test cases, or requirements. When looking at mechatronic systems, which combine software and electronic and mechanical hardware, such as cars, planes, trains, and the like, then additional views on the composition of mechanical parts, electric wiring, circuits, and so forth, arise. Obviously, all views from these view types need to be kept consistent at some stage during development. In many engineering disciplines, this is currently done manually. Not surprisingly, this often results in costly problems if changes in one view are not properly manually translated into the other views. The alternative, to return to a single view-type approach, for example as in so-called extreme programming, neither scales nor supports evolution or reuse, nor does it really have only a single view type: next to the code, test cases need to be kept consistent—manually. So what is the view on the horizon beyond Palladio? It is the systematic support of multiple views in a consistent way. This should result in tools that will automate consistency keeping as far as possible and that will advise the software developer about where to edit views to come to a consistent system, whenever automation is not possible. This is exactly the goal of the Vitruvius project, where Palladio plays itself the role of a case study.

Notably, while for Palladio mechanical engineering was a role model, in Vitruvius software modeling techniques are broadened and applied to the design of mechatronic systems. In this, we hope to give something back to Ferdinand Redtenbacher.

Epilogue: A Brief History of Palladio

The content of this book is based on our work on software modeling and simulation. This work comprises research, consultation with industry partners, and teaching at various universities. It was funded by several project grants and industrial partners.

Our work on Palladio started in 2003. Before this, Ralf Reussner worked with Heinz Schmidt and Iman Poernomo since 2001 on software architecture modeling and reliability prediction at DSTC Pty Ltd. in Melbourne, Australia. In this context, the ideas of a grant proposal to the DFG (German Science Foundation) were born: Can we compositionally reason about software quality attributes such as performance or reliability, and is the software architecture a good base for this kind of reasoning? Lacking a good abbreviation of the short title, "Methods and Tools for Systematically Constructing Component-Based Software Architectures with Predictable Quality Attributes," the grant proposal was, for obvious reasons, short-named Palladio.

After this proposal was granted in 2003, Palladio started as an Emmy Noether Project (a specific program of the DFG dedicated to support and award young scientists) at the University of Oldenburg in northern Germany. Oldenburg has in addition to its faculty an institution (the OFFIS Institute) specifically oriented to bring academic research results into industrial practice. Through this, Palladio was from its beginnings directly grounded in applicability through real-world design challenges. At those times, however, the first researchers associated with Ralf Reussner, namely, Viktoria Firus and Steffen Becker, were concerned with basic research challenges. Under which assumptions can we compose performance models of software components in analogy to the composition of the components themselves? What are the influences on software component performance of the execution context? This "phase 1" Palladio research resulted in highly parameterized performance models that were context independent (Reussner et al. 2004) and compositional (Reussner et al. 2005). As a technology base, Microsoft's .NET Framework was intentionally chosen, mainly because of the good support for components. The research group was considerably strengthened through the graduate school "TrustSoft" established by Wilhelm Hasselbring and Ralf Reussner in 2005, also funded by the DFG (Hasselbring et al. 2006). As TrustSoft scholarship holders, Jens Happe and Heiko Koziolek now worked on modeling hardware parallelism (Jens) and the influence of the usage profile (Heiko) on application-level performance (Koziolek et al. 2008; Happe et al. 2009). With Ralf following the call to a professorship in software engineering at the University of Karlsruhe, the whole group moved to Karlsruhe in southern Germany. With the FZI-IT research center, strong and established links to industry partners could be used from the first moment on, similar to the work in Oldenburg. On the scientific side, it became clear, in particular through Steffen's initiative, that it was necessary to explicitly meta-model Palladio with the MetaObject Facility (MOF). With the initial usability of Eclipse frameworks such as the Eclipse Modeling Framework (EMF) and the Graphical Modeling Framework (GMF) and the increasing scalability of Eclipse 2.0, the technology base of Palladio was shifted from C# / .NET to Eclipse / Java. To increase applicability in industrial practice, Klaus Krogmann investigated reengineering approaches and built tools such as SoMoX (Krogmann et al. 2010). Concurrently, Michael Kuperberg was concerned with approaches to abstractly describe resource demands in terms of Java Virtual Machine (JVM) instructions. This also resulted in a generated benchmark for JVMs (Kuperberg et al. 2009). Anne Koziolek added to Palladio a new layer allowing automated optimizations of deployments and the presentation of Pareto-optimal sizing options in relation to their costs (Koziolek et al. 2011a). We realized that many abstractions introduced for performance, such as SEFFs and stochastic usage profiles, also form a well-suited base for reliability modeling and prediction, which was investigated and realized by Franz Brosch (Brosch et al. 2011). Chris Rathfelder added events as first-class entities in PCM and enabled the analysis of event-based systems (Rathfelder et al. 2013). With the use of Palladio to predict quality before the actual system realization, software design made a step toward an engineering discipline. On this road, the next milestone would be software certification, with "certification" in the strong meaning of established engineering disciplines; namely, the trusted demonstration of quality properties of a technical piece. The use of Palladio for component certification was investigated by Henning Groenda (Groenda 2010). Coming to the present time, recently virtualized resources are measured, modeled, and included in Palladio predictions, such as virtual processors by Micha Hauck (Hauck et al. 2013) and storage systems by Qais Noorshams (Noorshams et al. 2015). Zoya Durdik was concerned with the relationship of requirements and architectural design and formed a pattern-based approach to link requirements via design decisions to Palladio models (Durdik et al. 2013). Benjamin Klatt investigated the recovery of architectural variability in software and its use for product lines (Klatt et al. 2014).

In the meantime in April 2010, Steffen was appointed as assistant professor at the University of Paderborn. In Paderborn, as previously in Oldenburg and Karlsruhe, Palladio had an impact on a Fraunhofer project group and the s-lab Software Quality Lab, which is directed toward industrial applications of research results. Under the supervision of Wilhelm Schäfer and Gregor Engels, Steffen helped in acquiring the Collaborative Research Center 901 grant "On-The-Fly Computing," in which the Palladio language formed the basis for the Service Specification Language (SSL); this grant was extended especially by Marie Christin Platenius with approaches for service matching and composition (Platenius et al. 2014). In addition, Markus von Detten extended Palladio by the Archimetrix approach to also support reverse engineering of eroded architectures (Detten et al. 2013). Under the influence of another meta-model developed at the University of Paderborn, MechatronicUML, Matthias Becker started to extend the Palladio modeling language with self-adaptation modeling constructs leading to SimuLizar. As cloud computing is a particular instance of a self-adaptive system, SimuLizar allowed extensions for scalable systems on the basis of cloud technologies (Becker et al. 2013). Sebastian Lehrig started working on a reusable library of self-adaption architectural styles and aims at making them easily available to the software architect (Lehrig 2014b). Finally, Frank Brüseke added an automated testing approach to Palladio, allowing one to spot and analyze performance deviations found during testing (Brüseke et al. 2014). Since 2014, Steffen is a full professor in Chemnitz, where his group continues to work on Palladio and plans to extend it for multicore and many-core systems.

Through the use of model-driven techniques in the development of the Palladio workbench and also for the performance simulations themselves, we started to do research in model-driven techniques themselves. Lucia Happe added higher-order transformations (HOTs) and a mechanism to generate completions, a kind of "modeling macro" that is also used in Palladio. Andras Rentschler created a new modularity concept for model transformations (Rentschler et al. 2014). Thomas Goldschmidt was concerned with a framework to define multiple concrete syntaxes as a means to define views on software systems (Goldschmidt et al. 2009). From this line of work on views, the Vitruvius project originated in 2013 with Erik Burger as head and Max Kramer and Michael Langhammer as current members. This group forms a new line of research that is concerned with view consistency and is using Palladio as a case study as such.

All dissertations contributing to Palladio as presented in this book can be found in the Karlsruhe Software Design and Quality series or at the homepages of the researchers.

The work of the authors of this book and the contributors were financed through various public funding organizations in different projects. The ones with the strongest influence on Palladio are the following:

- Palladio, DFG, 2003–2008
- Q-Impress, EU, 2009–2011
- SLA@SOI, EU, 2009–2011
- Ferdinand, DFG, 2010–2013
- Collaborative Research Center 901 "On-The-Fly Computing," DFG, since 2012
- CloudScale, EU, 2012–2015

A current list of industrial references for the use of Palladio and our research partners can be found online at www.palladio-simulator.org.

References

Abbott, Martin L., and Michael T. Fisher. 2009. *The Art of Scalability, 559*. Reading, MA: Addison-Wesley.

Aleti, Aldeida, et al. 2013. Software Architecture Optimization Methods: A Systematic Literature Review. *IEEE Transactions on Software Engineering* 39 (5): 658–683.

de Alfaro, Luca, and Thomas A. Henzinger. 2001. "Interface Automata." In *Proceedings of the Joint 8th European Software Engineering Conference and 9th ACM SIGSOFT Symposium on the Foundation of Software Engineering (ESEC/FSE-01)*, 26(5): 109–120. ACM SIGSOFT Software Engineering Notes. New York: ACM Press.

Ambler, Scott. 2002. *Agile Modeling: Effective Practices for Extreme Programming and the Unified Process.* New York: John Wiley & Sons.

Atkinson, Colin, and Oliver Hummel. 2012. "Iterative and Incremental Development of Component-based Software Architectures." In *Proceedings of the 15th ACM SIGSOFT Symposium on Component Based Software Engineering*, 77–82. CBSE '12. Bertinoro, Italy: ACM.

Avgeriou, Paris, et al. 2011. *Relating Software Requirements and Architectures*. Berlin: Springer-Verlag.

Avizienis, Algirdas, et al. 2004. Basic Concepts and Taxonomy of Dependable and Secure Computing. *IEEE Transactions on Dependable and Secure Computing* 1 (1): 11–33.

Bachmann, Felix, et al. 2005. Designing Software Architectures to Achieve Quality Attribute Requirements. *IEE Proceedings. Software* 152 (4): 153–165.

Balsamo, Simonetta, et al. 2004. "Experimenting Different Software Architectures Performance Techniques: A Case Study." In *Proceedings of the Fourth International Workshop on Software and Performance*, 115–119. Redwood Shores, CA: ACM Press.

Banks, Jerry, et al. 2000. *Discrete-Event System Simulation*. 3rd ed. Englewood Cliffs, NJ: Prentice Hall.

Barbacci, Mario, et al. 2003. *Quality Attribute Workshops (QAWs)*. Tech. Rep. 3rd Ed., CMU/SEI-2003-TR-016. Software Engineering Institute, Carnegie Mellon University.

Basili, Victor R., Gianluigi Caldiera, and H. Dieter Rombach. 1994. "The Goal Question Metric Approach." In *Encyclopedia of Software Engineering*, 528–532. New York: John Wiley & Sons.

Bass, Len, Paul Clements, and Rick Kazman. 2003. *Software Architecture in Practice*. 2nd ed. Reading, MA: Addison-Wesley.

Bass, Len, Paul Clements, and Rick Kazman. 2012. *Software Architecture in Practice*. 3rd ed. Reading, MA: Addison-Wesley Professional.

Beck, Kent. 2003. *Test-Driven Development: By Example*. Reading, MA: Addison-Wesley Professional.

Beck, Kent. 2005. *Extreme Programming Explained*. 2nd ed. Reading, MA: Addison-Wesley.

Becker, Matthias, Markus Luckey, and Steffen Becker. 2012. "Model-Driven Performance Engineering of Self-Adaptive Systems: A Survey." In *Proceedings of the 8th International ACM SIGSOFT Conference on Quality of Software Architectures*, 117–122. QoSA '12. Bertinoro, Italy: ACM.

Becker, Matthias, Steffen Becker, and Joachim Meyer. 2013. "SimuLizar: Design-Time Modelling and Performance Analysis of Self-Adaptive Systems." In *Proceedings of Software Engineering 2013 (SE2013)*. Vol. P-213, 71–84. Lecture Notes in Informatics (LNI). Aachen: Gesellschaft für Informatik e.V. (GI), Bonn, Germany.

Becker, Stefan. 2011. *Performance Modellierung des 1&1 Mail-Systems*. MA thesis, Karlsruhe Institute of Technology (KIT).

Becker, Steffen. 2008. *Coupled Model Transformations for QoS Enabled Component-Based Software Design*. Vol. 1. The Karlsruhe Series on Software Design and Quality. University of Karlsruhe.

Becker, Steffen, Jens Happe, and Heiko Koziolek. 2006. "Putting Components into Context: Supporting QoS-Predictions with an Explicit Context Model." In *Proceedings of the 11th International Workshop on Component Oriented Programming (WCOP'06)*, 1–6.

Becker, Steffen, Heiko Koziolek, and Ralf Reussner. 2009. The Palladio Component Model for Model-Driven Performance Prediction. *Journal of Systems and Software* 82:3–22.

Bengtsson, Per-Olof, et al. 2004. Architecture-Level Modifiability Analysis (ALMA). *Journal of Systems and Software* 69 (102): 129–147.

Berntsson Svensson, Richard, et al. 2011. "Quality Requirements in Industrial Practice—An Extended Interview Study at Eleven Companies." *IEEE Transactions on Software Engineering* (Washington, DC) 38 (4): 923–935.

Beugnard, Antoine, et al. 1999. Making Components Contract Aware. *Computer* 32 (7): 38–45.

Boehm, Barry W. 1984. Software Engineering Economics. *IEEE Transactions on Software Engineering* SE-10 (1): 4–21.

Boehm, Barry W., and Richard Turner. 2004. "Balancing Agility and Discipline: Evaluating and Integrating Agile and Plan-Driven Methods." In *Software Engineering, 2004. ICSE 2004. Proceedings of the 26th International Conference*, 718–719. Washington, DC: IEEE Computer Society.

Boehm, Barry W., and Ricardo Valerdi. 2008. Achievements and Challenges in COCOMO-Based Software Resource Estimation. *IEEE Software* 25 (5): 74–83.

Boehm, Barry W., John R. Brown, and Myron Lipow. 1976. "Quantitative Evaluation of Software Quality." In *Proceedings: 2nd International Conference on Software Engineering*, 592–605. New York: IEEE Computer Society Press.

Boehm, Barry W., et al. 2000. *Software Cost Estimation with COCOMO II*. Upper Saddle River, NJ: Prentice Hall PTR.

Bondi, André B. 2014. *Foundations of Software and System Performance Engineering: Process, Performance Modeling, Requirements, Testing, Scalability, and Practice*. Reading, MA: Addison-Wesley Professional.

Braga, Regina M. M., Marta Mattoso, and Cláudia M. L. Werner. 2001. "The Use of Mediation and Ontology Technologies for Software Component Information Retrieval." In *Proceedings of the 2001 Symposium on Software Reusability: Putting Software Reuse in Context*, 19–28. SSR '01. Toronto: ACM.

Brataas, Gunnar, et al. 2013. "CloudScale: Scalability Management for Cloud Systems." In *4th International Conference on Performance Engineering*, 335–338. ICPE '13. Prague, Czech Republic: ACM.

Brosch, Franz. 2012a. *Integrated Software Architecture-Based Reliability Prediction for IT Systems*. Vol. 9. The Karlsruhe Series on Software Design and Quality. Karlsruhe: KIT Scientific Publishing.

Brosch, Franz, et al. 2012b. Architecture-Based Reliability Prediction with the Palladio Component Model. *IEEE Transactions on Software Engineering* 38 (6): 1319–1339.

Brosig, Fabian, Samuel Kounev, and Klaus Krogmann. 2009. "Automated Extraction of Palladio Component Models from Running Enterprise Java Applications." In *Proceedings of the 1st International Workshop on Run-time Models for Self-managing Systems and Applications (ROSSA 2009)*. 10:1–10:10, Pisa, Italy. New York: ACM.

Brosig, Fabian, Nikolaus Huber, and Samuel Kounev. 2013. *Architecture-Level Software Performance Abstractions for Online Performance Prediction*. Elsevier Science of Computer Programming Journal *90*, Part B:71–92.

Brosig, Fabian, et al. 2015. Quantitative Evaluation of Model-Driven Performance Analysis and Simulation of Component-Based Architectures. *IEEE Transactions on Software Engineering* 41 (2): 157–175.

Bruneliere, Hugo, et al. 2014. Modisco: A Model Driven Reverse Engineering Framework. *Information and Software Technology* 56 (8): 1012–1032.

Brüseke, Frank, et al. 2014. PBlaman: Performance Blame Analysis Based on Palladio Contracts. *Concurrency and Computation: Practice and Experience*.

Burger, Erik. 2013. "Flexible Views for View-Based Model-Driven Development." In *Proceedings of the 18th International Doctoral Symposium on Components and Architecture*, 25–30. WCOP '13. Vancouver: ACM.

Burger, Erik, et al. 2014. View-Based Model-Driven Software Development with ModelJoin. *Software & Systems Modeling* 14:1–24.

Buschmann, Frank, et al. 1996. *Pattern-Oriented Software Architecture—A System of Patterns*. New York: John Wiley & Sons.

Canal, Carlos, et al. 1999. "Adding Semantic Information to IDLs. Is It Really Practical?" In *Proceedings of the OOPSLA'99 Workshop on Behavioral Semantics.*

Cheesman, John, and John Daniels. 2000. *UML Components: A Simple Process for Specifying Component-Based Software.* Reading, MA: Addison-Wesley.

Cherkasova, Ludmila, et al. 2009. "Automated Anomaly Detection and Performance Modeling of Enterprise Applications." *ACM Transactions on Computer Systems* 27(3): 6.1–6.32.

Chikofsky, Elliot J., and James H. Cross. 1990. Reverse Engineering and Design Recovery: A Taxonomy. *IEEE Software* 7:13–17.

Clements, Paul C., and Linda Northrop. 2001. *Software Product Lines: Practices and Patterns. SEI Series in Software Engineering.* Reading, MA: Addison-Wesley.

Clements, Paul, Rick Kazman, and Mark Klein. 2001. *Evaluating Software Architectures: Methods and Case Studies*, 1st Ed. SEI Series in Software Engineering. Reading, MA: Addison-Wesley Professional.

Clements, Paul C., et al. 2003. *Documenting Software Architectures. SEI Series in Software Engineering.* Reading, MA: Addison-Wesley.

Conway, Melvin E. 1968. How Do Committees Invent? *Datamation* 14:28–31.

Cortellessa, Vittorio, Fabrizio Marinelli, and Pasqualina Potena. 2008. "An Optimization Framework for 'Build-or-Buy' Decisions in Software Architecture." Part Special Issue: Search-Based Software Engineering. *Computers & Operations Research* 35 (10): 3090–3106.

Deb, Kalyanmoy, et al. 2000. "A Fast Elitist Non-Dominated Sorting Genetic Algorithm for Multi-Objective Optimization: NSGA-II." In *Parallel Problem Solving from Nature PPSN VI*, 1917/2000: 849–858. Berlin: Springer-Verlag.

von Detten, Markus. 2013. *Reengineering of Component-Based Software Systems in the Presence of Design Deficiencies.* Dissertation, Software Engineering Group, University of Paderborn.

von Detten, Markus, and Sebastian Lehrig. 2013. "Reengineering of Component-Based Systems in the Presence of Design Deficiencies—An Overview." In *Proceedings of the 15th Workshop Software-Reengineering*, 2. Bad Honnef, Germany: Gesellschaft fuer Informatik.

von Detten, Markus, Marie Christin Platenius, and Steffen Becker. 2013. Reengineering Component-Based Software Systems with Archimetrix. *Software & Systems Modeling* (April): 1–30.

Douglass, Bruce Powel. 2002. *Real-Time Design Patterns. Object Technology Series.* Reading, MA: Addison-Wesley Professional.

Durdik, Zoya, and Ralf Reussner. 2013. "On the Appropriate Rationale for Using Design Patterns and Pattern Documentation." In *Proceedings of the 9th ACM SIGSOFT International Conference on the Quality of Software Architectures (QoSA 2013) .*

Erl, Thomas. 2009. *SOA Design Patterns.* Englewood Cliffs, NJ: Prentice Hall PTR.

Faber, Michael. 2011. *Software Performance Analysis Using Machine Learning Techniques*. MA thesis, Karlsruhe Institute of Technology (KIT).

Fagan, Michael E. 1976. Design and Code Inspections to Reduce Errors in Program Development. *IBM Systems Journal* 15 (3): 182–211.

Finkelstein, Anthony, et al. 1992. Viewpoints: A Framework for Integrating Multiple Perspectives in System Development. *International Journal of Software Engineering and Knowledge Engineering* 2 (1): 31–57.

Fowler, Martin. 2003. Who Needs an Architect? *IEEE Software* 20 (5): 11–13.

Fowler, Martin, and Rebecca Parsons. 2010. *Domain Specific Languages*. 1st ed. Reading, MA: Addison-Wesley.

Fowler, Martin, et al. 2002. *Patterns of Enterprise Application Architecture*. Reading, MA: Addison-Wesley Professional.

Franks, Greg, et al. 2009. Enhanced Modeling and Solution of Layered Queuing Networks. *IEEE Transactions on Software Engineering* 35 (2): 148–161.

Friedman, Jerome H. 1991. Multivariate Adaptive Regression Splines. *Annals of Statistics* 19 (1): 1–141.

Frølund, Svend, and Jari Koisten. 1998. *QML: A Language for Quality of Service Specification*. Technical Report HPL-98-10. Hewlett-Packard Laboratories.

Gamma, Erich, et al. 1995. *Design Patterns: Elements of Reusable Object-Oriented Software*. Reading, MA: Addison-Wesley.

Georges, Andy, Dries Buytaert, and Lieven Eeckhout. 2007. Statistically Rigorous Java Performance Evaluation. *SIGPLAN Not. (New York)* 42 (10): 57–76.

Giacinto, Daria, and Sebastian Lehrig. 2013. "Towards Integrating Java EE into ProtoCom." In *Proceedings of the Symposium on Software Performance: Joint Kieker/Palladio Days 2013, Karlsruhe, Germany, November 27–29, 2013*. 1083: 69–78. CEUR Workshop Proceedings. Available at www .CEUR-WS.org.

Glass, Robert L. 1998. *Software Runaways: Monumental Software Disasters*. Englewood Cliffs, NJ: Prentice Hall.

Glinz, Martin. 2007. "On Non-Functional Requirements." In *15th IEEE International Requirements Engineering Conference, 2007. RE '07*, 21–26. Washington, DC: IEEE Computer Society.

Glinz, Martin. 2008. A Risk-Based, Value-Oriented Approach to Quality Requirements. *IEEE Software* 25 (2): 34–41.

Glinz, Martin. 2011. *A Glossary of Requirements Engineering Terminology: Standard Glossary for the Certified Professional for Requirements Engineering (CPRE) Studies and Exam*. Technical Report. International Requirements Engineering Board. Available online.

Glinz, Martin, and Samuel A. Fricker. 2014. "On Shared Understanding in Software Engineering: An Essay." *Computer Science—Research for Development* 30 (3): 363–376.

Gödel, Kurt. 1931. Über formal unentscheidbare Sätze der Principia Mathematica und verwandter Systeme I. *Monatshefte für Mathematik und Physik* 38:173–198.

Gokhale, Swapna S. 2007. Architecture-Based Software Reliability Analysis: Overview and Limitations. *IEEE Transactions on Dependable and Secure Computing* 4 (1): 32–40.

Goldschmidt, Thomas, Steffen Becker, and Erik Burger. 2012. "Towards a Tool-Oriented Taxonomy of View-Based Modelling." In *Proceedings of the Modellierung 2012*. Vol. P-201. 59–74. GI-Edition—Lecture Notes in Informatics (LNI). Bamberg: Gesellschaft für Informatik e.V. (GI).

Goldschmidt, Thomas, Steffen Becker, and Axel Uhl. 2009. "Textual Views in Model Driven Engineering." In *Proceedings of the 35th EUROMICRO Conference on Software Engineering and Advanced Applications (SEAA)*. IEEE.

de Gooijer, Thijmen. 2011. *Performance Modeling of ASP.Net Web Service Applications: An Industrial Case Study*. MA thesis, Mälardalen University, School of Innovation, Design and Engineering.

de Gooijer, Thijmen, et al. 2012. "An Industrial Case Study of Performance and Cost Design Space Exploration." In *Proceedings of the 3rd ACM/SPEC International Conference on Performance Engineering*, 205–216. ICPE '12. ICPE Best Industry-Related Paper Award. Boston: ACM.

Gorton, Ian. 2011. *Essential Software Architecture*. 2nd ed. Berlin: Springer-Verlag.

Goseva-Popstojanova, Katerina, and Kishor S. Trivedi. 2001. Architecture-Based Approach to Reliability Assessment of Software Systems. *Performance Evaluation* 45 (2–3): 179–204.

Greenberg, Albert, et al. 2008. The Cost of a Cloud: Research Problems in Data Center Networks. *Computer Communication Review* 39 (1): 68–73.

Groenda, Henning. 2010. "Usage Profile and Platform Independent Automated Validation of Service Behavior Specifications." In *Proceedings of the 2nd International Workshop on the Quality of Service-Oriented Software Systems*, 6: 1–6:6. QUASOSS '10. Oslo, Norway: ACM.

Groenda, Henning. 2011. "An Accuracy Information Annotation Model for Validated Service Behavior Specifications." In *Models in Software Engineering*, 6627: 369–383. Lecture Notes in Computer Science. Berlin: Springer.

Groenda, Henning. 2012a. "Improving Performance Predictions by Accounting for the Accuracy of Composed Performance Models." In *Proceedings of the 8th International ACM SIGSOFT Conference on Quality of Software Architectures (QoSA)*, 111–116. QoSA '12. Bertinoro, Italy: ACM.

Groenda, Henning. 2012b. "Path Coverage Criteria for Palladio Performance Models." In *Proceedings of the 38th EUROMICRO Conference on Software Engineering and Advanced Applications*, 133–137. SEAA '12. Washington, DC: IEEE Computer Society.

Groenda, Henning. 2012c. "Protecting Intellectual Property by Certified Component Quality Descriptions." In *Proceedings of the 2012 Ninth International Conference on Information Technology—New Generations*, 287–292. ITNG '12. Washington, DC: IEEE Computer Society.

Groenda, Henning. 2013. *Certifying Software Component Performance Specifications*. Vol. 11. The Karlsruhe Series on Software Design and Quality. Karlsruhe: KIT Scientific Publishing.

Grunske, Lars, and David Joyce. 2008. Quantitative Risk-Based Security Prediction for Component-Based Systems with Explicitly Modeled Attack Profiles. *Journal of Systems and Software* 81 (8): 1327–1345.

Happe, Jens. 2008. *Predicting Software Performance in Symmetric Multi-core and Multiprocessor Environments.* Dissertation, University of Oldenburg.

Happe, Jens, et al. 2008. "A Pattern-Based Performance Completion for Message-Oriented Middleware." In *Proceedings of the 7th International Workshop on Software and Performance (WOSP '08)*, 165–176. Princeton, NJ: ACM.

Happe, Jens, Henning Groenda, and Ralf H. Reussner. 2009. "Performance Evaluation of Scheduling Policies in Symmetric Multiprocessing Environments." In *Proceedings of the 17th IEEE International Symposium on Modelling, Analysis and Simulation Computer and Telecommunication Systems (MASCOTS'09)* .

Happe, Jens, Heiko Koziolek, and Ralf Reussner. 2011. Facilitating Performance Predictions Using Software Components. *IEEE Software* 28 (3): 27–33.

Happe, Lucia, Barbora Buhnova, and Ralf Reussner. 2013. Stateful Component-Based Performance Models. *Software & Systems Modeling* 13 (4): 1319–1343.

Hasselbring, Wilhelm, and Ralf H. Reussner. 2006. Toward Trustworthy Software Systems. *IEEE Computer* 30 (4): 91–92.

Hauck, Michael. 2009. *Extending Performance-Oriented Resource Modelling in the Palladio Component Model.* Diploma Thesis, University of Karlsruhe (TH).

Hauck, Michael, et al. 2013. Deriving Performance-Relevant Infrastructure Properties through Model-Based Experiments with Ginpex. *Software & Systems Modeling* 13 (4): 1345–1365.

Heger, Christoph, Jens Happe, and Roozbeh Farahbod. 2013. "Automated Root Cause Isolation of Performance Regressions During Software Development." In *Proceedings of the 4th ACM/SPEC International Conference on Performance Engineering*, 27–38. ICPE '13. Prague: ACM.

Heidenreich, Florian, et al. 2010. "Closing the Gap Between Modelling and Java." In *Software Language Engineering*, 374–383. Berlin: Springer.

Heinrich, Robert. 2014. *Aligning Business Processes and Information Systems: New Approaches to Continuous Quality Engineering.* Berlin: Springer.

Heinrich, Robert, et al. 2015a. Integrating Business Process Simulation and Information System Simulation for Performance Prediction. *Software & Systems Modeling* 1–21.

Heinrich, Robert, et al. 2015b. *Run-time Architecture Models for Dynamic Adaptation and Evolution of Cloud Applications. Forschungsbericht, Technical Report.* Kiel: Kiel University.

Hoare, Charles Anthony Richard. 1969. An Axiomatic Basis for Computer Programming. *Communications of the ACM* 12 (10): 576–580.

Hofmeister, Christine, Robert Nord, and Dilip Soni. 1999. *Applied Software Architecture.* Reading, MA: Addison-Wesley.

van Hoorn, André, Jan Waller, and Wilhelm Hasselbring. 2012. "Kieker: A Framework for Application Performance Monitoring and Dynamic Software Analysis." In *Proceedings of the 3rd ACM/SPEC International Conference on Performance Engineering (ICPE 2012)*, 247–248. New York: ACM.

Hu, Lei, and I. Gorton. 1997. "A Performance Prototyping Approach to Designing Concurrent Software Architectures." In *Proceedings of the Second International Workshop on Software Engineering for Parallel and Distributed Systems*, (Washington, DC): 270–276.

Huber, Matthias. 2010. "Towards Secure Services in an Untrusted Environment." In *Proceedings of the Fifteenth International Workshop on Component-Oriented Programming (WCOP) 2010*, 2010–14: 39–46. Interne Berichte. Karlsruhe: Karlsruhe Institute of Technology, Faculty of Informatics.

Huber, Nikolaus. 2009. *Performance Modeling of Storage Virtualization*. MA thesis, University of Karlsruhe (TH).

Huber, Nikolaus, et al. 2010. "Performance Modeling in Industry: A Case Study on Storage Virtualization." In *Proceedings of the 32nd ACM/IEEE International Conference on Software Engineering—Volume 2*, 1–10. ICSE '10. New York: ACM.

Hummel, Oliver, and Colin Atkinson. 2004. "Extreme Harvesting: Test Driven Discovery and Reuse of Software Components." In *Proceedings of the EEE International Conference on Information Reuse and Integration*, 66–72. Washington, DC: IEEE Computer Society.

Hummel, Oliver, and Colin Atkinson. 2006. "Using the Web as a Reuse Repository." In *Reuse of Off-the-Shelf Components, Proceedings of the 9th International Conference on Software Reuse, ICSR 2006*, 298–311. Berlin, Heidelberg: Springer.

Hummel, Oliver, and Colin Atkinson. 2010. "Automated Creation and Assessment of Component Adapters with Test Cases." In *Component-Based Software Engineering*, 6092: 166–181. Lecture Notes in Computer Science. Berlin: Springer.

Hummel, Oliver, Werner Janjic, and Colin Atkinson. 2007. "Evaluating the Efficiency of Retrieval Methods for Component Repositories." In *SEKE*, 404–409. Skokie, IL: Knowledge Systems Institute Graduate School.

Humphrey, Watts Sherman, Terry R. Snyder, and Ronald R. Willis. 1991. Software Process Improvement at Hughes Aircraft. *IEEE Software* 8 (4): 11–23.

Hüttermann, Michael. 2012. *DevOps for Developers, 176*. New York: Apress.

IEEE Std 610.12–1990. 1990. *IEEE Standard Glossary of Software Engineering Terminology*. New York: IEEE Standards Board.

Immonen, Anne, and Eila Niemelä. 2008. Survey of Reliability and Availability Prediction Methods from the Viewpoint of Software Architecture. *Software & Systems Modeling* 7 (1): 49–65.

ISO/IEC 25010:2011(E). 2011. *Software Engineering—Software Product Quality Requirements and Evaluation (SQuaRE) – System and Software Quality Models*. Geneva: International Organization for Standardization.

ISO/IEC 25030:2007(E). 2007. *Software Engineering—Software Product Quality Requirements and Evaluation (SQuaRE) – Quality Requirements*. Geneva: International Organization for Standardization.

ISO/IEC/IEEE Std 42010:2011. *Systems and Software Engineering—Architecture Description*. Los Alamos, CA: IEEE.

Jain, Raj. 1991. *The Art of Computer Systems Performance Analysis: Techniques for Experimental Design, Measurement, Simulation, and Modeling*. New York: Wiley.

Jansen, Anton, and Jan Bosch. 2005. "Software Architecture as a Set of Architectural Design Decisions." In *5th Working IEEE/IFIP Conference on Software Architecture (WICSA'05)*, 109–120. Pittsburgh, PA: IEEE Computer Society.

Jézéquel, Jean-Marc, and Bertrand Meyer. 1997. Design by Contract: The Lessons of Ariane. *Computer* 30 (1): 129–130.

Kapova, Lucia, et al. 2010. "State Dependence in Performance Evaluation of Component-Based Software Systems." In *Proceedings of the 1st Joint WOSP/SIPEW International Conference on Performance Engineering (WOSP/SIPEW '10)*, 37–48. San Jose, CA: ACM.

Khoussainov, Bakhadyr, and Anil Nerode. 2001. *Progress in Computer Science and Applied Logic*. Vol. 21. Automata Theory and its Applications. Boston: Birkhäuser.

Kindel, Olaf, and Mario Friedrich. 2009. *Softwareentwicklung mit AUTOSAR: Grundlagen, Engineering, Management in der Praxis*. Heidelberg, Germany: dpunkt.verlag.

King, James C. 1976. Symbolic Execution and Program Testing. *Communications of the ACM* 19 (7): 385–394.

Kircher, Michael, and Prashant Jain. 2004. *Pattern-Oriented Software Architecture: Patterns for Distributed Services and Components*. New York: John Wiley & Sons.

Kiselev, Ivan. 2003. *Aspect-Oriented Programming with AspectJ*. Indianapolis, IN: Sams.

Klatt, Benjamin, Klaus Krogmann, and Christoph Seidl. 2014. "Program Dependency Analysis for Consolidating Customized Product Copies." In *IEEE 30th International Conference on Software Maintenance and Evolution (ICSME'14)*, 496–500. Victoria, Canada.

Klaussner, Christian, and Sebastian Lehrig. 2014. "Using Java EE ProtoCom for SAP HANA Cloud." In *Proceedings of the Symposium on Software Performance: Joint Descartes/Kieker/Palladio Days 2014*, 17–27. Stuttgart, Germany.

Knuth, Donald E. 1997. *Fundamental Algorithms*, 3rd Ed. Vol. 1. The Art of Computer Programming. Redwood City, CA: Addison-Wesley Longman.

Kornyshova, Elena, and Camille Salinesi. 2007. "MCDM Techniques Selection Approaches: State of the Art." In *Proceedings of the 2007 IEEE Symposium on Computational Intelligence in Multicriteria Decision Making (MCDM'2007)*, 22–29. Honolulu: IEEE Press.

Koziolek, Heiko. 2008. *Parameter Dependencies for Reusable Performance Specifications of Software Components*. Vol. 2. The Karlsruhe Series on Software Design and Quality. University of Karlsruhe.

Koziolek, Heiko. 2010. "Performance evaluation of component-based software systems: A survey." *Performance Evaluation* 67 (8): 634–658.

Koziolek, Anne. 2013. *The Karlsruhe Series on Software Design and Quality*. Vol. 7. Automated Improvement of Software Architecture Models for Performance and Other Quality Attributes. Karlsruhe: KIT Scientific Publishing.

Koziolek, Heiko, and Jens Happe. 2006. "A QoS Driven Development Process Model for Component-Based Software Systems." In *Proceedings of the 9th International Symposium on Component-Based Software Engineering (CBSE'06)*, 4063: 336–343. Lecture Notes in Computer Science. Berlin: Springer-Verlag.

Koziolek, Anne, and Ralf Reussner. 2011. "Towards a Generic Quality Optimisation Framework for Component-Based System Models." In *Proceedings of the 14th International ACM Sigsoft Symposium on Component Based Software Engineering*, 103–108. CBSE '11. Boulder, CO: ACM.

Koziolek, Heiko, et al. 2008. "Evaluating Performance of Software Architecture Models with the Palladio Component Model." In *Model-Driven Software Development: Integrating Quality Assurance*, 95–118. IDEA Group Inc.

Koziolek, Heiko, Bastian Schlich, and Carlos Bilich. 2010. "A Large-Scale Industrial Case Study on Architecture-Based Software Reliability Analysis." In *Proceedings of the 21st IEEE International Symposium on Software Reliability Engineering (ISSRE'10)*, 279–288. Washington, DC: IEEE Computer Society.

Koziolek, Anne, Heiko Koziolek, and Ralf Reussner. 2011a. "PerOpteryx: Automated Application of Tactics in Multi-Objective Software Architecture Optimization." In *Joint Proceedings of the Seventh International ACM SIGSOFT Conference on the Quality of Software Architectures and the 2nd ACM SIGSOFT International Symposium on Architecting Critical Systems (QoSA-ISARCS 2011)*, 33–42. Boulder, CO: ACM.

Koziolek, Heiko, et al. 2011b. "An Industrial Case Study on Quality Impact Prediction for Evolving Service-Oriented Software." In *Proceeding of the 33rd International Conference on Software Engineering (ICSE 2011), Software Engineering in Practice Track*, 776–785. Acceptance Rate: 18% (18/100). Honolulu: ACM.

Krogmann, Klaus. 2012. *The Karlsruhe Series on Software Design and Quality*. Vol. 4. Reconstruction of Software Component Architectures and Behaviour Models Using Static and Dynamic Analysis. Karlsruhe: KIT Scientific Publishing.

Krogmann, Klaus, Michael Kuperberg, and Ralf Reussner. 2010. Using Genetic Search for Reverse Engineering of Parametric Behaviour Models for Performance Prediction. *IEEE Transactions on Software Engineering* 36 (6): 865–877.

Kruchten, Philippe. 2003. *The Rational Unified Process: An Introduction*. 3rd ed. Boston: Addison-Wesley Longman.

Kruchten, Philippe, Patricia Lago, and Hans Van Vliet. 2006. "Building Up and Reasoning About Architectural Knowledge." In *Quality of Software Architectures*, 43–58. Berlin: Springer.

Kuperberg, Michael, Fouad Omri, and Ralf Reussner. 2009. "Using Heuristics to Automate Parameter Generation for Benchmarking of Java Methods." In *Proceedings of the 6th International Workshop on Formal Engineering approaches to Software Components and Architectures*, York, UK, 28th March 2009 (ETAPS 2009, 12th European Joint Conferences on Theory and Practice of Software).

Kuperberg, Michael, Martin Krogmann, and Ralf Reussner. 2011. "Metric-Based Selection of Timer Methods for Accurate Measurements." In *Proceedings of the 2nd ACM/SPEC International Conference on Performance Engineering 2011*, 151–156, New York: ACM.

Langhammer, Michael, Sebastian Lehrig, and Max E. Kramer. 2013. "Reuse and Configuration for Code Generating Architectural Refinement Transformations." In *Proceedings of the 1st Workshop on View-Based, Aspect-Oriented and Orthographic Software Modelling*, 6: 1–6:5. VAO '13. Montpellier: ACM.

Laprie, Jean-Claude. 1985. "Dependable Computing and Fault Tolerance: Concepts and Terminology." In *Proceedings of the 15th IEEE Symposium on Fault Tolerant Computing Systems (FTCS-15)*, 2–11. Washington, DC: IEEE Computer Society.

Larman, Craig. 2005. *Applying UML and Patterns—An Introduction to Object-Oriented Analysis and Design and Iterative Development*. 3rd ed. Upper Saddle River, NJ: Pearson Education.

Law, Averill M., and W. David Kelton. 2000. *Simulation, Modelling and Analysis*. 3rd ed. New York: McGraw-Hill.

Lazowska, Edward D., et al. 1984. *Quantitative System Performance—Computer System Analysis Using Queuing Network Models*. Englewood Cliffs, NJ: Prentice Hall.

Lazzarini, Lemos, et al. 2011. A Test-Driven Approach to Code Search and Its Application to the Reuse of Auxiliary Functionality. *Information and Software Technology* 53 (4): 294–306.

Leach, Ronald J. 1990. Software Metrics and Software Maintenance. *Journal of Software Maintenance: Research and Practice* 2 (2): 133–142.

Leffingwell, Dean. 1997. Calculating Your Return on Investment from More Effective Requirements Management. *American Programmer* 10 (4): 13–16.

Lehman, Meir Manny. 1979–1980. On Understanding Laws, Evolution, and Conservation in the Large-Program Life Cycle. *Journal of Systems and Software* 1:213–221.

Lehman, Meir M., and Juan F. Ramil. 2001. Rules and Tools for Software Evolution Planning and Management. *Annals of Software Engineering* 11 (1): 15–44.

Lehrig, Sebastian. 2014a. "Applying Architectural Templates for Design-Time Scalability and Elasticity Analyses of SaaS Applications." In *Proceedings of the 2nd International Workshop on Hot Topics in Cloud Service Scalability*, 2: 1–2:8. HotTopiCS '14. Dublin: ACM.

Lehrig, Sebastian. 2014b. *Quality Analysis Lab (QuAL): Software Design Description and Developer Guide Version 0.2*. Technical Report. U FP7 CloudScale.

Lehrig, Sebastian, and Thomas Zolynski. 2011. "Performance Prototyping with ProtoCom in a Virtualised Environment: A Case Study." In *Proceedings to Palladio Days 2011, Karlsruhe Reports in Informatics 32*. 7–14. Karlsruhe, Germany: KIT, Fakultät für Informatik.

Lyu, Michael R. 1996. *Handbook of Software Reliability Engineering*. New York: McGraw-Hill.

Marino, Jim, and Michael Rowley. 2009. *Understanding SCA (Service Component Architecture)*. 1st ed. Reading, MA: Addison-Wesley Professional.

Martens, Anne, et al. 2010. "Automatically Improve Software Models for Performance, Reliability and Cost Using Genetic Algorithms." In *Proceedings of the First Joint WOSP/SIPEW International Conference on Performance Engineering*, 105–116. WOSP/SIPEW '10. San Jose: ACM.

Martin, Robert. 1994. *"OO Design Quality Metrics—An Analysis of Dependencies."* Object-Oriented Programming Systems, Languages / Applications. OOPSLA.

McCall, James A., Paul K. Richards, and Gene F. Walters. 1977. *Factors in Software Quality, Volume I, II, and III*. Tech. Rep. RADC-TR-77–369. Griffiss AFB, Rome, NY: Rome Air Development Center. [Available from Defense Technical Information Center, Cameron Station, Alexandria, VA, order number ADA049014, ADA049015, and ADA049055.]

McConnell, Steve. 2004. *Code Complete: A Practical Handbook of Software Construction*. 2nd ed. Redmond, WA: Microsoft Press.

McIlroy, Malcolm Douglas. 1969. "'Mass Produced' Software Components." In *Software Engineering*, 138–155. Report of a conference sponsored by the NATO Science Committee, Garmisch, Germany, 7th to 11th October 1968. Brussels: Scientific Affairs Division, NATO.

Mell, Peter, and Timothy Grance. 2011. The NIST Definition of Cloud Computing. *NIST Special Publication* 145 (6): 7.

Menascé, Daniel A. 2003. Workload Characterization. *IEEE Internet Computing* 7 (5): 89–92.

Menascé, Daniel A., and Virgilio A. F. Almeida. 2001. *Capacity Planning for Web Services: Metrics, Models, and Methods, 2*. Englewood Cliffs, NJ: Prentice Hall.

Menascé, Daniel A., Virgilio A. F. Almeida, and Larry W. Dowdy. 1994. *Capacity Planning and Performance Modeling: From Mainframes to Client-Server Systems, 432*. Englewood Cliffs, NJ: Prentice Hall.

Menascé, Daniel A., Virgilio A. F. Almeida, and Lawrence W. Dowdy. 2004. *Performance by Design: Computer Capacity Planning by Example*. Englewood Cliffs, NJ: Prentice Hall.

Meyer, Bertrand. 1992. Applying 'Design by Contract.' *IEEE Computer* 25 (10): 40–51.

Meyer, Bertrand. 1986. *Design by Contract, Technical Report TR-EI-12/CO*. Goleta, CA: Interactive Software Engineering Inc.

Microsoft Corporation. 2004. *Improving. NET Application Performance and Scalability (Patterns and Practices)*. Redmond, WA: Microsoft Press.

Montealegre, Ramiro, and Mark Keil. 2000. De-escalating Information Technology Projects: Lessons from the Denver International Airport. *Management Information Systems Quarterly* 3:417–447.

Murugesan, San. 2008. "Harnessing Green IT: Principles and Practices." *IT Professional* 10(1): 24–33.

Musa, John D. 2004. *Software Reliability Engineering: More Reliable Software Faster and Cheaper*. 2nd ed., Bloomington, IN: AuthorHouse.

Nelson, Michael L. 2005. "A Survey of Reverse Engineering and Program Comprehension." *Computing Research Repository* abs/cs/0503068.

Nierstrasz, Oscar. 1993. "Composing Active Objects." *Research Directions in Object-Based Concurrency* 151–171. Cambridge, MA: MIT Press.

Noorshams, Qais, et al. 2015. "The Storage Performance Analyzer: Measuring, Monitoring, and Modeling of I/O Performance in Virtualized Environments." In *Proceedings of the 6th ACM/SPEC International Conference on Performance Engineering*. ICPE '15. Austin, Texas.

Nuseibeh, Bashar. 2001. Weaving Together Requirements and Architectures. *IEEE Computer* 34 (3): 115–117.

Östberg, P.-O., et al. 2014. "The CACTOS Vision of Context-Aware Cloud Topology Optimization and Simulation." In *Proceedings of the Sixth IEEE International Conference on Cloud Computing Technology and Science (CloudCom)*, 26–31. Singapore: IEEE Computer Society.

Parnas, David Lorge. 1972a. A Technique for the Specification of Software Modules with Examples. *Communications of the ACM* 15 (5): 330–336.

Parnas, David Lorge. 1972b. On the Criteria to Be Used in Decomposing Systems into Modules. *Communications of the ACM* 15 (12): 1053–1058.

Paulish, Daniel J. 2001. *Architecture-Centric Software Project Management: A Practical Guide*. Reading, MA: Addison-Wesley.

Platenius, Marie Christin, Markus von Detten, and Steffen Becker. 2012. "Archimetrix: Improved Software Architecture Recovery in the Presence of Design Deficiencies." In *16th Conference on Software Maintenance and Reengineering*, 255–264. Szeged, Hungary: IEEE.

Platenius, Marie Christin, Steffen Becker, and Wilhelm Schaefer. 2014. "Integrating Service Matchers into a Service Market Architecture." In *Proceedings of the 8th European Conference on Software Architecture (ECSA 2014)* .

Pohl, Klaus. 2010. *Requirements Engineering—Fundamentals, Principles, and Techniques*. Berlin: Springer.

Prechelt, Lutz, et al. 2002. Two Controlled Experiments Assessing the Usefulness of Design Pattern Documentation in Program Maintenance. *IEEE Transactions on Software Engineering* 28 (6): 595–606.

Rathfelder, Christoph, et al. 2012. "Workload-Aware System Monitoring Using Performance Predictions Applied to a Large-Scale E-Mail System." In *Proceedings of the Joint 10th Working IEEE/IFIP Conference on Software Architecture (WICSA) & 6th European Conference on Software Architecture (ECSA)*, 31–40. Helsinki, Finland: IEEE Computer Society.

Rathfelder, Christoph, et al. 2013. "Modeling Event-Based Communication in Component-Based Software Architectures for Performance Predictions." *Journal of Software and Systems Modeling* 13 (4): 1291–1317.

Rentschler, Andreas, et al. 2014. "Designing Information Hiding Modularity for Model Transformation Languages." In *Proceedings of the 13th International Conference Modularity (AOSD '14)*, Lugano, Switzerland, April 22 - 26, 2014, 217–228. New York: ACM.

Reussner, Ralf H. 2001. "The Use of Parameterised Contracts for Architecting Systems with Software Components." In *Proceedings of the Sixth International Workshop on Component-Oriented Programming (WCOP'01)*.

Reussner, Ralf H. 2003. Automatic Component Protocol Adaptation with the CoCoNut Tool Suite. *Future Generation Computer Systems* 19 (5): 627–639.

Reussner, Ralf H., et al. 1998. "SKaMPI: A Detailed, Accurate MPI Benchmark." In *Recent Advances in Parallel Virtual Machine and Message Passing Interface: 5th European PVM/MPI Users' Group Meeting, Liverpool, UK, September 7–9, 1998*, 1497: 52–59. Lecture Notes in Computer Science. Berlin: Springer-Verlag.

Reussner, Ralf H., Viktoria Firus, and Steffen Becker. 2004. "Parametric Performance Contracts for Software Components and their Compositionality." In *Proceedings of the 9th International Workshop on Component-Oriented Programming (WCOP 04)* .

Reussner, Ralf, Jens Happe, and Annegreth Habel. 2005. "Modelling Parametric Contracts and the State Space of Composite Components by Graph Grammars." *In Fundamental Approaches to Software Engineering (FASE)*, 3442:80–95. Lecture Notes in Computer Science. Springer-Verlag Berlin Heidelberg.

Reussner, Ralf H., et al. 2007. *The Palladio Component Model*. Interner Bericht, 2007–21. University of Karlsruhe (TH).

Reussner, Ralf, et al. 2011. *The Palladio Component Model. Tech. Rep., Karlsruhe Reports in Informatics; 2011, 14*. Karlsruhe: KIT Faculty of Informatics.

Rhinelander, Richard. 2007. "Components Have No Interfaces!" In *Proceedings of the 12th International Workshop on Component Oriented Programming (WCOP 2007)*. Vol. 2007–13. Interne Berichte. Karlsruhe: University of Karlsruhe, Faculty of Informatics.

Rostami, Kiana, et al. 2015. "Architecture-Based Assessment and Planning of Change Requests." In *Proceedings of the 11th International ACM SIGSOFT Conference on the Quality of Software Architectures (QoSA'15)*. QoSA'15. Montreal: ACM.

Rozanski, Nick, and Eoin Woods. 2005. *Software Systems Architecture: Working with Stakeholders Using Viewpoints and Perspectives*. Reading, MA: Addison-Wesley.

Saaty, Thomas L. 1980. *The Analytic Hierarchy Process, Planning, Priority Setting, Resource Allocation*. New York: McGraw-Hill.

Schmidt, Douglas C. 2006. Guest Editor's Introduction: Model-Driven Engineering. *Computer* 39 (2): 25–31.

Schmidt, Douglas, et al. 2000. *Pattern-Oriented Software Architecture—Volume 2—Patterns for Concurrent and Networked Objects*. New York: John Wiley & Sons.

Schmietendorf, Andreas, and André Scholz. 2001. Aspects of Performance Engineering—An Overview. In *Performance Engineering: State of the Art and Current Trends*. Vol. 2047. Lecture Notes in Computer Science. Berlin: Springer-Verlag.

Schumacher, Markus, et al. 2005. *Security Patterns: Integrating Security and Systems Engineering*. New York: John Wiley & Sons.

Schwaber, Ken, and Mike Beedle. 2002. *Agile Software Development with Scrum*. Englewood Cliffs, NJ: Prentice Hall.

Shaw, Mary, and David Garlan. 1996. *Software Architecture. Perspectives on an Emerging Discipline*. Englewood Cliffs, NJ: Prentice Hall.

Siedersleben, Johannes. 2004. *Moderne Software-Architektur: Umsichtig planen, robust bauen mit Quasar*. Heidelberg, Germany: dpunkt.verlag.

Smith, Connie U., and Lloyd G. Williams. 2001. *Performance Solutions: A Practical Guide to Creating Responsive, Scalable Software. Addison-Wesley Object Technology Series*. Reading, MA: Addison-Wesley.

Smith, Connie U., and Lloyd G. Williams. 2002. *Performance Solutions: A Practical Guide to Creating Responsive, Scalable Software*. Reading, MA: Addison-Wesley.

Stachowiak, Herbert. 1973. *Allgemeine Modelltheorie*. Vienna: Springer-Verlag.

Stahl, Thomas, and Markus Völter. 2006. *Model-Driven Software Development*. Hoboken, NJ: John Wiley & Sons.

Stier, Christian, Henning Groenda, and Anne Koziolek. 2014. *Towards Modeling and Analysis of Power Consumption of Self-Adaptive Software Systems in Palladio. Tech. Rep.* Stuttgart: University of Stuttgart, Faculty of Computer Science, Electrical Engineering, and Information Technology.

Szyperski, Clemens, Dominik Gruntz, and Stephan Murer. 2002. *Component Software: Beyond Object-Oriented Programming*. 2nd ed. New York: ACM Press / Addison-Wesley.

Taylor, Richard N., Nenad Medvidovic, and Eric M. Dashofy. 2009. *Software Architecture: Foundations, Theory, and Practice*. New York: Wiley.

Trivedi, Kishor Shridharbhai. 2001. *Probability and Statistics with Reliability, Queuing and Computer Science Applications*. 2nd ed. New York: John Wiley & Sons.

Urdaneta, Guido, Guillaume Pierre, and Maarten van Steen. 2009. Wikipedia Workload Analysis for Decentralized Hosting. *Elsevier Computer Networks* 53 (11): 1830–1845.

Westermann, Dennis, and Jens Happe. 2011. "Performance Cockpit: Systematic Measurements and Analyses." In *ICPE'11: Proceedings of the 2nd ACM/SPEC International Conference on Performance Engineering*. Karlsruhe: ACM.

Westermann, Dennis, et al. 2010. "The Performance Cockpit Approach: A Framework for Systematic Performance Evaluations." In *Proceedings of the 36th EUROMICRO Conference on Software Engineering and Advanced Applications (SEAA 2010)*, 31–38. Washington, DC: IEEE Computer Society.

Willnecker, Felix, et al. 2015. "Using Dynatrace Monitoring Data for Generating Performance Models of Java EE Applications." In *Proceedings of the 6th ACM/SPEC International Conference on Performance Engineering*, 103–104. New York: ACM.

Wood-Harper, Trevor, Lyn Antill, and David Ernest Avison. 1985. *Information Systems Definition: The Multiview Approach. Computer Science Texts*. Malden, MA: Blackwell Scientific.

Woods, Eoin, and Nick Rozanski. 2011. "How Software Architecture Can Frame, Constrain and Inspire System Requirements." In *Relating Software Requirements and Architectures*, 333–352. Berlin: Springer.

Woodside, Murray, Greg Franks, and Dorina C. Petriu. 2007. "The Future of Software Performance Engineering." In *Proceedings of ICSE 2007, Future of SE*, 171–187. Washington, DC: IEEE Computer Society.

Xu, Jing. 2010. "Rule-Based Automatic Software Performance Diagnosis and Improvement." Special Issue on Software and Performance. *Performance Evaluation* 67 (8): 585–611.

Xu, R., and D. Wunsch. 2008. *Clustering. IEEE Press Series on Computational Intelligence*. New York: Wiley.

Yourdon, Edward, and Larry LeRoy Constantine. 1979. *Structured Design: Fundamentals of a Discipline of Computer Program and Systems Design*. Upper Saddle River, NJ: Prentice-Hall.

Züllighoven, Heinz. 2005. *Object-Oriented Construction Handbook—Developing Application-Oriented Software with the Tools and Materials Approach*. Heidelberg, Germany: dpunkt.verlag.

Tools and Webpages

1. http://www.google.com/analytics/

2. http://newrelic.com

3. http://www.appdynamics.com

4. http://www.dynatrace.com

5. https://scoutapp.com

6. http:/www.nagios.org

7. https://www.dotcom-monitor.com

8. http://kieker-monitoring.net

9. http://sopeco.github.io/AIM/

10. http://www.oracle.com/technetwork/articles/cico-wldf-091073.html

11. http://www.r-project.org

12. http://www-01.ibm.com/software/analytics/spss/

13. http://www.mathworks.com/products/matlab/

14. http://www.emenda.eu/en/products/understand

15. http://www.klocwork.com

16. http://findbugs.sourceforge.net

17. http://www.sonarqube.org

18. http://www.visualstudio.com

19. http://eclipse.org

20. *Accuracy Influence Analysis.* https://sdqweb.ipd.kit.edu/wiki/Accuracy_ Influence _Analysis

21. *Behavior Validation Effort Estimation.* https://sdqweb.ipd.kit.edu/wiki/Behavior_Validation _Effort_Estimation

22. Briegleb, Volker. 2007a. *Bericht: Probleme bei SAPs neuer Mittelstandssoftware.* Heise online. 2007-04-16. http://heise.de/-167703

23. Briegleb, Volker. 2007b. *SAP soll für den Mittelstand attraktiver werden.* Heise online. 2007-01-17. http://heise.de/-135709

24. Charette, Robert. 2008. *The Software Issues Behind Heathrow's T5 Meltdown.* IEEE Spectrum Blog: The Risk Factor. 2008-05-12. http://spectrum.ieee.org/riskfactor/computing/it/the _software_issues_behind_hea

25. CIO Wirtschaftsnachrichten. 2011. *SAP enttäuscht trotz Umsatz- und Gewinnplus-Erwartungen.* CIO. 2011-04-28. Archived by WebCite. http://www.cio.de/news/wirtschaftsnachrichten/ 2273391/index2.html

26. *Dynatrace—Application Performance Management and Monitoring.* 2011. http://www .dynatrace.com

27. Eriksdotter, Holger. 2010. *SAP-Projekt abgeschlossen—Business by Design eingeführt.* http:// www.cio.de/saas/it-anwender/2238157/

28. Object Management Group (OMG). 2011. *UML Profile for MARTE: Modeling and Analysis of Real-Time Embedded Systems, version 1.1.* http://www.omg.org/spec/MARTE/1.1/PDF

29. *Meta Object Facility (MOF) Core.* 2011. Object Management Group. http://www.omg.org/ spec/MOF/2.4.1/

30. *MoDisco.* 2015. https://eclipse.org/MoDisco/

31. *Neotys Neoload Load Testing Tool.* 2011. http://www.neotys.com/product/overview -neoload.html

32. *Object Management Group (OMG). 2007. CORBA 3.0—OMG IDL Syntax and Semantics chapter.* http://www.omg.org/docs/formal/02-06-39.pdf

33. *Palladio-Bench Add-Ons.* 2015. http://www.palladio-simulator.com/tools/add%5C_ons/

34. *PCM Coverage*. https://sdqweb.ipd.kit.edu/wiki/PCM_Coverage

35. Robertson, David. 2008. *BA loses 220,000 passengers following T5 debacle*. Times Online. 2008-05-06.   http://business.timesonline.co.uk/tol/business/industry_sectors/transport/ article3881109.ece

36. *Sawmill—Universal log file analysis tool*. 2011. http://www.sawmill.net

37. *Stateful Software Performance Engineering*. 2014. https://sdqweb.ipd.kit.edu/wiki/ Stateful%5C_Software%5C_Performance%5C_Engineering

38. Storm, Ingo T. 2008. *SAP-Co Léo Apotheker räumt Fehler ein*. Heise resale. 2009-05-16. http://heise.de/-219358

39. *Test-Based Validation*. https://sdqweb.ipd.kit.edu/wiki/TestBasedValidation

40. Thomson, Rebecca. 2008. *Update: lack of software testing to blame for Terminal 5 fiasco, BA executive tells MPs*. http://www.computerweekly.com/Articles/2008/05/09/230629/ Update-lack-of-software-testing-to-blame-for-Terminal-5-fiasco-BA-executive-tells.htm

Contributors

Fabian Brosig, University of Würzburg

Erik Burger, Karlsruhe Institute of Technology

Axel Busch, Karlsruhe Institute of Technology

Zoya Durdik, ABB Corporate Research

Lucia Happe, Karlsruhe Institute of Technology

Christoph Heger, Novatec Consulting GmbH

Jörg Henss, FZI Research Center for Information Technology

Nikolaus Huber, University of Würzburg

Oliver Hummel, iQser GmbH

Benjamin Klatt, inovex

Martin Küster, Senacor Technologies AG

Michael Langhammer, Karlsruhe Institute of Technology

Sebastian Lehrig, Chemnitz University of Technology (TUC)

Philipp Merkle, Karlsruhe Institute of Technology

Florian Meyerer, iQser GmbH

Qais Noorshams, IBM Germany Research & Development GmbH

Kiana Rostami, Karlsruhe Institute of Technology

Simon Spinner, University of Würzburg

Christian Stier, FZI Research Center for Information Technology

Misha Strittmatter, Karlsruhe Institute of Technology

Alexander Wert, Novatec Consulting GmbH

Index

Note: numbers in **bold** refer to definitions or term introductions; numbers in *italics* refer to figures, tables, and digression boxes.